ENHANCING COUNSELOR INTERVENTION STRATEGIES

ENHANCING COUNSELOR INTERVENTION STRATEGIES:
An Integrational Viewpoint

Sterling Gerber, Ph.D.
Eastern Washington University

USA	Publishing Office:	ACCELERATED DEVELOPMENT *A member of the Taylor & Francis Group* 325 Chestnut Street Philadelphia, PA 19106 Tel: (215) 625-8900 Fax: (215) 625-2940
	Distribution Center:	ACCELERATED DEVELOPMENT *A member of the Taylor & Francis Group* 47 Runway Road, Suite G Levittown, PA 19057-4700 Tel: (215) 269-0400 Fax: (215) 269-0363
UK		ACCELERATED DEVELOPMENT *A member of the Taylor & Francis Group* 1 Gunpowder Square London EC4A 3DE Tel: +44 171 583 0490 Fax: +44 171 583 0581

ENHANCING COUNSELOR INTERVENTION STRATEGIES: An Integrational Viewpoint

Copyright © 1999 Taylor & Francis. All rights reserved. Printed in the United States of America. Except as permitted under the United States Copyright Act of 1976, no part of this publication may be reproduced or distributed in any form or by any means, or stored in a database or retrieval system, without prior written permission of the publisher.

1 2 3 4 5 6 7 8 9 0

Printed by Edwards Brothers, Ann Arbor, MI, 1999.
Cover design by Joe Dieter.
A CIP catalog record for this book is available from the British Library.
The paper in this publication meets the requirements of the ANSI Standard Z39.48-1984 (Permanence of Paper).

Library of Congress Cataloging-in-Publication Data
Gerber, Sterling K.
   Enhancing counselor intervention strategies : an integrational viewpoint / Sterling Gerber.
     p. cm.
   Includes bibliographical references and index.
   ISBN: 1-56032-739-1 (pbk.: alk. paper)
   1. Crisis intervention (Mental health services)   2. Counseling.
I. Title.
   [DNLM: 1. Counseling—methods. 2. Learning. WM 55 G362e 1999]
RC480.6.G47   1999
616.89′14—dc21   98-47897
                                                                           CIP

CONTENTS

Preface vii

PART I. CLIENT CIRCUMSTANCE AND INTERVENTION SELECTION

Chapter **1**   Philosophical Foundations for Integrationism   3

Chapter **2**   Congruence: A Perceptual Frame for Intervention   14

Chapter **3**   Perspective   30

PART II. INTERVENTION THEORIES

Chapter **4**   Four Families of Intervention Theories   43

Chapter **5**   Association Learning Approaches to Intervention   50

Chapter **6**   Reinforcement Learning Approaches to Intervention   68

Chapter **7**   Perception Learning Approaches to Intervention   87

Chapter **8**   Cognitive Learning Approaches to Intervention   120

PART III. CONTEXTUAL CONCERNS

Chapter **9**   Contextual Issues: Circumstance and Style—
Personality and Developmental Dynamics   155

Chapter **10**   Contextual Issues: Circumstance and Style—
Social and Spiritual Dynamics   172

PART IV. ASSESSMENT, STRATEGY SELECTION, AND IMPLEMENTATION

Chapter **11**   Assessment and Strategy Selection   195

References	207
Index	213
About the Author	223

PREFACE

Theoretical Bases for Therapeutic Interventions

Intentionality is the descriptor for a widely held value in counseling. To truly be professional, the therapist must know what he or she is doing and the rationale for doing it, and be able to anticipate realistic outcomes as a result of that action. Interventions must be selected intentionally to fit the client and the particular problem being confronted by the client. Within the context of this book, reference is made to the identification of client circumstance and style. As applied, circumstance reflects problem dynamics and available resources, while client style represents the manner in which dynamics of the circumstance are perceived by the client, and the preferred, client-specific approaches to solving problems.

While clients represent integrated systems, counselor preparation programs have tended to isolate parts of the client system and have addressed those parts as almost independent entities. Courses in learning, counseling, personality, and developmental theories are offered, with few formal attempts made to integrate between and among them. Furthermore, they have generally evolved as surveys of theoretical frameworks—a smorgasbord of theoretical tidbits from which the consumer may pick and choose as suits his or her fancy. Skills courses and practica have tended toward an atheoretical development of micro-skills and weak or no evaluation of counselor intentionality. The intent of this work is to integrate many theoretical strands into workable patterns, providing a high degree of effectiveness in the intentional intervention process. In doing so, the bias is toward a foundation in learning theories because behavioral change fundamentally results from learning.

Textbooks and classes on learning traditionally have provided either a description of theorists and an elaboration of their positions or an amalgamation of learning principles with research foundations and elaboration. This book is different. Its foundation is an applied learning stance based on the premises that (a) intervention approaches in counseling work best when they are grounded in theory, and (b) professionals differ from technicians and amateurs in their ability to know the theoretical underpinnings of an approach and their precision in using applicable strategies in a theory-pure context.

Textbooks and classes on therapeutic or counseling theories traditionally have given a brief introduction to the biography and philosophy of major theorists, then described their theories and provided case examples for clarification. Little, if any, recognition is given to linking learning principles with therapeutic change modalities. This book posits that all human behavior—action, cognition, perception, and probably affect—is a product of genetics, biochemistry, or learning. Since society has guarded the area of manipulation of human genetics through ethical proscriptions and has relegated chemical interventions to the medical profession, counselors are restricted to producing change through application and management of learning principles and procedures. All counseling or therapy approaches produce change in clients or client systems as a result of employing learning principles. These approaches are effective because of their learning theory context. Each possesses a learning theory "tap root" that provides power to every counseling theory structure which, in turn, supports each intervention strategy.

Practica and internships in counselor preparation programs have relied on the supervisor's experience and expertise, occasionally augmented by a book or books that focus on particular applications in the therapeutic setting. There are few books, if any, that treat the selection and application of intervention strategies in the press of everyday professional practice. This book provides examples and theory-bound interventions for a variety of clients and is easily generalized for use in a wide range of therapeutic and training settings.

The process of beginning to develop a perceptual awareness of client circumstance and style requires consideration of the developmental level of the client. It also requires sensitivity to dynamics inherent in social, familial, and religious contexts. Change processes are modified by developmental and personality characteristics. They are impacted by contextual and systemic factors. Intervention strategies—intentional applications of learning principles to client change—are improved to the extent that they take into account the central learning dynamics as evidenced in their developmental and social contexts.

Another difference between this and other intervention-oriented books is a consistent bias toward integrationism, that is, the necessity for a practicing professional to be able to apply different theory-pure interventions to different clients, each experience making sense within its theoretical context. This is markedly different from eclecticism, which operates without a unifying theoretical base. Rather than selecting techniques from many approaches and using them without reference to their source or to each other, the integrationist employs a strategy—a series of integrated assessments and techniques—intact in its theoretical context. This strategy is applied to a client whose circumstance and style foreshadows the success of the strategy. As an extension of the Gestalt maxim, "Meaning comes from context," (Perls, 1969) the guiding principle of an integrationist approach is that the power of intervention strategies comes from recognizing and honoring their theoretical context. This bias requires considerable cognitive flexibility in avoiding the tendencies (a) to see only one theoretical "truth" and (b) to deny the power extant in all other approaches. It requires competence on the part of the practicing professional to work within several markedly different theoretical structures, separately applied to different clients.

The book is organized in the following manner. Chapter 1 establishes the philosophical foundation for integrationism. It is followed by Chapter 2, which introduces a congruence model as a conceptual gestalt for assessing client circumstance and style and for selecting appropriate intervention strategies. This model provides structure for applications within each of four families of intervention theories. Chapter 3 offers some historical perspectives for the state of learning theory, while Chapter 4 is an introduction to and comparison of four families of intervention theories: association, reinforcement, perception, and cognition. The following four chapters, Chapters 5 through 8, elucidate each of the four families and include representative theorists—both learning and counseling—and their work. Chapters 9 and 10 treat contextual concerns, evidenced in client circumstance and style, that underlie modifications in the applications that were featured in previous chapters. Included are sections on developmental structures, personality dynamics, social processes, and spiritual influences. The final chapter, Chapter 11, describes the processes of assessment, selection of strategy, and employment of strategy in a theory-pure context.

While the scope of this approach is wide enough to appeal to all human service providers and educators, it is written for the narrower audience of counselors and therapists. Because the foundational dynamics of both counseling and psychotherapy are identical, coming from learning based approaches to change of client behavior, no attempt is made to differentiate these two areas of application. Wherever reference is made to therapy, counseling is inherently included; references to counselors pertain equally to therapists.

A counter-theme has been incorporated into the text to take into account Blosser's (1973, 1975) taxonomy of thinking: cognitive memory, convergent thinking, divergent thinking, and evaluative thinking. In Chapters 5 through 8, practical examples have been given with directions to identify theory dynamics (recall) and their application (convergent thinking) through an intervention strategy for each example. In Chapter 11, practical problems have been given along with two directives: (a) within the framework of each problem, arrive at two intervention strategies from different theory families (divergent thinking), and (b) compare/contrast/evaluate the selected strategies (evaluative thinking).

A set of objectives for a class in intervention theories and applications (including an amalgamation of learning and counseling theories) might look like this:

☐ Blosser's Cognitive Memory

Upon completion of the course students will:

- describe the dynamics of change according to each of the four families of intervention theories;
- identify prominent theorists and practitioners in each of the four families of intervention theories, giving a description of the model of each and examples of its application; and
- discriminate between one- and two-stage theories of learning.

☐ Blosser's Convergent Thinking

Given cases appropriate to each of the four families of intervention theories, students will:

- correctly describe an intervention approach according to the specific family and theoretical bias therein; and
- defend their intervention by reference to theoretical principles.

☐ Blosser's Divergent Thinking

Given random case vignettes, students will:

- describe at least one approach from each of two or more different families of theory for each case; and
- explain/defend their interventions by reference to the appropriate theoretical dynamics.

☐ Blosser's Evaluative Thinking

From the interventions processed in Blosser's Divergent Thinking, students will:

- compare and contrast two or more interventions for each case vignette; and
- select a preferred approach for each case and give reasons for its selection over the other alternative(s).

PART

I

CLIENT CIRCUMSTANCE AND INTERVENTION SELECTION

CHAPTER 1

Philosophical Foundations for Integrationism

The process of applying theoretical knowledge to practical situations presents some major ideological problems. If there is a single, unified truth that governs application in the human services or in education, then finding the theory that circumscribes this truth and consistently applying it is the only defensible option. Many professionals behave as though they have discovered the one true theory, and become devout disciples of its major proponent. While successful in many instances of application, they occasionally encounter clients who do not fit, or for whom they are unable to adapt, their procedures. Other professionals find a single theory to be either too confining or not to their taste, and choose, instead, to take parts from many theories that seem to work for them or that appeal to their preferences and combine them into a personalized approach. Such practice has an advantage of fitting a broader sample of potential clients but at the cost of reducing the power that comes from a unified theoretical context. The approach fits more people, more loosely.

In addition to the options of ignoring all theories that do not parallel the one "true" one or of discarding parts of theories in order to incorporate the remaining parts into a comfortable box, there is a third option. It is to accept all functional theories, intact and completely, and to selectively apply them in appropriate circumstances. In effect, every theory is the one true theory for the circumstance and style of the client for whom it fits. This option is called the integrationist approach. From the standpoint of a treatise that includes many differing theoretical formulations as viable and significant, it is the most defensible of the three options. It requires consideration of a range of differing client circumstances and differing styles of perception and problem-solving, combinations of which will fit the various theoretical presentations.

Aldous Huxley, in *The Doors of Perception* (1956), made a case for the brain and nervous system having one major function, that being the reduction or elimination of input. From his experience following the ingestion of mescalin, he wrote:

> Reflecting on my experience, I find myself agreeing with the eminent Cambridge philosopher, Dr. C. D. Broad, "that we should do well to consider much more seriously than we have hitherto been inclined to do the type of theory which Bergson put forward in

3

connection with memory and sense perception. The suggestion is that the function of the brain and nervous system and sense organs is in the main *eliminative* and not productive. Each person is at each moment capable of remembering all that has ever happened to him and of perceiving everything that is happening everywhere in the universe. The function of the brain and nervous system is to protect us from being overwhelmed and confused by this mass of largely useless and irrelevant knowledge, by shutting out most of what we should otherwise perceive or remember at any moment, and leaving only that very small and special selection which is likely to be practically useful." According to such a theory, each one of us is potentially Mind at Large. But in so far as we are animals, our business is at all costs to survive. To make biological survival possible, Mind at Large has to be funnelled through the reducing valve of the brain and nervous system. What comes out at the other end is a measly trickle of the kind of consciousness which will help us stay alive on the surface of this particular planet. To formulate and express the contents of this reduced awareness, man has invented and endlessly elaborated those symbol-systems and implicit philosophies which we call languages. Every individual is at once the beneficiary and the victim of the linguistic tradition into which he has been born—the beneficiary inasmuch as language gives access to the accumulated records of other people's experience, the victim in so far as it confirms him in the belief that reduced awareness is the only awareness and as it bedevils his sense of reality, so that he is all too apt to take his concepts for data, his words for actual things (1956, pp. 22–23).

Whether or not you are inclined to accept the notion of Mind at Large, it is difficult to ignore Broad's assertion that language has limitations in its power to communicate all experience. Similarly, theories serve to sharpen awareness of critical factors and, at the same time, blur or reject awareness of factors that are alien to their scope. Rollo May echoed this theme:

. . . every scientific method rests upon philosophical presuppositions. These presuppositions determine not only how much reality the observer with this particular method can see—they are indeed the spectacles through which he perceives—but also whether or not what is observed is pertinent to real problems and therefore whether the scientific work will endure. It is a gross, albeit common, error to assume naively that one can observe facts best if he avoids all preoccupation with philosophical assumptions. All he does is mirror uncritically the particular parochial doctrines of his own limited culture. The result in our day is that science gets identified with *isolating* factors and observing them from an allegedly *detached base*—a particular method which arose out of the split between subject and object made in the seventeenth century in Western culture and then developed into its special compartmentalized form in the late nineteenth and twentieth centuries (May, Angel, & Ellenberger, 1958, p. 8).

In his 1974 presidential address to the American Psychological Association, Albert Bandura said:

What we believe [people] to be affects which aspect of human functioning we study most thoroughly and which we disregard. Premises thus delimit research and are, in turn, shaped by it (p. 859).

Proponents who recognize only external consequences [as reinforcement contingencies] restrict their practice to such influences and thus generate evidence that reinforces their conceptions. Those who acknowledge personal influences as well tend to select methods that reveal and promote self-directing capabilities in [people] (p. 863).

If we allow that a theory is nothing more than a refined and tested description of somebody's perception of reality, then we can allow for its being valid, true, and useful. That we find inconsistencies between or among theories is only a problem if we insist on there being a single unified truth. It seems possible to take a step or two back from the theories we see as inconsistent, and incorporate them into a broader frame, one in which they can dwell compatibly. It is possible that we can move from an either-or or neither-nor mentality to one in which both extremes plus their middle ground can and do make sense. Rather than limit oneself to a single, narrow view of a complex reality, with the necessity either of forcing people into that view or ignoring those who do not fit, a professional with an integrationist mindset is competent to work within several theoretical frameworks and to select the framework that most nearly accommodates the circumstance and style of any particular person.

To return to Huxley's ideas as an analogy for theory, the mind selectively reduces input in order to protect us from being overwhelmed and confused by the mass of largely useless and irrelevant knowledge that is accessible through our senses. Similarly, a theory focuses our attention on certain salient aspects of a much larger and confusing reality. Huxley praises languages for giving access to the accumulated records of other people's experience and criticizes languages for creating the illusion that the reduced awareness encompassed by the language is the only awareness. It is a common experience for students of foreign languages to find that some words defy direct translation and that differences in the structures of languages require different ways of looking at reality. Similarly, students of theory find marked differences in the way theories explain reality. To cope with differences in language, people become bilingual or multilingual, using the particular language that is appropriate to the context. To cope with differences in theory, many people become eclectic. They seek to combine uncomplimentary views with the result that they either must distort important factors or ignore significant differences—change or leave out the pieces that do not fit. Another option, superior in the mind of the integrationist, is to become bi-theoretical or multi-theoretical and to use the particular theory that is appropriate to the context.

The basic posture of an integrationist is to accept the probability that many theories describe a portion of the larger reality. Interventions based on their descriptions and applied to clientele from which their conclusions are drawn are legitimate, appropriate, and recommended to the extent that they are applied within the context from which they were derived (theory-pure, complete, and not diminished by combination with theory-alien techniques). This suggests, for example, that modification of habituated responses can be directly and efficiently accomplished by use of operant conditioning techniques. Techniques that impact affective responses or cognitive changes will not have the same efficiency or strength when used instead and, if used in combination with operant techniques, they probably will cause inefficiency at best, ineffectiveness in amelioration, or even aggravation of the circumstance at worst. An instance that demonstrates this is the experience of a neophyte therapist employed to conduct behavior management at an institution for delinquent youth. The basic therapeutic strategy was a token economy with relatively few rules and with clear consequences for obeying or failing to obey them. The therapists were to award tokens for compliance, tokens that could be accumulated and later cashed in for privileges or goods. In an attempt to bond with the clients (contradictory to the operant approach), the therapist adopted an "unconditional positive regard" mindset and expressed concern, disappointment, and caring when one of the clients failed to earn a token. The emotional response from the counselor far offset the power of a mere token, with the result that noncompliance on the part of the client increased.

Another example of mixed models causing failure of a potentially strong intervention involves the use of cognitive restructuring to combat depression. Such an approach requires a strong and consistent disputing of uncovered beliefs that precipitate the undesirable emotions. The therapist did a good job of identifying the activating event that preceded the emotional episode. Likewise, the underlying beliefs that justified the defeating emotion were formalized. The therapist proceeded skillfully to loosen the client's cognitive structure, introduced some strong and convincing counter-beliefs, then, instead of cementing the shift with action or homework asked, "How are you feeling now?" The client stopped processing the restructured beliefs, disassociated from the immediacy of the situation, re-entered the strong and vividly remembered emotional state of the recent past, and became depressed. In an attempt to be sensitive and supportive, the therapist not only did not access changed feelings, but directed the client to think about something other than what had just been successfully established. Asking, "How do you feel now?" is a violation of every theoretical model except for a Gestalt integration effort. It is an example of theoretical cluttering that happens within an eclectic frame.

The attitude of allowing for more than one description of reality to be valid and useful permits the practitioner to avoid the difficulties in choosing and defending a singular position. In an extreme sense, it could be argued that by accepting all positions, it is unnecessary to reject any. The integrationist does not frivolously accept all positions. He or she can afford to accept the possibility of usefulness in all theories, yet will of necessity select and use those that have a foundation of support, that have been tested and their applications found to be productive. In this regard, the criteria for evaluation may be broader than the empirical tradition of psychology would indicate. Since the eventual validation of a particular model will come through its application by the practitioner, its initial selection may result from rigid empirical support, from a convincing logical foundation, or as a result of experiential awareness. The integrationist would not reject, out-of-hand, an approach that has yet to generate research support if it makes sense and fits within a logical framework appropriate to its application. Similarly, he or she would not deny the evidence of personal experience or of the accumulated experience of other similar professionals.

Even on a much broader, philosophical level it is possible to adopt an integrationist position. Take, for example, the debate between those who choose to see people as monistic, unified creatures who operate as sort of biological–existential Gestalts, and those who adopt a mind–body or soul–body dualism. At various periods across time, there has been alternation between which of the two positions are in vogue, and at any point in time there are devotees of both positions. In contemporary times, we hear phrases such as "Treat the disease" versus "Treat the patient," and "The symptom is the disease" versus "The symptom is an evidence of an underlying dysfunction." Segmented and specialized care is played off against holistic health. As long as a dichotomy is perceived, there will be competition for disciples. What if both positions are accepted as true? What if, at some level, everything is integrated and functions with regard to the whole and responds to interventions that foster integrated action, *and* what if parts of the whole can be addressed, accessed, impacted, and altered by direct intervention? If both are true, it is not necessary to rule out either global or specialized interventions.

Consider another philosophical conundrum, determinism versus free will. Many philosophers and theorists structure the human condition as one of external locus of control wherein the person is an amalgamation of conditioned responses and is predictable when the external forces can be defined. In contrast are those who allow for, even insist upon, internal locus of control, freedom to choose their actions, and power to influence/determine their conditions. What if both are true or partially true? What if people are neither totally controlled nor totally free? What if people have the possibility of some degree of choice, and what if exercising that choice is a function of awareness? Those who are unaware of choice will behave as though determined; those who perceive choice may exercise options. Choice may be limited either by the availability of options or by the degree of awareness of options and the belief that, in fact, any exist. Belief in freedom to choose in situations where alternatives are nonexistent or severely limited is delusional; denial of choice in situations where options are numerous and mutually attractive is also delusional. It is possible to have a basically realistic philosophy overlayed by a phenomenal factor that explains individual differences and variability across individuals and across situations. It is possible to manage the behavior of most people in some situations of restricted options by behavioral engineering; it is possible to help most people in some situations of multiple options to recognize options and to make choices. Implications of the above for human services and educational intervention are delineated in the following sections.

☐ Psychoeducational Design

In his book, Snelbecker (1985) posited a professional specialty called Psychoeducational Design. He believed that there is need for a specialist to translate general principles of pure theory into situation-specific applications that may be managed by technicians. His analog is the physical sciences where research physicists and research chemists discover or create general scientific principles or laws, where engineers create general principles or laws of application, where an engineering technologist combines those two sets of general laws into a specific application strategy for a specific manufacturer and, at which point, a technician carefully employs that strategy to enhance production.

In the discipline of psychology, and with eventual application in the clinic, classroom, or other behavioral change context, there are two levels of general theory corresponding to the physicist and the engineer: learning theory and instructional theory. The learning theorist engages in "pure" science in an attempt to discover general laws of learning. Learning theory focuses on how behavior is changed through experience and usually accounts for the behavior of a wide range of species and a range of behavior from the most simple to the most complex. "Learning theories are conceptual devices for organizing information primarily at the research level" (Snelbecker, 1985, p. 171). Explanation and prediction of changes in behavior, experience/meaning, and experience/perception are the purposes of this type of theory. Pavlov, Thorndike, Skinner, and Wertheimer are well-recognized learning theorists.

Instructional theorists are concerned with how to facilitate or manage learning by other people. They are "applied" scientists or the "engineers" of the learning process, their focus being the description of strategies for implementing change. An instructional theory is a set of statements based on research that allows one to predict how particular changes in the educational environment—classroom, clinic, industrial setting, agency—will affect student or client learning. Gagné, Bruner, Ausubel, Rogers,

Perls, Meichenbaum, and Yates are instructional theorists. A distinction between these two groups of theorists and the specialties to be considered next is that they study specific processes under careful scrutiny so as to extract principles that then are generalized to all learning contexts. General principles form the products of their work.

Counselors have the option of working either as technicians or as professionals. A technician performs at the service delivery level. He or she creates change in behavior or thought or awareness on the part of clients. As long as the correct techniques are used in the appropriate circumstances, the learning/teaching enterprise is successful. What seems to be relatively simple in the general terms of the scientist often becomes confusing within the context of application to a specific individual or group. The clean reality of the laboratory is often "muddied" in the specific application setting. Differences between and among theories lead to confusion in the clinic or classroom. Technicians will be successful only to the extent that their techniques are appropriate to the demands of the application context.

One major difference between a successful technician, one who applies appropriate techniques effectively, and the professional is that the professional understands (a) the circumstance and style of the client or student, and (b) the theoretical dynamics for producing or enhancing change. He or she then selects or creates intervention strategies that are tailored to the client or student and that are used in a theory-pure context. Snelbecker's (1985) *Psychoeducational Design* (see Figure 1.1) is the creation

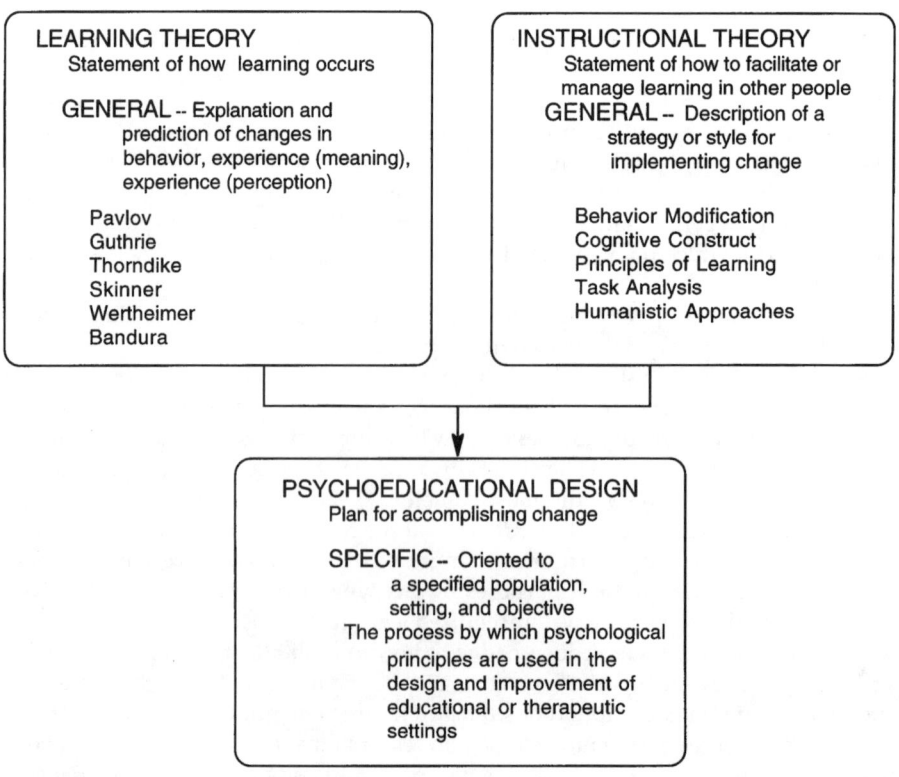

FIGURE 1.1. A Comparison of Two Theory Bases With Each Other and With Psychoeducational Design.

of a plan for accomplishing change that is oriented to a specific person or population, setting, and objective. It is the translation of general principles, the realm of the scientist, to specific applications, the realm of the technician. A middle position between psychological theoretical research and counseling practice would include (a) clarifying objectives, (b) delineating intervention methods, and (c) troubleshooting.

There are references to programs that prepare counselors as counselor *training* programs. The rubric, "training," suggests the preparation of technicians—people who can apply a specific technique within a specific setting. The complexities of clients militate against a technician mindset. Professionals are needed either to perform the tasks of therapy or to direct and supervise others who deliver those services. The preparation or education of therapists and counselors requires their gaining an understanding of the general principles of learning and of intervention plus extensive and intensive practice in applying the principles to a variety of contexts. This skill of perceiving client circumstance and style and selecting or creating an intervention that fits the needs of the client and yet can be applied within the full power of the theoretical context is the foundation for success as a professional. Technique follows understanding. The power of an intervention comes from its theoretical context.

☐ The Parts and the Whole

Similar to the swings between monism and dualism in philosophy, there have occurred shifts in definition and emphasis on the part of psychologists. Early in its history, psychology went through a "schools" era wherein empiricists were involved in identifying and studying the structure of experience or the function of behavior. This was countered by those of a gestalt persuasion who professed that to divide into parts was to destroy the essence of what is being studied. Preferences for laboratory research were played off against naturalistic observation. In the 1960s and 1970s, much interest in clinical endeavors was evidenced by identifying and separating out techniques that would address specific parts of the client. The most frequent division included the affective, behavioral, and cognitive functions. One evidence of this movement is a text by Kjell E. Rudestam, *Methods of Self-Change: An ABC Primer* (1980), the ABC denoting affective, behavioral, and cognitive modes within an integrated person, modes that can be influenced separately and apart from one another. Major proponents of change in each category flourished and attracted disciples. Behaviorists such as Wolpe (1969) formed one camp. The cognitivists, led by Ellis (1962, 1971, 1980) and his Rational-Emotive Therapy, formed another. Humanists such as Rogers (1951, 1961), with a credo of faith in the inherent capacity of the unfettered human to behave in progressively socialized and self-enhancing ways, constituted a third group. The psychodynamic group was another, with two branches: Freudian/neo-Freudian psychoanalysis and Gestalt facilitation of personal integration.

Under the influence of the American empiricist tradition, the various camps competed, not very successfully, for "scientific" credibility. In fact, only the behaviorists with their single-subject design application faired consistently well. The humanists generated some support for relationship as a factor in therapeutic encounters that were deemed to be effective. Seemingly as a response to the success of behaviorist research, a number of previously labeled cognitive specialists relabeled themselves as "cognitive–behavioral" therapists and either added or put focus on homework or on observable activities as a result of therapy. Simultaneously they cast the former behaviorists into a mold labeled "radical behaviorism." Interestingly, compared to their previous status, there is nothing any more behavioral about cognitive–behaviorists nor is there anything any more radical about radical behaviorists. The name-changing presents an illusion of differences that is more shadow than substance. Like the language concerns of Huxley, psychologists from differing persuasions engage in attempts to reduce awareness by their use of terminology and to consider it as the only awareness.

Subsequent to these developments, a more focal effort to return to monism appeared wherein it was recommended that any program of change must address all modes of the individual and their integration. Mueller, Dupuy, and Hutchins (1995) developed the TFA Counseling System which stresses the interaction among the think-feel-act aspects of human behavior. "It differs from other theories . . . by focusing on the interaction of thinking, feeling, and acting and defining this interaction as individual and situation specific" (p. 573). They referenced several sources to conclude that, "The blending of cognitive, affective, and psychomotor behavioral strategies is considered by many to be essential for maximizing the effectiveness of counseling interventions" (p. 573).

From an integrationist standpoint, this contrast of treating the dysfunctional sub-part by itself or only in the context of treating the whole person also may be recast from an either-or framework to an inclusive one. At times, and for some things, a monistic approach may be indicated and, at other times or for other things, clients may respond more adequately to an intervention directed at one aspect of being. As Rudestam (1980) suggested, sometimes a change in one mode will be mirrored by immediate or subsequent change in other modes. If this is the case, it could be argued that it does not matter which mode is the object of therapy since all will respond in an integrated way. It also can be argued that even though all modes may be affected, the most rapid, efficient, and effectual change process will address that mode that seems to be the focus of maladjustment or maladaptation.

Rudestam also contended that, "Sometimes, however, change in the affective, behavioral, or cognitive realm does not automatically lead to change in the other two areas" (1980, p. 11). To the extent this is true, the only defensible change strategy is one directed at that mode that requires adjustment. Furthermore, two or more modes may be out of adjustment. "The fact that the affective, behavioral, and cognitive levels of functioning at times operate relatively independently suggests that a total treatment package may need to consider all three modes in order to be optimally therapeutic" (p. 12).

Is the universe of human adaptation large enough to contain maladjustment in an isolated sub-system, in two or more sub-systems with related or different maladaptations, and whole-system encompassing concerns? Is it possible that sometimes an intervention into one sub-system will have important effects in the other sub-systems and at other times it will not? Could it be possible that Truth lies in some other explanation but that the intervention strategies just considered might work anyway—that phenomenal or experiential evidence supports their use? Adopting a tentative "yes" to these questions, the integrationist selectively incorporates, intact, those theoretical positions and their interventions into a repertoire of treatment strategies. Technique follows understanding. The power of an intervention comes from its theoretical context.

☐ Types of Learning

While the tradition in psychology has been to consider only three modes or three sub-systems, there appears to be reason to increase that vision. Furthermore, since this is a learning-based treatise, sub-systems should be different in relation to ways of knowing or to ways of learning. It is asserted that the traditional categories of affective and behavioral learning are understandable and defensible; that the traditional cognitive state requires division into cognitive learning and perceptual learning; and that two additional sub-systems be added: social learning and spiritual learning. Each type of learning has unique characteristics and dynamics and, hence, can be studied independently from one another. This description will begin with the most familiar and progress from that base to differential comparisons with the less familiar.

Cognitive Learning

Cognitive learning is that type of learning that people associate with acquisition of information. It is learning about things, people, and experiences in logical, language-mediated ways. From a study of concept formation, particularly as promoted by David Ausubel (1963), it is possible to know about something or someone without ever having had direct experience with that object or person. It is possible to "know about" without actually "knowing." This may be the kind of knowing Rogers (1969) referred to as insignificant knowledge—that which has no immediate personal relevance, that which forms the great bulk of formal schooling. It is attained through listening, reading, analyzing, and thinking. The result of this learning is a conceptual bank or a cognitive closet filled with information. For it to be useful, it must be structured. Gagné (1965) posited a systemic process whereby multiple discriminations predate concepts, concepts relate with other concepts to form principles, and principles combine in relation to context in the problem-solving process. Chomsky (1975, 1977) analyzed language into structural components, while Försterling (1986) demonstrated the power of the structure of thoughts to impact behavior and the dynamics of cognitive restructuring as a form of intervention.

Perceptual Learning

Direct experience somehow produces a different kind of knowing. Unlike cognitive learning, it seems possible to really "know" something or someone without "knowing much about" it or him or her. *Perceptual learning* is understanding, awareness, contextual relatedness, and qualitative uniqueness—the gestalt, the totality, the more than sum of parts. This defines perceptual knowing. It has additional differences inasmuch as perception of similar events varies from person to person. Unlike language, which can be standardized in denotative, dictionary-like precision, the phenomenological assumptions of perception recognize a degree of futility in cataloging or standardizing experiences.

Perceptual learning is the "right brain," holistic, motivation-centered something (Watzlawick, 1978) that defies logical or cognitive analysis. Images and perceptual "frames" can be stored in memory and can be altered—re-imaged or re-framed—with an accompanying change in awareness or understanding. The insight produced in such an experience is different from the change in knowledge coming from a language-mediated intervention.

Behavioral Learning

Behavioral learning consists of the adoption of actions in response to some environmental occurrence. It is habitual in that it tends to recur under the same or similar environmental situations, and it may be explained through the connection of contiguous cues and responses (Guthrie, 1952) or through reinforcement by consequent stimuli (Skinner, 1953). Locus of control is outside the individual, while acquisition or change in response is accomplished through conditioning, most usually imposed from an external situation or agent.

Affective Learning

Affective learning presupposes that emotional experience and expression are parts of a learned phenomenon. The expression of emotion may be conditioned in behavioral ways, and it may be elicited by self-statements. Emotion itself, though, has some features that set it apart from other ways of learning. The early development of emotion tends to occur in reaction to environmental conditions such as comfort- or discomfort-eliciting calmness or agitation (Berndt, 1997). Subsequent differentiation of a wide range of emotional experience and expression comes through interaction with people. It is relationship-mediated. It has a function in communication. An expressed and accurate understanding of someone's emotional state usually results in an abatement or cessation of that state (Gerber, 1986). Affective learning tends to fall into two separate categories: (a) management or expression of intense emotions, and (b) acquisition or development of desirable emotional states. Emotion is both a product of and a factor in interpersonal relationships.

Social Learning and Spiritual Learning

Social learning and *spiritual learning* are categories that are not traditionally treated in this context. They may not be categories of learning at all, or they may be understudied categories. There seems to be sufficient information, though, to describe them here and to make reference in other sections of this treatise. Social learning is more than the vicarious learning described by Bandura (1969). In fact, early descriptions of social learning described the various phenomena in cognitive, perceptual, and behavioral language—phenomena such as vicarious reinforcement, modeling, and principle-mediated learning. Of importance within the present context is the kind of learning that is an integral part of group dynamics. Janis (1967) spoke of "Groupthink," a descriptor for behavior that is unique to the group interaction. Schutz (1958, 1966, 1973) talked of needs that are satisfied in groups, one of which is social behavior on a continuum from "oversocial" through "psychotic." Harvey (1974) discussed the Abilene Paradox, which is a manifestation of giving up the logical problem-solving of the cognitivist and the perceptual validation of perceptual learning (yet operating on assumptions of the phenomenal reality of other group members). It ignores affective elements and may only border tangentially on behavioral factors. Current interest in systemic dynamics delineates varying influences on behavior as a result of the social system. Maybe social learning is an amalgamation of the other types of learning, yet the systematic differences argue for treating it as a category unique in itself.

Spiritual learning has little or no credibility in traditional learning theory discussions. It is seen as mystical at best, illusory or delusional at worst. Yet there seems to be considerable expression of personal change through subscription to religious dynamics or religious rituals. Believers speak of a quality of knowledge that is different from and more complete than cognitive or perceptual learning (James, 1960). They talk of a way of becoming convinced that, by its very difference from traditional experience, makes it either patently unique and different or patently false. Life-changing experiences connected with conversion, behavior predicated on faith that turns out to be self-enhancing, and attribution of strength in a higher power contributing to personal strength on the part of addicts (gaining power by giving up power—an interesting paradox), as practiced in the 12-Steps of Alcoholics Anonymous, all provide informal data and support a logical argument for the existence of yet another form of learning. One statement of a formula for managing spiritual discernment and learning suggests that (a) confusing issues be studied carefully, (b) tentative decisions be made, and (c) an appeal to deity be made while exercising the faith or expectation of receiving a response; this results in (d) a spiritual validation or sureness if the decision is correct or (e) a confounding of thought if the decision is errant (LDS Church, 1830). Interest in spirituality as an important aspect of life has broadened from the fads of the 1960s—transcendental meditation and Yoga—to a legitimized interest in Christian Counseling, Native American forms of intervention, Eastern religion-based therapies, and revived interest in asceticism and other manifestations of the spiritual side of humankind. If there is a commonality of experience produced by adherence to a formula or standard process, then there is either an entity of discovery or of mass delusion. Because it parallels other types of learning, allowing for the possibility of its existence and subjecting it to further study seems warranted.

CHAPTER 2

Congruence: A Perceptual Frame for Intervention

If there is substance to the Gestalt claim for a structural foundation for all "Truth," then the exposition of such a frame will provide a validation for this intervention model. It also will be a way of understanding the dynamics of an integrationist model and a tool for selecting or creating intervention strategies that have a high probability of success. This chapter employs a congruence model of positive mental health for the foundation; examples of patterns of incongruence are described, and a view of differential strategies of intervention for the various kinds of incongruence is given. The chapter closes with a consideration of client problem-solving styles.

☐ Congruence Model of Mental Health

"Congruence" is a mathematical construct with denotative significance in science and with analog power in the counseling arena. In its native context, congruence refers to the exact correspondence of two geometric figures when compared to one another. Two triangles with equal legs and equal angles may be said to be congruent. Carl Rogers (1942) employed the label, congruence, to explain the degree to which a client's perceptual version of reality replicates empirical or consensual reality. Clients whose perception is narrowed or distorted as a result of defensiveness are incongruent. The therapeutic atmosphere of genuineness, warmth, and unconditional positive regard permits the client to feel accepted and validated, resulting in a decrease in defensiveness and corresponding refinement—increased congruence—in his or her perception of reality.

Building on the foundation set in Chapter 1 regarding five ways of knowing, and employing triangles from the context of geometrical congruence, one can visualize the congruence/mental health analogy (see Figure 2.1).

If a person's cognitive, affective, behavioral, social, and spiritual selves are balanced, "in synch," and correspond to one another in respective content and strength, the person is congruent. Such a person is internally consistent and demonstrates a high

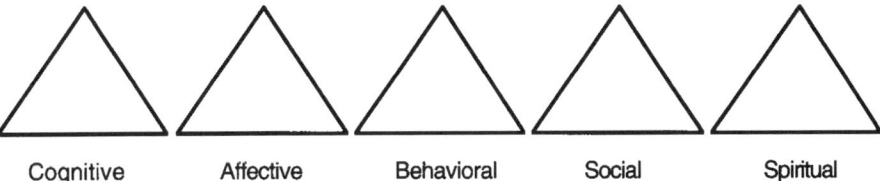

FIGURE 2.1. Five Ways of Knowing Expressed as Equilateral Triangles.

degree of positive mental health. Such a person shows no contradictions in thought, feeling, action, interaction, and spirituality.

Conversely, a person who is inconsistent, by virtue of any one or more of these five selves being out of phase with any others, is incongruent and demonstrates less than optimal mental health. An example of such incongruence is an individual who claims to be scrupulously honest (cognitive), cheats at the weekly poker games (behavioral), feels chagrined when caught (affective), rationalizes it as insignificant because it is just a game (cognitive), while blushing and grinning (behavioral) in discomfort (affective). The initial duplicity impacts his or her openness in communication with the group (social), while the subsequent getting caught and minimizing its significance impacts future relationships within the group (social). The degree to which the person has internalized the value of honesty affects his or her perception of worthiness/hypocrisy and diminishes the inclination to engage in spiritual activities (spiritual). Admittedly, this is a contrived example, yet it reflects the dynamics of internal inconsistency and self-defeat that marks incongruence.

There is a history of empirical activity devoted to those learning principles and change dynamics that are focused on the cognitive, affective, and behavioral segments of human experience. Therefore, they are considered as promising and legitimate domains within the intervention realm. Social and developmental psychologies have a traditional place within the academic and professional community and yet, as pertains to intervention, they are considered more as contextual elements rather than as being central to the process of behavioral change. Spirituality has received less attention from the mainstream of research and analysis. It has been relegated by many psychologists either to the realm of imprecision, where it shares a common berth with philosophy or to that category of experience referred to as "maybe significant but unmeasurable with our current state of assessment technology" and pushed aside as less promising or less worthy of investment than those areas of more precision and more empirical accessibility.

While many commonalities exist across cognitive, affective, behavioral, developmental, social, and spiritual areas as they pertain to intervention dynamics, there is a sufficient inequity of research, application, and respect to warrant selective consideration of some or all of them. Convention favors emphasis on the cognitive, affective, and behavioral realms, and clinical experience reinforces the importance of developmental, social, and spiritual areas, at least to the extent that their dynamics affect the processes of learning and change on the part of consumers of psychological services. In recognition of this professional duplicity, that may only be a manifestation of our *Zeitgeist*, this book includes separate emphases, one on learning-based change dynamics and the other on contextual factors, the management of which will facilitate successful interventions.

While history or convention is used as a reason for separate focus on developmental, social, and spiritual realms of experience and learning, they will be violated in the separation of the cognitive area into two portions: perceptual and cognitive. During the 1930s, in American psychology there were but two conceptual emphases in learning theory: behavioral and perceptual-cognitive. The behavioral dynamics tended to be carefully explicated because of a preference for empirical validation while the thought-mediated approaches, difficult to study directly, were clumped together. It was almost like there were behavioral approaches and "other." Subsequent shifts in professional and research focus have elaborated cognitive dynamics and distinguished them from the more purely behavioral ones; however, there is yet to be a strong division between perceptual and cognitive emphases. This professional evolution receives further treatment in Chapter 3. For reasons that will become obvious in subsequent chapters, there will be four areas in the organizational scheme for the learning-based interventions: perceptual, cognitive, affective, and behavioral (see Figure 2.2).

One additional focus or frame needs to be established before proceeding. It is the contrast between deficit and surplus states of learned behavior. Learning often is seen as the accomplishment of new and different views, thoughts, feelings, and actions. There is a developmental perspective that tends to be seen as additive in nature. Piaget and Inhelder (1969) described the processes of assimilation and accommodation as means by which the developing intellect organizes new information into the cognitive repertoire or apperceptive mass. There are two additional processes that are not additive. One is forgetting, or the subsequent inability to retrieve awareness of previously known information or perception. The other is the learning of new information or the shift in perceptual awareness that does not replace or obliterate former awareness, but rather renders it useless, invalidates it, or moves it into a category of being incorrect, foolish, improper, or self-defeating. Ausubel (1963) uses variations of the term "subsumption" to describe cognitive shifts that explain differences in retrieval of information. Correlative subsumption "locates" new information close to older and similar information; obliterative subsumption combines or blends information, new and old, that is so similar as to be difficult to differentiate and, hence, gets lost in or obliterated by other "too similar" information. Watzlawick (1978) suggests the creation of mutually exclusive perceptual experiences, the process of reframing, that results not in forgetting or obliterating previous frames but replaces previous, self-defeating frames with more functional ones. Försterling (1986) describes similar dynamics for replacement of thought patterns or structures, the process of restructuring.

To restate in different words, there are processes by which new thoughts, views, feelings, and actions are accomplished. When a person is without these and would benefit from their accomplishment, such person is in a deficit state. Terms such as

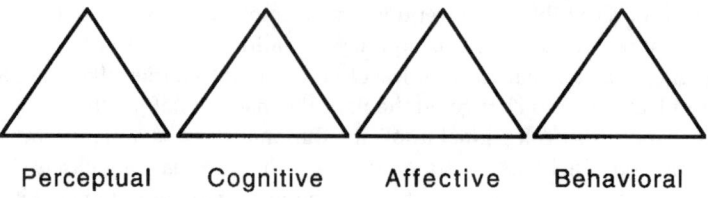

FIGURE 2.2. Four Learning-Based Intervention Areas

framing, structuring, guiding, or *establishing* refer to these additive processes. They are used to rectify deficit states.

Often people have views, thoughts, feelings, or habits that are problematic and lead to self-defeating responses. Such conditions are, at worst, damaging and, at best, excess baggage leading to inefficiency or to less than optimal satisfaction. Having excess baggage is a surplus state, one rectified by holding a "garage sale" of the mind to purge the outmoded, unuseful, and nuisance belongings. Terms such as *reframing, restructuring, ventilation* or *emotional management,* and *behavioral change techniques* address these modification processes. It is to be noted that there are different techniques for addition and for modification dynamics and that there are differing techniques for perceptual, cognitive, affective, and behavioral change.

☐ Patterns of Incongruence

The basic intervention model that follows logically from the above foundations includes eight categories of conditions in the learning-based focus: perceptual deficit, perceptual surplus, cognitive deficit, cognitive surplus, affective deficit, affective surplus, behavioral deficit, and behavioral surplus. Similarly there are six categories in the contextual areas of focus: developmental deficit, developmental surplus, social deficit, social surplus, spiritual deficit, and spiritual surplus (see Figure 2.3).

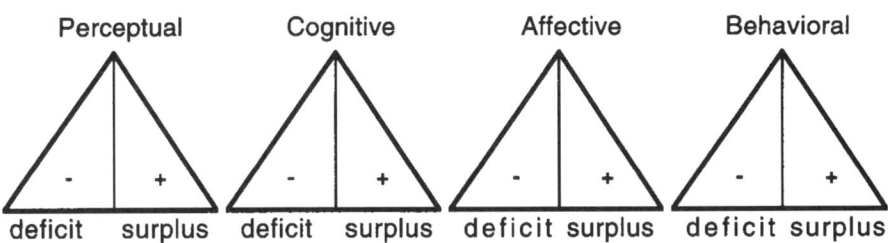

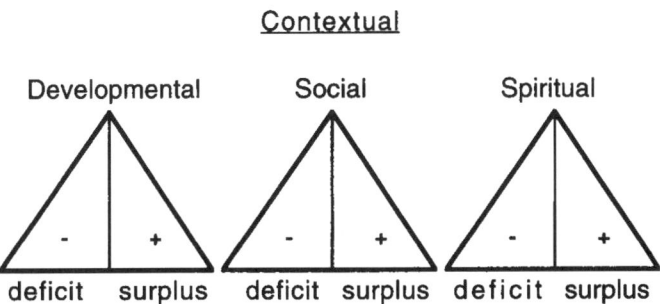

FIGURE 2.3. Surplus and Deficit Conditions in Four Areas of Learning-Based Focus and Three Contextual Areas of Focus.

Some examples in each category will help elucidate the model. A perceptual deficit state is experienced by anyone who enters into an entirely new circumstance. Two phrases are in the common vernacular that refer to this experience: "I didn't have a clue!" and "When in Rome, do as the Romans do." By virtue of their relative inexperience, children encounter more frequent deficit states than do adults. In order to survive, children tend to be more vigilant or observant than are adults. Various kinds of modeling or "teaching by example" are useful in dealing with perceptual deficits. The seminal study by Bandura and Walters (1963) demonstrates the dynamics of filling a perceptual deficit for children introduced to a new context after having seen a model perform constructive or aggressive play.

Perceptual surplus has been experienced by a great number of parents who find themselves doing to a child the very act that they vowed never to do. The author's father had a tendency of saying, "Shut up that crying or I'll give you something to really cry about," whenever he encountered crying. As the author choked down the convulsive sobs, he vowed again and again to never do that to his children. It wasn't until he caught himself saying those very words that he was able to correct that response. He had carried that surplus frame for years, ready to implement it in a similar context to which he experienced it. The perceptual memory seems to be able to capture and store global experiences to be recalled and to be used as the basis for response far into the future.

"I don't know what to make of this" and "I haven't figured it out yet " are two sentences that allude to the commonality of experience called cognitive deficit. Gagné (1965) spoke of verbal association that is requisite to multiple discrimination. That, in turn, precedes concept learning, then principle learning. The development of language permits people to talk to each other and to themselves about conceptualizations of direct experience, observations, and of logic- or symbol-mediated relationships. The absence of labels for objects of perception prevents the sharing of those perceptual experiences. Insufficient concept formation precludes coding and symbol manipulation, and that makes higher reasoning impossible. Constructs such as congruence cannot be recognized or used by the person who does not know them or is in a deficit state as regards them. A great amount of upper elementary school work and secondary education focuses on filling deficits that are deemed by curricula makers to be of importance. Everyone has at least one encounter with severe and resistant cognitive deficit as they try to master a school subject that seems to be impossibly difficult on the acquisition side and incredibly simple after mastery. For a portion of psychologists, the term "statistics" triggers memory of such an experience.

Cognitive surplus has received considerable attention in the literature (Beck, Rush, Shaw, & Emery, 1979; Ellis, 1969; Försterling, 1986). A basic assumption for theorists and therapists in this group is that all responses are thought-mediated and that by changing the thoughts that precede responses, the subsequent actions will be modified. Personal experiences of determined persistence in the face of discouraging feedback suggest self-statements in the nature of, "It will be catastrophic if I fail, or even if I do less than a perfect job" or "I'll just die of shame if I let my father down." Restructuring of the self-statements results in alteration of the behavior, often in the direction of enhanced performance. The statement, "While it will be moderately disappointing to me and while my father may withhold enthusiastic praise, it will not be catastrophic, nor even of much lasting consequence if I do a less than perfect job," permits the person to move ahead with more efficiency and toward resolution of the challenge.

A surface description of affective deficit would be a state of having no feelings or of being unable to experience certain specific feelings. Such may be an accurate description, though this area is more obscure than all of the others. Affective deficit is not synonymous with "flat affect" or with depression, both conditions involving the presence of emotion, the expression of which is severely dampened. A simplistic description of depression is that a person with this condition refuses to feel anything in order to protect himself or herself from the extremes of discouragement or hopelessness engendered by the circumstances; it is necessary to avoid positive feelings because to feel anything is to risk feeling everything. Because of the presence of feelings that are suppressed, depression is not an affective deficit condition. There is one context, frequently encountered in therapy, that seems to fit the dynamics of affective deficit (Gerber, Pederson, & Selby, 1996). Two foundation pieces need to be set for its description

First, Maslow (1954) postulated a hierarchy of needs. Satisfaction of these needs is important for continued existence and for progress toward self-actualization. Of critical importance is the true hierarchical nature of this system. It is impossible to be successful at a higher level until the requisite needs are met. It is possible to use the techniques of a higher level, but the effort will be futile because higher-level techniques do not satisfy lower-level needs; unsatisfied lower-level needs will preclude satisfaction of higher-level needs. At the middle of his hierarchy, Maslow sees needs for love and belonging. These needs are satisfied in children who are raised in an emotionally healthy context, one in which parents give love, cherish their children, and create for them a psychological/emotional home. Love is given. The child has validity simply by virtue of his or her being. The child has position in the family simply because he or she exists there. This love and belonging cannot be earned. In contrast, the needs for self-esteem, the next higher level, are accomplished through feedback from other people. Good impression on others results in internalized good impression of self. Self-esteem is "earned" or is contingent on appearance, performance, or possessions.

The second foundational piece is an awareness of the strong focus in our society on contingency relationships. Advertising communicates the message, "You will be happy, loved, admired, successful if you weigh the right amount, drive the prescribed vehicle, wear the appropriate and stylish apparel, use the recommended toothpaste, and chew a specific brand of chewing gum." Whatever the content of the advertisements, the underlying message most frequently is an "if–then" contingency. Observations of parenting techniques, fueled by a bribery misinterpretation of positive reinforcement doctrine, show contingency relationships: "You may borrow the car when you have completed your studies or chores," "You may go out to play after you have practiced on the piano for thirty minutes," "You may sleep over at your friend's house if you get a good report card," "You will be okay if . . ." and "I will love you if . . ." are examples of such relationships.

Harris (1967) described the universal position of childhood as "I'm not ok, you're ok" because of the obvious differences in ability and stature between child and parents and between child and older siblings. Because older people in the context will always be older, catching up is not likely, and becoming as ok as they are is unlikely. It is up to the older people in the context to give to the child the message, "You are ok as you are. You needn't be different." This is noncontingent validation, or personal validation

The absence of personal validation, or the deficit in feelings of being ok as is, describes one condition of affective deficit. The contrast between personal validation and esteem is the difference between "I know *you* and I accept/tolerate/like *you*" and "I see your *image/behavior/act* and I evaluate *it* as appropriate/desirable/pleasing." The only way to experience the emotion that comes with personal validation is to engage deeply in a noncontingent relationship. This means allowing another person (one who has sufficient status to matter) to know the good, the bad, the pretty, the ugly, and the neutral, and to experience acceptance of all by that significant other person. Rogers (1961) coined the phrase, unconditional positive regard, to describe a therapeutic relationship; such a relationship has the dynamics of being a personally validating one

A surplus of affect is a condition wherein a person feels intensely and cannot/will not do what is necessary to diminish the intensity. One characteristic of emotion is the need to communicate it (Gerber, 1986). Many clients spend the initial portion of their therapy in a gush of emotional expression, a venting process that seems necessary as a prelude to focusing on problem dynamics. Some people "stuff" emotions because the expression of them is prohibited by earlier conditioning: "It's not good to show anger," "Grown people don't cry," and "Any show of emotion is a sign of weakness" are examples of such prohibitions. Some people are afraid to express emotion for fear of total loss of control, of "having a mental breakdown." Intervention for affective surplus involves two phases: (a) the first is to help the client vent those emotions that are blocking effective functioning, and then (b) the second is to facilitate emotional expression (integrate perception and cognition) so that denotative expression that promotes understanding will replace less direct and less explicit ways of showing emotion. Intervention into affective surplus states involves both cognitive and behavioral dynamics as well as the experiential aspects tied to affective dynamics.

Traditionally, operant techniques such as behavior modification have taken a unified approach to all behavior change, allowing for differences only in the definition of the behavior to be impacted: the target behavior. There are two kinds of target behavior: (a) that which is desired and absent (deficit) and (b) that which is not desired and present (surplus). The traditional organization is entirely workable. There may be some advantages in differentiating approaches for deficit and surplus states. Doing so will preserve the parallel nature of this integrative model. Behavioral deficit is marked by the absence of some desired, stimulus-controlled or habitual response. Identification of the desired response may come from authority figures or from clients themselves. Ethical considerations require that human clients be aware of and a party to definition of target responses. Once identified, intervention consists either in waiting until the target response occurs naturally and reinforcing its repetition, or in shaping the response from "sort of what's desired" toward the target response through a series of successive approximations until the desired response is emitted and can be reinforced to a highly consistent pattern. The absence of study skills in university students is an example of behavioral deficit. Another is the demeanor of some people that is devoid of propriety—absence of social sensitivity and appropriate response.

Behavioral surplus requires additional dynamics because it is marked by existing and undesired habits. The existing habit needs either to be extinguished or to be rendered inoperative due to the conditioning of a competing, mutually exclusive response. Extinction requires manifestation of the habit in the absence of any reinforcers for enough trials to render it inoperative. Because of the tendency for seemingly extinguished responses to pop up unexpectedly in the future (spontaneous remission), replacement with mutually exclusive responses keyed by the same stimulus conditions is preferred. One example is the tendency of a person to make large numbers of self-references while interacting with others, resulting in ostracism or social isolation. Self-reference can be extinguished through conditioning techniques for certain contexts; however, encountering a non-extinction context might re-establish the tendency toward excessive self-reference. Conditioning the habit of either making reference to others or of asking questions regarding others' interests would simultaneously increase focus on others while decreasing self-focus. Caution must be exercised in the selection of substitute responses so as to avoid conditioning another self-defeating habit. The "lemon drop" technique for stopping smoking involves conditioning the sucking of candy in place of smoking. The potentially resultant problems with dental hygiene and weight control may diminish the accomplishment of cessation of smoking.

The learning-based focus has four components that incorporate all of the change dynamics for selecting and managing intervention strategies in general. Each of the components has different variations depending on the context in which it is applied. The following paragraphs delineate aspects of client circumstance that require sensitive modifications of change techniques if they are to work optimally.

Developmental psychology is best seen as a descriptive or normative science. By very careful observation of the characteristics and responses of people at specific chronological ages and across periods of change, it is possible to catalog those characteristics and responses that are typical or normal for the age and condition of people. Having established normality, it is possible to describe, assess, and sometimes even quantify differences from the norm. Exceptionality is a term used in reference to people who are sufficiently subnormal or supernormal to draw attention to themselves. Development across individuals is inconsistent such that many people of the same chronological age will manifest variations in characteristics and responses. Development within a single individual is asynchronous, meaning that each separate person will show a range of maturity across characteristics, in some cases including some subnormal and some supernormal characteristics and responses.

Developmentalists such as Havighurst (1949) contend that human development is the result of both biological and experiential conditions. Successful toilet training, for example, depends on physical maturation to the point of sphincter control plus the learning of socially determined propriety. As a result of this interplay between biology and experience, there are two aspects of development that are significant in counseling. The first is the assessment and remediation of characteristics or responses that are at a subnormal level because of lack of experience or learning. The second is the taking into account of normal developmental states in the selection of interventions for other concerns. It is ineffectual to use an intervention that requires a higher developmental level than the client possesses.

A developmental deficit state is one where the client is subnormal in some way that is leading to self-defeat and that can be enhanced by coached experience. Of course, in this as in other areas, if there is some structural condition or health state that is preventing desired responses, medical or surgical procedures may be required prior to or simultaneous with therapeutic interventions. In this deficit situation, the client's developmental level is the focus of therapy. Another condition that fits the dynamics of developmental deficit is where the client has not progressed sufficiently to gain from the intervention being applied by the counselor. In this case, the deficit is in regard to the task that is required, not in relation to the age group norms for the client. Since this is a mismatch of technique with developmental level, the technique should be discarded in favor of one that is within the range of the client to perform. Similarly, a client who is operating at a subnormal level will respond better to interventions that match his or her level than to those typically applied to normal clients of his or her age group.

Developmental surplus is simultaneously more difficult to conceptualize and of less concern. For most conditions, being overly mature is not a handicap. Perhaps the concern most easily understood with developmental surplus is when a client elicits expectations well above her or his reference group in one aspect of performance; this then gets generalized to all aspects of her or his performance. An intellectually precocious child may be misplaced in a social environment that labels his or her age-natural responses as immature.

The descriptor, social, is problematic because it has many and varied uses. In this case, it will refer to the major interpersonal context in which individual responses occur. From social psychology and personality there are foundational concepts such as:

- self-concept is formed from the feedback we get from interactions with other people (Sullivan, 1953).
- individuals develop patterns of response to others shown as the tendency to move toward, away from, or against others (Horney, 1945, 1950).
- two urges dominate the behavior of people: the need for union with and the need for individuation from other people (Fromm, 1941, 1956).
- our personality is established as a result of the place we make for ourselves in our family of origin (Ansbacher & Ansbacher, 1956).
- the individual's needs for inclusion, affection, and control show up in behavior in the group context ranging from over-expression to isolation, suspicion, and/or neurosis (Schutz, 1958, 1966, 1973).

Whether there are unique responses produced by the social context or manifestations of other kinds of learning to social circumstances is a difficult issue. It is possible to see in oneself and in others a variation in response when "talking to oneself" in contrast to interacting with one other person, or as compared to relating in a group of several, that may vary from responses in a large group. Some people tend to show a relatively narrow range of behavior across social situations. Others seem to be "different people" from one situation to another. To the extent that some or all clients are a product of their social context, it is necessary to consider such contexts in regard to applying intervention strategies. Perhaps the most attention to this issue is currently given by the systems theorists (Bateson, 1958; Minuchin, 1974, 1984; Minuchin & Fishman, 1981; Ruesch & Bateson, 1968).

In addition to the change in dynamics resulting simply from the addition of more people to the equation are the concerns of gender and culture. This is particularly true for individuals who manifest gender confusion or those who subscribe to practices that deviate from the norm. Similarly, minority versus majority status involves difficulties in learning and in behavioral change due to variations in perceptual sets and standards of acceptability for behavioral expression. While there are little verifiable data to suggest that the processes of learning are different across cultures and genders, there is much to suggest that what is accessible by way of perception and what is permissible by way of expression must be taken into account in an intervention strategy.

Social deficit would be indicated when the client is unresponsive to his or her social context. "Clueless" is a word from the vernacular that describes this kind of person. Absence of social awareness and insensitivity to subtle and sometimes strong feedback from the social environment are typical of this condition. The use of perceptual and behavioral deficit intervention techniques often are effective in this area, but must incorporate contextual dynamics.

Social surplus is seen either as over-reliance on contextual definition or persistence in a social response that is counter to the present setting. Individuals who use an external locus of control framework and who evidence needs that they (a) perceive (perceptual surplus), (b) believe (cognitive surplus), or (c) have been conditioned toward (behavioral surplus) satisfaction only through group response, will rely too much on the group setting for gratification. They often "turn off" their most promising source of response by being too demanding, too clinging, too ever-present, or too dependent.

In contrast, those who operate from past programming (behavioral or cognitive) to ignore social feedback, to stand firm, or to not need people will alienate potential supporters by their unresponsiveness to or disregard of their social context. This pattern often incorporates a cognitive surplus state and lends itself to cognitive restructuring and practice within the current contextual dynamics

Some of the more powerful intervention strategies for both social deficit and social surplus conditions occur in group counseling. A range of groups—sensitivity, support, assertion training, psychoeducational, and therapy—incorporate social change dynamics as a primary focus.

The spiritual domain is evident in many contexts, yet it is obscured by the many philosophical and sectarian frameworks in which it is expressed. Certainly, the traditions and forms of religious expression form important considerations in dealing with clients who subscribe to or have been indoctrinated or programmed by them. In the familiar 12-step approach of Alcoholics Anonymous, a Higher Power is accessed in a very structured manner and for purposes that facilitate change. Native Americans invoke sensitivity to supreme powers and indulge in rituals such as those involving sweat lodges. Asceticism is a means seen by some to transcend their venal nature and rise to a more highly valued, spiritual plane. There is an interest in Asian religions and related therapies within the counseling profession. Christian counselors invoke change through an appeal to a unified higher authority. Some produce change through exorcisms or other traditional rituals. Charismatic Christians mix interpersonal sensitivity with spiritual sensitivity. The late sixties and seventies witnessed the popularity of Yoga and of transcendental meditation as techniques for stretching consciousness. Zen was prescribed reading in some therapy training programs. Even Satan worship and psychological investment in interactive fantasy games carries some dynamics of ritualistic and traditional spirituality. If there is something significant to any or to all of these experiential manifestations, then those who manage the principles in accomplishing a leap of faith or a communion with another power have something not enjoyed or used by others. It, too, can be experienced in two ways: (a) a deficit state, with problems arising out of the inability to engage in potentially self-enhancing behavior and (b) a surplus condition, wherein over-reliance on spiritual ritual or technique or interpretation results in overriding the evidence of other systems to the detriment of the individual.

A spiritual deficit state exists when a person is unsuccessfully persistent in coping with crises or growing through blocks, the solution to which is spiritual in nature. This may be indicated by expressions that life lacks meaning or that personal activities and efforts, though successful, are not fulfilling. A sense of being ungrounded in a diverse and changing environment is an expression of spiritual deficit. In contrast, the description by a professor of Buddhist Studies at Dongguk University in Seoul Korea, in personal conversation with the author, defined spiritual centeredness as the ability to "be calm with oneself."

Spiritual surplus conditions require sensitive interpretation. To a person who is a strong advocate of a religious or spiritual position, it is impossible to be "too spiritual" or too much in touch with a higher power. In a pragmatic sense, there are individuals who put so much emphasis on what they believe is spiritual that they systematically over-rule evidence of a cognitive or experiential nature and limit themselves in their progress. Fanaticism may be a descriptor though it would be necessary to differentiate the spiritually "unbalanced" person from the one with an extreme cognitive surplus belief script. A spiritually balanced person expresses his or her spirituality in ways that are consonant with his or her circumstance and manages that circumstance better as a result of faith in, communion with, and validation by the higher power.

☐ Differential Strategies for Intervention

There are three views of problem solving that are pertinent here. One view assumes a unified, monistic nature of people and claims that any change to a sub-part of the system will produce changes throughout the person; other sub-parts accommodate for the changes to one sub-part. This enables therapists to use their favored approach on all clients. The behaviorist, for example, focuses on the observable symptom or target response with the belief that the client will rationalize (cognitive) the new response as appropriate or best in the situation and will get used to the new response and begin to feel (affective) comfortable with it. For the cognitivist, thought precedes all action, whether it be overt behavior (behavioral) or covert feeling (affective). From this view, change in cognition is the only defensible approach. Specialists in relationship therapies claim that the affective state resulting from a positive therapeutic relationship will permit the client or student to martial his or her own cognitive and perceptual resources resulting in behaving, automatically or intentionally, in more self-enhancing ways.

A second viewpoint recommends therapy or teaching that involves all sub-parts. It is multi-modal, incorporating perceptual, cognitive, affective, and behavioral parts in all therapy. Some cognitive-behavioral therapists assume that the addition of an action phase to the standard cognitive restructuring procedure accomplishes this goal. While this is a logical response in recognition of duplicity or of a dualistic nature in people, it runs counter to contemporary emphasis on differing learning styles or perceptual styles and a preference for individualized education or client-specific therapy.

The third position is that of the integrationist who takes a much broader view of individual differences than do practitioners with either of the previous views. This permits the mastery and use of therapies or strategies that are very different one from another. This position places or integrates these diverse strategies into a repertoire or "tool chest" that allows the practitioner to select one that is appropriate to the circumstance and style of a given client. Such an approach requires careful observation of the client by the practitioner until an awareness of circumstance and style is accomplished. Then the selection of that theory-pure, specific problem-solving strategy most appropriate to the case at hand is made. Technique follows understanding

Clients present an incredible array of individual differences—in native capacity, in living style or problem-solving style, and in circumstance. Some categorizing is possible, yet there are always exceptions who defy the categorical system. Of particular concern to the integrationist is to perceive and understand client differences and to know the dynamics of specific interventions well enough (a) to select the most promising technique or techniques as fit the client and (b) to avoid using techniques out of context or combining two or more techniques with incompatible dynamics. It is necessary to keep in mind the range of individuality and complexity of people so as to avoid a view of integrational therapy that is too simplistic, yet some organizational model is necessary to permit the therapist to cope with the magnitude of information about each client.

One approach would be to look at client characteristics in each of the seven areas introduced earlier. A second, simpler yet effective method, would be to render a two-level decision. The first decision would be concerned with focal dynamics of learning/behavioral change. This would look at circumstance and style in terms of behavioral, affective, cognitive, and perceptual dynamics. The second decision-level would be the contextual or qualitative aspects of the client's circumstance and style. This would define the developmental, social, and spiritual elements that prescribe modifications in the behavioral change strategies of decision one.

The following is a brief review of the focal categories of the model with the addition of logical intervention examples for each. Chapters four through eight will expand consideration of these focal areas. Chapters nine and ten will treat the contextual categories.

Behavioral Deficit

This condition is marked by the absence of a stimulus cued response, the presence of which would improve the condition of the client or student. Two factors are of importance here: (a) whether or not the response is in the client's repertoire, and (b) if present, how to associate it with the environmental cues intended to control it. If the person can do the target response but is not doing it when desired, a Guthrian association learning strategy might be best. Suppose a worker "forgets" to attach safety devices before proceeding with the job. A series of directed repetitions with awareness of environmental cues that are always present in the work context would result in the habitual response of attachment of the safety devices as cued by the identified environmental features.

If the client has never performed the target response and if it is difficult to do with only one or two trials or demonstrations, then an operant shaping process would be appropriate. While in the performance context, the client/learner would attempt to perform the target response. The counselor would ignore gross misperformance but would reinforce any activity that is a "move in the right direction" or a weak approximation of the target response. The process of coaching skill performance such as in athletics or music or drama or surgery also fits these dynamics.

Behavioral Surplus

Bad habits are those automatic responses that result in embarrassment or defeat. They are frustrating to the performer because of their seemingly automatic nature. Good intent to avoid doing them or reliance on "will power" more often than not results in failure and self-deprecation (another self-defeating habit). The procedure of response extinction or the conditioning of mutually exclusive responses as used in operant conditioning should work well. Overeating or getting hooked into excessive television viewing are examples of externally cued behavioral surpluses.

Affective Deficit

The lack of personal validation that seems to limit the quality of a person's experience in virtually every aspect of life is an example of affective deficit. It is immune to being rationalized away or distracted by excessive activity. Intense experience or consistent experience over time in a non-contingent relationship is the therapy of choice. This is practiced by many Rogerian counselors and others of a Humanistic bent such as Jourard.

Affective Surplus

Being "pent up" with emotion is very disabling until it is rectified. Intense and unexpressed or not understood affect tends to control the consciousness and motivation of the person so affected. There are several approaches to dealing with this concern. The particular strategy would be dictated by the style of the client. Psychodrama (Kellermann, 1992) provides a "stage" for experiencing the emotions, communicating them, and seeing the results in a coached context. Gestalt techniques (Passons, 1975; Perls, 1969) that require detachment and isolation of sub-parts and then re-integration of those parts provide expression of many emotions. Careful and denotative reflection of feelings by the therapist permits client expression and success in being understood as well as some cognitive knowledge for labelling feelings. This may then be followed up with practice in definition of affective states with more accurate communication of the emotional experience.

It should be pointed out that sometimes feelings are stimulus-cued responses and, as such, may respond to techniques that ordinarily are categorized elsewhere. Phobias are an example of this. An illogical and self-defeating fear that is triggered by environmental conditions and results in avoidance behavior or in intense discomfort follows a Pavlovian or classical conditioning paradigm in its inception and in its remedy. The onset of an emotion can be understood as a conditioned reflex with a phobia resulting when a previously neutral stimulus substitutes for its accompanying emotion-producing stimulus. The systematic desensitization and reciprocal inhibition method of Wolpe's (1969) works very well in deconditioning stimulus-cued, maladaptive emotional responses.

Perceptual Deficit

This is apparent in the client who is expected to perform an act for which he or she has no prior awareness. The historical Gestalt processes of insight and the discovery learning emphasis of Bruner (1966) are examples of strategies that provide a client with experiences from which he or she may form perceptual impressions. The modeling approaches typical of Bandura (1969), with attention to model characteristics that will be effective with a given client, are powerful techniques for filling in major perceptual gaps. Bibliotherapy and movie/videotape modeling are often useful in creating vicarious experience for the person with perceptual deficit. For any client faced with entering an environment or context that is foreign, totally or in some significant part, these techniques will be beneficial.

Perceptual Surplus

Perceptual "set" is the tendency for an individual to perceive a situation in a certain way. If hungry, the individual might select, from a complex stimulus experience, those cues that relate to food. For an individual who has had previous experience in a context, he or she often is "set" to perceive a new and similar experience in the same way as the old one. Like people with decremental losses over time in sight or hearing, this individual can only respond to what he or she "sees." Like the person with gradual erosion of vision who gets corrective glasses, the perceptual surplus person often is shocked by a sudden shift of perception or clarification produced by the lens of a "reframing" technique. Such reframing may be accomplished through the suggestion to look at things from a different perspective or from role playing or role reversals. Sometimes the client is resistant to such techniques and requires a paradoxical disconnection of cognitive restriction or a hypnotic "bypass operation." Watzlawick (1978) and Erickson (1967) describe techniques for reframing. Gestalt figure-ground reversals and separation of confused sub-parts are useful in producing new perceptual frames. Maximum dissociation techniques of Ausubel (1963) produce clarity when two images are difficult to discriminate one from the other.

Cognitive Deficit

This category deals with basic ignorance—lack of knowledge of something necessary to know. The principal considerations in this category have to do with the developmental level of the learner and the methods for organization/presentation of information. Piagetian (1969) principles relative to the developmental stage of the learner are useful. The preference for experiential bases for learning (Bruner, 1966) in younger learners in contrast to the more logical, structured approaches for older learners (Ausubel, 1963) is important. Entry level skills and knowledge (Gagné, 1965) and behavioral objectives (Mager, 1962, 1972) are pertinent in this context. The great majority of effort in instructional theory is directed at resolving cognitive deficits. With a client showing cognitive deficit, the therapist either becomes a teacher or refers the client to a person who can intervene by the use of instructional techniques.

Cognitive Surplus

When what you know, is wrong, and you insist it be right, you are in a state of cognitive surplus. The known gets in the way of the correct. It is necessary to eliminate the known and incorrect and replace it with the unknown and correct. The major problem in this area is dealing with the intensity of need or the insistence that what is known be correct. Ellis (1969, 1971) and Beck, Rush, Shaw, and Emery (1979) are foremost applied theorists in this area, though they tend to be oriented toward emotive responses in contemporary application. Försterling (1986) and other social psychologists (Abramson, Seligman, & Teasdale, 1978; Anderson, Horowitz, & French, 1983; Kelly, 1971; Kelley & Michela, 1980) have a broader theoretical base and are useful in dealing with cognitive surplus. They work most efficiently on cognitive issues

There are three steps to addressing problems of cognitive surplus. The first is to identify or deduce the specific and inaccurate cognitive element. Ellis (1958, 1969) refers to this as "a sentence we tell ourselves." Once it is known, the next step is to loosen the structure in which it is embedded. This may be done by creating doubts through the introduction of dissonant information (Festinger, 1957) or by stronger methods of confrontation—directly attacking the belief or challenging the client to an empirical verification of the belief. The third step is to introduce a replacement belief that is more adaptive for the person in the given context. This three step process is called cognitive restructuring.

☐ Client Style Considerations

The first stage in an integrationist approach to therapy is to understand the client's circumstance and style. The above material addresses circumstance: what is the condition of the client? Style, in contrast, refers to the person's usual or preferred way of dealing with circumstantial conditions.

Client patterns of response tend to be consistent; that is, each client will have a preferred pattern of dealing with life circumstances. One may meet a crisis in the present and immediately shift to a futuristic frame and respond with catastrophizing or with self-reassuring optimism. Another may rationalize away the significance of either the problem or the importance of his or her position. One may fantasize, while another may invest in overt and intensified action—keep busy. Even the seeming nonstyle of changing to meet the demands of different situations is an externally oriented, "satisfy the situation" style. Each person has a style

For the sake of consistency in the model and to demonstrate the dynamics of same circumstance–same style and of mismatch between circumstance and style, four classes of style will be considered: cognitive, affective, behavioral, and perceptual.

Cognitive

The person with a cognitive style solves problems through thinking about them. He or she relies on the cognitive processes of rational, logical, meaningful structure: If it doesn't make sense, it can't be correct. Sometimes, when the cognitive person says, "I just can't figure it out," it is because the problem is affective and not responsive to cognitive processes. Myths such as the Rumpelstiltskin Effect, wherein giving a name to it is supposed to make it go away, are confounding aspects for a person with this style.

Affective

Feeling right about a solution is the key to acting on it for the person with an affective style. He or she works on intuition and "gut feelings." While the dynamics of this are unclear, as are most things of an affective nature, to a cognitive styled person, it appears to be a workable style. Choices may seem illogical, yet they are selected and employed with some success.

Behavioral

Doing what the situation demands is the response set of the person with a behavioral style. Response to an external locus of control, both for cue and evaluation, defines this style. It is a reactive style with initiation set up by cues within the context. Responses tend to be spontaneous and rapid with no time required for processing. As long as the person's repertoire contains situation-specific responses, the person does okay. When the cues are novel, the process of stimulus generalization sets in and the person selects that response that has worked in similar situations.

Perceptual

In response to some personally established perception of what should be, the person with a perceptual style constantly scans the environmental context. He or she looks for discrepancies in old contexts and, if in novel circumstances, looks for familiar cues so as to select a frame for interpretation. What fits is what's right. The person with a perceptual style is led by insight. The response may be delayed until the "incubation" time for an insight to "hatch" has transpired. Then the action taken will be spontaneous, confident, and complete. Options closest to the "good form" of the client are those that are selected. The four style considerations are summarized in Figure 2.4.

One strength of the integrationist approach is in the capacity to match cognitive interventions to cognitive problems, affective interventions to affective problems, perceptual strategies to perceptual problems, and behavioral approaches to behavioral concerns. While it is possible that change in cognition may follow a behavioral intervention, or emotional responses might adapt to cognitive changes, the matching of intervention strategy to circumstance will likely be more efficient and effective. Similarly, marked efficiency comes when the client or learner style matches the circumstantial problem. The cognitive style person will be most receptive to a cognitive intervention and the same carries through with matching other styles and problems. Life is complex, however, and many of the problems that clients bring to therapy result from trying to use their preferred style to solve problems of another kind. For instance, clients may try to think their way through non-logical emotions or resolve habits through will-power. The therapist must be ready to teach non-preferred resolutions while simultaneously engaging the client in the preferred style.

Another complication occurs when the client has difficulties that involve more than one type of problem and his or her style may not correspond to any of the difficulties. In addition to having a repertoire of intervention strategies that address varying circumstances, the professional must have flexibility both in awareness and approach for clients of differing styles.

- Cognitive: What makes sense.
- Affective: What feels right.
- Behavioral: What the situation calls for.
- Perceptual: What fits the context.

FIGURE 2.4. Criteria by Personal Style.

CHAPTER 3

Perspective

Since meaning comes from context, it will be helpful to establish a conceptual framework for this treatment of intervention theories. This chapter will provide a definition of learning, a description of theory and its purpose or function, a grounding in philosophy, a brief treatment of some historical roots, and sketches of two historically prominent theorists and their models. Other theorists will be considered within an application context in subsequent chapters.

☐ Definition

Because the types of intervention in counseling are strategies for changing behavior, dynamics of learning form the focus for analysis and application. The nature of a structural frame often is apparent in its label and definition. Students of psychology are familiar with definitions of learning similar to the following:

- learning is a change in behavior as a function of experience; or
- learning is the capacity of a system to react in a new or modified way as a result of experience; or
- learning is a process by which an organism modifies its behavior or acquires entirely new behavioral patterns as a result of interactions with the environment.

These definitions usually contain a disclaimer to exclude biological or physiological conditions such as growth, maturation, aging, fatigue, receptor adaptation; changes in arousal, attention, or motivation; and disease.

A casual perusal of the three definitions above indicates that the first focuses on outcomes of learning, the second emphasizes the ability to change, and the third stresses the procedure for bringing about change. An integrationist would have to allow that all are accurate and that all are useful. Instead of being mutually exclusive as these definitions are, an integrational definition will have a large enough frame to incorporate all of them, plus more. For purposes of this book, learning is considered to be a construct, meaning that it is not accessible to direct empirical assessment and, hence, is implied or inferred from changes in behavior; cognition, both in ways of thinking (process) and in results of thinking (products); perception; and/or affect, including feelings, attitudes, and values. The definition excludes changes due to drugs, fatigue, illness, instinct, and maturational changes in readiness. Learning occurs following or as a result of experience, direct or vicarious; thinking; and/or insight. It is relatively permanent, usually is enhanced by practice, and usually is purposeful for self-maintenance, survival, and/or prediction or anticipation of future conditions. Often, there are physiological correlates: learning either causes or results from changes in the central nervous system. In outline form, learning is:

1. a construct inferred from
2. changes in
    (a) behavior,
    (b) cognition,
    (c) perception, and/or
    (d) affect;
3. not due to drugs, fatigue, illness, instinct, and maturational changes in readiness;
4. follows or results from
    (a) experience,
    (b) thinking, and/or
    (c) insight;
5. relatively permanent,
6. usually enhanced by practice, and
7. usually is purposeful for
    (a) self-maintenance,
    (b) survival, and/or
    (c) prediction or anticipation of future conditions.
8. Often there are physiological correlates.

☐ Theory

He who has imagination without learning has wings but no feet (Chinese fortune cookie).

Learning theory represents the organizational underpinning for all behavioral change strategies. It is the organizational context for interventions. From a therapeutic framework, Lovinger (1984) emphasized the importance of a theory base. He said

> Because the material a patient produces is of so vast an array, the emotions so varied in range and intensity, the demands on the therapist so complex, and the nature of what will be helpful so often uncertain, a theory is needed to reduce the cognitive and emotional burdens on the therapist. A theory aids therapy by, at the very least, reducing the therapist's anxiety and confusion to manageable levels so that it is possible to continue to hear the patient (p. 43).

Just what is a theory that makes it a necessary part of the therapy process? A simple description is that theory is a refined statement of the theorist's observations or experiences. The dynamics may be seen clearly in an analogy. An artist perceives some piece of reality that he or she wishes to communicate. The rendition in oils or some other medium is intended to recreate the essence of the artist's experience. Suppose ten artists were commissioned to render a common experience, and suppose they were given a lecture on a psychological principle with the task of communicating that lecture in graphic form. It is probable that the result would be ten different pieces of art, each distinctly different one from another yet with some perceived commonality.

32 Client Circumstance and Intervention Selection

Such an exercise has been conducted by the author a number of times in the context of a theory class. After the initial renderings, the students ("artists") were subgrouped and challenged to select or recreate a model upon which they could agree and refine or make a new rendition representative of the subgroup. Models were described and critiqued. With the shift in perceptual frame from an artistic creation to a graphic model of the lecture content/experience, the following conclusions were drawn:

- A theory is simply a description of somebody's reality.
- Content is selectively added or subtracted as a result of the model-building process.
- The communication mode limits or distorts reality.
- Even if given common stimuli, each observer receives something different. In actuality, no two theorists sample the same behavior yet most generalize freely to all people.
- Data, once received, are interpreted according to the background of the observer; the meaning is a product of the observer.
- The cognitive style of the observer affects the form of presentation (e.g., a tendency to think in analogies, formulas, simplistic terms, complex interactions, pictures, etc.).
- Models are changed by subsequent input; they evolve.
- A tendency exists to solidify a position and defend it as "True" (schoolism).
- Theories represent, more than anything else, the theorist. To understand the reality he/she experienced, one must consider his/her position, look beyond the theorist to the data observed and to the purposes in describing them. Also, one must know oneself in order to assess the limitations one places on his or her own perceptions and interpretations of reality; therefore, it makes sense to refer to the theory by the name of the theorist.

Theory can be a useful yet imperfect instrument in the study of conditions and in the selection of interventions. Time-tested theories tend to be more useful than individual, idiosyncratic ones. The unquestioned intervention or method or strategy has a high probability of being whimsical and ineffective. Written exposition of methods allows for the possibility of broad support and validation, and for the risk of reasoned or empirical criticism that would invalidate it. The mark of a professional is to know what is being done, for what purpose it is being done, and what theoretical context gives it power. Some theory is necessary, and "good" theory is preferable over "bad" or uncommunicated theory. By studying time-tested theories, a practitioner may either select one with a reasonably good chance of being effective or create one within the context of comparison. Theory provides the feet that are needed to launch interventions into successful flight.

☐ Philosophy

Rollo May indicated that ". . . every scientific method rests upon philosophical suppositions" (May, Angel, & Ellenberger, 1958, p. 8). If theory is the context that gives meaning to application, then philosophy is a larger context that lends meaning to theory. Morris Bigge (1964) proposed a simplified scheme for identifying philosophical foundations. He proposed that selection of two words, one from each of two continua, would circumscribe a person's philosophical position. Relative to the "basic nature of people," is it bad or neutral or good, and is it passive, interactive, or active?

A cursory look at some of the categories thus defined will demonstrate the relationship between philosophy and method. The Bad–Active category is based on the Judeo-Christian premise that natural man is the enemy of God. The natural tendency to embrace evil must be countered by strong and severe educational methods. Spare the rod and spoil the child; corporal punishment is an aid to therapeutic change. People naturally seek pleasure (hedonism); this can be offset by denial of bodily pleasure, avoidance of comfort to temper the spirit and tame the evil tendencies (asceticism). Progress, learning, remediation come from established, firm programs of change managed by the professional on behalf of the client: "Teacher, counselor, father knows best."

Within the Neutral–Passive category would fit John Locke and his *tabula rasa* or blank slate belief. People are born as but blank slates upon which life's experience writes. Minds are to be molded. Children must be educated for desired perceptions and socialized behavior. Control or power is in the environment. Therapy is contingency mediated with locus of control outside of the client (i.e., in or with the therapist).

A Good–Active assumption credits people with being fundamentally programmed for self-enhancement within proper social contexts. Locus of control is internal, and difficulty with self actualization as shown by under-social or anti-social behavior and self-defeat is caused by negative environmental influences and restrictions. Rousseau's treatment of the French boy, Emile, wherein he removed him from the corrupt city environment and permitted him to unfold at his own rate and direction is a reflection of this position. A. S. Neill's *Summerhill* (1964) was a group experiment in non-directive schooling. Carl Rogers (1942) built a therapeutic approach based on neutralizing relationship negatives that preclude natural growth.

Such thinking can be expanded into large philosophic systems called paradigms of science or world views. One posits that organisms are like machines, and to know how classes of organisms operate is to be able to control them through manipulation of critical factors. Another suggests that organisms are pre-programmed, and the therapist works to enhance natural functions and to remove obstacles. A third sees a mutual interaction between person and environment so that changes in either have impact on the other. The personal philosophy or world view of the therapist will influence his or her theoretical bias and choice of interventions. Being aware of his or her base of biases is important to the professional. Understanding the client's philosophical set will enable the counselor to enlist more active effort on the part of the client in support of his or her therapy.

☐ Historical Roots

Accounts of psychological history begin most often with Wilhelm Wundt and his laboratory in Leipzig, Germany in 1879. Credited to him was a shift away from the reliance on logic to establish truth toward the insistence on empirical demonstration as the only defensible source of knowledge. He used introspection in an attempt to describe consciousness. Atomism was the scientific venture of his day, the attempt to reduce everything to its smallest particle or atom in order to understand it. Wundt was looking for the atoms of consciousness.

Other developments prior to or contemporary with Wundt include extirpation experiments on animals (removal of parts or of all body organs including the brain), establishment of a nervous basis of reflex behavior, and Weber's law dealing with the relationship of stimulation to sensitivity (just noticeable difference experiments). Circa 1870, Sir Francis Galton (under the influence of Darwin) developed case study techniques, developed "test" as a measure of a particular trait, and started using correlation as a statistical approach.

In France in 1792, Pinel took mental cases out of the dungeons; Mesmer's work (circa 1779) set up Charcot (circa 1872) and Janet (circa 1906) in pioneering hypnosis. In America, the turn of the century saw activity by Hall and the child study movement, Cattell in mental testing and differential psychology, and William James working with memory and transfer of training, and with basic education approaches.

During the 1900 to 1930 time frame, various trends were solidified by their advocates into five major thrusts: the four "schools" of psychology, and psychoanalysis. The impetus of Wundt was divided into two schools: structuralism and functionalism. The structuralists emphasized the "what" of experience and continued on with introspective techniques. Titchener is identified as prominent in this school. The functionalists studied the "how" and the "why" of learning. They focused on mental operations in contrast to the elemental focus of the structuralists. Ebbinghaus and his studies of the effects of the nature of the learning curve and of dynamics involved with overlearning, using nonsense syllables and the memory drum, is one prominent functionalist. Others include John Dewey (progressive education), Edward S. Robinson (work decrement, fatigue, boredom), and John McGeoch (retroactive inhibition).

A third school of psychology was behaviorism, touted by John Watson. Rats became a favored vehicle for the study of learning. Since rats learn and since it was hard for Watson to attribute consciousness to them, the focus was firmly placed on empirically verifiable behavior as the only acceptable evidence of learning; consciousness was an unnecessary concept.

The fourth school of psychology was Gestalt psychology. Proponents of this position decried the reductionistic approaches of American empiricism and insisted that experimental control changed the important aspects of reality, resulting in conclusions not generalizable beyond the laboratory. The dictum, "the whole is greater than the sum of its parts," pretty well phrases the major ideological difference between Gestalt and the other three schools.

Psychoanalysis, championed by Sigmund Freud in Vienna, was not so much a departure from philosophy as were the other schools. It was a fledgling medical specialty with numerous violations of the empirical mandate in American psychology. Freud relied on a case study approach that assumed broad generalizability to other cases, perhaps to all other people. He did not take rigorous case notes, preferring to write up remembrances and impressions at the end of the day, after seeing many patients. His philosophical set was of the Bad–Active variety, assuming the existence of a personality component, the *Id*, that generates energy in service of basic gratifications; its oppositional unconscious force, the *superego*, that is the socializing force; and the conscious *ego*, working on the reality principle.

Over the years, the emphasis or "center stage" of psychology has moved from one to another focus. For a time it seemed that Behaviorism was the only true psychology, then Cognitive Psychology took the spotlight. Humanism had a resurgence followed by a brief renaissance of Behavioral Empiricism in response to a societal concern for mathematics and physical sciences and in winning the space race. Cognitive approaches resurfaced and emphasized an action component, changing their designation to "cognitive behavioral" and labelling the previous users of the behaviorism title as radical—radical behaviorists. From an integrationist viewpoint it is important to remember that each of these theoretical and research biases has retained its vitality, even during times that another had the center stage position. Though temporarily less popular than another position, none was less true or less useful than at times of being in vogue. Rather than arguing what is the best position, with an assumption of mutual exclusiveness and a developmentally primitive insistence that if one is valid, all others must be invalid, the integrationist can use the strengths of each position on those clients and for those circumstances where each is most applicable.

☐ Theorists of Historical Significance

There are two theorists who have been of such prominence and influence to warrant special consideration, yet whose works are of more historical significance than of contemporary applicability. These are Edward L. Thorndike and Clark L. Hull.

Thorndike

Thorndike was born in 1874 in Wesleyan, Massachusetts and died in 1949. His father was a Methodist clergyman. He completed the Bachelor of Arts at Wesleyan University and was elected to Phi Beta Kappa. At Harvard, he completed a master's degree (in 1897) under the supervision of William James. His first laboratory was housed in James' basement, where he started studying children. That proved to be a little too progressive for society at that time. Nobody seemed to care when he switched to "experimenting on" chickens. In 1898, he completed the doctorate at Columbia University where he studied under James McKeen Cattell. He spent most of his professional career at Columbia Teacher's College. He was a dedicated researcher and prolific writer, authoring over 500 books, monographs, and journal articles.

The geneticist, Galton, with his directive that whenever you can, count, and the quantitative bias of Cattell influenced Thorndike, who said,

> Whatever exists at all, exists in some amount. To know it thoroughly involves knowing its quantity as well as its quality. Education is concerned with changes in human beings; a change is a difference between two conditions; each of these conditions is known to us only by the products produced by it—things made, words spoken, acts performed, and the like. To measure a product well means so to define its amount that competent persons will know how large it is, with some precision, and that this knowledge may be conveniently recorded and used (1918, p. 16).
>
> A [person's] nature and the changes that take place in it may be described in terms of the responses—of thought, feeling, action, and attitude—that he makes, and of the bonds by which these are connected with the situations that life offers. Any fact of intellect, character or skill means a tendency to respond in a certain way to a certain situation— involves a situation or state of affairs influencing the [person], a response or state of affairs in the [person], and a connection or bond whereby the latter is a result of the former (1913a, p. 1).

The most characteristic form of learning of both lower animals and people was identified by Thorndike as trial-and-error learning, or learning by selecting and connecting.

Influenced by British association psychology, Thorndike developed a system of learning predicated on Jeremy Bentham's philosophy of psychological hedonism. . . . Individuals, by virtue of their human nature, pursue pleasure and avoid pain (Sahakian, 1984, p. 103). Responses to a situation that are followed by a rewarding state of affairs will be strengthened or stamped in as habitual responses to that situation; responses that are unsuccessful will be weakened or stamped out as responses to that situation (Sahakian, 1979, p. 31).

The theory was derived mostly from studying maze-running in chickens and puzzle-box escaping in cats. There were three major laws and five minor ones.

Major Laws. *Law of readiness.* This was influenced by William James, who said that psychology should be close to physiological correlates. Thorndike postulated the existence of "conduction units" between sensory stimuli and response activation. The readiness of conduction units to operate varies:

- if ready, firing is experienced as satisfying;
- if not ready, firing is experienced as annoying;
- if not ready, not firing is satisfying;
- if ready, not firing is annoying.

This law gave a logical and physiological definition to the experience of being satisfied or annoyed. It was not accessible to empirical verification and tended to fade in significance in Thorndike's later theorizing.

Law of effect. The distinction here applies to whether the state of affairs is positive or negative, satisfying or annoying. "When a modifiable connection between a situation and response is made and is accompanied or followed by a satisfying state of affairs, that connection's strength is increased; when made and accompanied or followed by an annoying state of affairs, its strength is decreased" (Thorndike, 1913b, p. 4). The operational definition of "satisfying state of affairs" is one that the animal does nothing to avoid, often doing things that maintain or renew it. An "annoying state of affairs" is one in which the animal does nothing to preserve, often doing things that put an end to it. According to Thorndike,

If a mental state or bodily act is made to follow or accompany a certain situation with resulting satisfaction it will tend to go with that situation in the future . . . Put together what you wish to go together. Reward good impulses. Conversely; Keep apart what you wish to have separate. Let undesirable impulses bring discomfort (Sahakian, 1984, p. 104).

Later Thorndike de-emphasized the effect of an annoying state of affairs as being inconsistent and probably of no influence at all. In effect,

Rewards in general tend to maintain and strengthen any connection which leads to them. Punishments often but not always tend to shift from it to something else, and their educative value depends on what this something else is . . . Punishment does not weaken the connection leading to it at all—does not strengthen the tendency to any other connection than in the slightest degree (Thorndike, 1932, p. 277).

Law of exercise. Thorndike (1932) noted that, other things being equal, learning tends to occur to the extent that particular acts are practiced. He later discounted this entire law, concluding that "the mere repetition of a situation is, in and of itself, unproductive for learning" (p. 64).

Minor Laws. *Law of multiple response or varied reaction.* Instead of persisting with only one response in a new situation, most subjects display multiple (numerous) responses or varied reactions.

Law of set or attitude. After a time, certain aspects of the situation (certain stimuli) seem to be more crucial in influencing the subject's behavior.

> The principle that in any external situation, the responses made are the product of the "set" or "attitude" of the animal, the satisfyingness or annoyingness produced by a response is conditioned by that attitude, and the "successful" response is, by the law of effect, connected with that attitude as well as with the external situation per se, is general. Any process of learning is conditioned by the mind's "set" at the time (Thorndike, 1913b, p. 13).

Law of partial activity (prepotency of elements). A part of the situation may become so prepotent or salient that some responses may become partially bound to those stimuli no matter what else is happening in the situation. This is similar to superstitious behavior where a response gets hooked to a specific part of a larger stimulus context and, when that sub-part is experienced, it elicits the response.

> Such a partial or piecemeal activity on the part of a situation is, in human learning, the rule. Only rarely does [a person] form connections, as the lower animals so often do, with a situation as a gross total—unanalyzed, undefined, and, as it were, without relief... Such prepotent determination of the response by some element or aspect or feature of a gross total situation is both an aid to, and a result of, analytic thinking; it is a main factor in [a person's] success with novel situations; the progress of knowledge is far less a matter of acquaintance with more and more gross situations in the world than it is a matter of insight into the constitution and relations of long familiar ones (Thorndike, 1913b, pp. 26–27).

Law of assimilation or analogy. When confronted with a novel situation, an organism will respond as it would to situations that are most similar to those it had encountered in the past.

Law of associative shifting. Any response of which a learner is capable can become associated with any situation to which he is sensitive (e.g., one can get a cat to stand by holding food and saying, "Stand up." Later the cat will stand to the position of hand or even to the command alone).

Thorndike was concerned with the establishment and testing of a theory of learning. Breaking a larger theoretical structure into sub-parts such as major and minor laws and then testing them empirically was the pattern for successful scholarship in his era. He also was interested in applications of theoretical knowledge. He said, "Learning is connecting, and teaching is the arrangement of situations that will lead to desirable bonds and making them satisfying" (Snelbecker, 1985, p. 228). The procedure is to break down complex acts into simpler ones and systematically reward practice to build up connections. He preferred an "identical elements" explanation for transfer of training over the prevalent notion of strengthening mental faculties. For instance, it's fruitless to study Latin in order to improve one's ability to do hard thinking in other areas.

Hull

Clark L. Hull is known for the magnitude and thoroughness of his theory. Often called a monolithic theory, his model was thorough, large in scope, and provided the impetus for a large quantity of follow-on research. Dr. Hull was born in 1884 near Akron, New York. His youth was spent in what has been described as pioneer conditions on a farm in Michigan. He contracted typhoid fever that resulted in partial memory loss and, at age 24, was stricken with poliomyelitis. The residual paralysis in his lower extremities forced him to change his career track from mining engineering to psychology. His university preparation was prolonged by economic problems resulting in his interrupting his education while teaching in rural schools to work his way through college. His undergraduate degree was from the University of Michigan. He was a graduate assistant at the University of Wisconsin where he completed the Ph.D. in 1918. He stayed on for 11 years as a faculty member, then worked at Yale's Institute of Psychology from 1929 to 1952. In addition to his work in learning, he wrote a book on aptitude testing in 1928 and one on hypnosis in 1933. He was president of the American Psychological Association in 1936. Through his work on a hypothetico-deductive theory of learning, he was a major power in the 1930s and 40s.

Apparent influential forces in his training and professional work were Darwin and his survival theory, Newton and mathematical methodology, Thorndike and the law of effect, and Tolman, a contemporary, who postulated intervening variables. Certainly his early training in the physical sciences influenced his research and theorizing. His major thrust was to establish a small set of primary laws from which additional secondary laws could be established.

Truly a scientist who was willing to test his position, Hull arranged for Kurt Koffka, one of the primary advocates of Gestalt Psychology, to spend a year at the University of Wisconsin. The richness of educational experience for their students is attested to by Gengerelli (1976) who endured a master's oral examination conducted by Hull, Koffka, and one other faculty member. His article provides a window for seeing the spirited interaction between Hull, the reductionist, and Koffka, the Gestalt wholist. Hull's summary of Koffka was that he was a "reasonably well-informed critic of behaviorism—mainly acting as corrective influence rather than offering a viable alternative" (Snelbecker, 1985, p. 256).

Essentials of Hull's theory. Psychology is a "natural science" with quantitative laws of behavior. "He contended that every science involves a continuous interaction between tentatively formed principles based on logically derived assumptions and interpretations of data and ongoing laboratory studies that are designed to test and to modify the theory" (Snelbecker, 1985, p. 257). The theory is based on a conceptualization of the learner (his research subjects were white rats) as an adaptive organism. All organisms are self-maintaining systems. Behavior occurs and is modified relative to need state (deprivation) and to the goal of equilibrium (a homeostatic or cybernetic model). The organism's behavior is controlled by environmental stimuli that guide it to need gratification. Hull assumed that organisms have, at birth, some existing receptor–effector connections (S/U/R) that provide a baseline behavior ability.

Upon the basic construct of the adaptive organism, Hull identified three classes of variables and sixteen postulates. The three classes of variables represent a research analog for the learning process: independent variables, intervening variables, and dependent variables. The interinvolvement of these variables is complex, yet subject to empirical study and verification. What an organism does in a given situation (dependent variable and the outcome variable for research) depends jointly on the condition of need (deprivation or disequilibrium) in the organism (independent variable or internal precondition) and the characteristics of the environment (independent variable, external precondition). Intervening variables are primarily organismic variations that influence the amount of motivational energy toward a goal and any factors that inhibit action toward the goal.

Dependent variables for Hull had to be subjected to careful empirical assessment. He looked at amplitude of response (amount or strength), latency of response (time elapsed between stimulus and response), resistance to extinction (number of trials to suppression of response), and frequency of response (rate, number of responses in standard time interval).

The independent variables consisted of all controlled and pre-existing conditions. These would include all stimuli that impinge on the organism, such as noise, color and sizes of visual stimuli, foods, liquids, and the organism's previous experience in similar conditions. Such previous experience influences the amount of learning or "habit strength" for pursuing a specific goal in a specific condition. Habit strength mediates the organism's response to a certain stimulus condition. In other words, the probability of a given response is a function of the need state, or drive, and the habit strength, or previous history of reinforced trials. These two independent variables can be estimated in units from one to one hundred and the product of multiplying these estimates is an assessment of reaction potential (available energy to be expended in pursuit of the goal).

The sixteen postulates define characteristics of the three classes of variables. They will be incorporated here in a brief description. For a more detailed enumeration and description see Sahakian (1984). The reaction potential ($S^E R$) is an intervening variable produced by drive (D) and existing habit strength ($S^H R$). Reaction potential is reduced by conditioned and physiological inhibitors ($S^I R$) and becomes effective reaction potential; this in turn is influenced by oscillation in electro-chemical status ($S^O R$) resulting in momentary reaction potential. The probability and strength of a response is a function of the momentary reaction potential being strong enough to surpass the energy threshold ($S^L R$) required to overcome inertia.

The Hullian model is mechanistic, assuming that an organism's response is set in motion by a combination of need and environmental conditions and that differences in response from time to time or across organisms are variously inhibitory functions of intervening variables. Complex behavior, including apparent "choice," are a result of habit family hierarchies—alternate behavioral routes to the same goals. The accomplishment of subgoals (rgs) that are part of habit family hierarchies allows for a sense of awareness of the process, even of prediction or foreknowledge of eventual outcomes.

The reviews of Thorndike and Hull provide a grounding in historical learning theory. Some of their concepts will be apparent in subsequent chapters, largely because of their strong influence on other theorists. Their work does not fit application models as well as that of some other theorists.

PART II

INTERVENTION THEORIES

CHAPTER 4

Four Families of Intervention Theories

This chapter will formalize common dynamics across theories that can be fit into each of four groups. It will describe the commonalities for each group and establish a base for interventions into problem circumstances that are congruent with each group. It is a "mini-theory" of theories, a model of models or a meta-model.

The four families are association, reinforcement, perception, and cognition. Association and reinforcement are one-stage models, while perception and cognition are two-stage models.

☐ One-Stage and Two-Stage Models

From a historical bias for scientific or empirical processes, psychologists are used to the symbols S->R indicating a cause and effect relationship between stimulus and response. Some theories see the human being as a biological machine that "runs" depending on which switches are engaged or which buttons are pushed. To elicit a different behavior, you must press a different button

Sometimes the person or organism under observation is included in the formula: S->O->R. This recognizes that there are organismic qualities or characteristics that might have an impact on the response. Since the workings of the organism are not open to direct observation and measurement, they are inferred from systematic observation of differences in S->R trials. The simplest of models says that S causes R, or that S cues the organism to give the predictable R. This is a single-stage, unitary process, triggered by the stimulus. A slightly more complex model suggests that the probability of R is enhanced or diminished by conditions in the organism, S->O->R. This also is a single-stage model in that the response is initiated by the stimulus, the "button is pushed and the machine responds." The response might be one of lowered intensity because of "dirty bearings" or "frayed connections," but a specific response has been initiated by the occurrence of the stimulus.

Sometimes the probability of a particular stimulus eliciting a specific response can

43

be affected by whatever happens after the response. This formula is S->R->S. The change in stimulus condition, subsequent to and consequent on the response, acts to increase the probability of recurrence of the response upon another presentation of the original stimulus. This also is a single-stage dynamic, since the relationship between S and R is a one-step, highly predictable one. Individual differences across observations of different organisms in similar stimulus circumstances and in the same individual across time are explained by organismic changes that inhibit or enhance normal response or by changes in consequential stimulus conditions that impact the probability of responding, an external locus of control.

Another way of looking at the dynamics across an S->O->R event is to see the organism as an active agent. This usually means attribution to the organism of the ability to perceive, think, judge, and decide. This is a two-stage process. The first stage is the occurrence of S and its perceptual impact on O (S->O). What does O perceive and how clear or accurate is that perception? This allows for variations in factors such as attention, sensory receptor differences, and perceptual set across individuals and in the same individual over time. In effect, the same physical event in the "real world" may be perceived at a variance from its physical science properties. The second stage is the decision and action process (O->R). The organism initiates action based not on the stimulus but, rather, on the decision it has made. Stage one is stimulus and perception. Stage two is decision and action. Variations in response across individuals in similar stimulus circumstances and in the same individual across repetitions of a similar stimulus situation are explained as resulting from decision, an internal locus of control.

☐ The Association Theory Family

Association theories, of which those of Pavlov and of Guthrie will be examined in a subsequent chapter as primary referents, have the following dynamics in common:

- The stimulus event occurs prior to or at the same time as the response and either elicits or cues the response.
- A connection or bond is established between the stimulus and response (afferent–efferent neural events) or between two stimuli and a reflexive response (afferent–afferent–efferent neural events).
- Contiguity—the simultaneous or overlapped, or closely proximate occurrence of the stimulus and response—is the single and powerful condition for the bond or association of the two to be made.
- Teaching or conditioning is a process of arranging stimulus and response events to occur contiguously to one another.

The establishment of a phobia is an example of association learning. A phobia is the experience of fear in an illogical context. Imagine a child of four or five years of age accompanying a parent on a shopping trip. Upon entering a crowded elevator, the child is pushed up against the parent by an overly ample person wearing a bulky coat. Momentarily the child is smothered in the coat and experiences trouble breathing. Though the experience is brief, ending at the next elevator stop, it is long enough for the child to experience panic from the threat of suffocation. Previously neutral stimuli would include people, relatively confining spaces, and bulky coats. It is possible for any of those stimuli to become associated with the panic experienced by the child so that future encounters with any of them would call out the panic response. This would be a manifestation of claustrophobia, agoraphobia, or "bulkycoataphobia."

Similarly, most people come to associate smells with favorite and not so favorite foods. Experiencing the smell calls up memory of the food and may cue a seeking response. Encountering a different smell, particularly if it is offensive, when in close proximity to the favorite food is an unsettling experience, a violation of the previously learned association.

While the dynamics of simple verbal association can be explained in reinforcement terms, it is likely that the attaching of the spoken word to a referent and, later, the attaching of the printed word to the spoken word are examples of association learning. The young child sees a small furry animal, hears the sound of the spoken word, "kitty," and attempts to reproduce the sound. Subsequent encounters with kittens elicit similar sound production from the child. (It is helpful to recognize that proponents of different theoretical viewpoints will generate logical explanations for learning events based on their models. Some explanations are reasonable and efficient while others are far-fetched and extremely unparsimonious. For the integrationist who can understand the logic in several approaches, the simplest one that works becomes the explanation of choice. This is an expression of the conventional use of parsimony.)

☐ The Reinforcement Theory Family

Reinforcement theories, of which that of Skinner will serve as primary referent in a subsequent chapter, have the following dynamics in common:

- Learning is a process of the contiguous occurrence of three related or contingent events: the stimulus, the response, and the consequent stimulus or reinforcer.
- Specific stimuli that are intended to become controls for specific responses must be discriminated by the learner from among other similar but not identical stimuli.
- The desired response or target behavior must be caused to occur contiguously to the discriminated stimulus; this may be accomplished by selective reinforcement or by the conditioning of successive approximations of the target response.
- A reinforcer is any event subsequent to the response that has the effect of increasing the probability of the discriminated stimulus calling out the target response.
- The consequent stimulus must be caused to occur contiguously to the target response.
- Teaching or conditioning is a process of managing the contiguous relationship of the three contingent events.

The most frequently given example of reinforcement learning is that encountered by most people—learning to avoid touching a hot stove. The stimulus to be discriminated is stove (later on in the sequence when it may be useful to touch a cold stove, the means of discriminating hot stove from cold stove is learned). The response is avoidance of contact or moving away from or halting any movement toward the stove. The consequent stimulus from touching the hot stove is a burning sensation. This is not a really good example of reinforcement learning because it is a punishment paradigm.

It works, theoretically, because of the immediacy and severity of the consequent and punishing stimulus. A better example would be that of a parent giving positive words, physical strokes, or culinary treats (consequent stimulus) when the child moves away from or halts movement toward (target response) the stove (discriminated stimulus).

Another example of reinforcement in an escape learning mode is the proverbial whistling in a cemetery. These dynamics occur when a person is walking through a cemetery in the darkness of night and experiences fright or anxiety. The combination of cemetery, darkness, and fright is the discriminated stimulus. The person proceeds to whistle a happy tune (response), the doing of which results in cessation of fright (consequent stimulus). This paradigm will be recognized later as an example of negative reinforcement.

Various applications of the "grandma law" fit the dynamics of reinforcement learning. For example, grandchild is not particularly fond of eating rutabaga and likes very much to eat truffles. In the presence of rutabaga, truffles, and grandma, the child is told, "You may have truffles after you eat your rutabaga." This sequence is caused by grandma to happen; indeed, truffles are received upon completion of eating the rutabaga. Rutabaga is intended to be the discriminated stimulus, eating same is the target response, and getting truffles to eat is the consequent stimulus or reinforcer. If, however, the *combination* of grandma, rutabaga, and truffles is the discriminated stimulus, then rutabaga eating is less likely to happen in any other stimulus circumstance.

☐ The Perception Theory Family

Perception theories, of which those of Wertheimer, Köhler, Koffka, Tolman, and Bandura will serve in a subsequent chapter as primary referents, have the following dynamics in common:

- What a person perceives varies with the properties of physical stimulation.
- The perceptual variations or distortions follow patterns or "rules."
- Perception and understanding are molar events that cannot be reduced without altering their meaning.
- Learning is a process of varying perceptual frames until one is accomplished that corresponds to a universal structure.
- Perceptual learning is not incremental; it happens in an all-or-none fashion and is experienced as a revelation.
- Past perceptual units or gestalts are stored in memory and become data for future decisions.
- Teaching or conditioning is a process of managing experiences, real or vicarious, until the learner accomplishes insight or perceptual "homeostasis."

Everyone from time to time has an "aha!" experience when, following a period of confusion and frustration, "things fall into place" and clarity is achieved instantaneously. When struggling to understand new conceptual material, students are encouraged to let it incubate for a while, to put their minds on something else, to let their computer grind out its concatenations. Presumably the mind continues to "turn things over" until some order is accomplished, if it is to happen at all. Insight is something that is extremely difficult to define or to describe in language; language is uninsightful, unperceptual. One relies on the experience of having insight to understand insight.

Another example of perceptual learning is the acquisition of a new way of being or of doing as a result of watching someone else. Imitation learning, particularly on the part of young children who have yet to develop analytical skills, is a function of perceiving a complete behavioral sequence in context and replicating it in the same or a similar context. When pressed to perform a new task and be able to do it successfully, a person might be heard to say, "I didn't know that I knew how to do that!" This would be the result of having seen a person perform the task and imitating that performance. Many of the skills of childhood—mumbly peg, hopscotch, jumping rope, conning authority figures—are picked up as a result of seeing a peer perform them successfully. Few are analyzed in a language-mediated way, and are seldom performed as a result of decision or plan.

☐ The Cognition Theory Family

Cognition theories, of which those of Festinger, Försterling, and Rokeach will serve in a subsequent chapter as primary referents, have the following dynamics in common:

- Experience becomes coded and remembered; humans rely to a great extent on language codes.
- Language permits labelling of referents and of experience; it also permits progressively higher levels of abstraction resulting in organization or structure of knowledge.
- People can modify or combine structures to arrive at new and creative knowledge.
- Reasoning skills permit analysis of past and present experiences and prediction of future outcomes.
- Thought precedes action; most behavior results from cognitive analysis of data and from decision.
- Teaching or conditioning is a process of providing (a) *standardized* labels and/or descriptions for experiences and referents; (b) organizational structures of abstractions to enhance memory retrieval, reasoning, and classification of new experiences; and (c) supplanting of inefficient or self-defeating structures with new ones.

Most children encounter an adult who, when asked for the solution to a problem, says, "You figure it out." Most adults can remember or recreate the awareness of accomplishment when becoming able to figure things out. Piaget claims the need for a level of intellectual development that he calls the formal operations stage (Wadsworth, 1971). The learning of logical patterns such as, "*If* I spill spaghetti on my shirt, *then* I will be embarrassed," is an example of cognitive learning, of using formal operations. Syllogistic reasoning is another example: All dogs have dog breath; Phydeaux has dog breath; Phydeaux is a dog. Of more concern in a therapeutic context is the acquisition of imperatives, the use of which is self-defeating. Examples would include, "I must be perfect in order to be acceptable" and "Only foolish klutzes spill spaghetti on their shirts."

☐ Categorizing

One of the frustrations and weaknesses of building a meta-model of pre-existing theories is that not all of the theories will fit neatly into categories. This is particularly true in the area of learning theory where many theories attempt to explain the same phenomena. In the following four chapters, each of the families of intervention theory will be examined. Those theorists used as major referents for each theoretical position are selected on the basis of a primary dynamic that warrants their inclusion in a particular context. When another major characteristic of a given theory is viewed, the assignment may seem questionable. Were the theorists themselves able to make the assignments to category, there likely would be discrepancies from this model. It is hoped that the structural dynamics of the categories will be clear and that they will survive the potential dissonance of different interpretations of the theories included in each.

The good side of categorizing is the ability to make sense of large amounts of information and to be more efficient in decision-making. An organizational scheme, such as the following grid (see Figure 4.1), provides an overview of the entire field. It allows for an entry point in the analysis of problem dynamics and in the selection of an intervention strategy.

This particular model suggests the existence of 160 separate intervention strategies. A compulsive attempt to fill all of the cells seems unwise. Interventions based in each of the theory families are not universally effective across client circumstances and styles, nor across application settings. One would predict that perception-based interventions would load heavily into perceptual deficit and surplus cells and that cognitive interventions would be more numerous for cognitive problems. Reinforcement approaches are most adaptable to behavioral targets, and association methods address affective surpluses. Historically, broader uses of strategies from each family have

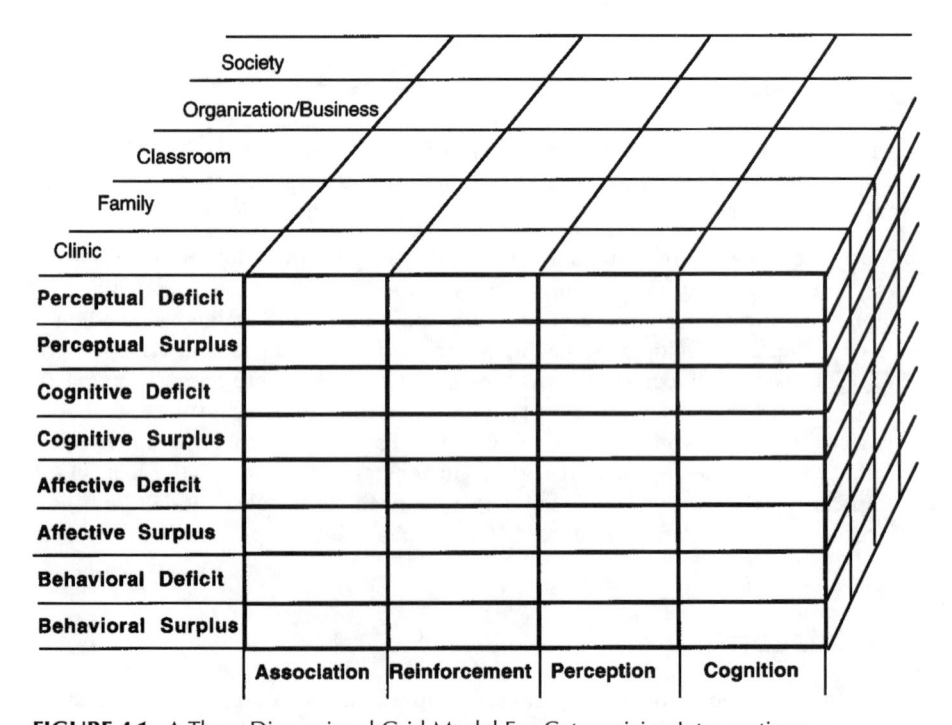

FIGURE 4.1. A Three-Dimensional Grid Model For Categorizing Interventions.

demonstrated success. In addition to showing which techniques are most appropriate to certain client circumstances, further study and development of this grid will demonstrate which interventions are least appropriate or least efficient or of little merit for certain problems. Chapters 5 through 8 will include applications for interventions based on the respective theory families. Chapters 9 and 10 deal with contextual concerns attributable to differences in personality, developmental, social dynamics, and spiritual aspects of the client's circumstance. Chapter 11 will show the strength of an integrational model for dealing with complex circumstances and atypical patterns of circumstances and style.

CHAPTER 5

Association Learning Approaches to Intervention

This is the first of four chapters that address intervention approaches from their learning theory foundations. Beginning with identification as one- or two-stage models, there follows an introduction to learning theorists and their works that are germinal to the examples of interventions that ensue. Each chapter includes analyses of applications of typical intervention strategies and finishes with sample problem scenarios for the reader's practice. Because counselors apply their knowledge and skills in a variety of settings, sometimes in a consulting capacity, a variety of application scenarios is included.

☐ Focus

Association theories are one-stage models that operate on a belief in stimulus control of behavior. Once learning or conditioning has taken place, the person will emit essentially the same response when he or she next encounters the trigger stimulus. Basically two approaches exist for associational conditioning, represented by the works of Pavlov and Guthrie. The first approach focuses on substituting a new stimulus for an already functional one. Stimulus substitution, or S-S conditioning, is particularly useful in managing emotional expression. In this form of conditioning, it is imperative that the old stimulus and the new stimulus occur contiguously one to another. Since the old stimulus calls out an unconditioned response or a reflex, the response also will occur contiguously to both the old and the new stimulus.

The second approach focuses on making a contiguous relationship between any situational stimulus and the response that the counselor wishes the client to make. This is S-R conditioning. Theoretically, any target response can become a conditioned response to any specified stimulus if certain conditions are met, the most important of which is contiguity.

☐ Foundation Theories

The two classical theorists whose work most clearly demonstrates the dynamics of association learning are Ivan Petrovich Pavlov and Edwin R. Guthrie. Pavlov focused on stimulus substitution; Guthrie was concerned with stimulus-response conditioning.

Pavlov

Ivan Petrovich Pavlov (1849–1936) was born in Ryazan, Russia, the son of a parish priest. He attended an ecclesiastical seminary in St. Petersburg, then went to the University of St. Petersburg to study physiology. Later he studied medicine at the Medico-Chirurgical Academy, graduating in 1879. He worked as director of the physiological division of the Institute of Experimental Medicine in St. Petersburg, then he became a professor of physiology at the University of St. Petersburg. The highlight of his first career was being awarded the Nobel Prize (1904) for his work on gastric secretions (Lectures on the work of the Principle Digestive Glands, 1897, in Pavlov, 1955).

As a physiologist, Pavlov viewed the organism as a biological machine. He assumed that, while there are obvious individual differences, the basic mechanisms and operations are the same across individuals. He was looking for the characteristics of digestion. An accomplished scientist, Pavlov was a master at isolating variables. His work on "sham feeding" of his canine subjects called for separation of the activities of mastication, salivation, swallowing, and stomach distension in search of determinants of hunger and satiation. What causes the dog to eat a certain amount and then stop eating? It seems unlikely that sufficient time would elapse between starting to eat and the digestion and subsequent change in body chemistry to signal cessation of eating. Therefore, there must be some kind of physical condition that signals the organism to stop eating

Pavlov surgically severed the esophagus of his canine subject, harnessed the dog, and conducted various experiments. He fed the dog which, after chewing the food, swallowed it only to have it drop into a dish. He fastened tubes to collect saliva so he could measure the amount of that salivary solution. He introduced pre-masticated food directly into the stomach through the severed esophagus to isolate stomach distension from the other activities of eating

It was during the height of his first career that his second one, that of psychologist, began. He was influenced to believe that organisms had a psychical system, somewhat akin to other bodily systems, such as the respiratory system, the digestive system, and the integumentary system. One of his influencers, Ivan Mikhailovich Sechenov, wrote, "All psychical acts, without exception, if they are not complicated by elements of emotion . . . develop by way of reflex. Hence, all conscious movements resulting from these acts and usually described as voluntary are reflex movements in the strict sense of the term" (*Reflexes of the Brain*, 1863 in Sechenov, 1965).

If there is a psychic system, it operates according to predictable dynamics. While observing his dog just prior to introduction of food into its mouth, Pavlov noticed an amount of saliva dropping from the collection tube. If the organism is a machine, it requires a switch to start the salivation mechanism. Previously, Pavlov had believed that food in the mouth triggered salivation. With nothing introduced into the dog's mouth, there was no physical stimulus for salivation. Pavlov deduced that the psychic system operated in anticipation of previously conditioned events. For example, being harnessed and having food placed in the dog's mouth was a conditioned sequence, anticipated by the psychic system's signalling the onset of salivation.

Given (a) the belief of a psychic system and (b) Sechenov's edict that all conscious and voluntary movements are reflexes, Pavlov set out to describe the relationship between physical and psychical events. Experimentally, he isolated factors until he arrived at the classical conditioning formula: the unconditioned stimulus elicits the unconditioned response (reflex); the conditioning stimulus, when paired contiguously and repeatedly with the unconditioned stimulus comes to elicit a diminished manifestation of the unconditioned response. The conditioned stimulus, a previously neutral stimulus as pertains to the target reflex, can substitute for the natural trigger, the unconditioned stimulus. By this method, behavior can be brought under the control of selected and experimenter-managed stimuli. This relationship, stated as a paradigm is:

$$US \rightarrow UR$$
$$CS \rightarrow CR$$

Additional principles established by Pavlov through his experiments include the following:

- Extinction. He found that after a response had been brought under control of the substitute stimulus, continued presentation of the conditioning stimulus and no pairings with the unconditioned stimulus resulted in cessation of the response. At first he believed the association was eliminated, extinct. Subsequent experiments led him to alter this conclusion to one of conditioned inhibition of response.
- Spontaneous recovery. After "extinction" plus sufficient elapsed time, presentation of the substitute stimulus again elicited the response.
- Stimulus generalization. The response occurred not only to the substitute stimulus, but in lesser amounts to stimuli similar to the substitute stimulus. The similarities were of the nature of a bell of a different tone, higher or lower metronome frequencies, and eliptical versus round visual signals.
- Stimulus discrimination. It was found that the dog could be conditioned simultaneously to salivate to the substitute stimulus and to inhibit salivation to similar stimuli that previously were generalized elicitors.
- Combined stimuli. By conditioning the dog to salivate to two or more different substitute stimuli, the amount of salivation could be increased when both substitute stimuli were given together, though not of a magnitude equal to the sum of both presented separately. Combining of a conditioned stimulus and a conditioned inhibitor resulted in inhibition of response.
- Higher order conditioning. Pavlov found that he could substitute a second new stimulus by pairing it with the original substitute stimulus. For example, salivation could be elicited by presentation of a circular visual card by pairing it with a bell that had previously been paired with the unconditioned stimulus of food. This was called second order conditioning. Third order conditioning was demonstrated by Pavlov, though with each successively higher order, the magnitude of the response declined. Theoretically, a long chain of conditioning could explain complex behavior that is far removed from an unconditioned reflex.

Pavlov was a scientist. His focus was on identifying and isolating factors in the conditioning process. He did not invest much time, if any, to ideas of practical application. To the extent that consistent, predictable, and controllable relationships exist between environmental cues and reflex or habituated behavior, such relationships can be managed in regard to any reaction that is to be brought under stimulus control.

Examples of Pavlovian-Type Association Learning. *Lamaze birthing.* Proponents of natural childbirth, the delivery of a child without medical or pharmacological intervention, claim that the pain that is a natural part of the process can be inhibited greatly by training. For some time prior to the onset of labor, the pregnant woman practices activities that can be carried out incidental to delivery (e.g., lying in a certain position, breathing in a panting fashion, holding hands with a "coach"). These activities are done in a group setting that is managed to be a pleasant social experience. By associating pleasant emotional responses that are naturally elicited by the pleasant group atmosphere with previously neutral stimuli for those emotions—lying in a certain position, breathing exercises, presence of coach saying key phrases—it is posited that the natural pain cues of the actual childbirth will be partially offset by the conditioned positive reactions cued by the substitute stimuli.

The simultaneous presentation of stimuli that call out competing responses will result in a modification of the usual responses when the stimuli are presented singly. In the case of Lamaze, the stacking up of substitute stimuli that call forth positive emotional responses and the fact that tension and fear cannot be expressed by the mother at the same time as positive emotional responses, the birthing mother will be less tense, will feel less pain, and will tend to evaluate her delivery experience as more positive than will an unprepared mother (see Figure 5.1).

Environmental control. One way of explaining some of the dynamics of Attention Deficit Hyperactivity Disorder (ADHD), is to see an accumulation of stimuli effects on the child. In other words, the child has learned to respond with an energetic action to many separate environmental cues—color, sound, time of day, food, companions, etc. When these separately conditioned cues occur at the same time, their additive effect is to elicit an activity level that is inappropriate and self-defeating. More normal children will have learned finer discriminations between and among stimuli and contexts with the result of behaving more acceptably. Proponents believe that by limiting the number and intensity of environmental stimuli, the child can be conditioned to behave at an acceptable activity level. The number and/or intensity of stimuli then can be increased gradually, each time below the threshold for triggering over-response, until an ordinary level of stimulation is matched by an ordinary response.

Alcohol treatment with anabuse. A common experience for many people who ingest alcoholic beverages is an emotional state of comfort or relaxation, or a freeing up of inhibitions. The taste and smell of alcoholic beverages becomes associated (substituted) with the emotional response and, just as Pavlov's dog salivated at the substitute stimulus, experienced alcohol ingesters are calmed by the smell or taste of alcoholic drinks (and maybe the bar or club or brand logo or other previously neutral stimuli that have become associated with the response). In the attempt to change desire for alcohol to an aversion to alcohol, the client or patient is given a drug, anabuse, the presence of which in the system of the drinker will produce nausea when combined

54 Intervention Theories

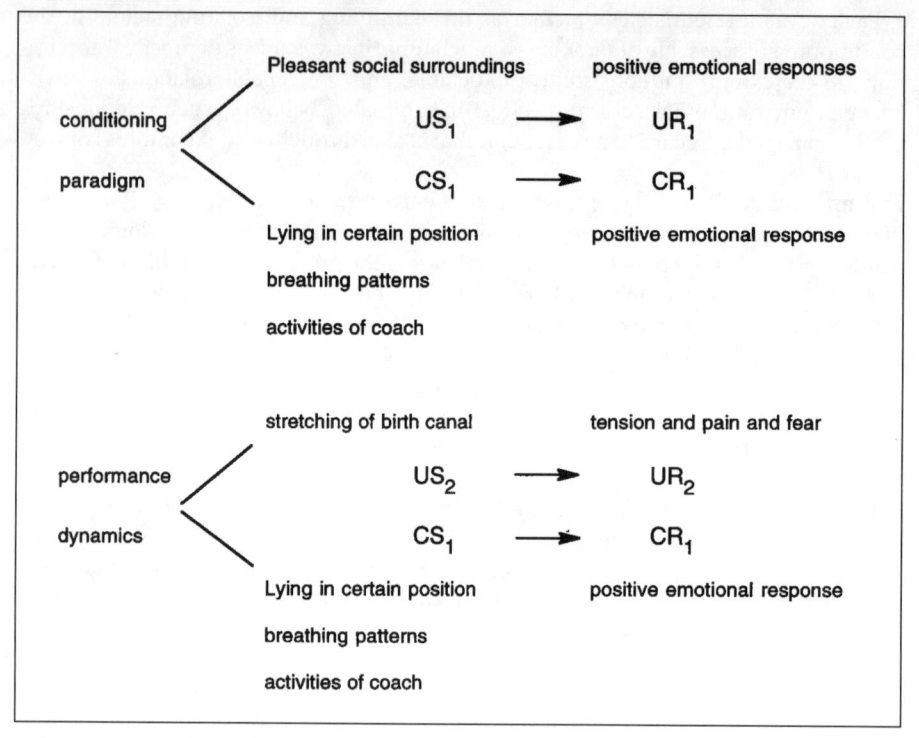

```
                    Pleasant social surroundings    positive emotional responses
conditioning                  US₁          ⟶            UR₁
paradigm                      CS₁          ⟶            CR₁
                    Lying in certain position        positive emotional response
                    breathing patterns
                    activities of coach


                    stretching of birth canal       tension and pain and fear
performance                   US₂          ⟶            UR₂
dynamics                      CS₁          ⟶            CR₁
                    Lying in certain position        positive emotional response
                    breathing patterns
                    activities of coach
```

FIGURE 5.1. Analysis of Pavlovian Explanation for Lamaze Birthing Technique.

with alcohol. Stimuli that previously called out positive emotional reactions now become associated with negative physical and emotional reactions.

Initially, the pairing of stimuli calling out a positive response will reduce the discomfort of the nausea; however, with repeated pairings of the previously conditioned stimuli and the discomfort of nausea, those stimuli become associated with illness and tend to call out the nauseous response. The diminished but noticeable experience of nausea when encountering the smell, logo, bar, or club is sufficiently aversive to produce avoidance responses and prevent the ingestion of the alcoholic beverage (see Figure 5.2).

Enuresis. An associationist approach to coping with bedwetting in clients is to manage stimuli in a Pavlovian pattern. Presumably the enuretic client sleeps so soundly that the normal discomfort of bladder distension prior to voiding the bladder is not sufficient to awaken the client, though it signals sphincter relaxation and the subsequent wet bed. A device that is placed on the bed under the client can be employed, with the result of moisture from the enuretic episode completing an electrical circuit that rings a loud bell, awakening the client. Whatever stimuli occur just prior to the bell's ringing will become attached to the waking up response.

The contiguous occurrence of bladder distention discomfort and the loud bell provides substitute stimulus power to the bladder distention discomfort in eliciting enough arousal from sleep to enable the client to be aware of his or her biological condition and to urinate in the preferred location (see Figure 5.3).

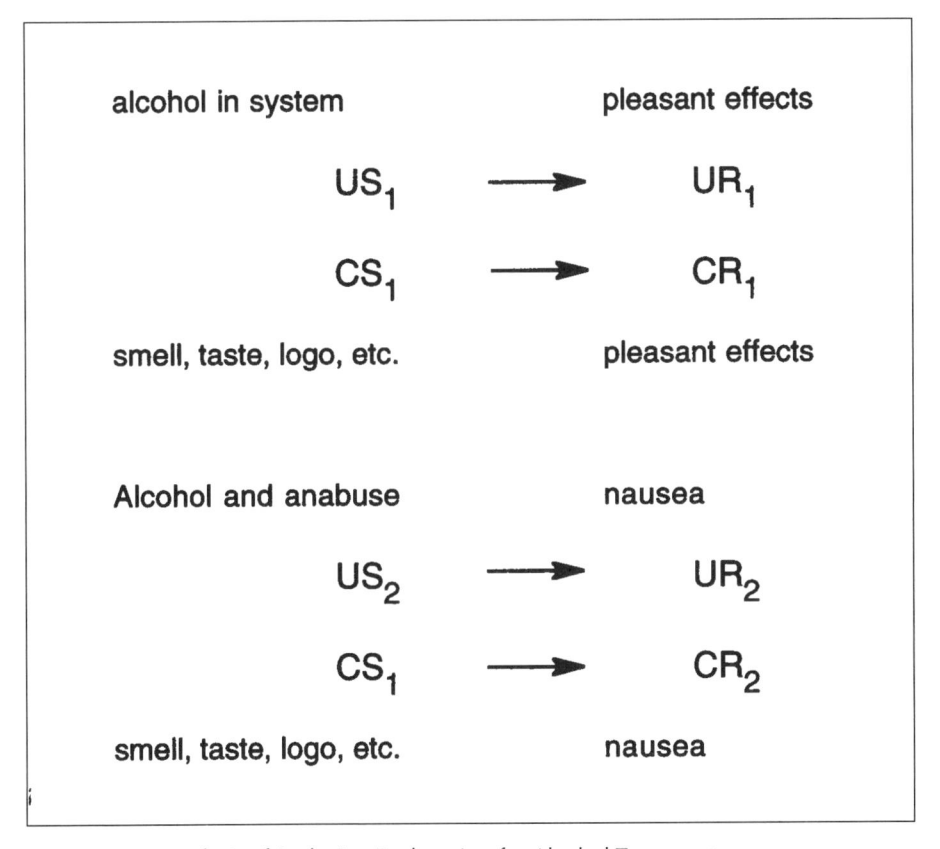

```
alcohol in system              pleasant effects

        US₁           ⟶            UR₁

        CS₁           ⟶            CR₁

smell, taste, logo, etc.        pleasant effects


Alcohol and anabuse              nausea

        US₂           ⟶            UR₂

        CS₁           ⟶            CR₂

smell, taste, logo, etc.          nausea
```

FIGURE 5.2. Analysis of Pavlovian Explanation for Alcohol Treatment.

Neuro-Linguistic Programming (NLP). NLP (Bandler & Grinder, 1975) is a therapeutic system that features covert access to a client's problem state by mirroring representational modes (visual, auditory, kinesthetic) to create an experience of positive relationship. The client is not required to verbalize the details of his or her condition, but he or she must be able to recreate the experiences through imagery. The client will be directed to relive a problem situation from a position inside the imaginal re-creation. By observing physiological cues such as changes in pace of breathing, color of skin, or muscle tension, the therapist can identify that point in the re-creation at which an emotional response is elicited by the replay of the experience. At precisely the time of emotional response, the therapist introduces a neutral cue, such as a touch on the client's left shoulder. This is called anchoring. It is the substituting of the touch on shoulder for the portion of re-created experience that produced the emotional response.

After anchoring is accomplished, the emotional response can be called out by a touch on the shoulder. A second anchor is established for a competing emotional state. This is done by having the client relive the problem situation again with one major change. The client is directed to imagine a response he or she wished had been made in place of the dysfunctional one. Again the therapist watches carefully for physiological indicators of an emotional experience, this time a positive one. The right shoulder is touched as a substitute stimulus for eliciting the positive emotional state.

```
    bladder distention discomfort        sphincter relaxation, bed wetting

                 US₁          ──▶          UR₁


    wet bed ──▶ loud noise                waking up

                 US₂          ──▶          UR₂

                 CS₂          ──▶          CR₂

    bladder distention discomfort, a

    previously neutral s for waking up     waking up
```

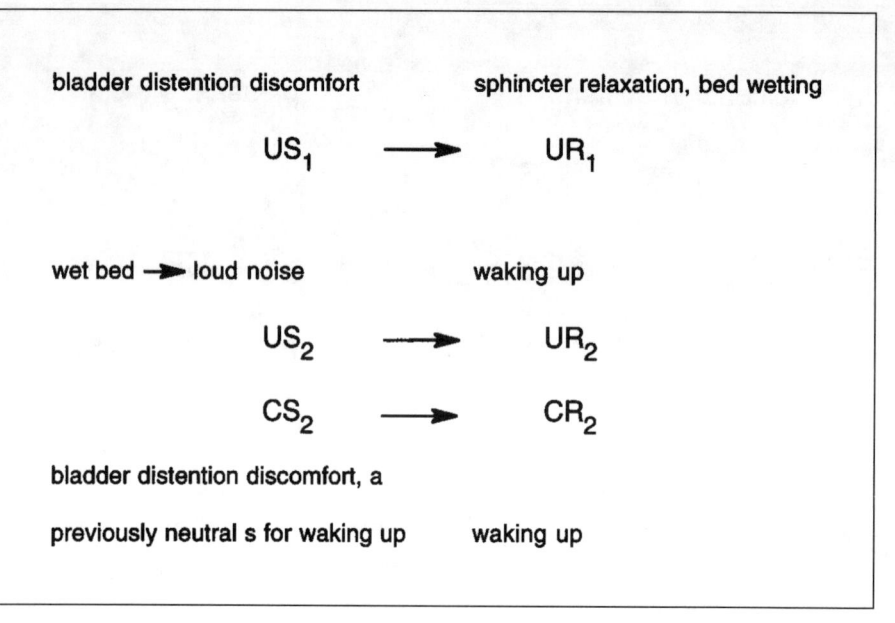

FIGURE 5.3. Analysis of Pavlovian Explanation for Treatment of Enuresis.

At this juncture, the client will respond with negative emotions to a left shoulder touch and positive emotions to a right shoulder touch.

To complete the therapy, the counselor again instructs the client to relive the situation. At the critical moment for emotional response, the counselor touches both shoulders (bridges), simultaneously calling out mutually exclusive responses.

It is postulated that the neural system creates a response somewhere between positive and negative and the client is now programmed away from an unlikely positive creation and the undesired negative one and toward a more functional reaction (see Figure 5.4).

Commercial advertising. Many print and television commercials employ a Pavlovian strategy in attempting to pair the brand logo with an existing stimulus that elicits strong and positive emotion. Perhaps the most blatant are the inclusion of sexually stimulating images contiguously with the brand name or logo of the product being advertised. A fairly elaborate scheme to condition brand loyalty is used by beer makers. The beer company representative contacts student representatives on college and university campuses and offers financial support of a major activity, such as a springfest, in return for exclusive rights to sell his or her product at reduced prices and to display the brand logo conspicuously and in prominent places. The belief is that the previously neutral stimulus of brand logo will elicit memories or emotions from major happy events and will sway decisions as to which brand to buy when faced with various brands. Similar "guilt by association" or "validity by association" ploys are used by commercial sponsors of major tennis tournaments, football bowl games, and entertainment extravaganzas.

```
Anchor 1
        stimuli in replay that elicit response      negative emotional response
                        US₁  ⟶  UR₁
                        CS₁  ⟶  CR₁
            touch on left shoulder           negative emotional response.

Anchor 2
        stimuli in replay that elicit response      positive emotional response
                        US₂  ⟶  UR₂
                        CS₂  ⟶  CR₂
            touch on right shoulder          positive emotional response.

Bridge
        stimuli in replay that elicit response      negative emotional response
                        US₁  ⟶  UR₁
                        CS₁  ⟶  CR₁
                        CS₂  ⟶  CR₂
            touch on both shoulders          new emotional response.
```

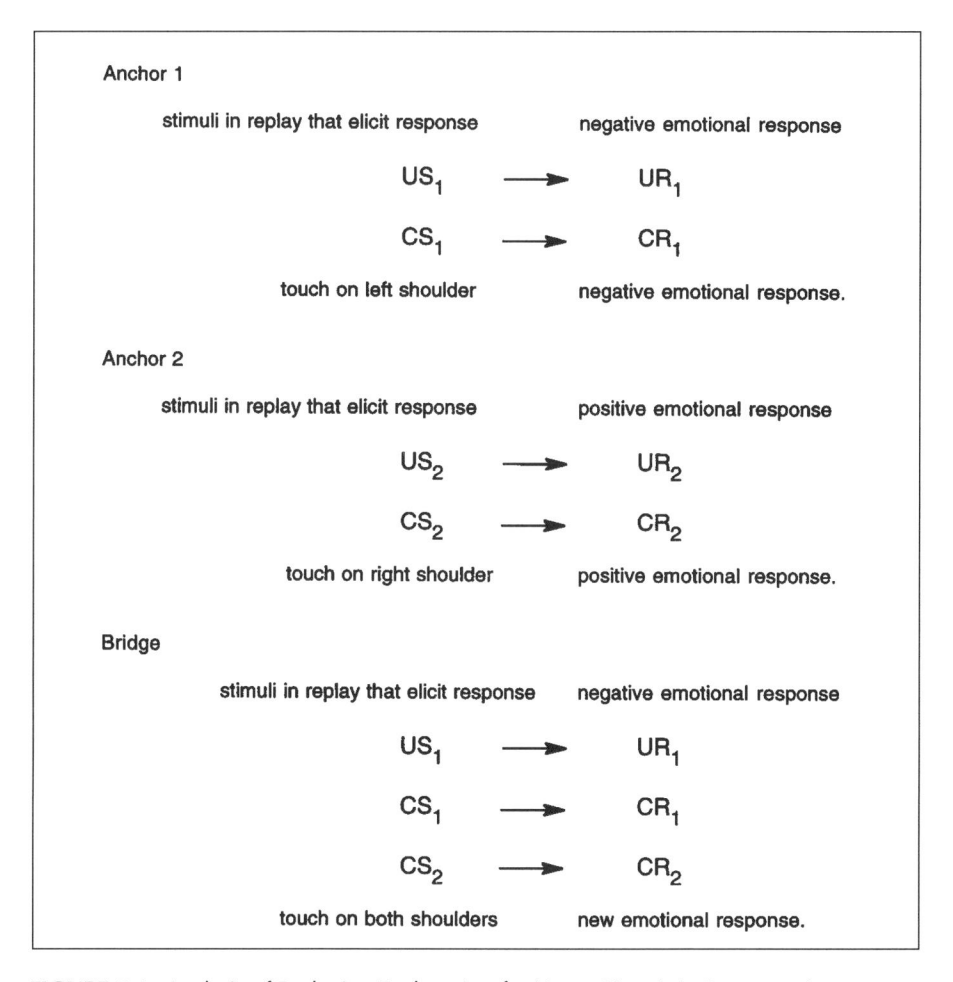

FIGURE 5.4. Analysis of Pavlovian Explanation for Neuro-Linguistic Programming.

Systematic desensitization and reciprocal inhibition. Joseph Wolpé is a major proponent of the application of Pavlovian techniques to the alleviation of anxiety and, hence, the removal or inhibition of responses resulting from anxiety. His definition of the reciprocal inhibition principle is: "If a response inhibiting anxiety can be made to occur in the presence of anxiety-evoking stimuli, it will weaken the bond between these stimuli and anxiety" (1969, p. 17). The best known context for application of Wolpé's methods is in combatting phobias. A phobia is an irrational fear, meaning the attaching of a fear response to a stimulus that logically should not elicit fear. This can be described using the Pavlovian mechanism of stimulus substitution. Whenever a genuine fear-producing situation occurs, there are contextual stimuli that may be conditioned to the fear response. Remember or imagine an experience common to many people. As a child, you are standing on the observation platform of a tall structure such as the Space Needle in Seattle or the World Trade Center in New York City. As you look down you are impressed with how tiny the objects at ground level appear.

Suddenly, your older sibling grabs your shoulders, pushes you forcefully and perilously over the edge of the guard rail and loudly shouts, "Booo!!!" For some time thereafter, maybe a lifetime, you experience sensations of fear whenever your are in high, exposed places.

One approach to alleviating this irrational fear is to create a mutually exclusive emotional state to fear, then introduce the conditioned stimuli in amounts below the fear trigger threshold. Relaxation is mutually exclusive to fear. The phobic client is taught to relax through use of progressive relaxation techniques. These are carried out in the therapist's office, amid many stimuli that are neutral both to fear and to relaxation. Repeated pairings of relaxation procedures and those stimuli create a context conducive to relaxation. One variation is to have the client record the progressive relaxation sequence in his or her own voice so that future relaxation can be cued by talking to him or herself.

In order to help the client experience progressively stronger presentations of fear-producing stimuli, the therapist instructs the client to establish a hierarchy of stimuli from neutral to highly charged with fear. In the case of the phobia for heights, the hierarchy would look something like this:

11. looking over rail
10. approaching rail
9. leaving elevator
8. riding up in elevator
7. pushing top floor button
6. entering elevator
5. approaching elevator
4. entering building
3. approaching building
2. leaving automobile
1. riding in automobile

After relaxation has been brought under stimulus control in the therapist's office, the client is asked, while in a relaxed state, to imagine a sequence of events that involves riding in an automobile. The sequence then includes leaving the automobile and approaching the building. The therapist and the client monitor the client's relaxation. At the first indication of change, the imaginal sequence is stopped, the relaxation state is re-established, and the imaginal sequence is begun again. Eventually, the client will be able to imagine himself or herself looking over the rail while experiencing no fear.

The stimuli that previously were neutral and conditioned to call out fear are now neutral to relaxation and being conditioned to call out relaxation. When completed, the height-related stimuli will elicit relaxation, an emotional state that is mutually exclusive of fear (see Figure 5.5).

Implicit in the Pavlovian approach to associationist learning is the prominence of reflexive learning. Pavlov believed that all learning was reducible to the reflex; the relationship between reflexive and non-reflexive responses was not demonstrated successfully by Pavlov. The associationist model has another major component, advocated by Edwin Guthrie. The major departure for this component is the allowance for stimulus control of any response, especially those that are hard to define as reflexive in nature.

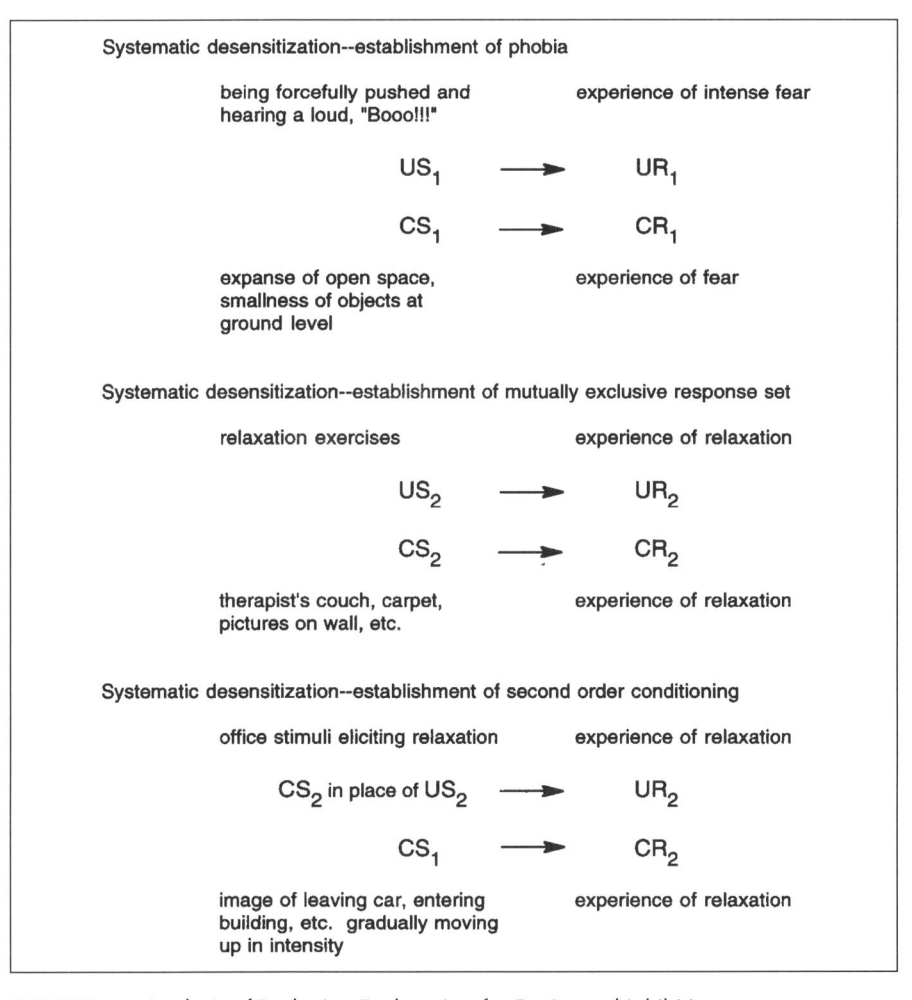

```
Systematic desensitization--establishment of phobia

         being forcefully pushed and         experience of intense fear
         hearing a loud, "Booo!!!"

                    US₁      ⟶       UR₁

                    CS₁      ⟶       CR₁

         expanse of open space,              experience of fear
         smallness of objects at
         ground level


Systematic desensitization--establishment of mutually exclusive response set

         relaxation exercises                experience of relaxation

                    US₂      ⟶       UR₂

                    CS₂      ⟶       CR₂

         therapist's couch, carpet,          experience of relaxation
         pictures on wall, etc.


Systematic desensitization--establishment of second order conditioning

         office stimuli eliciting relaxation    experience of relaxation

                 CS₂ in place of US₂   ⟶     UR₂

                    CS₁      ⟶       CR₂

         image of leaving car, entering      experience of relaxation
         building, etc. gradually moving
         up in intensity
```

FIGURE 5.5. Analysis of Pavlovian Explanation for Reciprocal Inhibition.

Guthrie

Edwin R. Guthrie (1886–1959) was born in Lincoln, Nebraska. He completed bachelor and master degrees at the University of Nebraska in mathematics and philosophy and the Ph.D. in Philosophy at the University of Pennsylvania. He spent 42 years at the University of Washington: 1914–1919 in the philosophy department, 1919–1943 in the psychology department, and the remainder of his career as dean of the graduate school and academic dean. He served as president of the American Psychological Association in 1945.

Guthrie was influenced by philosophers such as Aristotle, John Locke, and particularly David Hume, who argued that cause and effect relationships were not consequential relationships, but merely sequences of events. As a mathematician, he certainly was aware of the correlational argument defining covariance as not necessarily causative.

It is possible to summarize Guthrie's model into major principles with several subpoints (Sahakian, 1976):

- Learning occurs by the linked or associated occurrence of a physical stimulus (cue or signal) and a response.
- Stimuli occur in patterns. In normal reality and even in the laboratory, stimuli rarely occur in an isolated and pure form. They are imbedded in a context of accompanying stimuli that vary from time to time and across situations.
- Stimuli must be viable cues. To be viable to the learner, which is necessary for the cues to be attended to and perceived, the cues must be meaningful to the learner.
- Contiguity is *the* dynamic agent. Learning by association requires only the contiguous occurrence of perceived cue and response. No reduction in need as a result of the response (a major contention of Hull) and no psychic signal system tied to reflex (as believed by Pavlov) are necessary. *Only* the perceived cue and response as contiguous events are necessary. A paradigmatic expression of Guthrie's model would be Cue -> Response. Where Pavlov focused on the contiguous relationship between the unconditioned stimulus and the conditioning stimulus, Guthrie's interest regarding contiguity was its occurrence between the stimulus and the response (see Figure 5.6). Even in the conditioning of reflex responses to a new stimulus (cue), of importance is the fact that the response occurred immediately following the presentation of the conditioning stimulus.
- Attention is a necessary condition. Whatever is being noticed by the learner at the time a response is elicited may become a cue for that response.
- Learning is an all-or-none, single-trial bonding of cue and response. This principle was a cornerstone of Guthrie's theory. It is a rational conclusion and not readily open to empirical verification. If pure stimulus events could be managed and if the requisite attention and viability of the pure stimulus could be made to occur contiguously with the target response, then that response would be cued again in identical circumstances. In reality, many repetitions of the sequence between complex stimulus events and the target response must occur to increase the probability of the learner attending to that portion of the complex cue that has been associated with the target response. The more repetitions of similar response to a similar complex cue, the more elements of that complex cue are associated with the response and, hence, become signals for manifesting that response.
- Causality is not assumed. The stimulus does not necessarily cause the response. It is merely a signal or cue for the emission of the response.
- Conflicting cues result in suspended associational responses. The typical response to encountering cues that signal competing responses is for the learner to suspend the associated responses and to become hyperattentive.
- Error in predicting behavior results from the complex nature of its causes. If the stimulus does not necessarily cause the response, then some variation in eliciting that response to the same cue will occur from time to time. It is safer to say that the learner will probably make the specified response when cued; estimates of the probability of the response occurring on cue correspond to the strength or completeness of the learning.
- Movement or activity is a necessary condition. The learner must be making a response, doing something, in the contiguous presence of the attended cues in order for an association to be made. Movement is not limited to gross motor activity. It can include subvocal speech or thinking
- Forgetting and Inhibitory Conditioning work on the same mechanism. In other words, forgetting is not a result of disuse or of fading of neural traces; it occurs from learn-

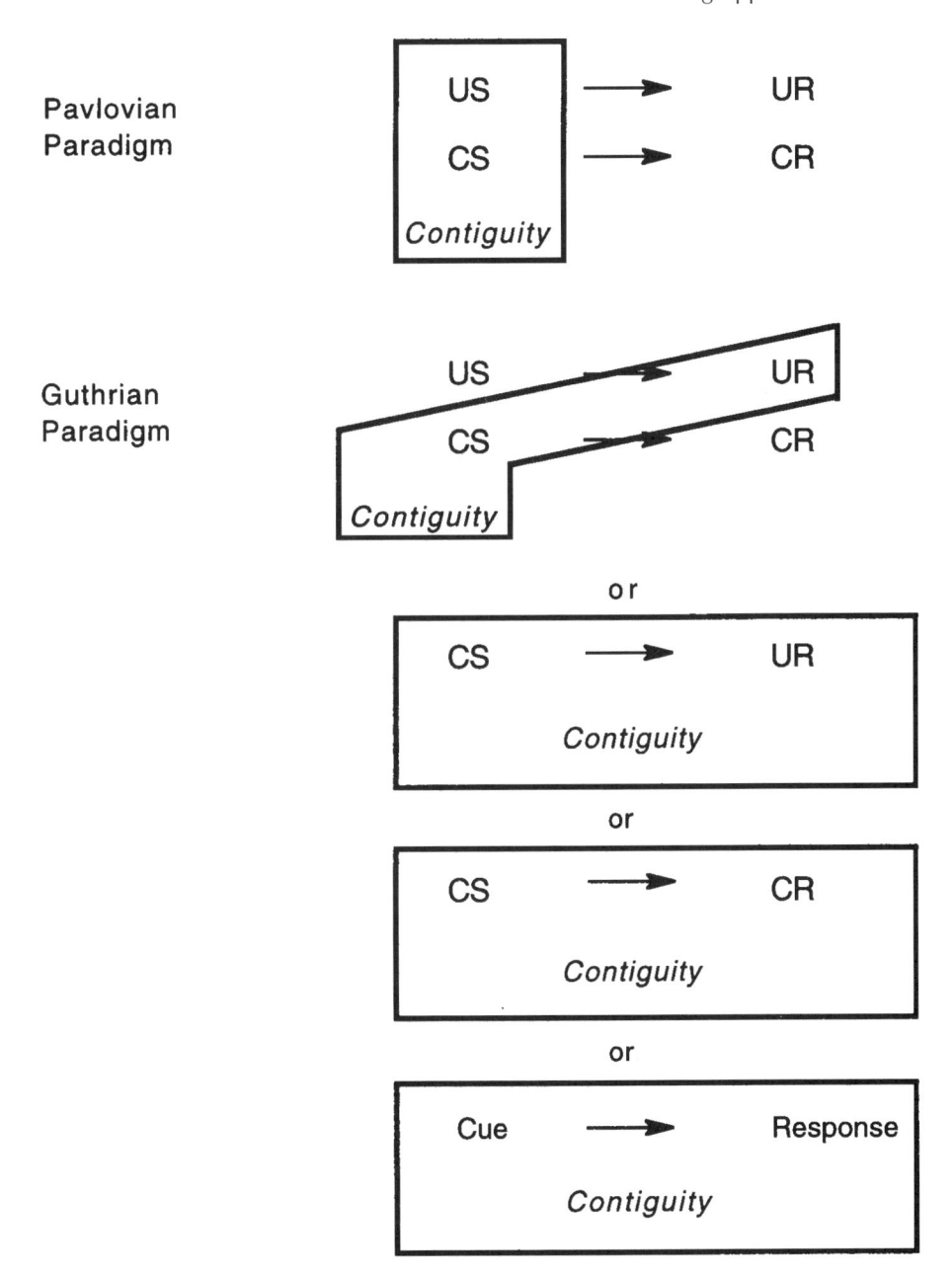

FIGURE 5.6. Contiguity in Pavlovian and Guthrian Paradigms.

ing new responses to cues that previously signaled the "forgotten" responses. There are three approaches:

1. Increasing threshold. A previously associated response may be inhibited by presenting the cue in diminished intensity, lower than that required to elicit the

response. The presentation is gradually increased in the absence of response until it no longer has cue strength for that response. One example is the so called "blanket breaking" of a horse wherein a light blanket is placed on the horse's back with no reaction from the horse; the weight of blanket and other objects is gradually increased until a person can mount the horse without eliciting bucking behavior. Similarly a hunting dog can become desensitized to the sound of a rifle discharge by giving it the experience of hearing distant gunfire and gradually reducing the distance and increasing the sound volume of such gunfire.
2. Exhaustion or fatigue. Because the last response made to an attended cue is the one that will be made in future encounters with the cue, a response may be inhibited by allowing the response to be made until the learner is exhausted in making that response. Exhaustion of response equals greatly diminished response or nonresponse, that is now the action being made contiguously to the cue. Theoretically a person with a strong aversion to snakes could be enclosed with many such reptiles and allowed to make whatever sounds or avoidance responses he or she wanted to make. Eventually those responses would fatigue and a more relaxed response would be cued by the snakes. Some readers will recognize this method as having been effective in "curing" their fear of the dark; upon resistance to entering their darkened bedroom, their parent shut them in and waited for the noise to subside. Subsequent encounters with dark rooms produced greatly inhibited expressions of the fear if not an absence of the fear experience itself.
3. Incompatible activity. If a person can be caused to make a response that is mutually exclusive to a less desired response in the presence of cues for the less desired response, those cues will come to signal the more desired response. The airline industry has long combatted fear of flying on the part of customers by presenting meals and entertainment in flight. The non-fear responses to eating or listening to music are made to occur in the context of the passenger compartment with all of its unique characteristics and with the cues of noise and motion resulting from flying.

- Habit is a tendency to respond in a specific way to a great variety of circumstances. It is having learned the same response to many different cues. The habit of smoking, for example, is manifest by doing so in many circumstances: before and/or after eating, going to bed, sitting at one's desk, and getting up from one's desk. Similarly, because people tend to eat in many different situations, they may be cued to eat when studying, going to a movie, lying on a beach, visiting a friend, or sitting at a table.
- The value of reward and punishment is in directing the learner to the desired behavior, and has no reinforcing power. Reward or punishment is an inducement to behave in a certain way. Either can be useful in getting the learner to do what is wanted and made to do so in the contiguous presence of the cue that is to become its signal in the future. Reward may mark the end of a learning event, in that it may take attention away from the learning event, thus preventing another response from being associated with the cue.

Examples of Guthrian Type Association Learning. The ability to attach specified responses to selected stimuli makes it possible to signal or cue the specified response by management of the cue. By arranging the contiguous cue and response with the criteria of viability, attention, and movement, it is possible to condition many types of responses to many kinds of cues. Almost all of Guthrian conditioning can be considered to be signal learning.

Classroom management. Making the transition from playground energy level to classroom focus in elementary school children is an important goal. Teachers may use consistent verbal cues like saying, "Okay! Quiet down. It's time to go to work." If they pair this verbal cue during several repetitions of training with demanding quiet response, eventually the verbal cue will signal the desired response. Another approach to the same goal is to use changes in lighting to signal the transition. If the teacher puts the students through a series of turning the lights down and directing them to thirty seconds of quiet, the students will come to associate lights down with response of quietness. The change in illumination is a more distinctive cue than is verbal direction and often results in quicker conditioning and more consistency over time.

A music teacher was able to cue differential attention by use of a small platform on which he would stand when directing the entire group. He instructed the students and put them through a number of practice trials such that when he was off the podium, they could talk quietly, silently finger through sections of the music, or engage in other non-disruptive behavior; when he stood on the platform, everyone was to pay attention and be ready to perform. As long as he was consistent in his behavior, the cue worked very well in producing efficient use of rehearsal time.

Multiple cuing. In natural situations, there are many cues in the environment that can be attached to a certain response (see Figure 5.7). This can be seen easily in responses such as fastening seatbelts in automobiles or in handwashing after toileting. Both of these responses seem to fit in a sequence of activity, yet neither seem to be necessary to subsequent parts of the sequence. With the presence of several cues and the probability of variations in attention to any of them, repetition of the entire sequence so that the target response will occur as signaled by different cues from time to time is necessary. To condition the fastening of seat belts it is recommended that the

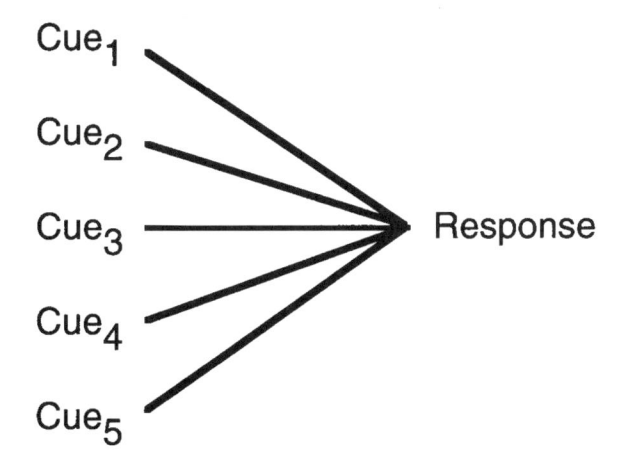

FIGURE 5.7. Multiple Cues.

learner be directed to retrieve keys from pocket or purse, enter vehicle, fasten seat belt, insert keys into ignition, and start the engine; this entire sequence is repeated several times. If ever the seat belt is not fastened as part of the sequence, it is important to stop the sequence and begin it again, and to avoid inserting a verbal cue just prior to the target response. In this fashion, seat belting will be cued by things such as the sight of the vehicle, the feel of the keys, the opening of the door, the feel of the seat cushion, and/or any other stimulus that frequently occurs as part of the sequence and to which it may be differentially attended.

Handwashing as part of toileting has dynamics similar to seat belting. If a concerned parent notices the absence of hand washing after his or her child uses the toilet, the parent directs the child to pull down trousers, sit on toilet, get up, flush toilet, pull up trousers, wash hands, dry hands, exit bathroom; this sequence is repeated several times to associate different cues to the target response—sensation of getting up, sight of paper dispenser, feel of flush handle, room characteristics.

Breaking multiple-cued responses. Smoking, for example, happens contiguously to many situations—before meals, after meals, at bedtime, at changes in work routine, and after intimate relations. To break such a habit it is necessary to associate some other response to all of the cues that have come to signal smoking. This is done by refraining from smoking for a period of time (the "cold turkey" approach) long enough for all previous cues to occur and be attended to or by substituting some other action for the actual smoking (the "lemon drop" or "chewing gum" approach). The first substitutes non-response to the cues or a separate response to each cue context and the second substitutes another habit for the one being deconditioned.

Place conditioning. Once associated, responses become strongly joined with cues. Consider the common experience of many students who claim to be unable to study unless listening to loud music, watching television, being with friends, sitting at kitchen table, etc. That these contexts are inefficient for focused concentration is obvious, yet they seem to be conditional cues for successful study. Formal study skills approaches direct students to create an environment that is devoid of objects such as pictures, momentos, food, etc. that are cues for other activities, and to study at that place, and only study at that place, for several days. The rationale is that the place characteristics will come to cue the study response.

Another common experience of many people is to condition themselves to become drowsy when reading a book because they have repeatedly read while reclining in bed and just prior to going to sleep. Instead of the place (bed) becoming a cue for reading, book reading becomes the cue for going to sleep.

Unintentional association. Surprising and sometimes puzzling connections get made unintentionally. Guthrie noted non-functional, superstition-like behavior in cats learning to escape from puzzle boxes. Whatever posture or movement preceded their release tended to be repeated as part of the release sequence. The author noted the strange effect of musty books provoking bathroom-seeking behavior. After some analysis, he remembered that during graduate school, he spent lots of time in the library finding and reviewing articles pertinent to his research work. In the atmosphere of musty books, he was forced to bend and stoop frequently to retrieve books from the lower shelves and, also, to climb up and down stairs from floor to floor and to climb ladders to get books from higher shelves. The bending and climbing triggered peristaltic responses in the lower bowel. The smell of musty books was viable, hard not to attend to, and contiguous to peristalsis over repeated experience, hence, the cue-response association was established.

Habit breaking. Guthrie proposed three methods for breaking habits: threshold, fatigue, and incompatible response. The threshold method involves presenting the cue in a greatly reduced intensity, below that required to elicit the response and then gradually increasing the intensity of the cue. For example, consider a person with a fear of spiders (arachnophobia). A series of experiential stations that move from little to much involvement with spiders would be identified. The first might be working at a library where people request books about various kinds of spiders. Next would be classifying pictures of spiders according to categories and names. Then the task of being a receptionist at the zoo and being located in the front of the arachnid house. Successively, the person would be involved with showing people through the arachnid collection, assisting the caretaker in feeding the spiders, feeding them alone, and eventually letting them crawl over his or her hands.

The fatigue method requires direct contact with the cues that elicit the habitual response, creating whatever that response is, in its complete and full-blown intensity. The response is continued until exhaustion, at which time the person is showing something other than the habitual response in the presence of the cues. For the person with fear of spiders, the treatment would be confinement in a room full of spiders until the fear response—screaming, panic, diaphragm tension, sweating—ceased to occur from fatigue. Such a treatment raises questions of an ethical nature. The same dynamics occur, however, in cases where a student who talks out in class is instructed to keep doing so for a long period of time until he or she tires of doing so, or where a person with aversion to speaking in public is required to talk at length until the fear experience or aversion subsides.

To employ the incompatible response method it is necessary to cue a mutually exclusive response contiguously with the habit that is to be overcome. Children often are acclimated to darkness or other fearful experiences by taking a favored blanket or teddy bear, from which is cued a sense of security, with them into the feared context. For the arachnophobic person it is hard to come up with a cue for a non-phobic response that is strong enough to compete with the power of the spiders in cuing the phobia.

Several problem scenarios will be presented for the purpose of assisting the reader in mastering the first two levels of Blosser's taxonomy of thinking abilities, cognitive memory and convergent thinking. Since there are two basic associationist approaches, Pavlov's and Guthrie's, it will be necessary first to (a) identify which is more appropriate for the problem scenario; then it is helpful to (b) list the principles involved in change according to the chosen approach and, finally, to (c) give a detailed description of the intervention strategy.

If the response to be modified or to be brought under differential stimulus control is reflexive, it is generally best to use a Pavlovian-based approach. If the client is sufficiently mature, a vicarious strategy may be appropriate (ala Wolpé). A Guthrian "threshold" method can be applied to some reflexive retraining. If the response is not reflexive, a Guthrian-based approach is preferred.

Pavlovian-based interventions have two applications: (a) elicitation of a desired reflex to a new stimulus and, (b) replacement of an undesirable conditioned response to an existing stimulus.

a. Existing reflex–new stimulus
   1. Identify the US for the existing reflex (UR).
   2. Select a substitute stimulus (CS) to which the reflex is to be conditioned.
   3. Pair the US and the CS contiguously over many trials until presentation of the CS alone elicits the reflex that is now the CR.
b. Existing stimulus–undesirable conditioned response
   1. Identify the US for that undesired reflex (UR_1) that has become a conditioned response (CR_1) elicited by the existing stimulus (CS_1).
   2. Determine a desired reflexive response (UR_2) that is mutually exclusive of the undesired reflex (UR_1).
   3. Find the stimulus (US_2) that elicits the desired reflex (UR_2).
   4. Pair US_2 with several previously neutral stimuli (CS_2) so as to gain stimulus control over the UR_2.
   5. Present CS_2 to elicit CR_2 at the same time as a diluted form of CS_1, resulting in only the elicitation of CS_2.
   6. Gradually increase the intensity of CS_1 while CS_2 is eliciting CR_2 until CS_1 becomes an eliciting stimulus only for the desired reflex, now CR_2.

With Guthrian-based interventions, the intitial determination is whether (a) a new response is to be conditioned to a specified context or (b) an existing response is to be replaced in a prescribed context.

a. New response
   1. Identify or create obvious contextual elements that consistently occur and can be used as cues.
   2. Cause the desired response to occur in the presence of the cues, making certain that the cues are viable and are attended to by the learner.
   3. Repeat step two numerous times so that the various elements of the complex cues can be associated with the desired response.
   4. Change the situation so that no subsequent response is associated with the same cues.
b. Replace response
   1. Determine a response that is to replace the undesirable response. Note that non-response (e.g., remaining quiet and still) is an option as a replacement response for inappropriate activity.
   2. Identify the situation that cues the undesirable response.
   3. In the presence of those cues, cause the substitute response to occur. This can be done by direct manipulation or by using the threshold, fatigue, or incompatible response approaches to habit change.
   4. Change the situation so that no subsequent response is associated with the same cues.

☐ Sample Problem Situations

School Phobia

Sally is ten years old and in the fourth grade. She has developed an extreme aversion to being in school and has not attended since the second week of the current school year—two months prior. Just after her initial refusal to go to school, she was forced to attend one day which resulted in her crying and screaming so intensely that she vomited all over her desk, materials, and an adjacent student. Since that time, her parents have made an attempt at home schooling, with only marginal satisfaction. Her father has been promoted to a new job that demands more of his time and energy and her mother has returned to the university in an advanced degree program. They want desperately for Sally to return to school.

"Where Did I Put My Keys?"

Tom is a building maintenance engineer for a large custodial service. He is responsible for overseeing the cleaning of six different facilities. The number of keys he uses is too great to carry all at the same time. He habitually places keys in a variety of places and, as a result, frequently can't remember which keys are where. This creates annoyance and inefficiency. He has hired a psychologist to, "help me improve my memory."

Return Tools Promptly

Chris is an industrial arts teacher in a high school woodworking class. His major concern is getting students to return tools to the correct place immediately after they use them so that the tools will be available for another student's use.

Fear of Flying

Susan is an agent for a major electronics firm. She has made rapid progress in moving through beginning and intermediate levels of her work and is seen by management as a candidate for a central management position. Her career path lies through regional sales coordination that requires her to cover a six-state area. She is extremely phobic about flying, yet cannot hope to perform successfully by driving between locations. Unless she can get over this fear, she will be forced to change careers or relegate herself to continuing at her present level.

Bring in the Mail

George and Carly live with their thirteen year old son, Zach, in a new home in a rural area. Zach rides the school bus to and from school each day. George and Carly are commuting to the city, leaving at about the same time as Zach and returning at about 6:00 p.m. each workday. Recently there has been a rash of incidents where someone, apparently a student or students, has taken mail from boxes. George has asked Zach to pick up the mail when he arrives home from school, but Zach frequently forgets.

CHAPTER 6

Reinforcement Learning Approaches to Intervention

☐ Focus

Reinforcement theories are one-stage models based on the belief that behavior is caused or controlled by external conditions including those that precede and those that follow the behavior. In natural or intrinsically reinforcing circumstances, responses to discriminated stimuli are always followed by a consistently reinforcing event. An example might be the appearance of a typically sugary treat responded to by eating it and resulting in the sensation of sweetness. It must be recognized, however, that such a sequence is culturally bound. One has only to travel to foreign locations to discover that visual cues of sweetness are not universal, that sweet-appearing morsels may not deliver sweet tastes upon being eaten. Sequences of events that culminate in an environmental occurrence that increases the probability of a certain response include an antecedent condition, a response, and a consequence. In natural sequences, the consequence is automatic. It contains the power, intrinsically, to influence conditioning of the response to recur in the same or similar circumstances.

Any sequence of antecedent condition, response, and consequence that can be managed, can produce controlled behavior. When the consequence is not a natural outgrowth of the response, it is said to be extrinsic. The notion of reward and punishment, intentionally applied by one person to another as a result of the second person's behavior, is an extrinsic consequence. It must be pointed out, however, that not all actions described as reward or punishment are reinforcing events; reinforcement must follow specific and particular guidelines if it is to work.

Reinforcement models focus on the relationship between and among three events: the antecedent condition, the response to that condition, and the resultant condition or consequent event resulting from the response. It is the relationship among these three events, the contingencies of reinforcement, that must be understood and managed for behavior to be created and controlled (see Figure 6.1).

```
antecedent event  →  response  →  consequent event
       S         →      R      →        S
```

FIGURE 6.1. Reinforcement Contingencies.

Foundation Theory

One person has been so dominant in this area of learning research and theory that he alone will serve as the referent for reinforcement learning. Burrhus Frederic Skinner (1904–1990) was born in the Susquehanna area of Pennsylvania. His father was a lawyer. Reportedly he grew up in a context of high expectations and little physical punishment. He graduated from Hamilton College with a degree in English Literature. Following graduation he spent a year in Greenwich Village in New York in pursuit of literary production. His writing inclinations resulted much later in two nonscientific books: *Walden II* and *Beyond Freedom and Dignity*. Said to have been influenced by Bertrand Russell's criticism of Watson's behaviorism, Skinner returned to school, completing a Master's degree in 1930 and the Ph.D. in Psychology from Harvard in 1931.

In his historical context, Skinner could be considered somewhat of a rebel. He rejected the schools of psychology and mentalistic concepts of his time; he rejected the hypothetico-deductive approach to research; he avoided physiological explanations for behavior; and he objected to statistical studies. His preferred research approach was a single subject design. His insistence that psychological principles be based on sound observations about behavior led him in pursuit of explanations of behavior that rested only on empirical observations. Concepts or experiences of emotion, logic, mentalism, and imagination were either too complicated to define and measure or, as he thought, unnecessary in a thorough explanation of behavior and its causes. His aim was to predict the behavior of organisms on the basis of external events without dependency on knowing what was going on inside the organism.

Antecedent Events

Skinner recognized two types of learning. Type 1 is what came to be called classical conditioning, the kind so well researched by Pavlov. It focused on eliciting reflexive responses through conditioning to a previously neutral stimulus. As such, it is a process of stimulus substitution and focuses on the relationship between unconditioned and conditioning stimuli. For Pavlov, the effects of basic conditioning were to bring an involuntary response, such as salivation or eye blinking, under intentional control by connecting it to various manageable stimuli such as a bell, metronome, or visual symbol. That Pavlov had a basic paradigm that empirically demonstrated influence on behavior with no reliance on mentalistic concepts was appealing to Skinner. Skinner's aim, though, was to predict a wider range of behavior. The Pavlovian model provided answers regarding only a narrow segment of behavior, namely, reflexive responses.

With such a strong focus on the relationship between classes of stimuli, this provided Skinner with the structure for intensive study of one third of the contingencies of learning, the antecedent conditions.

Building on Pavlov's work in teaching dogs to (a) differentiate one stimulus from another, (b) learn to salivate to the bell and not to the metronome, and (c) make relatively fine discriminations between presentations of the same stimulus—salivation to a bell, of one pitch and non-response to another bell, or salivation to metronome clicks of 100 beats per minute and not to 90 bpm or to 110 bpm—Skinner refined the stimulus side of his equation. He found that he could condition a rat to press a bar for the reinforcement of food under various specific stimulus conditions, for example when and only when a light was turned on. The rat learned to distinguish or discriminate the conditions that signalled a high probability of reinforcement. In the Skinnerian formula, $S^d \rightarrow R \rightarrow S^{reinf}$, the S^d signifies an antecedent condition that can be determined and made operational by the scientist or therapist and used to signal and control the emitting of a prescribed response by the experimental subject or client. The discriminated stimulus, S^d, is distinguished from other stimuli and other variations of the same class of stimuli that are referred to as S^Δ.

One particular practical problem in working the antecedent stimulus side of the equation is in the case where the client has difficulty discriminating the particular form of the stimulus. The pairing of subtle sounds with obvious lights until the conditioning to the lights has occurred and then progressively dimming out the lights until the subtle sound is left as the lone S^d is an example of cuing and fading of cues. A practical example is the use of colored letters in teaching discriminations necessary for reading. The lower case letters—b and d, p and q—often are hard for young readers to discriminate. The letter q is not as much of a problem because it rarely if ever occurs without the following letter u, though the pu combination is often seen in words such as put and pudding. Particularly with the b and d letters, it is possible to create reading materials that include at the beginning the rendition of the letter b in a bright blue color, the letter d in an orange hue. A third of the way through the letters are gray-blue and gray-orange; two-thirds of the way through both letters appear in gray and at the end, they appear in the same print as all other letters. The vivid color is easy to discriminate. As the color is changed by progressive amounts of gray, the shapes of the letters become more useful and eventually remain as the only discriminated stimulus for correct pronunciation and correct reading of each letter in its word contexts.

Consequent Events

Skinner found that the dynamics of stimulus substitution could apply to responses, both reflexive and "intentional," or voluntary. Organisms learn to respond to a restricted range of antecedent conditions. They discriminate among sensory cues and make responses that are useful in some situations and self-defeating in others. This occurs in many situations, some as simple as comparing the relative size and strength of another child to one inclined to be a bully.

Pavlov provided an answer to what produced the reflexive response, and demonstrated techniques for pairing its elicitation with another previously neutral stimulus. He found that the substituted stimulus lost its power to elicit the reflexive response unless the connection between the conditioning stimulus and unconditioned stimulus was "reinforced" periodically by having them occur together. It was difficult for

Skinner, and others, to generalize the classical conditioning paradigm to voluntary responses, yet the discriminated stimulus dynamics obviously were applicable. What "reinforced" the power of those discriminated stimuli from other similar but noneffective stimuli? This question permitted Skinner to look to consequent events for an answer. He found a strong relationship between events following a response and the probability of recurrence of that response. He noted, also, that only some consequences had power to reinforce the relationship between the discriminated stimulus and the specified response. This opened up an intensive study of consequent conditions, initially developed around manipulation of conditions impacting rats in a controlled environment, the "Skinner box," and later generalized successfully to a wide range of behavior across species of organisms and individual subjects within species.

Several conclusions regarding management of the consequent events or "reinforcers" in the Skinnerian paradigm, $S^d \rightarrow R \rightarrow S^{reinf}$, include:

- The reinforcing event must be perceptible to the learner and must occur contiguous to the response.
- A consistent application of the reinforcer on every occurrence of the desired or target behavior tends to produce more rapid conditioning of the response to the discriminated stimulus. This is called a continuous reinforcement schedule.
- An intermittent relationship between response and reinforcement, as in a reinforcement for every fifth or every tenth manifestation of the response, a fixed ratio schedule, or the reinforcement of the first response following a time lapse—a fixed interval schedule—produces slower acquisition and has varying effects on the durability of the conditioning.
- The schedule of reinforcement that produces most durability of conditioning is a variable reinforcement schedule wherein the reinforcing event has no consistent pattern, yet occurs as a result of the target response. The strongly-resistant-to-extinction pattern of response of gambling machines is an example of the power of a variable reinforcement schedule.
- Combining the continuous reinforcement for early acquisition with transition to a variable schedule for maintenance seems to be the most efficient procedure in managed conditioning.

With rats and pigeons, Skinner could control conditions such as deprivation of food (three days for rats, 80% ad lib weight for pigeons) and use the offering of small bits of food as a powerful consequent event for producing bar pressing or disk pecking and even for creating long and complex sequences of response such as teaching two pigeons to play ping-pong. A practical application of consequence management for people requires a different strategy. One can rely on the reinforcement definition that anything that, upon presentation consequent to a target response, increases the probability of the recurrence of that response in the same antecedent conditions is a positive reinforcer. The task is to try out various consequences that can be controlled by the therapist to determine which has reinforcing power, then use that consequence in the process of conditioning.

In the process of determining what is a positive reinforcer and which is the most reliable form of reinforcer, it is possible to encounter several patterns for managing the consequent contingency of reinforcement. Not all of the patterns work as well as others. Usually these patterns are described by four terms: positive reinforcement, negative reinforcement, punishment, and extinction. They can best be understood through analysis of their application in the *antecedent* to response, *response*, and *consequent* to response sequence.

Upon the occurrence of a discriminated stimulus, the target response is emitted. Upon emission of the target response, something is added to the situation, the addition of which increases the probability of the target response recurring the next time the discriminated stimulus is presented. It is important to attend, in a *post hoc* fashion, to the dynamics and not to any preconceived notion about the characteristics of the reinforcer. This is a critical differentiation between the dynamics of reinforcement and those of reward and punishment. When presented in this format, rats have been conditioned to bar press to a reinforcement of painful stimulation. Children have been known to increase their acting out responses when shouted at, made to sit in the dunce chair,* sent to the office, spanked, and given other consequences the judgment of which is that they are punishing and will either prevent or suppress recurrence of the response. *Anything* that follows and increases the likelihood of repetition of the response is a positive reinforcer (see Figure 6.2).

When the discriminated stimulus occurs in a context that includes a condition that is negative or aversive to the organism/person and, upon emitting the target response, the aversive condition subsides and the probability of a repetition of the same pattern is increased, negative reinforcement has occurred. It must be recognized that negative reinforcement is positively reinforcing. In an awkward sort of way, it can be said that the removal of the aversive condition is the addition of relief from the aversive condition. The terms positive and negative as modifiers of reinforcement have nothing to do with quality, as in "that was a negative experience;" they are mathematical in nature. In *positive* reinforcement, something is *added* as a result of the response; in *negative* reinforcement, something is *subtracted* as a result of the response. Both are positively reinforcing in that they both increase the probability of response recurrence to the discriminated stimulus (see Figure 6.3).

When the consequence of the response is the addition of something aversive to the behavior, one form of punishment has been attempted. Being forced to sit in the dunce corner, being sent to the office, being struck or spanked, and being imprisoned are examples of this form of punishment. The results of punishment are unpredictable. Social examples on a large scale include a high rate of recidivism in criminals who have been incarcerated, and the belief that children who are spanked merely suppress the target response and learn to repeat the spanking on their subsequent offspring.

Antecedent Condition	Target Response	Consequent Condition
S^d →	R →	S reinf
		+++

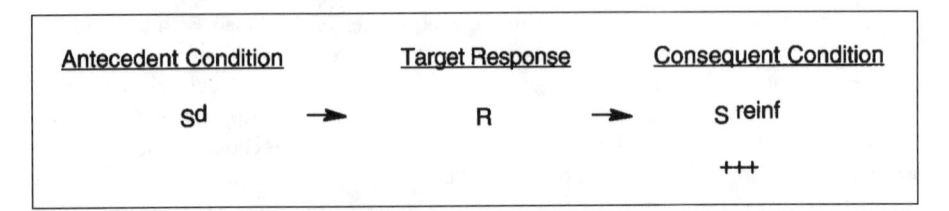

FIGURE 6.2. Positive Reinforcement.

---

*The dunce chair was intended to elicit derision and pressure to conform from classmates. This is a form of negative attention. The use of time out is more than a contemporary form of the dunce chair. When properly used, time out results in absence of attention and of any other consequent and reinforcing event.

Antecedent Condition	Target Response	Consequent Condition
S^d →	R →	S^{reinf}
addition of aversive condition		removal of aversive condition
+ (-1)		- (-1) = 0

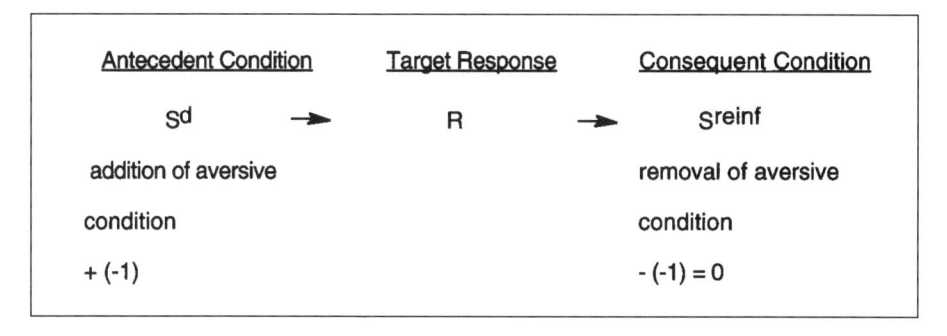

FIGURE 6.3. Negative Reinforcement.

The factor that prompted Skinner to profess against any form of punishment as a behavior control is that it fits the dynamics that often produce a stronger response, namely, the addition of something consequent to the response that increases rather than decreases the probability of recurrence

The claim is that intrinsic punishment works, that punishment as employed by "mother" or "father" nature, as the case may be, is effective. One major difference between intrinsic punishment and managed or extrinsic punishment is that the former is immediate and severe and that it follows a continuous reinforcement schedule. Presumably, if immediate, severe, and consistent punishment were permitted by society, it would be effective. A further limitation of punishment is its effect, when it works at all, to only suppress the particular manifestation of the target response. It communicates only what should not be done, permitting the behaver to emit other equally undesirable responses. Recognizing the limitations in both the paradigm and the inconsistent application of punishment, it is safe to conclude that, while punishment may work in some cases, positive reinforcement is a far superior technique for modifying behavior in a prescribed direction.

When the consequence of the response is the removal of something perceived to be powerful or important to the behaver, a second form of punishment has been attempted. Taking away privileges, "grounding," and levying monetary fines are examples of this type of punishment. This kind of attempt to modify behavior suffers from the same dynamics as the previous, with the added problem of being relatively impossible to perform without simultaneously calling attention to the behavior that is being punished. This paying attention to the offense, or negative attention, is added consequent to the response and, hence, fits the pattern of positive reinforcement for recurrence of the offensive behavior. This is especially problematic if the only attention received by the behaver is negative attention (see Figure 6.4).

If punishment is, at worst, ineffective and, at best, unpredictable, what technique(s) can be used to eliminate or repress an unwanted response? Skinner found, as did Pavlov, that unreinforced responses gradually diminished until they were no longer measurable. Extinction is the process of permitting the response to the discriminated stimulus to occur with no severe consequence (see Figure 6.5).

Repetitions of this dynamic removes the power for its continuation and the response fades out. Often ignoring a response is sufficient to eliminate it. When the environment includes reinforcing elements that are difficult or impossible to remove, the behaver can be expelled for a brief period. Time out, the procedure of removing a

Antecedent Condition	Target Response	Consequent Condition
S^d →	R →	S^{reinf}
		addition of aversive condition
		+(-1) = -1
Antecedent Condition	Target Response	Consequent Condition
S^d →	R →	S
Presence of favorable condition		Removal of favorable condition
+1		-(+1) = 0

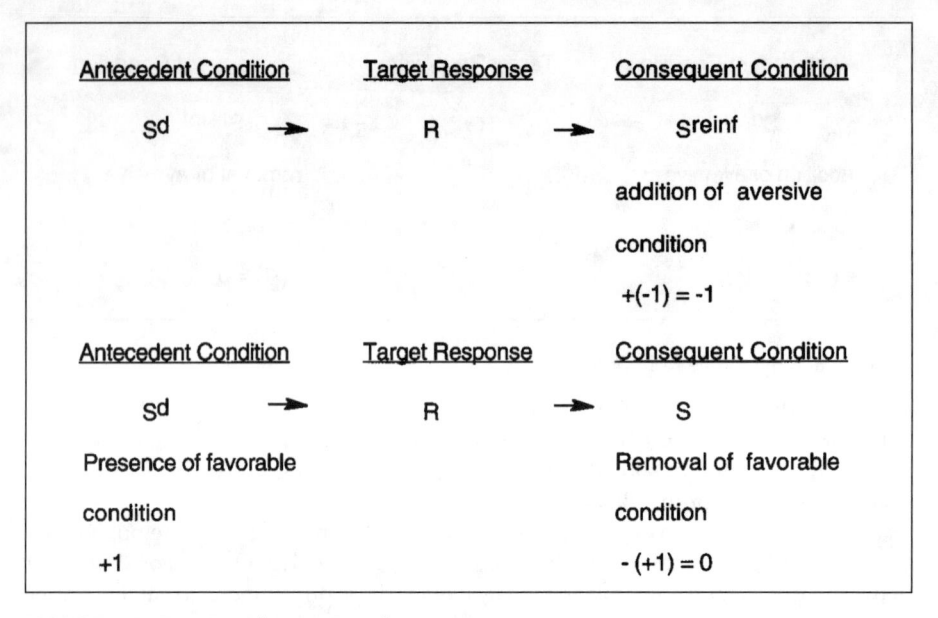

FIGURE 6.4. Two Punishment Paradigms.

child from a reinforcing context for several minutes, is the creation of a "nothing" space following the offense; obviously this must be done in the absence of negative attention.

A second technique for dealing with an unwanted response is to condition a mutually exclusive and desirable response to the same discriminated stimulus. The positive reinforcement of the new target response should offset whatever is maintaining the unwanted behavior. Obviously, a combination of extinction and counterconditioning would be another viable option. An example is the conditioning of on-task-behavior that is mutually exclusive of disruptive responses.

Responses

Given the importance of selecting and managing the discriminated stimuli that permit initiation of the process in a predictable manner, and given the necessity to understand and manage the powerful dynamics of the consequent, reinforcing events that cement the conditioning, it is necessary now to consider the third part of the contin-

Antecedent Condition	Target Response	Consequent Condition
S^d →	R	nothing added or removed
		0 +/- 0 = 0

FIGURE 6.5. Extinction.

gencies of reinforcement—the response. Pavlov managed to create the response he wanted by presenting an unconditioned stimulus that elicited the predictable reflex. Having control over the manifestation of the response allowed him to manipulate elements of the antecedent context assuring a contiguous occurrence with the response. Skinner had a different problem as he moved his attention to non-reflexive, voluntary emissions of behavior: How do you get the organism to emit the prescribed target response?

There are two simple answers to this question. Wait until the target response is given, then reinforce it. With children in a classroom, if one waits long enough, there will come a brief period of quiet. Upon the occurrence of that quiet, if being quiet is the target behavior, a reinforcing event may be introduced. One approach, then, is not to manage the response but to time the reinforcement so that it happens only when the response is randomly made. This approach works on responses that already exist in the repertoire of the behaver, and the attempt is to bring them under stimulus control. It is not useful for creating a new response.

The approach for working on new responses or speeding up the process of control of existing responses is to reinforce successive approximations of the target response. This is called shaping. In an animal example, it is unusual for pigeons to peck at ping-pong balls in a vertical plane. Casual observation of pigeon pecking shows that they peck still or slowly moving objects from the ground, a horizontal plane. One could wait endlessly for a pigeon to encounter an object that is moving toward him or her and impel it to move in the opposite direction. The process of conditioning involves a series of approximations beginning with moving toward a vertical plane; posturing so as to eventually peck at the vertical; pecking at a stationary object on the vertical plane; responding to an object moving toward it in a non-evasive way; pecking at the moving object in any direction other than downward; and pecking at it so as to move it back in the direction it came. That this can be done at all is impressive. With people, having some perceptual and communicative ability, their responses can be directed or instructed or modeled. Still, the successful performance of a skill such as competitive tennis playing or efficient keyboarding on a computer requires considerable repetition with reinforcement of successive approximations of a skilled performance. The directing, shaping, and reinforcement of successive approximations of response is the process for managing the occurrence of that response in a contingent relationship with the prescribed discriminated antecedent stimulus and the effective consequent stimulus, the reinforcer.

☐ Applied Theories

There are many variations of operant conditioning or behavior modification or continuous measurement or whatever other rubric is used to refer to change through management of reinforcement contingencies. In reality, the single subject bias of Skinner is a benchmark for successful use of operant techniques. The technique of choice will be the one that works on the single subject or individual client at hand. Once a therapist understands the rudiments, he or she can build applications for the particular situation. Because of this fact, a very simple approach will be given. Variations of approach can be ascertained from the examples of applications that appear in a subsequent section.

This six-step method comes from synthesizing information on operant techniques from sources such as Mink (1970) and Sherman (1973).

1. Identify the target behavior in terms of discrete units. This target behavior may be from two categories: responses that are self-defeating and need to be removed, and responses that are absent, the presence of which would be self-enhancing. Defining them in discrete units requires identifying either countable instances of each or of defining discrete time intervals that contain their occurrence. Suppose that the client wishes to quit his or her smoking habit. The act of smoking can be defined in number of cigarettes, number of puffs on a cigarette, number of minutes/hours/days between cigarettes. For a bulimic client with a binge and purge pattern, the number of sub-binge meals is a discrete quantity or the number of hours or of days without a purge episode is a discrete time lapse indicator. Other discrete events include number of times putting away tools after their use, flossing teeth, bringing sharpened pencil to class, speaking respectfully to parent, time segment devoid of profanity, washing of hands after toileting, and instances of daydreaming.
2. Determine if the target behavior is to occur in a restricted context, for example, while at school desk, on the playground, in response to authority figure, when challenged, in response to angry spouse. Identify major features of the stimulus event that are always present when you want the target response to occur. These form the discriminated stimuli that you wish to become signals for emission of the target response.
3. Establish a baseline. The baseline is the number of discrete occurrences within a specified time, such as, Johnny flosses his teeth on the average four times per week; Sally profanes fourteen times per hour of awake time. Another measure of baseline is the usual time lapse between instances of the target response occurrence, for example, hardly an hour passes between times that Jennifer daydreams. Taking a baseline measurement for a reasonable time period, say a week, provides an awareness of the severity of the problem and permits subsequent evaluation of changes that result from conditioning.
4. Identify reinforcers. A reinforcer must be something that can be given immediately following the manifestation of the desired change in target response. Anything that requires a waiting period before getting it may still be an incentive, but it is not a reinforcer. The promise of a new car if and after graduating with honors is a bribe; however, dollars or tokens or check marks received after every hour of study time and that can be cashed in toward purchase of a new car are reinforcements. It is not the nature of the object or privilege that is reinforcing, rather it is the contiguous time relationship between response and consequence that makes something reinforcing. Reinforcements generally are small objects or tokens that can be managed easily and delivered readily upon occurrence of the target response.

   A story that is almost legendary or apocryphal is of a time of operant techniques, perfected on rats, being generalized to use with human subjects. It is alleged that patients in an institution for the mentally retarded were difficult to manage, had poor hygiene, and failed to appear on time for meals. Attendants in one wing of the facility were issued a pocket-full of M&M chocolate candies each day with two instructions: (a) don't eat the M&Ms yourself, and (b) without saying anything, place an M&M in the mouth of any patient who makes a rudimentary attempt at being out of bed on time, straightening the bed, washing hands and face, etc. The second technique was to lock the doors to the dining room precisely at 8:00 a.m., permitting those on-time patients to eat, and depriving latecomers of the food reinforcement for being on time. In impressively short order, patients who had been relegated to a hopeless status were performing hygienic activities and arriving on time for meals. If there is a "universal reinforcer" it might be M&Ms, though there may be people who find them aversive and the dental and dietary consequences of frequent ingestion of chocolate candy militate against overreliance on M&Ms. Allegedly, the same institution substituted plastic chips for the M&Ms, chips that could be traded in following the evening meal for M&Ms or other goodies or articles. The results continued to be positive and impressive.

Any item or event that can be managed to occur contiguously to the target response and results in an increase in the probability of recurrence of the response can be an effective reinforcer. When conditioning people, it is helpful to discuss with them and even negotiate reinforcers. Not all reinforcers will be manageable or effective; however, the negotiation provides a place to start. Access to a variety of incentives works well when the reinforcing event of receiving a token or a "point" occurs immediately upon the making of the response, and the tokens or points can be saved up and cashed in on an item of choice from the incentive "store."

5. Run the learning trials. Operant conditioning usually requires many repetitions of the $S^d \rightarrow R \rightarrow S^{reinf}$ pattern, though sometimes change is fairly immediate and impressive. The author has both increased and decreased the frequency in number of self-references made by students in three-minute, extemporaneous speaking exercises when using a three-minute baseline test, a three-minute conditioning trial, and a three-minute posttest. Generally for change to become stable and resistant to change, many repetitions of the reinforced response must occur.

6. Perform a criterion test. A criterion measurement is a repetition of the procedure used to establish the baseline. Any change between baseline and criterion evaluation is an indication of the effectiveness or lack thereof of the conditioning program. Absence of desired change in the criterion measurement signals a need to alter the conditioning program, usually by changing the reinforcer.

☐ Examples

Since all problems are manifested in actions, theoretically all problems are susceptible to treatment through operant means. The key lies in adequately defining the problem in discrete terms of response. The integrationist either would disagree with the universality of operant intervention or would assert that, while operant techniques could be derived for all problems, sometimes an alternate approach is much more direct and efficient. The following examples are selected, not as a representative sample of behavioral applications, but rather as instances where the dynamics of operant intervention can be readily demonstrated. They are organized into clinic (individual and group) and classroom (individual and group) settings.

Clinic: Individual Applications

The first two examples are applications within the author's family. They will be described in first person, familiar form.

The Spelling Challenge. My oldest daughter, while in the fourth grade, brought home spelling tests with performances in the 25% to 35% range. The task required paying attention to the introduction of the new words for the week, practice in writing the words correctly, at least one practice test at midweek, and some use of the new words in class assignments and activities. It seemed to me that, with just a little effort, spelling test scores could be 100% or at least above 90%. I discussed with my daughter her performance and her response to the spelling preparation activities. She indicated that doing well was not high on her priority list and, that if it were more important to her, she could score higher.

Having determined that success would not require special teaching procedures, I told her that even though she did not care about the scores, I did, and that I would like her to improve. This revelation did not appear to have any significant impact, so I said, "What would it be worth for you to get perfect scores on those spelling tests?" The change in strategy left her without immediate reply. "How about my giving you a nickel for a 100% score?" Her stare became incredulous and she said something like, "Dad. You've got to be kidding." Recognizing that finding the workable reinforcing event sometimes requires negotiation, I quickly added, "And I'll double the payoff for each successive 100%." Her weakness was spelling, not mathematics. She took brief leave of me to get a pencil and paper. With fourteen weeks to go, she calculated that she could get $409.60 from me. She was eager to accept those terms; then it occurred to her, "What if I miss 100% on a test?" The agreement was to start over again at a nickel. The actual reinforcing event was a mutual accounting on her record of the amount she had gained (the debt I incurred) upon receipt of her weekly spelling test score. My recollection is that she did well the first couple of tests, did an 85% and started over. Eventually she received $51.55.

Of my five children, she is one of the better spellers. Apparently some natural reinforcers kicked in, such as praise by teacher and attention from schoolmates, that continued after the conditioning trials were finished.

> **Target behavior:** accurate spelling of words on spelling tests.
> **Baseline:** 30% average of scores over four-week period.
> **Reinforcing event:** calculation and accounting of money due.
> **Learning trials:** fourteen weekly spelling tests.
> **Criterion test:** 100% average on final four spelling tests.

Television Domination. For four months while on a professorial exchange assignment in Mexico, my family lived without television. Upon returning home, it was apparent that a pattern of "enter house, turn on television set, watch program" was immediately established or, perhaps, resumed. To alter that pattern and to teach judgment and control of television viewing, each member of the family was issued fourteen plastic chips on Sunday morning. The rules were that each member could watch whatever he or she chose at the "cost" of one chip per 30 minutes of viewing, payable in advance. A receptacle was located on the television set to receive the chips. Nobody could watch on another person's chip. Each member chipped in for his or her viewing. With a maximum of seven hours per week of viewing, the programming guide became a major reference tool, with weekly schedules established so that highly valued programs that occurred late in the week could be planned for. Two questions arose almost immediately: (a) "What if I have chips left over at the end of the week?

Can I save them for next week?" and (b) "What if I run out of chips and a really neat program or ballgame comes on Saturday?" I agreed to buy back unused chips at 5¢ each (tight budget) and to allow the earning of a chip for 30 minutes of extra reading, practicing of the piano, or household chores.

In relatively short order, I was buying back most of the chips. Operationally, few television programs were worth 5¢. Other activities took priority over watching the tube, such activities that became intrinsically reinforcing or were strengthened by positive parental or sibling reaction.

>   **Target behavior:** Decrease nonselective television viewing.
>   **Baseline:** All members of the family automatically turned on the television upon entering the room and watched, regardless of what was available and whether or not the program was beginning, or at various stages of completion.
>   **Reinforcing event:** Access to programs of choice, managed by the plastic chip system; later the receipt of 5¢ per unused chip became a support for not using the token.
>   **Learning trials:** Several weeks of chip-mediated viewing.
>   **Criterion test:** Average chip buy-back of 10 per week per family member.

Weight Control. All methods of losing unwanted weight consist of either limiting the intake of food or of increasing physical activity while holding food intake constant, or a combination of the two. Physiological or medical concerns generalize across methods and must be accounted for before beginning a weight-loss program. One patently operant approach identifies the target behavior as bites of food—trips of the eating utensil from plate to mouth. The genius of this method is that it requires no monitoring of calories, food preference, or size of bites. The baseline consists of counting and recording the number of bites taken daily for a one-week period and weighing and recording the weight at the same time/condition daily. The use of a golf-stroke counter is a convenient way for accounting for bites during the day. The program then requires adjusting the number of bites permissible while recording a weight loss of between one and two pounds per week. Usually the first week of the learning trials sees a 50% reduction in number of bites. Because bite size often increases, subsequent adjustments downward are required. It is not unusual for daily bite allowance to be as low as forty bites.

Fluids, other than water, are arbitrarily assigned four bites per 8 oz. serving. To allow for the occurrence of big appetite–low bite allowance, some "free" foods are allowed, such as raw carrots, undressed salad, or celery sticks. Bites can be managed according to preference only within a single day (i.e., bites cannot be saved from one day to the next). Sometimes a penalty for excess number of bites is helpful, something like twenty-five push-ups per bite over daily budget.

The program is continued until the desired target weight is reached, then the "bite budget" is gradually increased to determine a maintenance level. Daily bite accounting and daily body weight recording continue throughout the program.

>   **Target behavior:** Bites of food.
>   **Baseline:** Number of bites per day and daily body weight recording for one week.
>   **Reinforcing event:** Charting of bites each day; observance of decline of recorded weight amounts; attention from people who notice the recording of bites; even-

tually the comments of people who notice a change in appearance from losing weight.
Learning trials: Continuance of the program until target weight is reached.
Criterion test: Recording of weight with no increase for one week following accomplishment of target weight.

Encopresis. The client in this case is an eight-year old boy. He had experienced some delay in mastering toilet training, but was operating normally prior to starting kindergarten. Two months into the second grade, he started having "accidents" at school, with soiling occurring between two and nine times per week. He had similar difficulties at home and at church, but on a markedly less frequent occurrence. His behavior was manifest also upon his first visit to the psychologist's office. Information garnered from the client and from his mother indicated an unexpected assignment of his first grade teacher to be his second grade teacher; the teacher was stern and strict and controlling. The client's father was interested in outdoor activities, as was the client, though the father had refused to take the client on overnight outings because of the threat of an encopretic incident. A medical examination was entirely unremarkable in regard to bowel functioning as well as other potentially pertinent ailments. Though the client professed being unable to control his soilings, it was surmised that such behavior virtually was the client's only means of exerting any control over people in his environment. He successfully got attention and annoyance/sympathy from both adults and peers.

The intervention plan required working in four-hour time periods during his awake time. He showed no problems with nighttime incontinence. The target behavior was restraint from soiling during a four-hour time period. At the end of each time period without any "accidents," the client was given a sticker to place on a chart. Stickers could be accumulated and cashed in for a number of things, including food treats, toys, periods of attention from his mother or father (such periods to be at his discretion within a one-day timeframe), and with a large total of points, an overnight camping trip with his father. Parents and teacher were instructed to make the client responsible for cleaning up his messes. Procedures were outlined for school and home where, upon an incident of soiling, he would absent himself from the group and go to a bathroom, clean himself up, put on fresh clothing, place soiled clothing in a plastic bag, and return to the group. No attention was to be given around soiling incidents. Within four weeks, encopretic incidents dropped markedly and after another month, were completely absent.

Target behavior: Time without soiling.
Baseline: Eight incidents within a one-week time period, seven during school.
Reinforcing event: Receiving stickers to be placed on a chart and to be accumulated for access to a menu of things, including time and attention of parents.
Learning trials: Two months.
Criterion test: Client was incident-free for a period of one week.

Biofeedback. The client complained of periodic episodes of migraine headaches. A medical exam showed no organic or chemical causes for the symptoms. The client was instructed in relaxation techniques and desensitized to the room and the biofeedback apparatus. A temperature-sensitive device was strapped to his finger. He was directed, while in a relaxed state, to focus on a sound that was generated by a pure-tone oscillator attached to the temperature device. His task was to somehow cause the sound to move to a lower pitch. Such would result from the temperature in his fingertip rising. In essence, he was being told to warm his fingertip. The biofeedback device was necessary to cue the desired response because the client was not aware of minor changes in temperature in his extremities. Recall that cuing is the pairing of an obvious stimulus with one that is not yet distinguishable to the client. Relatively cooler temperature in the extremities accompanies the migraine symptoms because distended blood vessels in the head allegedly create pressure that is, in turn, experienced as a migraine headache. Distended vessels in the body core are paralleled by constricted vessels in the periphery of the vascular system. By raising the temperature in the fingers, blood is moved from the central to the peripheral vessels, thus releasing pressure in the head.

There seems to be no singular approach among clients to get the tone down. Some relax more; some visualize warm beaches; some may recall certain music. Whatever the client does to lower the sound is instrumental in raising the finger temperature. Knowledge of results (i.e., hearing the change in sound) is reinforcing of whatever it takes to lower the sound. Additional reinforcement may be administered in the form of praise or encouragement by the therapist. So the client was instructed to experiment with a variety of efforts to lower the tone. As he was learning to manage the pitch of the tone, he also was experiencing changes in his physiological systems that accompanied the raising of finger temperature. Over many learning sessions, he became quite adept at managing the pitch of the tone. He became increasingly sensitive to changes in his physiological condition. He became able to predict the onset of his migraines and to seek treatment promptly. As the apparatus was not always accessible, he made the connection between awareness of an oncoming episode and doing whatever it took to lower the tone, without the presence of the tone to lower. The artificial cue was faded, allowing the client to respond to the naturally occurring discriminated stimulus.

> **Target behavior:** Increase finger temperature.
> **Baseline:** No change in biofeedback equipment-generated tone in first twenty minutes.
> **Reinforcing event:** Change of pitch in tone.
> **Learning trials:** Daily sessions with equipment for two weeks.
> **Criterion test:** Ability to change pitch as directed and to maintain a lower pitch for three minutes.
>
> **Target behavior:** Reduce frequency of migraine episodes.
> **Baseline:** Average four migraines per month over the past six months.
> **Reinforcing event:** Change in pitch of tone; sense of control over symptoms.
> **Learning trials:** Daily practice for two weeks; bi-weekly practice for one month; access to equipment on request for six months.
> **Criterion test:** Client was able to interrupt the migraine occurrence totally or with a reduction of symptoms for the six months following active therapy.

Clinic: Group Application.

The use of operant techniques on a group is not possible. Groups do not behave; individuals behave. Group applications are those that are managed in a group setting to group members with some common concerns and who may benefit from the reinforcement possible in the group context, namely, feedback and support from other people. Assertiveness training is an example. The group members have in common responses in social encounters that are self-defeating and result in their being taken advantage of. Target responses such as firmly saying "No," using "I" messages, saying "I" choose to or not to" instead of "I can't" are identified and explained and modeled. Members take turns practicing the use of the target responses in a variety of role plays. The therapist and other members monitor the interactions, point out incidents of non-assertion and give praise when assertive responses are chosen.

> **Target behavior:** Increase assertive responses; decrease nonassertive responses.
> **Baseline:** Number of assertive responses, number of nonassertive responses in standard encounter situation.
> **Reinforcing event:** Ignoring of and redirection from nonassertive responses; praise, excitement, pat on back for use of assertive responses; eventual self-enhancement from reaction of others following effective use of assertive responses.
> **Learning trials:** Weekly or bi-weekly therapy/training sessions for several weeks.
> **Criterion test:** Number of assertive responses, number of nonassertive responses in standard encounter situation.

Classroom: Individual Applications

Attention Deficit Hyperactivity Disorder? The student was a fourth-grade boy with aptitude and achievement test scores between one and two standard deviations above the mean for his norm group. In a one-hour observation, he demonstrated forty-five different activities, none of them more than three minutes in duration. He did obey restroom rules of asking permission and being gone only three or four minutes. He waited, impatiently, for the teacher's attention in order to ask permission to leave. He correctly answered several questions from the reading assignment even though he appeared to be attentive to other things at the time of the lesson. None of his activities were of major disruption to the classroom, distracting at most one or two other students at a time, particularly when he engaged them in an activity.

An interview with the student's parents indicated similar though not as extreme response patterns at home. He reportedly viewed television for prolonged periods, built objects with toys and engaged in games with other children for appropriate lengths of time. His pattern was most annoying at times such as when accompanying his father to the father's bowling league matches. The parents were upset by the poor reports of his demeanor and lack of achievement at school and had tried a variety of contingent rewards for better performance; the results of their efforts were disappointing.

The counselor elected to work on two issues with this student: personal validation from an affective deficit viewpoint and increased time on task from a behavioral viewpoint. It was postulated that the boy was in the developmental phase, from a Maslovian context, of seeking to fill his love and belonging needs (Maslow, 1962), yet he was confronted exclusively with contingent relationships—everyone was concerned with his performance; no one seemed to be very accepting of him as an individual. The parents were instructed to spend thirty minutes per day with him in non-contingent activities such as playing games, watching TV, letting him tag along on shopping trips, and reading stories.

The problem of time on task was approached at school. The teacher was instructed to simplify the stimulus environment by placing him in a desk immediately in front of her's, removing everything from his desk, and giving him only the materials needed for the task at hand. The teacher was to work out a secret signal system (assuming that his getting attention would be a positive reinforcer) with which she could reinforce his appropriate actions without detracting from the learning of other students. The system they worked out was that she would touch him on the shoulder as she was passing by or, if she were in another location in the room, she would catch his attention and wink at him to let him know she was watching and that she liked his behavior. Of course, when convenient and appropriate, she gave him the same verbal praise as was given to other students for desired responses. She was instructed to ignore instances of off-task responses.

>**Target behavior:** Decrease instances of off-task behavior.
>**Baseline:** Forty five activities in one hour, of which five may have been briefly on task.
>**Reinforcing event:** Ignoring of off-task behavior (extinction schedule); it is assumed that the restriction of materials reduced the stimuli that had been signals for off-task activities and supported a focus on a narrower range of stimuli that were being discriminated as cues for on-task responses.
>**Learning trials:** Ongoing and continuous conditioning during all time in classroom.
>**Criterion test:** After two weeks, another observation period resulted in zero off-task responses in a one-hour period.
>
>**Target behavior:** Increase on-task responses and increase time on task.
>**Baseline:** In one hour of observation, the student was on task only five times and for very brief time spans.
>**Reinforcing event:** Attention from teacher given for on-task behavior; such attention through verbal praise and by way of secret signal system.
>**Learning trials:** Ongoing and continuous conditioning during all time in classroom.
>**Criterion test:** At the end of two weeks of conditioning, the teacher had moved the student to a position in the far left corner of the room and had given him back a full complement of study materials. During the criterion observation period, the student quickly began work as tasks were prescribed and stayed on task until directed to subsequent activities.

It is instructive to note here that the counselor directed the teacher to make modifications in all three of the contingencies of reinforcement: the discriminated stimulus, the response, and the consequent stimulus. To make it easier for the student to focus on the intended stimulus, the teacher removed all other potentially distracting stimuli. To support the student in performing the desired behavior, she moved him to a position where she could direct him and observe his responses very closely. In the process of managing the consequent stimuli, she arranged for some special consequences that pertained only to him and that had not been used previously.

Classroom: Group Application

Wampum. It is not easy to develop and keep straight enough secret systems of reinforcement to use on many students in the same class, nor is it advisable. There are a number of variations of "token economy" systems, any of which can be instituted and used with the full awareness of all students. A token economy is a menu of outcomes that can be accessed by the receipt of and the accumulation of objects or tokens. These tokens are something that can be delivered immediately upon manifestation of a target response and can be managed without disruption to the ongoing activity of all students. The token can be tangible or experiential; a tangible token is a plastic chip; an experiential token is a point on a tally sheet or a sticker on a chart.

One teacher created a token economy based on macaroni that she had colored to allow for various values of tokens. The system was introduced during a study of Native American groups that used objects as a medium of exchange. These objects were called wampum. The classroom system was arranged so that a variety of target responses could be reinforced by delivery of a piece of macaroni/wampum. For example, beginning a task promptly, raising a hand before speaking, having clean work space, putting name at top of worksheet as instructed, returning library materials, lining up in an orderly fashion at the end of recess, and being on task resulted in the award of a green macaroni, delivered by the teacher on a nearly continuous reinforcement schedule at the first instance and then changing naturally to a variable schedule. Green macaroni could be exchanged for red or blue or orange to make it easier for saving and accumulating enough wampum to trade in for a variety of things or privileges. The wampum could be redeemed for pencils, erasers, protracters, compasses, rulers, stickers, candy, gum, small toys, access to computer games during optional time, or the privilege of being the teacher's assistant.

A periodic class council was held to evaluate the system, hear requests for additional items to be added to the redemption center, and to negotiate the value of wampum for various activities. It is important to recognize that the group was not being conditioned; rather, each individual was being conditioned for a specific target response or responses in a context of others being conditioned simultaneously or alternately for similar or different target responses.

☐ Sample Problem Situations

As with the previous chapter, the directions for processing the following sample situations are similar: (a) list the principles involved in behavior modification through operant techniques, (b) create change procedures for a given sample problem, and (c) review the steps of your procedure with your list of dynamics. The six-step approach described in Chapter 5 will be a useful guide.

Seat Belt Use

A private foundation has granted you five million dollars to create a demonstration project involving your county. Create an approach based on positive reinforcement that will increase the incidence of voluntary seat belt use.

Driving Within the Speed Limit

Saul is a taxi driver in a large city. He prides himself in getting his passengers to their destinations in the shortest possible times. His pride and enthusiasm lead him to frequent and habitual driving in excess of the speed limit. He has had many tickets, and even more warnings over his three-year career but managed to stay just under the limit for losing his license or paying astronomical insurance payments. Last month he was in an accident, partially as a result of his speeding. His insurance company is threatening to cancel him; the police are threatening to suspend his license, and his new wife, a law-and-order crusader with three children who are old enough to read traffic signs and speedometers, is haranguing him almost beyond tolerance. All these detractors are willing to back off if he will get help for his problem.

Weight Loss

Henry is fifty pounds overweight. Because of other health problems it is not advisable for him to reduce or appreciably alter his eating regimen. Create for him an operant weight reduction program focusing on activity level.

Procrastination

Susan is a freelance writer. She has an excellent portfolio, is often sought out because of the quality of her work; however, she has a lifelong habit of procrastinating. She seems unable to meet any kind of deadline. Her spouse, a successful business executive who relies on her to entertain prime customers, has threatened to leave her because of her repeated failure to make timely arrangements. Because of the nature of his business, hiring a professional service is not an option.

Unexpected Change of Plans

Sam is a sales representative for a computer software company. He loves his work and is very good at it. As with many aspects of the software industry, his plans tend to be fluid with quick response required to customer needs and concerns. As a result, arrangements he makes with his spouse, children, community, and church groups are in constant jeopardy. Most of his family and acquaintances are aware of this and can usually allow for his absence if given notice. The problem is that Sam hardly ever remembers to call his spouse or to notify anyone when his plans change. Sally, Sam's spouse, has a history of tension neurosis and reacts unpredictably to changes in routine. Sometimes she is calm and gracious. At other times she may have an episode of uncontrollable crying, or of breaking household items, or of long and near-reckless drives into the country. Either Sam or Sally or both need help.

Social Isolation

Stephanie used to behave in a charming, vivacious, outgoing way. She felt at home in large gatherings as well as in small, close groups. Over the past year and a half, she has become reclusive, avoiding any occasion where she can afford to graciously do so, and being distant and non-communicative in those situations she cannot avoid. There are no major calamities in her life to support the notion of trauma as a cause. She did get a new, top-of-the-line computer system with software for managing her business and home, for designing interiors, and for playing Blackjack. Much of her elective time is spent at the keyboard.

Affection-Deficit

Marge has come to you for help with her relationship. Martin, her husband, was everything she wanted in a mate and companion before their marriage. Over the past five years, he has become distant and irritable. When she has confronted him with her concerns, he has reacted strongly and commented that she is impossible to please and if she doesn't like him, she should look elsewhere. She doesn't want to leave him or have an extramarital relationship. She believes that he still loves her and wants to please her. She has no reason to suspect that he is involved in another romantic liaison. Her plea is, "I've tried everything I know. Please teach me how to reclaim our relationship even without his willing assistance."

Take Your Pills

Davina suffers from a bipolar disorder. She is under psychiatric care and functions acceptably when she closely follows her medication regimen. The major problem comes when she moves from a depressed phase into a normal or mildly manic condition. At such times, she believes she is cured and stops taking her medication. She says, "Only sick people need medicine. I'm better now."

Smoking

You have been assigned to conduct a behavioral workshop on smoking control or cessation. There are twenty people signed up for the workshop. Some are chain-smokers of up to three packs per day, of which most would like to stop entirely, but two want to continue smoking in non-work settings. Two smoke infrequently, but mostly at times of emotional turmoil or tension; one wants to quit entirely; the other wants to stop smoking as a reaction to problems but to continue smoking in social situations. One heavy smoker doesn't want to quit at all, but his physician has told him that unless he quits immediately, his emphysema will kill him within six months.

CHAPTER 7

Perception Learning Approaches to Intervention

☐ Focus

Historically, cognitive and perceptual dynamics were included as a single set of dynamics, a two-stage model of learning. It is true that they are two-stage models; however, there are enough significant differences between the two to warrant discrimination and differential application. The two-stage nature of these approaches indicates that there is, within the learning and behaving organism, an important function—that of deciding. Mental functions such as interpretation, evaluation, remembering, and deciding are pressed into action by stimuli. These stimuli may either come from the internal or external environment. They may exist in the past or the present or as anticipations for the future. Stimulus input or information is processed by the organism. Decisions for action are made based on characteristics of that information and upon characteristics of the organism. The response or behavior that follows any stimulus condition is a function of the information processing and decision of the organism.

Perception theories focus on the nonlinguistic reception and processing of information from the environment through either sensory input, memory, or imaginal sources.

☐ Foundation Theories

Unlike the behavioral approach that was dominated by the work of one theorist, perceptual learning approaches to intervention have many theoretical roots. Five learning theorists will be considered as significant referents for perceptual learning. They are Wertheimer, Köhler, Koffka, Tolman, and Bandura. The first three were contemporaries and colleagues in the Gestalt movement. In addition, two representatives of Humanistic psychology who treated learning from a perceptual position were Maslow and Rogers. Jerome Bruner, the discovery learning advocate, interpreted perceptual learning for the classroom. Finally, the area of psychodynamics contributes a position touted by Perls (1969). Though none of these people defined himself as a "perceptual learning" theorist, all professed a two-stage model with the experiencing or observing human being as the key element in learning.

Wertheimer

Max Wertheimer's work is designated as "Productive Learning." He was born on April 15, 1880 in Prague, Czechoslavakia. His father was founder of a school with new methods of teaching. He graduated from Charles University (Prague) in 1900, having studied law, philosophy, and psychology. He then attended the University of Berlin where he studied philosophy and psychology with Carl Strumpf. In 1904, he completed the Ph.D. at the University of Würzburg under Oswald Külpe. He taught at the University of Frankfurt and at the University of Berlin. In reaction to Nazi persecution, he came to the USA in 1933 as a visiting lecturer at Columbia University, then became a professor at the New School for Social Research in New York City. He died in 1943.

Much of his professional attention was on the Phi Phenomenon, seeing motion in two-dimensional stimuli (i.e., the appearance of motion in a rapid succession of pictures such as occur in motion pictures or in neon light sequences). The Phi Phenomenon, A ø B—that which happens between A and B, is a perceptual experience that seems to be a universal connection between two successive stimuli, the connection perceived as movement, when the separate presentation of the independent stimuli are perceived as still, unmoving objects.

Wertheimer joined with Koffka, Köhler, Goldstein, and Gruhle to establish *Psychologische Forshung*, a professional journal. He also wrote poetry, music, and invented a lie detector. In his *Productive Thinking* (published posthumously, 1945) Wertheimer sought to distinguish between laws of logic (habitual or imitative behavior) and laws of thought, that is, creative or productive acts of thinking.

> Productive thinking is characterized by proceeding from the whole to the parts of which it is comprised; treating the problem as a whole; permitting the whole to dominate over the parts; and proceeding "from above," approaching a problem from a synthetic or bird's-eye view rather than from an analytic viewpoint (Sahakian, 1976, p. 270).

The whole is a phenomenon other than the parts in isolation. For example, a melody is not comprehensible in light of its notes considered separately. A melody-structure is important. Similarly, problems are embedded in structure. To solve them, one must understand their structure as a whole and view them according to fundamental laws of organization, such as the Law of Prägnanz.

Köhler

Wolfgang Köhler emphasized learning by insight. He was born on January 21, 1887, in Reval, Estonia, a country by the Baltic Sea. He completed the gymnasium in Wolffinbüttel in 1905, then attended the University of Tübingen, University of Bonn, and the University of Berlin where he completed the Ph.D. in 1909. He taught at the University of Frankfurt, and from 1913–1920 was director of an anthropoid station on Tenerife (Canary Islands). He published *The Mentality of Apes* in 1917 (Köhler, 1925/1917). After his experience on Tenerife, he went back to the University of Berlin as a professor of philosophy and director of the psychological institute. He was a visiting lecturer at Clark University during the 1925–26 school year, a William James lecturer at Harvard in 1934–35 (*The Place of Value in a World of Facts*) and he also lectured at the University of Chicago in 1935.

Later he left Germany to escape Nazi persecution and worked as a professor of psychology at Swarthmore College until 1958, when he retired. He was active in research at Dartmouth and Princeton until his death in 1967. He was president of the APA in 1959 and was honored by reception of the APA's Distinguished Scientific Contributions award, the Warren Medal from the Society of Experimental Psychologists, and the Wundt Medal from Die Deutsche Gesellschaft für Psychologie.

Koffka

Kurt Koffka worked on Perceptual Trace Theory. He was born in Berlin on March 18, 1886. He completed the Ph.D. in 1908 at the University of Berlin in philosophy and psychology. He spent one year studying at the University of Edinburgh, taught at the University of Würzburg (assisted Oswald Külpe), then at the University of Frankfurt in 1910 where he met Köhler and Wertheimer. In 1911, he went to the University of Giessen, became "Ausserordenlicher Professor" in 1918. He came to the USA in 1921, spending one year as a visiting professor at Cornell and one year at the University of Wisconsin. He taught at Smith College in Massachusetts for five years prior to his death in 1941.

Koffka (1963) believed that an infant experienced organized wholes with growth proceeding along a gradual increase in differentiation of structure, and that learning happened through insight, rather than by rote learning. He postulated three fundamental principles: (1) primary data are specific structures (gestalten); (2) patterns of stimuli are correlated with specific structural entities; and (3) brain functions, as molar events, correspond with structures in our experience (psychological parallelism).

Gestalt Concepts

The following are a collection of principles and concepts from the foregoing theorists. This is not intended to be an exhaustive nor complete discussion of Gestalt theorizing.

Insight. One of the most intriguing experiences common to all people and immune to any attempts to describe it within the constrictions of language, insight is a truly perceptual phenomenon. It is the revelation of a complete solution to a problem, consistent within its context, and happening suddenly and somewhat mystically. Attempts to reduce it to sequential steps or to identify separate, additive experiences have met with failure. Sometimes the insightful solution to a concern occurs after attempts to solve it have been abandoned, almost as though the brain continues working long after attention has shifted to something else.

Köhler noted insight on the part of the chimpanzees he studied. Sultan was able to use a box as a platform for reaching food that was suspended above him; he joined bamboo sticks together in such a way as to extend his reach to food beyond his grasp. In both instances he had tried other, unsuccessful ways of getting the food and apparently had given up on the quest prior to making a unified and successful, insightful effort.

The Relational Theory of Learning. What is learned in stimulus-cued behavior is a relationship, not a specific S->R bond. Some relational concepts are: larger than–smaller than; heavier than–lighter than; brighter than–duller than; darker (grey)–lighter (grey).

For example, chickens taught to peck at the lighter of two grey disks will continue to select the lighter one, even when it is the same shade of grey that was not selected in previous pairings. This is related to the principle of perceptual constancy, where we see or recognize objects even when orientation or color has changed; for example, we know a plate from any angle, from full circle to ellipse to straight line profile.

Productive Thinking. Creative thinking and understanding as opposed to formal logic and associationism proceeds from the whole (which gives meaning) to the parts of which it is comprised. Then, based on perceptual laws, it reorganizes (sorts) those parts into new structures or organizations. Wertheimer gives four features in productive thinking:

- SORTING—grouping, centering, reorganizing, and structuring the situation.
- REFERENCE—functioning in relation to characteristics of the whole rather than to piecemeal ones. This may be important in notions of perceptual field dependence and field independence.
- DIRECTION OR PURPOSE from perceiver—avoiding an "and-summative aggregation of a succession of piecemeal, chance happenings in which items, associations, operations just occur" (Wertheimer 1959, p. 235). There are three explanation structures for Gestalt thinking:
  (1) and-sums—the whole exactly equals the sum of its parts;
  (2) Gestalt factor—the whole is more than the sum of its parts; there is an added factor—a+b+c+d+Gestalt factor (structure or form) and;
  (3) trans-sums—the whole transcends the sum; the whole is quite different from the sum of its parts, some examples being electrical fields, soap bubbles, and personality. The whole is prior to its parts. It can be entirely different from its parts.
- REALITY BASE from environment—"structural truth" that leads to sensible expectations and assumptions

A person sorts through experience, relating parts to each other and to the entirety (phenomenal field) with a need or purpose (i.e., "looking for" something but within the limits set by reality). Meaning comes from within, hence, there can be different perceptions of the same experience. From an abnormal behavior standpoint, it could be said that schizophrenia is a distortion of the reality base and that paranoia is forcing the meaning of perception into a rigid, need-produced and incorrect form, a distortion of meaning.

A classical example of productive thinking is Wertheimer's experience with a five and a half year-old girl whom he had taught to figure the area of a rectangle using a crude measure of height times width (see Figure 7.1a). He then asked her to figure the area of a parallelogram (see Figure 7.1b). Her response was to struggle for a time, then say something like, "These ends are not right. Do you have some scissors?" She then cut off the end to the left and matched it to the other end, making a rectangle (see Figure 7.1c).

> Influenced by Lewin, Wertheimer regarded genuine thinking as resulting from problem situations. Structural features and requirements of the problem situation cause tension,

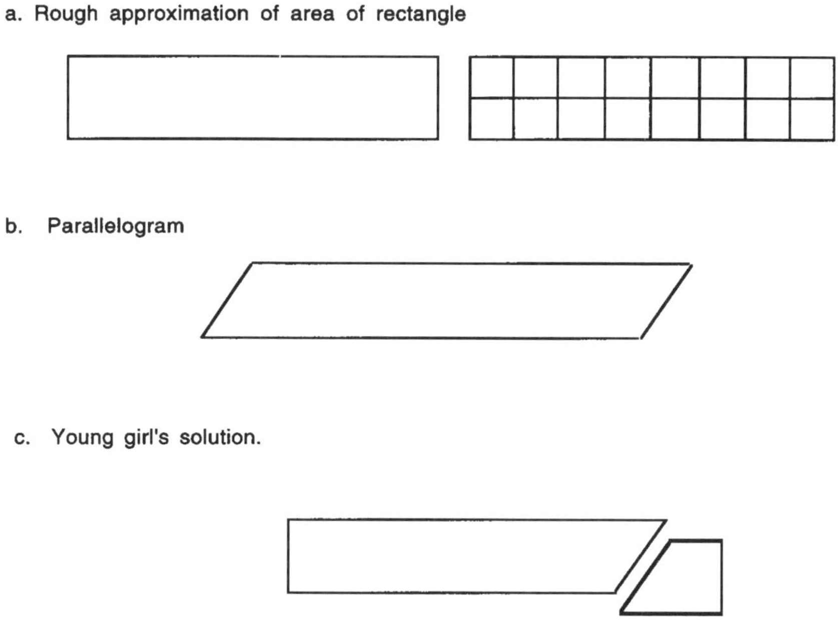

a. Rough approximation of area of rectangle

b. Parallelogram

c. Young girl's solution.

FIGURE 7.1. Wertheimer Lesson From Young Girl.

the strain of which produces vectors that prompt the individual to modify the situation in an improved direction [make an ugly gestalt into a beautiful solution]. An important first achievement is the realization that a problem exists. Correctly envisaging the problem is usually a more important achievement than solving it. (Sahakian, 1976, p. 272)

Perceptual sorting follows certain rules or Gestalt laws of organization. These include (see Figure 7.2):

- Prägnanz. The law of good form, the perception of meaningful wholes. Grouping tends toward maximal simplicity and balance, or toward the formation of "good form." This is a general law that includes the others.
- Proximity. Things seen together are perceived as belonging together.
- Similarity. Things that are alike are perceived as belonging together.
- Closure. We perceptually fill in the incomplete so as to accomplish good form.
- Objective Set. We perceive organization from previous stimulus arrangements.
- Continuity. Items that are a natural successor of a series will be seen as belonging to that series.
- Common Fate. Objects that are undergoing the same change are perceived as constituting a whole; for example, a band marching by a grandstand.
- Inclusiveness. The figure seen is the one involving the greatest number of stimuli; a small figure embedded in a larger figure is not seen.
- Figure and Ground. All perceptions are organized into Figure—principal object of attention, and Ground—background or context.

We perceive by contrast; we learn by contrast. Abstraction involves removing part from the whole, thus causing the part to lose its significance. Two learning problems result from abstraction:

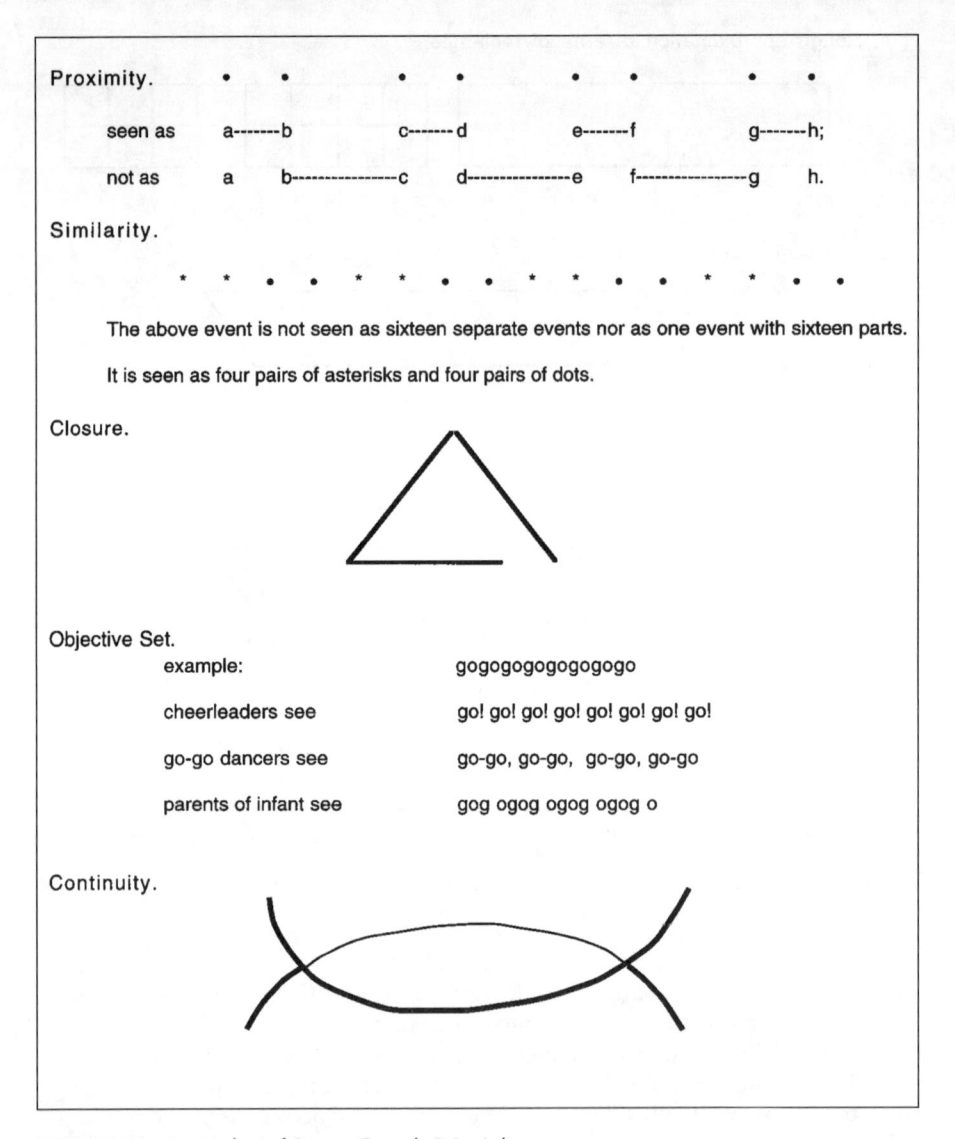

```
Proximity.     •  •       •  •        •  •         •  •

   seen as    a-------b   c-------d    e-------f    g-------h;

   not as     a    b----------------c  d--------------e  f----------------g   h.

Similarity.

              *  *  •  •  *  *  •  •  *  •  •  *  *  •  •

       The above event is not seen as sixteen separate events nor as one event with sixteen parts.
       It is seen as four pairs of asterisks and four pairs of dots.

Closure.

                         △

Objective Set.
       example:              gogogogogogogogo
       cheerleaders see       go! go! go! go! go! go! go! go!
       go-go dancers see      go-go, go-go, go-go, go-go
       parents of infant see  gog ogog ogog ogog o

Continuity.

                    ⟨⟩
```

FIGURE 7.2. Examples of Some Gestalt Principles.

1. inability to learn proper meaning in relation to the context, and
2. poor practical application.

Trace Theory. The natural reaction of the sensory system to a stimulus is to maintain a brief afterimage or trace of the stimulation. When learning occurs it leaves neurological changes in the form of a trace. Trace = retention of new learning. Memory is a perceptual trace. Consolidation of traces accounts for long-term memory and tends toward good form. What is remembered is not the object but how the object should be; therefore, well-structured material or lessons are retained intact.

It must be remembered that Gestalt psychologists were primarily interested in perception and in problem-solving processes. Learning was viewed as a secondary, derivative phenomenon of no special interest; what was learned was a product of and determined by the laws of perceptual organization; what was performed depended on how the mind, using its current problem-solving processes, analyzed the present situation and made use of traces of past experience (Bower & Hilgard, 1981, p. 299).

While Gestalt theorists would agree that past experiences will facilitate solution, they object to explanations in terms of the non-insightful use of previous experience without taking organization into account. More is needed than the necessary amount of information. Just knowing enough words does not enable one to write a poem (Bower & Hilgard, 1981, p. 319).

Tolman

Edward Chace Tolman was born in Newton, Massachusetts in 1886. He was of the Quaker persuasion. He attended the Massachusetts Institute of Technology (MIT) where his father was a trustee. After completing the Bachelors degree in electrochemistry, he attended Harvard, completing the MA in 1912, and the Ph.D. in Psychology in 1915.

Some influences in his formative period were (a) the philosopher, Ralph Barton Perry, who stressed "docility" (teachability, receptiveness), "behavior qua (as) behavior," and "Purposive Behaviorism," (b) the philosopher/psychologist, Donald C. Williams, who emphasized the "molar as opposed to molecular" scope of things, and (c) the psychologist, Kurt Lewin, who applied topological dynamics to a personal field theory.

While in graduate school, Tolman went to Germany and worked with Koffka for a short time. He was a pacifist, resulting in his losing his first job at Northwestern University because of his anti-war attitude during wartime; later he refused to sign a loyalty oath at the University of California at Berkeley and was dismissed for a time. He studied the behavior of white rats at Cal-Berkeley for most of his career. He died in 1959.

In contrast to mentalism (introspection) and a reaction to Watson (muscle twitchism) and as a recognition of higher mental processes, Tolman established a position he called Purposive Behaviorism (1949). This position was influenced by E. B. Holt, a former professor at Harvard.

> . . . the phenomena evinced by the integrated organism are no longer merely the excitation of nerve or the twitching of muscle, nor yet the play of mere reflexes touched off by stimuli. These are present and essential to the phenomena in question, but they are merely components now, for they have been integrated. And this integration of reflex arcs, with all that they involve, into a state of systematic interdependence has produced something that is not merely reflex action. The biological sciences have long recognized this new and further thing, and called it "behavior" (Holt, 1915, p. 366).

Tolman did not accept stimulus-response association as the basic category for explaining behavior. He relied on cognitive explanations such as sign learning and expectancy of objectives, based on experiments on latent learning and place learning.

"Individuals do more than respond to stimuli, they act on beliefs, conditions, and attitudes and strive toward goals. They learn spatial signs, map out their course of action, and act on their expectancy with a demand for certain goals" (Sahakian, 1976, p. 201).

94   Intervention Theories

Tolman looked at molar events (e.g., maze running, car driving) rather than molecular ones (e.g., S-R bonds, physiological base). He accepted "behavior qua behavior"—behavior as behavior (it does not need reduction); it is purposeful and whole. "The bulk of behavior cannot be reduced to responses to stimuli but must be seen as striving after goals" (Sahakian, 1976, p. 201). He believed that behavior is docile (teachable), not determined, but influenceable; it is a result of interaction between environment and organism.

> Purposive or cognitive aspects of behavior objectively are evident in respect to (1) the goals for which the subject strives (goal–objects relations), (2) the means for obtaining such goals (means–objects relations), and (3) the relation of the means to those goals (means–end relations) (Sahakian, 1976, p. 201).

Parenthetically, this vein of reasoning may be the major learning theory underpinning for what is called "Object-Relations" therapy. It also provides theoretical foundation for family therapies, particularly of the systems approaches wherein the people within a client's sign-gestalts are interactive and working from their own individual purposive processes.

That which is accumulated in the apperceptive mass is a collection of sign-gestalts or cognitive maps. A sign-gestalt is a complex cognitive pattern made up of:

- Signs—stimuli (external sensations and internal images);
- Significates—cues for significant goals, rewards;
- Discriminanda—the sense qualities of an object, that which allows us to discriminate one object from others—properties of the object;
- Discriminanda expectations—cognitive sets within the organism;
- Means–end relations—the path to reach goals;
- Manipulanda—characteristics of objects that make it possible to manipulate the object by motor activity (pick-up-ableness, throw-ableness, etc.); and
- Behavior supports—discriminanda, manipulanda, and means–end relations that encourage goal completion (cue the organism that it's on the right track).

Reinforcement is not the power in learning but, through its use, expectancies are created that provide learning power. Reinforcement is not a necessary condition for all learning. Confirmation of expectancies is the power. The organism emits behavior intended to accomplish a particular outcome (purposive behaviorism) as anticipated by the organism. Environmental characteristics—things, people—take on unique meaning within a given sign-gestalt relative to their usefulness in accomplishing the purpose.

Latent learning experiments were important to Tolman's position because they refuted the need for reinforcement. He wrote: "Under certain conditions, some discriminanda or the relationship between some discriminanda will be learned by the organism even though these discriminanda bear no differential relationship to reinforcement" (Tolman & Gleitman, 1949, p. 811). For example, he let sated rats wander through a maze for ten trials without reward, then made them hungry. They ran the maze again and, this time, found food at the end. By the twelfth trial they performed as well as rats that had been rewarded regularly over the initial ten trials.

Spence and Lippitt (1940) did an experiment wherein water and food-sated rats learned to run a Y maze that had a container of food in one goal-box and a container of water in the other. Since the rats were neither hungry nor thirsty, they did not eat nor drink, apparently learning to run the maze for the reinforcement of being removed and reunited with "friends" in the cage. Later, food-deprived rats took the food route, and water-deprived rats took the water route.

In addition to demonstrating latent learning, these experiments support the notion of cognitive maps, or of place learning. To establish the superiority of place learning over response chaining, several experiments were conducted. Rats learned the maze by swimming a flooded maze. The water was removed and the rats performed flawlessly; therefore, it's not the response (swimming to food) but rather the place (cognitive map). In MacFarlane's study (1930), rats were pulled through the flooded maze on rafts; then they ran the dry maze almost without error. In Lashley (1929), rats ran the maze, then received cerebellar lesions. Limited to running in circular motions, they still made it through the maze correctly.

By varying the kind of reinforcer, Tolman and his colleagues built a case for expectancy theory. Rats ran the maze for a particular kind of food (bran mash); when the food was switched between trials to a less preferred reward (sunflower seeds), the subjects displayed exploration behavior rather than eating the seeds. Similar results were found with primates in a banana-to-lettuce switch and with five year-old children when jelly beans were replaced by chocolate.

What is learned is a "probabilistic expectancy," not a habit nor a response to stimulus. "Learning as expectancy is that a given response will produce a particular consequence. Given a particular sign (S) responded to by a given behavior (R), the result is a particular consequence (S*)" (Sahakian, 1976 p. 214). Confirmation is the power in learning; each time the consequential event (expected reward) follows from the antecedent expectancy, then that expectancy is confirmed. With every success, the probability is increased for continued success.

Tolman coined the term "intervening variables" to account for the intermediate cognitive/perceptual events that occur between the stimulus and the response in his two-stage model (see Figure 7.3). In concert with Kurt Lewin's work, Tolman created a field theory formula to explain the dynamics: $P_V = (n_f, v_f, exp_f) - (n_W, v_W, exp_W)$. A performance vector ($P_V$) results from the need for food, attraction or value of food (v_f), and the expectancy of getting it (exp_f) minus the drive (need) against work (n_W), aversion (valence) against work (V_W), and expectation of work (exp_W).

A major differentiation of Purposive Behaviorism from S-R behaviorism was given by Tolman:

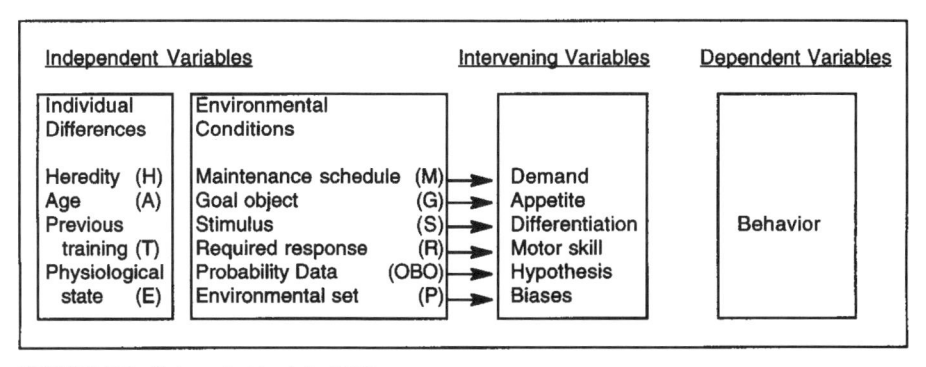

Independent Variables		Intervening Variables	Dependent Variables
Individual Differences	Environmental Conditions		
Heredity (H)	Maintenance schedule (M)	Demand	
Age (A)	Goal object (G)	Appetite	
Previous training (T)	Stimulus (S)	Differentiation	Behavior
Physiological state (E)	Required response (R)	Motor skill	
	Probability Data (OBO)	Hypothesis	
	Environmental set (P)	Biases	

FIGURE 7.3. Tolman's Model—1938.

In the process of learning, something comparable to a field map of the environment gets established in the rat's brain. We agree with the other school that the rat in running a maze is exposed to stimuli and is finally led as a result of these stimuli to the responses that actually occur. We feel, however, that the intervening brain processes are more complicated, more patterned and often, pragmatically speaking, more autonomous than do the stimulus-response psychologists. Although we admit that the rat is bombarded by stimuli, we hold that his nervous system is surprisingly selective as to which of the stimuli it will let in at any given time.

Secondly, we assert that the central office itself is far more like a map control room than it is like an old-fashioned telephone exchange. The stimuli, that are allowed in, are not connected by just simple one-to-one switches to the outgoing responses. Rather, the incoming impulses are usually worked over and elaborated in the central control room into a tentative, cognitive-like map of the environment. And it is this map, indicating routes and paths and environmental relationships, which finally determines what responses, if any, the animal will finally release (Tolman, 1948, p. 192).

As a final note for consideration of Tolman, here are his three laws that supercede Thorndike's Law of Effect:

- Law of motivation—the ultimate reason for learning seems to be the obtaining of final success or avoidance of final failures.
- Law of emphasis—both correct and incorrect responses are close to each other; emphasis (bell, shock, etc.) on the correct one will favor learning while accent on a wrong response will hinder desired learning.
- Law of disruption—any relatively violent negative emotional stimulus (punishment) coming in immediate sequence upon either right or wrong responses will disrupt learning.

Bandura

Albert Bandura is most noted for his work on observational learning. He was born in 1925 in Mundare, Alberta, Canada. He completed his BA at the University of British Columbia; the MA & Ph.D. in Clinical Psychology were accomplished at the University of Iowa. He spent a year of post-doctoral study at the Witchita Guidance Center in 1953. Except for the 1969–70 year at the Center for Advanced Study in Behavioral Sciences, Bandura has spent his professional career on the faculty of Stanford University. He was president of the APA in 1974. In a major break with philosophical tradition, Bandura rejected both linear assumptions of behavior resulting solely from environmental conditions and of behavior resulting only from individual intent. He postulated a reciprocal determinism wherein the conditions of the person, the environment, and the behavior act upon one another in mutually influential ways (see Figure 7.4).

There are perceptual/cognitive events that are symbolic representational systems, namely, thoughts and images. Behavior may be influenced or determined by several antecedent conditions, including:

- physiological and emotional variables;
- cognitive events (e.g., expectations, anticipations);
- inborn mechanisms of learning.

A brief description of the seminal research will set a foundation for this section.

```
        Person
          P
         ↗ ↖
        ↙   ↘
      B ←——→ E
   Behavior  Environment
```

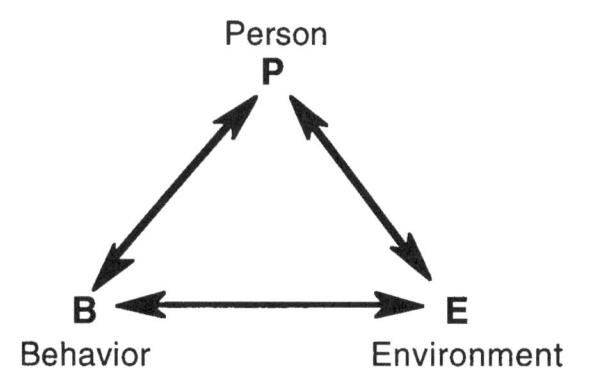

FIGURE 7.4. Bandura's Reciprocal Determinism.

Bandura and Walters (1963) created an experimental setting wherein groups of children would observe a child of about their same age interact with toys and other objects in an experimentally consistent playroom. The groups of children watched the model, through a one-way visual screen, behave in one of two ways, either aggressively or socially constructively. When members of the observation group were introduced, one at a time, into the playroom and their responses were observed and cataloged, it was demonstrated with meaningful and statistically significant levels of difference that those watching aggressive play performed more aggressive responses and those watching the socially constructive model tended to play constructively. The independent variable was the behavior of the model. The experimental subjects, in the absence of any reinforcement, either real or vicarious, were influenced through their observations.

Although aware of the empirical support for behavioristic approaches and sensitive to theoretical conventions for learning models to apply across species, Bandura believed that human learning has some unique and differential characteristics when compared to sub-human species, and that cognitive learning dynamics are important in the study of human learning.

> Contrary to popular belief, the fabled reflexive conditioning in humans is largely a myth. *Conditioning* is simply a descriptive term for learning through paired experiences, not an explanation of how the changes come about. Originally, conditioning was assumed to occur automatically. On closer examination it turned out to be cognitively mediated. People do not learn despite repetitive paired experiences unless they recognize that events are correlated (Dawson & Furedy, 1974; Grings, 1973). So-called conditioned reactions are largely self-activated on the basis of learned expectations rather than automatically evoked. The critical factor, therefore, is not that events occur together in time, but that people learn to predict them and to summon up appropriate anticipatory reactions (Bandura, 1974, p. 859).

The following exposition of Bandura's model draws heavily on Gazda and Corsini (1980). Much of human learning is cognitive.

> Humans like other animals, learn motor responses to environmental situations. But humans also have the capacity to acquire symbolic representations of external events, and

this allows the vastly superior variability and flexibility of human behavior compared with the behavior of infrahuman species (p. 379).

Once cognitions are developed, they become major factors in areas of functioning, such as perception, and problem-solving, and motivation. They enter into the process of determining which external events will be observed and which will be ignored, how external events will be perceived, and whether or not any lasting impressions of these events are made. They enter into the problem-solving behavior of humans and the construction of novel solutions. And finally they enter into the motivational process by providing incentives and sanctions not immediately present in the physical environment (p. 379).

There are two major sources of human learning—response consequences and observation. The direct experiences resulting from responses are the consequences, either positive, negative, or neutral, that exert influence on the behavioral repertoire of the person. Such influence might include:

- Information. "The informational nature of response consequences provides the person with the opportunity to construct hypotheses concerning which behaviors will result in successful outcomes under specific conditions. This hypothesis constructing function that information provides serves as a guide to future action based on the probabilities developed for different behaviors" (Gazda & Corsini, 1980, p. 379).
- Motivation. "Information already acquired can become an incentive condition for behavior in the present through anticipations and expectations . . ." (p. 379).
- Reinforcement. The third influence is to increase or decrease the frequency of the prior response. " . . . Bandura believes that at least for humans, the effects of consequences are mediated so much by cognitive structures that any instances of an automatic effect can be better understood within a framework that recognizes mental activities rather than within one that eschews them" (p. 380).

Observational learning or learning by way of vicarious experience is, "at least for humans, the major source of learning in contemporary culture, in which the environment is preeminently symbolic" (p. 380). There are four requisite processes: attention, retention, motor reproduction, and motivation. Different effects may occur from modeling. Higher order learning occurs as a result of observational learning.

In order for a person to learn through observation, he or she must pay attention to a model. Attention is influenced by characteristics of the model such as interpersonal attractiveness, perceived competence, status, social power, similarities in age, sex, and socioeconomic level. Characteristics of observer or learner that have demonstrated importance include dependency, level of competence, socioeconomic status, race, sex, and previous social learning experiences. "Incentive conditions have also been found to have influences on the attentional process in that they can enhance, impede, or channel looking or observing responses. Some forms of observational learning such as via television watching are so intrinsically rewarding that attention may be controlled for hours at a time" (p. 381).

It is important for the learner to be able to remember the results of his or her attentional observation. This retention may be eidetic or experiential, so-called "right-brain" memory, or it may be symbolically coded and rehearsed. An additional and obvious requirement for the appearance of a response from an observer is his or her ability to perform the response being modeled. Images and thoughts guide overt performance (response–guidance information). Any manifestation of actual behavior resulting from remembered observation is dependent on motor skills being available to the person.

Motivation has some special characteristics when looked at in Bandura's model. There are three influences on motivation: (a) external reinforcement, (b) vicarious reinforcement, and/or (c) self-reinforcement. External reinforcement comes from direct experience. It is the response consequence that makes up one major source of learning. This is Bandura's recognition that behavioral techniques are effective, though he posits a cognitive mediation between stimulus and response. Vicarious reinforcement happens when the observation of another person being reinforced for the behavior favors its acquisition; similarly, the observation of another person's being punished leads to behavioral suppression. Self-reinforcement is a uniquely cognitive contribution to motivational theory. "Modeled behavior may become manifest or inhibited in the absence of external sources of influence. In these self-regulating processes, the person experiences covert reinforcement or punishment based on evaluations of his or her own behavior, compared to standards that have been assimilated through observation" (p. 382).

There are considerable individual differences in the manifestation of observational learning. Bandura gives four categories. The observational learning effect (a) is simply the acquisition of novel responses. In this case, the learner performs in a way not previously done in the particular situation and after having seen a model perform the same action. The inhibitory effect (b) is manifest when the observer reduces a response tendency as a result of watching a model being punished for making that response. The disinhibitory effect (c) is seen when the observer re-introduces or increases performance of a generally inhibited behavior following the observation of rewarding consequences to a model for that response. With the social facilitation effect (d) no new response is acquired, but the observer emits a response different from the model's.

Bandura's model incorporates some aspects of reinforcement learning and cognitive learning as well as stressing perceptual learning. The response consequence dynamics reflect, at an empirical level, the same pattern as does reinforcement learning; Bandura posits a perceptual or cognitive component for most human learning. Vicarious reinforcement clearly requires a mental process that is easy to interpret as informational input that influences successive behavior. This information can be either eidetic or it can be coded into cognitive principles of an "If . . . then" nature—"If I do as the model did, then I will experience the same consequences as did the model." Similar information may be introduced to the learner through symbolic instruction. The direct teaching of concepts and principles fits into Bandura's category called higher order learning. It follows the dynamics that will be treated in the next chapter. Bandura believed that observational learning is a major source of integrating "rules or principles that go beyond the specific responses observed. What occurs is an abstraction of the common elements of the model's behavior that can be applied appropriately to situations in which the observer has never seen the model behave" (p. 384). He further contended that observational learning is a major source of creative behavior. "Creative expression is influenced when the observer is exposed to different models. Most often . . . behavior is not restricted to what has been observed; instead it is the result of a combination of features from various models that leads to responses that differ from any of the original individual sources" (p. 384).

Humanistic Learning Models

At least one author, Sahakian (1976, 1984), gives recognition to some theorists who emphasize adjustment from a Humanistic philosophy and who have devoted some attention to the learning process. Given the aspects of perceptual or cognitive learning that recognize attention and motivation as something that is at least partially a product of the learner, learner characteristics such as personality, values, and preferences impinge upon attention and motivation. That which impacts the perceptual or cognitive functioning of people becomes a factor in the learning process.

Especially concerning perception that may be subject to limitation or distortion resulting from emotional defensiveness, chemical imbalance, or threat, the condition of the learner is of critical concern. If one takes Bandura's reciprocal determinism model, then a focus on the condition of the person is warranted. If, at the very least, the humanists can clarify personal conditions that enhance learning, or even enhance only some kinds of learning, then including them in a study of learning becomes appropriate. A brief outline of Humanist qualities that affect the study of psychology will be given, followed by brief treatment of Abraham Maslow and Carl Rogers as referents for the Humanistic learning position.

Buhler and Bugenthal (Sahakian, 1976 pp. 379-380) listed four qualities of humanistic psychology:

1. Centering of attention on the experiencing person, and thus a focus on experience as the primary phenomenon in the study of humans.
2. Emphasis on such distinctively human qualities as choice, creativity, valuation, and self-realization, as opposed to thinking about human beings in mechanistic and reductionistic terms.
3. Allegiance to meaningfulness in the selection of problems for study; opposition to a primary emphasis on objectivity at the expense of significance.
4. An ultimate concern with and valuing of the dignity and worth of people and an interest in the development of the potential inherent in every person.

> There is no substitute for experience, none at all. All the other paraphernalia of communication and of knowledge—words, labels, concepts, symbols, theories, formulas, sciences—all are useful only because people already know experientially. The basic coin of the realm of knowing is direct, intimate, experiential knowing (Maslow, 1966, pp. 45-46).

One informal way of getting at the distinction of the Humanist position regarding learning is to contrast the concepts "knowing" versus "knowing about." It is possible to collect exhaustive amounts of data about someone, something, someplace and yet have an incorrect awareness that is immediately transformed upon a few moments of direct experience. Maslow contrasts experiential knowledge with spectator knowledge, an interesting analogy that parallels the difference between playing a sport or acting in a drama and just watching. Maslow posits inherent growth needs within every individual. Those needs to know and understand, beyond what is necessary for mere survival, are the essence of Humanistic knowing. Obviously in his system of hierarchical needs, other conditions may militate against the satisfaction of this level of knowing.

Maslow was born in 1908 in Brooklyn, New York. All of his university work was done at the University of Wisconsin. He taught at Brooklyn College from 1935 to 1951 and at Brandeis University until 1969. He died in 1970. He was president of the APA and was a major impetus in Third Force Psychology. He is best known for his system of hierarchical needs with four levels of instinctoid needs—physiological, safety, love and belonging, and self esteem—and a capstone of being needs—self-actualization (with knowing and understanding and with aesthetic needs as subsets). His major assumptions and those of other Humanists are that people come pre-programmed to do well; society encumbers natural progress; the work of therapists is to enhance natural tendencies and offset societal barriers.

Carl Rogers was born in 1902. He completed the Ph.D. in 1931, worked at the Rochester Guidance Clinic in Rochester, New York, was a professor of clinical psychology at Ohio State University, and counseling center director at the University of Chicago from 1945 to 1957. In 1957 he went to the University of Wisconsin as professor of psychology and psychiatry, was a resident fellow at the Western Behavioral Sciences Institute in the 1960s and went to the Center for the Studies of the Person in La Jolla, California in 1968. Mostly he was a therapist during, in, and around his professional settings. Non-directive or client-centered or person-centered are labels that have been applied to his approach. Based on a philosophy that people are basically good and that they are active in seeking their goals (becoming), his approach required the establishment of an atmosphere of unconditional positive regard, warmth, empathy, and understanding. He believed that, given a climate in which defensiveness can be released, clients will alter their perceptions in the direction of congruence with a more objective reality and act in ways that bring resolution to their problems. Progress, adjustment, and learning would come from within the client and be evaluated by the client as his or her behavior changed from self-defeating to self-enhancing.

To Rogers, important learning, "real learning," is significant learning. He contrasted significant learning—personally meaningful, experiential, resulting in change in behavior—with cognitive learning—learning by association, rote memory, acquisition of facts. Furthermore, significant learning has a quality of personal involvement, with both affective and cognitive parts involved. It is self-initiated; though the stimulus or impetus may come from without, the sense of discovery and of reaching out and of comprehending come from within.

Bandura's model moved people from the position of passive recipient of learning to being a major ingredient in the process. The Humanists moved the person from merely one of three ingredients (person, behavior, environment) to being the major actor in the formula, the most important factor.

☐ Applied Theories

Though it may be an oversimplification, all applications of perceptual learning fit into two categories: framing and reframing. In conditions of perceptual deficit, situations where the person has no prior experience, the task is to enter a way of dealing—a frame—into the perceptual closet. Direct experience is the prime method, though vicarious experience and even the perceptualizing of stories, descriptions, and precepts are effective. In circumstances where a client has previous experience that leads to self-defeating responses because it was a poor sample to begin with, or that it does not fit the present situation, or that dynamics have changed since its initial acquisition, a process of reframing is necessary. Reframing requires a loosening of responses based on the problematical frame long enough for a more functional frame to be introduced.

102 Intervention Theories

The theories already addressed in this chapter incorporate the dynamics necessary for accomplishing frames and reframes. Further delineation of the common foundations will be instructive.

There are primarily three theoretical foundation bases for the perceptual interventions referred to as framing and reframing. These are (a) a phenomenological philosophy, (b) the recognition of a mental processing system that is different from and separate from that which is dominated by language, and (c) the seminal work on rules of perception designated by the label, Gestalt.

Phenomenology

The American College Dictionary contains these definitions of phenomenon: "1. a fact, occurrence, or circumstance observed or observable: *the phenomena of nature.* . . . 3. *Philos.* a. an appearance or immediate object of awareness in experience. b. (in Kantian philosophy) a thing as it appears to, and is constructed by, us, as distinguished from a noumenon, or thing in itself" (Barnhardt, 1955, p. 909).

These two definitions set the stage for a comparison between the philosophies of realism, with its emphasis on empiricism as the basis of knowledge, and phenomenology, with its emphasis on experience as the source of knowledge. Empiricism permits and emphasizes community knowledge, that which can be subjected to controlled and replicable research. Experience involves a personal knowledge, one that is not readily accessible to other people, hence unverifiable except through language systems that appear to identify and label "common" experiences. A third philosophy probably fits somewhere between realism and phenomenology. It is rationalism. Truth or knowledge to the rationalist (or rationalizer) is verified to the extent that it fits within logical systems, namely, that it "makes sense." Realism and rationalism are rule-bound. Phenomenology is not rule-bound, though linguists talk of deep structure in language that attests to a commonality of experience across people even though their surface language may differ. Gestaltists subscribe to universal laws that operate on structural truth called Prägnanz, or good form, that undergirds the experiences of insight and agreement across individuals, and that allows for a differentiation from purely fabricated experience (as in hallucination) and experience that is grounded in a common context of reality.

Of particular significance in phenomenology are principles such as: (a) personal motivation and decision are based on phenomenal reality, (b) it is impossible to share another person's experience directly, and (c) everything is in a constant process of change.

Jourard (1968) wrote about the mental cycles between perception and cognition. A person is a *concept maker*.

> He forms *concepts* of the being of the world, and of his own self-being. A concept is an abstraction of what is. From a phenomenological and existential perspective, *a concept is a commitment to stop noticing the changing disclosures (disclosures of change) incessantly being transmitted by the beings in the world*. When I identify something as a cow, I rubricize it. I let it disclose enough of its being for me to classify it into the category cow. Then, I stop receiving, though the cow hasn't stopped sending (pp. 155–156).

In another section of the same work, Jourard describes a state of being more continually open to experience:

Generally we see the world in its conventional rubrics. We see someone and identify the person as a woman because she has the hair, curves, voice, and gait of women in general. We look at her long enough to assign her to some categories—e.g., pretty or ugly, willing or unwilling, marriageable or not—and then look at her no more. We usually observe the world under the impetus and direction of our needs, values, feelings, and purposes of the moment. Such need-steered perception certainly serves a vital role in our survival and adaptation; but it also tends to blind us to all features of the world that are not immediately relevant to our present hungers, desires, and values. "Desireless" or "undriven" [perception]—when we simply open our eyes, ears, noses, taste buds, kinesthetic and organic receptors, and let stimuli play upon them and impress them—seems to be the condition for the enriched mode of perception. Maslow (1962) calls this mode of perception "B-cognition," or "cognition of 'Being'"; and Schachtel (1961) refers to it as "allocentric" perception. It adds new dimensions to experience; or, rather, it permits new dimensions to "happen." Colors are seen more vividly; and things, animals, people, or scenes are perceived in their "suchness," in their concrete uniqueness, almost transfigured.

Moments of such perception are experienced by people as unforgettable. In fact, when people recall the past with vivid imagery, the content of their recollection is almost always the moments when they let the world impress itself upon their senses without selection. They let the world disclose itself to them. Such cognition, then, because it is rare and valued, may be called transcendent perception.

We may well ask, why is it so rare? Why is rubricized perception, perception of things and people as mere members of categories, so common and usual? The answer probably lies in the fact that average people are most often in the midst of many simultaneous conditions of privation, of need; and so their egos, their perceptual apparatus, remain a servant of unfulfilled desires (pp. 208–209).

Whether or not there is a special kind of transcendent perception, there are variations in the way people experience similar things from time to time and from person to person. There appears to be a difference between "rubricized" perceptions (categorized or explained perceptions) and the initial perceptions that are a part of experience. A standard explanation of perception is that it is what a person makes out of sensory input, taking into account variations or limitations in the person's receptive capacity and considering motivations and needs of the person. These perceptions can be divided into two kinds according to which system processes them—"How things look/seem to me in the combined images, smells, feelings of experience," and "How I describe them to others and/or file them away for further consideration in the rule-bound vehicle of language, or rubricized perceptions (cognitions)." Huxley wrote, "Systematic reasoning is something we could not, as a species or as individuals, possibly do without. But neither, if we are to remain sane, can we possibly do without direct perception, the more unsystematic the better, of the inner and outer worlds into which we have been born" (1956, p. 77).

Either processing system, recognizing even uniqueness in language usage, gives rise to some guidelines if one is to take into account the individualized world of another person. One set of guidelines is entitled the Eight Humanistic Assumptions of Behavior (adapted from Combs and Soper, 1963):

1. The way a person perceives (views or frames) the world is a major determinant of behavior.
2. People perceive the world differently.

3. To understand another person's behavior, you must view the world from his or her perceptual frame.
4. The most important perceptions a person has are those about self.
5. Threat narrows perception.
6. Motivation is best explained in terms of maintaining, protecting, and enhancing self.
7. The action a person takes is the most important/best response that the person can make at that moment in terms of the way he or she is perceiving or viewing the world at that moment.
8. In order for a person to change his or her behavior, he or she must change his or her perception or view of the world.

In conclusion, the phenomenological philosophy base requires recognition of individuality in the experiencing/processing/deciding dynamics that lead to behavior on the part of people. Attempts to intervene effectively in self-defeating actions of some people may be enhanced by knowledge about how the perceptual processing system works.

Perceptual Processing System

A phenomenological perspective allows for consideration of two processing systems: a perceptual one and a cognitive one. We experience in complex, multi-faceted ways. We analyze in simpler, linear, more logical ways. Experience and the perceptual processing of it happen instantly; "figuring something out" takes longer—sometimes minutes, hours, or days, and can be put aside and refocused even later still. In the prologue to *A Tale of a Tub*, Johnathan Swift wrote, "The eyes of the understanding see best when those of the senses are out of the way." You may contemplate any experience from which you drew conclusions and recognize that the experiencing and the concluding portions were very different from one another.

Paul Watzlawick (1978) refers to two language systems in humans. One is objective, definitional, logical, analytic; it is the language of reason, of science, of explanation and interpretation. This language is organized by grammar, syntax, and semantics. Symbols or words correspond to meanings by assignment or convention.

The second language is one of imagery and metaphor. It incorporates the totality of experiences in whole units. Rather than being organized and directed, it is undirected and often random. It includes dreams and fantasies and memories. It is experiential.

For a time, these two language functions were believed to be localized in different sections of the brain. The left hemisphere (for a right-handed person) was alleged to house the "verbal" language—logical, semantic, and phonetic. It was seen to be the dominant function and was demonstrated in competence in grammar, reading, counting, analyzing, and interpreting. The right hemisphere was said to house the "perceptual" or "experiential" function—the ability to operate with patterns, structures, and images. "The translation of the perceived reality, this synthesis of our experience of the world into an image, is most probably the function of the right hemisphere" (Watzlawick, 1978, p. 46).

While the so-called left brain was seen to be dominant in a symbol-intensive social context, it only is more obvious from the standpoint of Watzlawick's position. The left brain functions to rationalize the reality imaged by the right brain so as to permit some kind of communication with other people. This is in concert with the phenomenological belief that there is no direct access to another's experience. In reality, the right brain receives and synthesizes information and has the critical functions of understanding and motivation; hence, it is to the right brain that messages for change should be directed for the most efficiency.

It is an interesting twist of logic to suggest that reprogramming logical and meaningful segments of the verbal system will produce change only to the extent that the right brain receives and integrates them into its image of reality. ". . . it is known that a language does not so much reflect reality as create it" (Watzlawick, 1978, p. 16). So-called talk therapy of the cognitive restructuring variety or of informational transfer or of logically convincing for change, works, however unpredictably, based on the individual's partially distorted reception and incorporation into his or her phenomenal imaging system.

Based on the same logic that says verbalizing is an attempt to change through a filter, the more direct, efficient, preferred approach is to create images directly—through experience. Experiential techniques that invite a client's participation and lead to pre-scribed conclusions, as in discovery learning or guided discovery, provide the raw materials for the client to "frame" a segment of reality. Guided imagery or fantasy techniques are but vicarious experiences and may be as effective as direct experience.

Because people are so verbal, so practiced in translating everything into symbolic language, it often is difficult to engage them, particularly adults, in either direct or vicarious experience. Almost always they insist on knowing "why" before taking the chance. This is a little akin to reading the last chapter of a book first so as to decide if one wants to take the effort to go through it in its entirety. Watzlawick talks of the need to block the left hemisphere, disengage or disable the thinking function, in order to gain access to the right hemisphere. Paradox is one technique: ". . . the conscious effort to produce a reaction that can only occur spontaneously either makes impossible its occurrence or produces abnormal, unplanned, and unwanted reactions instead" (Watzlawick, 1978, p. 102). The direction to "be spontaneous" is such a paradox. "All prohibitions are prohibited" is another. Students of Zen Buddhism may recognize it for its power in fatiguing the left brain to the point of giving the right brain more prominence. Other techniques for disabling the logical function, as suggested by Watzlawick, include symptom displacement (feel the pain only on Monday; the pain will move to the other foot), illusion of alternatives (heads I win, tails you lose), injunctive language, and "anything but that" (see Watzlawick, 1978, for a more complete explanation).

The "language of change" or that which speaks to the right hemisphere generally cuts through the logical filter and creates an awareness or image. Verbosity is inversely related to meaning. Several categories of language that fit this definition include:

- Condensations—biodeplorable food, popullution, syphilization;
- Figurative language—hypnotherapy, embedded messages (ala Milton Erickson, 1980), imagery, poetry.
- Pars pro toto—substitute part for whole, for example, a piece of straw embedded in a door as result of a hurricane, or a photo of a war victim in a barren landscape, wherin the magnitude of the event is impossible to portray, and an isolated image represents the totality.
- Aphorisms—short, pointed sentences expressing wise or clever observations or gen-

eral truths: "Try easy!", "You can't live with him/her until you can live without him/her," "Too little to live on, too much to starve from."
- Ambiguities, puns, allusions—"secretary of defense" instead of "minister of war".

The preferred approach is experience, direct or vicarious, for a perceptual deficit condition. For a perceptual surplus, experience of a mutually exclusive kind is most efficient (reframing). Role reversal, substitute memory, looking from a different perspective, and identifying the positive are examples of perceptual reframing. Verbal reframing must confound the previous conclusion (disarm it) and simultaneously substitute another of sound logic. An example is the client who said, "I could be happy if only I could lose fifty pounds." The effective reframe for her was the therapist's response, "If only you would be happy, you might be able to lose fifty pounds."

Gestalt Rules of Perception

While there are many Gestalt rules of perception, this section will focus only on a few that are of significance to framing and reframing. Visual perceptions may be used as an analog for perceptions through other senses as well and through combinations of senses or total experiences. The eye is capable of sensing more at one time than the consciousness seems ready to tolerate. In fact, Huxley (1956) suggests that one function of the central nervous system is to reduce the potential perception of incoming stimuli to the small fraction of the total that can be assimilated. Gestaltists talk of organizing perceptions into *figure* and *ground*. That which is central to visual perception, or that which is in focus, is the figure. That which occurs in the periphery of awareness, the context in which the focus occurs, is called the ground or background. In theater the figure would be spotlighted, and the ground would be made up of other characters and stage settings. As applied to life, we can talk of central and peripheral life experiences, having trouble focusing on what's needed, competition for attention, or getting lost in details. There is a focus to almost everything; everything occurs in a context.

Meaning comes from context. One of the profound Gestalt contributions is the idea of widening the frame, realizing that narrowing our perception when puzzled or challenged is self-defeating. Making full use of all our senses, particularly in peripheral perception, is more self-enhancing. "Trying easy" allows for a wider field of vision or of awareness. Problems that seem similar when the focus is narrowly on them may be quite different from one another when seen properly in their various contexts. The "same" problem may be different in new contexts; this explains why old solutions don't always work. A new look at or a reframe of the circumstance often uncovers elements that are important. The phrase, "Wow! I never looked at it that way before," indicates insight that comes from the adjusted perception.

A number of so-called Gestalt techniques involve shifts in figure and ground. This is accomplished by taking an element from the context or the background and "becoming" that part. One example is to have the client notice a physical symptom—tight muscles, cramping stomach, sore feet—and talk as though he or she were that symptom. By giving it a voice, the symptom can offer a perception of relatedness to the prior problem of focus. Working "splits" within the personality structure permits the client to separate and own widely disparate views, beliefs, and even values. Addressing absent or dead people brings them from the "then and there" background into a "now and here" interaction, with the result being a creation of a new frame or reframe.

Recognition of the existence of insight and the reliance on it as a major avenue to learning is another contribution of Gestalt therapy to therapeutic intervention. Insight is based on the Gestalt law of Prägnanz. Simply stated, there is an underlying structure or truth to everything in the universe. Whenever a perception matches this truth, an unsettling and pleasing sensation of "Aha! I've got it!" occurs. There is sufficient freedom from doubt, as a product of insight, to allow people to move ahead, acting on their new-found and assured truth. This may be related in a larger sense to what Rogers (1951) referred to as congruence—that condition arrived at when the phenomenal awareness coincides with external reality. The experience of insight is managed or enhanced by encouraging or directing the client to non-defensively "try on" different frames of perception. Köhler, one of the early pioneers of the Gestalt school, spoke of "trying around" for solutions in a "half-understood" situation (Sahakian, 1976).

There are two aspects of insight and the law of Prägnanz that may be important. The first, referring back to Jourard's treatise in the section on phenomenology, is the fact that we live amid and contribute to constant change. Reality is so complex that even if our insight at one point in time and for one circumstance is infallibly accurate (i.e., corresponds with universal truth), conditions continue on their ever-changing path and our "rubricized" insight or the cognitive conclusion we file away immediately is outmoded. Fortunately, change is not so rapid or dramatic so as to invalidate all of our conclusions. Like the gradual decay of vision wherein one doesn't realize he or she cannot see as well as before, the gradual decay of knowledge is more fuzzy than obvious, until a reframe brings the focus back.

The second aspect of insight is not a Gestalt principle. It is rather a conjecture. Since individuals are very different from one another in many ways, it seems likely that the ability to experience insight varies from person to person. There is a statistical phrase, the line of best fit, that might serve as an analogue for insight as experienced by people. Particularly as we are developing from infancy, our initial insights might be sort of accurate or mostly accurate. If they are close enough to permit continued development, who is to know that they are not 100% congruent with universal truth. The conductor of a musical group may have in his or her phenomenal space an image of perfection toward which the group is being trained. If and when the production of the group coincides with the idealized perception, a type of insight experience ensues. As the conductor develops more expertise, the standards of that idealized perception improve, so that a "truer" performance is required at successively later periods. Might this also happen with all individuals in their development of living skills, particularly as they progressively reframe themselves and their evolving conditions?

The work of the therapist in helping clients who are "stuck" in some aspect of their context or of their development involves gaining access to the client's phenomenal reality, clarifying and expanding perceptions from within that space, and directing/initiating/influencing experiences that free the client to solve the problem or take the developmental step. It could be argued that perceptual learning preceded language development that, in turn, was necessary for cognitive acquisitions; therefore, perceptual learning is primary in changing clients as older children and as adults. Whether or not it is superior to any other approach, the mastery of intervention strategies based on perceptual principles contributes to the therapist's ability to better serve a more diverse clientele from a truly responsive framework.

Bruner

Another of the applied perceptual learning theorists for our focus here is Jerome Bruner. He was born in 1915, attended Duke University and Harvard, where he received the Ph.D. in 1941. He taught at Harvard from 1945 to 1972, and then went to Oxford as the Watts Professor of Psychology. He, too, was a president of the APA.

Bruner was identified by the rubric, "Discovery Learning." He believed that experience precedes understanding and that what is in the cognitive closet are sets of progressive abstractions built on foundations of empirical referents. A simple example might be a child sitting down for breakfast. Mother asks, "Would you like an apple this morning?" The child has direct experience with a referent of the concept, "apple." On successive mornings, mother presents an orange, a banana, grapes, and melon. Then one morning she asks, "What kind of fruit would you like today?" The child then has to operate at a higher level of abstraction. From direct experience with referents of level 1 concepts—apple, orange, etc.—the child moved to a level 2 concept—fruit—and similarly to higher levels such as food, edible/non-edible, fresh/processed, etc. Bruner contended that the strongest base for learning is direct experience, or what he called enactive learning—learning by doing. It is possible for people to learn by watching others or by seeing iconic representations of the activity (iconic learning); this is less powerful than enactive learning. A third type, less powerful than the first two, is called symbolic learning—learning through logical presentation of words, numbers, and formulas.

From an applied standpoint, Bruner advocated the spiral curriculum, an approach in which younger learners would be caused to interact with their environment on the enactive level, laying a foundation for future curricular encounters with the same material, but at iconic and progressively more abstract symbolic presentations. Teaching is a process of facilitating the learner to satisfy his or her innate curiosity by managing experiences carefully so that direct experience with referents occurs prior to introducing language abstractions. The teacher must pre-assess the level of student knowledge so as to introduce new material at a time when sufficient prior experience has prepared the student for successful mastery.

This approach fits particularly well the dynamics of perceptual deficit. For younger children, virtually all teaching should involve enactive components. From the standpoint of teaching older children and adults and from therapy, Brunerian approaches are especially appropriate. Perceptual deficit exists whenever a person is put into a situation for which he or she has no prior direct experience, such as going through a divorce, dealing with the death of someone close, becoming a parent for the first time, experiencing domestic violence, or being victimized in other ways. This particular way of thinking applies well to normal developmental challenges, things like entering school, first encounters with counselors, first job interview, first date. To the extent that therapy is pro-active, direct practice experience or vicarious experience by viewing a model go through the stage fills the deficit with socially constructive, self-enhancing responses. Problems with developmental passages result either from the client making a haphazard, trial and error type of response or from previous modeling of less than acceptable behavior. The fact that people who were abused as children tend to repeat the abuse may be simply explained by their having received an improper example of what to do in a given situation. When the situation recurs with them in the adult role, they have no perceptual map to go on other than their own previous, undesirable experience. Many parents have a very unsettling experience as they find themselves doing to their child the very thing they promised to themselves as a child, "I'll never do that to one of my children!"

Seligman

An applied model that addresses an extreme example of perceptual surplus is that of Martin E. P. Seligman: learned helplessness. Seligman was born in Albany, New York, in 1942. When he failed to make the eighth grade basketball team he turned to books. Freud's *Introductory Lectures* particularly impressed him. When Seligman was thirteen, his father suffered a series of strokes that left him permanently paralyzed and with cyclical mood swings. It appears that Seligman's observation of his father's struggle with helplessness foreshadowed the compelling interest and work that Seligman devoted to helplessness. A graduate of Princeton and The University of Pennsylvania (Ph.D., 1967), he taught at Cornell and at The University of Pennsylvania. Subsequent to the publication of *Helplessness: On Depression, Development and Death* (1975), he reformulated the helplessness model, saying that attribution governed the expression of helplessness. This shift in emphasis puts him more solidly in the cognitive interventions camp than here in the perceptual. The attributional emphasis will be treated in the next chapter.

From his initial work with animals, Seligman generalized that some forms of clinical depression result from a series of efforts resulting in failures and the generalized awareness that it somehow is less onerous to not try and not succeed than it is to try hard and fail. If a person is placed in a situation of noncontingency, that is, one in which any systematic effort has no relationship with success or failure, that person has an accurate perception of being helpless. Acting helpless or not trying is a natural response to a noncontingent situation. The person will generalize his or her nonresponse to situations that are similar and will continue the same pattern even though the situations may have changed dramatically. Seligman and his associates conditioned a dog to act helpless by harnessing it and administering non-lethal electric shocks. Were the dog not harnessed, it could have jumped over a barrier and escaped the shock. After a number of shockings and after the dog ceased resisting the shocks by straining against the harness, the harness was removed. Even though it was free to jump the barrier, it did not. The barrier was lowered, then removed altogether, and the experimenters even put food across from where the barrier once stood. The dog did not escape; it simply cowered in the corner and endured the shock. The act of forcefully dragging the dog across the barrier was necessary before it changed its perception of helplessness; it had to have an experiential intervention to overcome the surplus perception of helplessness

A similar set of dynamics can be presumed for depressed people, welfare dependents, able people supported by disability payments, and ineffectual parents dominated by strong-willed adolescents. While talk therapy may provide avenues to change for some, the perceptual shift that comes from direct experience is necessary for many.

Bandura Revisited

The major breakthrough validated by the experiments of Bandura and his colleagues was the notion of observational, vicarious learning. This established that, at least in the human learner, conceptual and behavior change can occur in the absence of direct experience. What the learner can be brought to perceive, he or she can learn from. While all means of creating perceptual experience cannot be traced to Bandura, and it is likely that he would not want to lay claim to many extant applications, the dynamics are common: created perceptual experiences that provide perceptual data for learning. Given a client who has either no frame or a problematic frame for dealing with a circumstance, a range of intervention techniques may be employed to produce for the client an integrated perception of one or some approaches to that circumstance. Bibliotherapy that focuses on biography, autobiography, or reality-based fiction is one avenue; this is different from self-help books that address the cognitive system. Videotaped presentation of circumstance-specific performance is another approach. Fantasy exercises employ the client's own creativity in making perceptions that are coached in ways to reframe the problematic client reality. Media-based techniques such as sand tray, clay, and pastels access and build on perceptual dynamics. Family sculpting—*en vivo* or with kokeshi dolls, psychodrama, role play, and role reversal are largely perceptual interventions.

Most activities engaged in when participating in encounter groups have an integral experiential/perceptual component. While most incorporate a cognitive processing activity, the primary focus of loosening existing frames and substituting alternate frames is a perceptual process.

Psychodynamics

While most learning and counseling theorists view people as integrated systems, some strong support exists for seeing them as an aggregation or compilation of sub-units. Divisions within the personality occur according to some personality theorists and some clinicians. The pioneer in psychodynamics was Sigmund Freud who observed the interplay of three personality components—the *id, superego,* and *ego*. He did not delve into the learning processes of these components, consigning two of them to the unconscious. His focus was on the interrelationships between and among them, the psychodynamics.

There are two models that are psychodynamic in nature and that fit within a learning based approach to intervention. These are Eric Berne's Transactional Analysis and Frederic Perls' Gestalt Therapy. Berne's approach will be examined in Chapter 8 as a contribution to cognitive learning approaches to intervention, primarily because the focus of therapy is on the definition and identification of the three conscious ego states—Child, Parent, and Adult—and a strengthening of executive power in the Adult. The Adult ego state works on logic and on empirically based prediction to solve problems; these are cognitive processes.

> Friedrich Saloman Perls was born in Berlin on July 8, 1993. His father, Nathan, was a wine salesman who had no affection and little interest in any of his three children, and he particularly despised his youngest child, Fritz (as he was known even then). The boy loved acting, hated school, and resented the anti-semitism that was endemic to life in

Germany then. World War I interrupted his training as a medical student; he became a soldier, was wounded and awarded the German Cross, which he threw away (Gaines, 1979, p. xii).

Perls returned to Berlin after the war and finished his medical degree at the University of Berlin in 1921. At various times he worked with Goldstein, Horney, and Reich and was acquainted with Fromm. Perls was an independent and charismatic man. He moved frequently, developing and practicing his therapy in Germany, Holland, South Africa, Canada, Israel, and the United States. He died in Chicago in March of 1970.

Perls' Gestalt Therapy (1969) is based on the assumption that clients are "dis-integrated," that is, they are split apart and they maintain separateness from their own integral parts and from other people. The aim of therapy is to help the client become integrated. Because many in our society are caught up in their intellectual "part," the phrase, "Lose your mind and come to your senses," is a prescription to shut off the distancing and depersonalizing effect of cognitive analysis and to experiment with experience. There is a consistent effort in this kind of Gestalt therapy to identify, separate, and live through the diverse "parts" of one's being. Techniques such as giving experiential voice to all of the parts of a dream, of giving experiential voice to various parts of the body, and of speaking from diverse and often polarized parts of a person's values, motivations, or memories, serve to identify and separate all of the parts, give them credence and value so as to take them into account in some kind of reorganization or re-integration of the personality. Whatever form our integrated self takes is evolutionary and okay, even when it may seem to go counter to past experience or to general reference anchors. Instead of a universal truth outside of the experiencing individual that undergirds insight (the Law of Prägnanz), the observing individual of the classical Gestaltist becomes a functional part of a greater Truth. As the client re-integrates within the self and within the greater context, an existential "Aha!" occurs to validate the new, harmonious fit.

Perls, as well as other theorists and practitioners of perceptual learning based interventions, stresses experimenting with or experiencing other new, alternative ways of seeing, doing, and being. From the creation or alteration of perceptual frames that comes as a result of such experiments, clients are freed to pursue their goals in an insightful and self-enhancing manner. The following section will give some examples of perceptual interventions.

☐ Examples

There are several dynamics involved in perceptual intervention. Not always are they readily apparent and, because perceptions vary across therapists, the same circumstances may be seen differently. Of importance is that the intervention be consistent with the perceptual frame of the interventionist so that it may be evaluated, or so that the perception may be reframed if the intervention fails. Basic to a perceptual intervention is the view of the circumstance and style of the client by the therapist. Obviously, a careful and systematic study of the client is superior to a snap judgment. Because the client's behavior will flow from his or her unique perceptual awareness, it is important to discover that frame of reference. In the process of active listening, several questions must be answered:

- What is the client doing or not doing that is self-defeating?
- What sense can be made of the client's behavior in the context of his or her situation?
- Is there a perceptual deficit? Is the client trying to do something for which he or she has no previous experience, either direct or vicarious?
- Does the client's behavior make sense from the client's distorted or incorrect perception? Is the client working from a misleading frame?
- From a perception of the client's style, what kind(s) of experience, direct or vicarious, would be effective in creating or helping the client to replace a perceptual frame?

Once the questions have been answered, a strategy that will fit the client's circumstance and style is adopted, adapted, or created. It is necessary to know that in instances where the client is using, though ineffectively, an existing perceptual frame, it will be necessary to loosen that frame before introducing a preferred perception. This is accomplished by having the client change focus within his or her perceptual framework by techniques such as role reversal, splits, and figure-ground shifts. Look for the above dynamics in the following examples of perceptual interventions.

Clinic: Individual Applications

It's Too Late. The client, Susan Strong, has complaints of emotional turmoil, fitful sleep, and loss of weight. The onset of her symptoms came when she received a telegram from her father's attorney telling her of the death of her father and of his bequeath to her, a modest yet significant sum of money and the family genealogical and historical records. Her mother had died seven years earlier, at which time Susan blamed her father generally for neglecting the family in favor of his demanding business and specifically for being out of town at the time that her mother's severe illness resulted in her death. Interactions with her father over the seven-year span had been hostile and full of strife, mostly due to her anger and her unwillingness to forgive. The contacts had become less and less frequent and Susan had an inner conflict, with part of her wanting to resolve the differences and rebuild a good relationship and another part of her still grief-stricken over her mother's death, and vindictive toward her father. Through this time her father had been surprisingly patient with Susan, sending her cards and letters on special occasions and suggesting that she get help in resolving her negative feelings. At the notice of his death, Susan was overwhelmed with her love and respect for her father that she had denied for those seven years.

Susan had previous experiences in being upset and angry when disappointed but she had no experience in grieving nor in forgiving. She was stuck with an emotional reaction that was not working. Now that her father had died, and especially since he had willed to her some money and the care of the family's historical treasures, she felt guilty, ashamed, unresolved, and somehow unworthy as a person. "Why was I so obstinate? Why was I so spiteful? Why did I waste seven years of a potentially good relationship with my father? Why didn't I fix things while he was alive?"

This sounds very much like an affective surplus problem—the presence of strong, self-defeating emotions. Indeed that is true. Also it is true that Susan had the perception that resolving interpersonal problems can only be done with the other person involved, and since he was dead, there could be no possible resolution. It was not so much the presence of negative emotions that was creating the turmoil, sleep loss, and weight loss. It was the perception of helplessness to do anything about it combined with the urgency to get resolution. She couldn't live with the emotions and she had no way to resolve them.

A second perception was that she could be content only after and if her father forgave her. She had experienced only situations where giving and receiving were consonant, that is where what was given was received with a show of appreciation. Until she could give her confession—her feelings of regret, her desire for forgiveness, and her expression of love—she would feel bottled up, stymied, and full of turmoil.

The initial intervention of choice was to teach her some new perceptions including that it is possible to talk to someone who is dead, and that the expression of emotion-laden content is curative even when no response is obviously made. She was instructed and coached in talking to her deceased father. She was helped to verbalize all of the feelings that she wanted him to hear, the request for forgiveness, and the confession of love for him and sorrow at his passing. She promised him that she would be a responsible custodian of the records and thanked him for his confidence in allowing her to do that. The expression of these emotions was a very natural resolution of the affective surplus. It could only be done as she gained a new perceptual frame regarding talking to the dead and one regarding earnestly giving without concern for a response.

Compulsive Shopper.   Marla was a self-referred client. She complained of years of wildly compulsive shopping that started, as near as she could remember, at a time she was feeling unhappy and empty. Her conclusion is that she was trying to fill the "enormous hole." She reported daily visits to shops all over the city, on a quest to buy something special, something to beautify herself. Sometimes she would experience an emotional pick-up; often she got no pleasure at all. The next day she would return to the stores and buy again. She told herself she "needed" the items, even though she had closets full of things she had never used.

In spite of her husband's frantic expressions of concern over how much money she was spending, she couldn't help herself. In regard to other aspects of her life, she described herself as well-off in every respect. She lived in a nice home in a good neighborhood, was a member of the country club, had enjoyed the benefits of education at a prestigious school—"Everything is Perfect!" she said. "So why am I so unhappy?"

A brief review of her early relationships disclosed her being the second child and only daughter of a prominent physician father and merchandising executive mother. She remembered being dressed elaborately for social events and being "paraded" among the guests amid comment of "What a beautiful child!" Her governess was a no-nonsense woman whom Marla supposed to be envious of her family's status and resentful of her role with the children, though she never did anything overtly to indicate such a feeling. Boarding school was a fun time, though there were no adults for whom she felt any closeness or even admiration. She learned to present the kind of image that got her by in encounters with authority figures. While she could recall numerous examples of success, she could find no instance in which she felt genuinely happy. Her conclusion, in retrospect, was, "I never had any reason to be unhappy, so I assumed I must be happy, yet I've always carried with me this emptiness, this hole that now seems enormous."

Marla outlined the characteristics of affective deficit or lack of personal validation. From a cognitive, analytical structure, since she could identify nothing as being wrong;

there was no reason to be unhappy. It did not make sense. This is the kind of statement that comes from a person with a cognitive style. Since affective deficit problems are not addressed by cognitive strategies, her attempts to explain away her difficulty consistently failed. From a perceptual deficit position, she had never experienced personal validation, therefore, she had no frame for it. She was in a state of perceptual deficit. Her relationships had all been contingent—positive attention when she was dressed beautifully, presentation of an impressive image that got her through encounters with authority figures. Her parents were too busy for her; her parent surrogate was either coldly indifferent to her or attended only to image and performance criteria.

The intervention of choice in this case is a relationship therapy of some length (maybe 18 months) during which time Marla is brought to disclose many positive, neutral, and negative actions, thoughts, and experiences to which the counselor gives unconditional acceptance. This provides the experience for Marla that no matter what she does, she is accepted as a person. The acceptance by the counselor is of *her*, not of her performance, and it is non-contingent. As she experiences this personal validation in all situations, the enormous hole fills and the compulsion to shop (behavioral surplus) and the insistence of trying to explain the problem away (cognitive style) subsides. Although explaining the dynamics to her would not serve to fill the emptiness, it probably would be useful to satisfy her cognitive style. Presenting Maslow's hierarchy, with a description of how Marla never filled her love and belonging needs (hence her inability to function at a higher level), is a straightforward cognitive approach that would work for her. Continued efforts to gain "esteem" through buying beautiful clothing would only aggravate the sensation of emptiness, as these efforts failed again and again, being the wrong solution for accomplishing personal validation.

Clinic: Group Application

The setting is a support group for people who had experienced incestual relationships as children. While there are several different strategies for conducting support groups, this one was person-centered with the leader promoting a therapeutic atmosphere, engaging in lots of furthering responses and paraphrases with frequent appeals to others in the group for disclosure or validation. As the first session began, participants were generally reticent to disclose anything except superficial information. The therapist used tracking skills to induce one then another participant into deeper disclosure. As a member gave more and more complete information, she experienced a perceptual shift regarding the permissibility to disclose and of her positive emotional response for doing so. Others experienced the same thing vicariously and soon all members were disclosing. The disclosures progressed through such expressions as confusion, anger, and guilt. As one focus was ventilated, a member of the group would naturally move to a successive focus, modeling for others whose experiences were similar.

The members moved from their initial isolation, from keeping the incestuous relationship a secret, through admitting its occurrence; dealing with their perceptions of somehow being responsible or at least having feelings of complicity; feeling and expressing self-pity from being victimized; to making decisions regarding future responses to themselves and to the other person relative to the incestuous relationship. In this particular group, some members decided to confront the other person, wishing to exact admission of guilt and an apology. Others thought it best to formally forgive the other person and to see him as a fallible, irresponsible person. Still others wanted simply to drop the issue from their store of important issues. Whatever their preference, they were involved in role plays of their position and that of the other person and of casual contacts who might bring the issue up in the future. No systematic attempts were made to analyze dynamics or to draw conclusions. Some shifts in the way clients described or rationalized their experience in fact did occur. These were by-products of perceptual shifts and of more significance as models of variations in the way other clients communicated their own meanings.

This group process incorporated perceptual learning in two categories: (a) perceptions about the process of coping, and (b) resolution of problems. It was necessary for participants to experience their position and to share that experience. Once they learned the process then they could evolve through several perceptual shifts until arriving at one that provided for them an acceptable, self-enhancing resolution. It is important to recognize that in a phenomenally based, perceptual model, all clients are not expected to arrive at the same solution. This approach honors individual differences and assumes no singular, best cure that applies across clients. In contrast, a cognitively based approach would likely move all participants toward a cognitive structure that would apply to all of them—a nearly universal conclusion.

Classroom: Individual Application

Stuart was a fourteen year-old transfer student from Grange Middle School located in a very small rural community. His family lived on an isolated farm and the combination of lengthy school bus rides and farm chores limited his social contact with non-family members to in-school interactions. Upon arrival at Metropolitan Heights High School, he was overwhelmed by the social diversity and sheer magnitude of both in-school and co-curricular activities. He perceived himself, quite accurately, as a "country cousin" and shied away from social contact.

The teacher, concerned with integrating Stuart into this new social setting, programmed in some units that would provide Stuart with credibility. One unit focused on individual and societal differences. It included sharing by students the unique features of their backgrounds. There were some children who came from Southeast Asian countries, as well as the usual mix of socioeconomic and familial variations. Another unit focused on food production and distribution. Stuart was a member of the committee that covered the farming focus. A third unit dealt with social interactions and involved descriptions and role plays regarding identity and preferences. Incorporated in this unit were some fantasy exercises in which all students assumed a different identity then acted as though they were that different person and played through introductions and other activities.

In this particular case, the primary focus was on Stuart yet the activities were such that all students could benefit and curricular objectives could be met. Stuart's perceptual shifts were from that of uninvolved outsider to participant in areas either of neutrality (fantasy roles) or of advantage (farm expert).

Classroom: Group Application

Cambridge High School was located in a university town and catered mostly to college-bound students from upper-middle class homes. The politics were conservative and there was a nominally Protestant majority in the community. One night in late October, three students—classmates, and apparently well-adjusted, judging from honor roll grades and involvement in school sports and student government—committed suicide. The following day, a team of mental health consultants came to facilitate the adjustment of the students and faculty. Their strategy included three parts: (a) enable expression of feelings and thoughts, (b) model personal ways of coping with ambivalence and confusion, and (c) teach a tentative, choice-mediated position.

Within homeroom classes, the consultants first enlisted several volunteers to verbalize what was going through their thoughts; the consultants used reflection and paraphrasing skills to enlarge the volunteers' awareness. Using the volunteers as models, the class was then divided into small sharing groups and asked to do the same thing—share what was going through their thoughts. The consultant then summarized and elaborated/formalized the confusion and ambivalence present in most of the sharing. This permitted the students to move from a perceptual place of "I don't know what to think" to one of "My thoughts are many and confused and so are the thoughts of my classmates." The consultants then modeled a tentative, choice-mediated position. While it varied according to the uniqueness of each consultant, the position was something like, "I don't really have answers to many of my questions. I can't quite understand how my friends could do this." Or, "I don't know what made them do so. I probably never will understand this entirely. For now I choose to focus on ways in which they enriched my life and on ways I can grow from this experience. I am upset at the finality of death and I promise myself that I will exhaust other ways of solving my problems before considering doing what they did. I think, maybe, that I will also express to my other friends how important they are to me and I will try to be more sensitive to them."

The intent of this intervention was to reframe perceptions of students from confused and helpless to confused but having constructive options. The filling in, or perceptual framing of looking on the positive and toward strengthening others is a creation of a frame for students, most of whom have not confronted death and otherwise would tend to frame the morbid and the self-sorrowing rather than the proactive and adjustive. A concern of these interventionists was that the absence of a perceptual frame might be filled by the example of the peers who had committed suicide, with suicide being perceived as the way to deal with overwhelming aspects of life.

Experiential Learning

In the context of classroom/workshop learning, there is an approach that, with variations, can be a perceptually-focused or a cognitively-focused technique. It is referred to as student-involvement teaching or as experiential learning. There are several common dynamics to most applications of experiential learning. Participants are given directions about their involvement in a coming activity. Then, they are involved in the activity. A period of "processing" the experience is given. Such an experience is perceptually based or purely discovery learning if the beginning directions are process oriented; namely, they describe what to do and how to heighten awareness. For example, "During this exercise you are going to stand in a circle, view video vignettes, and talk with two other people about selected topics. While you are doing this, I want you to monitor two things: what is going on around you and what is going on within you." Processing for perceptual learning is flexible, often divergent, accepting of all participants' responses; it is a chance for them to commit their perceptions to words and to share those words with others.

The perceptual focus in experiential learning primarily differs from a cognitive focus in the latter's including instructions about what to find (a content orientation) and what to conclude. Cognitive processing is convergent in drawing out experiences to support the prescribed conclusions.

As long as the dynamics of direction, experience, and processing are involved, experiential learning is happening. It may be applied to field trips, guest demonstrations, movies or videotapes, and contrived activities such as fantasy trips, encounter sequences, and psychodrama. An example of a contrived activity for trainees planning to work with children is to assign them in pairs to alternately kneel in front of the partner who is standing on a step and to conduct a prescribed interaction. With the directions to be aware of self and the other, and to remember what goes on between the partners and within self in both positions, the processing permits expression of personal awareness regarding size, position, and power that may be generalized to adult-children interactions.

☐ Sample Problem Situations

As with previous chapters, the directions for processing the following sample situations are similar: (a) list the principles involved in problem resolution through perceptual intervention techniques, (b) create change procedures for a given sample problem, and (c) review the steps of your procedure with your list of dynamics.

Sexual Harassment

Frank has been reprimanded by his superior for allegations of sexual harassment. He is totally surprised at the reprimand and initially defensive. He comes from a large Italian family and a background where touch is given freely and readily accepted. He prides himself on being a good conversationalist and has a wide repertoire of jokes, augmented by cable TV comedy shows. He is very much like his father, who was a "real ladies man." The complaints of co-workers do not deal with direct come-ons or with offers of increased pay or benefits in exchange for sexual favors, but rather are about a pervasive discomfort in working around him because of his physical "friendliness" and the quality of his jokes.

Recycling

You are the chief environmental officer of a large university. In addition to a personal belief that being environmentally conscious is a good thing, you have been asked to increase the rate of recycling disposable materials, especially paper. Your campus recently has been networked so that every office has computer access to electronic mail and electronic bulletin board service. The majority of the faculty are resistant to relying on the computer for communication, many don't know how to use it for class papers and projects, and the few who use it habitually make hard copies of all correspondence and bulletins, oftentimes reproducing those copies for students or colleagues.

Co-parenting

Jack and Julie have gone through a divorce. They prided themselves on being "adult" about the whole thing and managed to divide property and other assets in a mutually agreeable way. They also agreed to Julie having the legal custody of their two children, Julius and Jaqueline, and with Jack having very liberal visitation privileges. Some of the major pre-divorce problems centered around how to raise the children including what was appropriate entertainment and social activities. They now are having major battles over what the children are permitted to do in each other's domain. Both parents quiz both children about experiences with the other parent. Julie resists letting the children go with Jack and Jack is threatening court action to get Julie declared an unfit mother so he can have custody.

Cultural Diversity

Sarah is a manager for a large manufacturing concern. She considers herself to be extremely competent and has won many battles within a male-dominated industry. While not a professed feminist, she is acutely aware of gender biases, both at work and in the larger society. Her company recently formed an alliance with a similar company located in Iran. Her position is important in making the venture a success. Though she recognizes the huge discrepancy between her beliefs and those of the stereotypical Persian businessman, she is unwilling to step aside and permit Sam, her deputy, to assume the role as liaison person. She is afraid of losing the power and advantages she has battled so hard to achieve.

Littering

The state department of highways has contacted you to consult with them regarding the problem of litter on the highways. They are concerned with two possible target groups: (a) those who carelessly throw garbage on the roadways, and (b) those who have signed on to "adopt" a section of highway. They want you to come up with programs to reduce littering in general and to increase the frequency and thoroughness with which adoptive caretakers fulfill their agreement.

I Didn't Mean to Do It

The Smith family has been referred to you following Sharon's (the wife) brief stay at the domestic violence center. Tom (the husband), when confronted with Sharon's going to the center, implored her to return home. She agreed to do so only on the condition that he would go to counseling. They have three children, ages 5, 3, and 6 months. Other than being the recipients of stern discipline by both parents, there was no allegation of child abuse.

A pattern had evolved where Tom, who works a rotational shift job, would come home after the 4:00 p.m.-12:30 a.m. swing shift and desire/demand attention from Sharon. Sharon has never been a "night person" and after her work at a day care center and dealing with her own children, she "runs out of gas" by 9:00 p.m. She tries to be responsive to Tom's middle of the night demands, but is not convincingly doing so.

Tom had taken to drinking a "few" with a co-worker after the shift ended. Every so often, Tom loses his temper, beats up on Sharon, then sleeps off his inebriated state to find he has mistreated her. This has been followed by sorrow, begging forgiveness, and the promise to never do it again. Sharon's desperation and visit to the domestic violence center and Tom's agreement to go to counseling may be a sufficient break in the cycle to permit intervention.

Where Is the Manual?

This title is a common reference for people who are undergoing sudden and inflicted change. They are thrust into a situation that requires a response for which they have had no preparation or modeling, or for which their perceptual set is self-defeating. Support groups for domestic violence, death and dying, divorce, parenting, or retirement are examples of interventions that may deal with perceptual deficit people. You are a group counselor working on contract to a hospital unit that deals with diagnosed terminally ill patients. This is your first meeting with a new group of these five patients:

- a 73-year old woman who has Parkinson's Disease of a relatively mild manifestation. It is possible for most patients so diagnosed to function very well with a few limiting symptoms. She is acting as though her only option is a brief period of living, and being limited to constant nursing care and a wheelchair.
- a 50-year old man with lung cancer, given, at most, nine months to live. He acts as though nothing is wrong and is angry at you and everybody else for bothering him, even though he is confined to a wheelchair during the brief periods away from his room.
- a 60-year old minister, emaciated and dying from an intestinal disorder he contracted while serving in the Congo 20 years ago. His estimated longevity is anywhere from 3 months to 3 years. His energy, what little he has, is directed toward praying for his parishioners.
- a 49-year old woman, a stock broker by profession, with 6 months to a year remaining due to leukemia. Between chemotherapy treatments, she works on her portfolio of investments.
- a 90-year old man who insists the doctors are wrong and that he will get better and return to his Montana cattle ranch. Medically, his condition is such that, if he gets strong enough to leave the hospital, he will need to live in a nursing care facility close to hospital resources.

8
CHAPTER

Cognitive Learning Approaches to Intervention

☐ Focus

Cognitive learning approaches to intervention are two-stage models. Stimuli provide information. They may exist in the external world or they may come from within the person. Information forms the input function of a cybernetic model such as that modified from McDonald (1965) (see Figure 8.1). The information or input is processed by the person. References to information-processing components are identified with titles of constructs such as interpreting, remembering, evaluating, learning, and deciding. As constructs, these only can be verified through a network of converging operations that have an empirical base. The output resulting from the information processing function is behavior or action toward a goal.

Looking further at the modified McDonald model, it can be said that perception is the product of sensing and interpreting, of registering impulses on our receptors and of making sense out of the experience. Decision rests on perception. Decisions are subject, then, to errors in sensation and to errors in interpretation. MacDonald (1965) postulated several systems that interact to permit or produce goal-oriented actions. The first is a "self-system," likened to a semipermeable membrane that selectively allows some agents to pass while excluding others. This self-system reflects the biases, fears, inclinations, and habits that determine to what extent we notice something in our environment. Whether or not there is an entity such as a self-system, people do behave as though one exists. Some things just do not get sensed.

A second system is the interpretive system. Sensory data that are permitted in by the self-system are interpreted relative to past experience (contributed by the memory system) and to importance to the person (contributed by the evaluative system), or they receive an interpretation appropriate to the newness of the data. Interpreting can be seen as the result of either one of two processes (or a combination of both). Piaget (Phillips, 1969; Piaget & Inhelder, 1969) spoke of assimilation and accommodation, of fitting new information into old structures if it will fit nicely, and of altering

Cognitive Learning Approaches 121

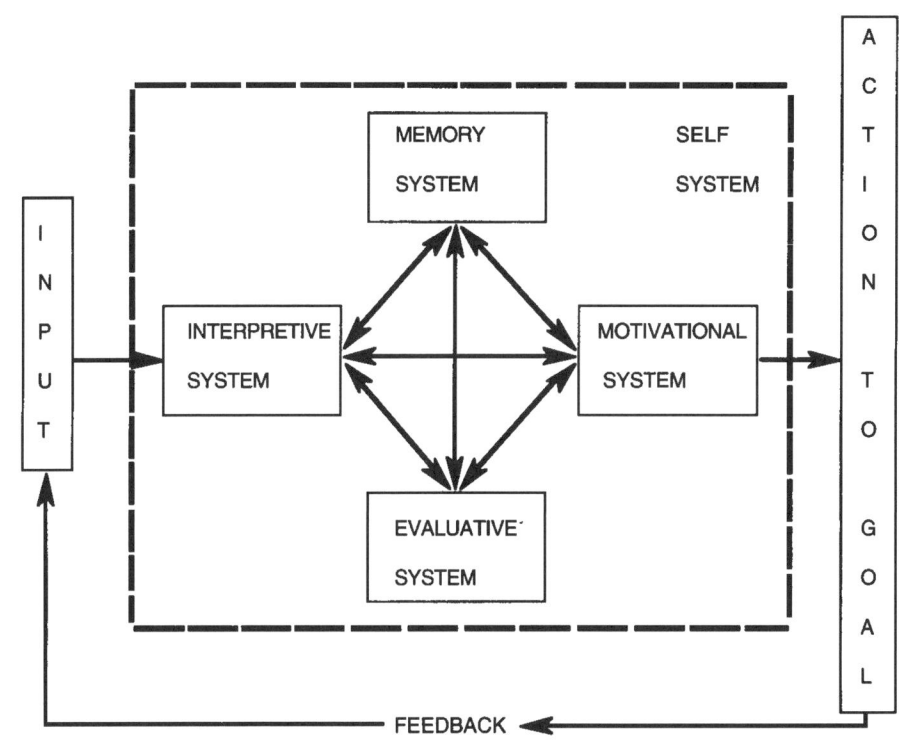

FIGURE 8.1. Dynamics of Decision Making. Adapted from *Educational Psychology* by F. MacDonald. Copyright © 1965 by Wadsworth Publishing Company, Belmont, California. Reprinted with permission.

old structures or building new structures for information that doesn't fit (doesn't "make sense"). Attribution theory (Försterling, 1986) suggests that people persist in making explanations about "what causes what" and seek to find meaning in experience. Whenever a situation is encountered or experienced, people compare it to previous similar situations. If the recently experienced situation is very much like something from the past, it tends to receive the same interpretation as the past one. If the new experience is unique or dissimilar to prior experiences, then a new interpretation will be made according to the principles of attribution theory.

The memory system operates somewhat like the memory banks of a computer. Information from past experience is coded verbally or perceptually and "filed away." Similarities in subsequent experience may trigger a recollection of the old. Conscious attempts to search the "files" may result in the remembering of critical components of past experiences. Obviously, only that which is filed can be retrieved, and the contents of memory result from individual, personal experiences. They may or may not correspond to an empirical reality. Adler (Ansbacher & Ansbacher, 1956) adds one other important awareness with his observation that memory is "creative," that is, people systematically distort the past to be harmonious with their individual personality.

If data are meaningful, they are processed by the evaluative system that determines whether they are important enough to warrant action at that particular time. According to Rokeach (1973), there is a somewhat systematic progression from experience through interpretation and attitude to value formation. Values are the personal conclusions of what should be or what should happen (terminal values) and of how a person should go about accomplishing those valued conditions (instrumental values). Examples might include: "I deserve to (should) live comfortably (terminal value), but I should accomplish that goal honestly (instrumental value)."

The fifth system is the motivational system. It responds to the primary issue of "enough" as applied to results of the other systems. Does my interpretation indicate that the opportunity is strong enough or that the threat is sufficiently great to warrant action? Does my memory system provide enough data to support probable outcomes? Does my evaluative system indicate that I care or should care enough to take action? If the situation produces enough concern or attraction or if my present system state indicates enough deficit (boredom, hunger, attention-deficit), then the motivational system will provide the degree of movement or action appropriate to the occasion.

The McDonald model summarizes much research and analysis of cognitive processes. Its orientation is toward human learning or human decision-making. If one allows for two mental systems that are similar, yet have one or two critical differences, then it is logical to postulate two learning systems, one perceptual and one cognitive. A digression into the study and experience of memory will illustrate these differences. Ebbinghaus did some pioneering work in memory by using nonsense syllables and his "memory drum" (1913). Among other things, he concluded that practice enhances retrieval and that overlearning enhances memory. This exemplifies a cognitive position. In contrast, most people have experienced a flood of memories, largely experiential in nature, from smelling an odor or hearing a song or visiting a location that triggers memories of events from the past. There was no practice nor overlearning nor even an intent to remember. This typifies the perceptual position. Another position, still largely cognitive, suggests that memorizing nonsense syllables is a different task than is required in most cognitive learning, in that nonsense syllables exclude meaning; something that is meaningful may be remembered without much practice or overlearning.

With two learning systems, it is possible to allow that sub-human species may learn perceptually, ala Tolman, and that human and animal learning may be similar or identical as regards perceptual learning and perceptual memory. The rich language of people is difficult to explain as a by-product or extension of conditioning. A more parsimonious position allows for different learning principles that explain cognitive, language-mediated learning. Learning theories have suffered in the past from limiting their focus to animal or child learning and insisting that the theory must apply to various phylogenetic levels of creatures and to human adults. Cognitive learning applies only to older children and adults. This is supported by developmental theory that documents orderly changes in cognitive abilities that culminate in the ability to manipulate abstractions. During the formal operations period of Piaget, ". . . the child's cognitive *structures* reach their greatest level of development, and the child becomes able to apply logic to all classes of problems" (Wadsworth, 1971, p. 27).

There seems to be some overlap between conditioned verbal responses and the successful use of verbal abstractions. The teaching of accurate labels can be explained by association learning or reinforcement learning dynamics. Knowing labels is fundamental to a language system. It is easy to see the dynamics of naming when a given referent is addressed by only one term; however, more commonly, a number of different classes of referents are signalled by a term such as, for example, key or table. Even when there is a restricted range of application for a given term, the use of the term becomes abstract as more and more referents are signalled. Taking a simple example, a child may learn the word "cat" in response to a specific cat, "Tabby," and later use the same word to apply to other referents—"Boots," "Whiskers," and "Georgina." When the term gets generalized or "rubricized," it belongs in formal operations. Cat refers neither to its referent nor as a refinement of stimulus generalization to other referents, but to "catness."

Given the existence of a cognitive system and given the human potential for a highly elaborated belief system full of abstractions and logical connections, there remains the requisite assumption for cognitive intervention that thought precedes action. An extreme position is that thought precedes all action. Its antithesis is that action is externally cued and thought is merely a product of awareness and unnecessary as a mediator of behavior. The unsophisticated person, when caught in an error, often says, "I'm sorry. I just wasn't thinking." This assumes that thinking does impact some behavior. [The same person would relate instances of highly practiced responses for which thinking is unnecessary. If thoughts were to occur in the process of those highly practiced responses, they might even impede or prevent effective behavior.] The integrationist can allow that at least some behavior is cognitively mediated and for that domain, cognitive models support intervention strategies that can and do provide changes in client responses from self-defeating ones to self-enhancing ones.

☐ Foundation Theories

There are three theorists, among many who have prominence in cognitive theory, who form a complimentary foundation for understanding cognitive interventions. They are Leon Festinger, Friedrich Försterling, and Milton Rokeach.

Festinger: Cognitive Dissonance

Leon Festinger's work, *A Theory of Cognitive Dissonance* (1957), is the major reference source for this explanation of the dynamics involved in the sensing and making sense of events and experiences. Cognition is "knowledge, opinion, belief about the environment, about oneself, or about one's behavior" (p. 3). It is primarily an individual, unique set of accumulations, although Festinger is a realist to the extent that he believes in a consistent, accessible reality. What is "out there" really is out there. This provides the possibility of common cognitions across individuals. He is enough of a phenomenologist to recognize that, even given a consistent physical environment, people sometimes get distorted perceptions of that reality. Those distortions are not common across people (except for illusions that tend to be somewhat universal sensory or perceptual distortions). Information comes from what the person does and feels, as well as from the physical environment. "Elements of cognition correspond for the most part with what the person actually does or feels or with what actually exists in the environment" (p. 11). "The reality which impinges on a person will exert pressures in the direction of bringing the appropriate cognitive elements into correspondence with that reality" (p. 11).

Elements occur in batches; they are not isolated. They can be said to be relevant to one another (It is snowing/I am cold) or irrelevant (The wind is blowing/I like modern art). Relevance can be seen as a continuum from "extremely relevant" or "always experienced together" to "very irrelevant" or even "antithetical." The degree of relevance can be called cognitive consonance. Moving through the irrelevant to the antithetical end of the continuum produces increasing degrees of cognitive dissonance. Two elements are dissonant if they do not fit together, yet they appear together. There is an innate preference for consonance such that, "The existence of dissonance, being psychologically uncomfortable, will motivate the person to try to reduce the dissonance. When dissonance is present, in addition to trying to reduce it, the person will likely avoid situations and information that would likely increase the dissonance" (p. 3). This accounts for the motivation to "make sense" of things, the persistence at thinking through issues when they don't make sense, and/or resisting new input that threatens the state of understanding. Even in the presence of disconfirming data, there is a tendency for people to hang onto their "comfortable ignorance." By the same token, the way to alter someone's cognitive organization is to introduce undeniable dissonance so that he or she is pressured, from within, to make a change. "The presence of dissonance correlates with the tension or urge to reduce or eliminate the dissonance. The strength of the pressure to reduce the dissonance is a function of the magnitude of the dissonance" (p. 18).

Achieving consonance and/or avoiding dissonance are somewhat universal goals. There are times that form an exception to the rule when life is so consonant that people seek dissonance. Alteration of choice of food to include something more or differently spiced, traveling to new places or even altering the route home are examples of seeking dissonance. Too much dissonance is intolerable; too much consonance is boring. Most of the time, for most people, the balance tends toward the presence of more dissonance than is desired. Cognitively, as well as experientially, they change or progress in the direction of resolving dissonance.

Festinger provides three options for achieving consonance and three for avoiding dissonance. To achieve consonance, one must do or have done for him or her:

- a change in the behavioral elements;
- a change in the environmental elements; or
- addition of a new cognitive element that will give consonance and avoidance or denial of elements that increase dissonance.

For avoidance of dissonance, one must:

- be selective about seeking or adding new information;
- be selective of whom is approached; or
- avoid doing anything new or different.

These notions underscore the importance of consistency to children through their years of development. Consistency provides an environment stable enough to permit understanding and some experiments at control and self-direction. Under conditions of inconsistency, such as evidenced by the syndrome attributed to children of alcoholics, efforts to achieve consonance or to avoid dissonance are unpredictably sabotaged, thus requiring the child to float in a nonsensical world. Another manifestation of these principles is the seeming displeasure and difficulty of aged people coping with surprises, even very pleasant ones. Expectations of constancy are consonant; requirements to respond spontaneously produce dissonance that, in turn, demands adjustment.

Försterling: Attribution Theory

Friedrich Försterling, in an article in the *American Psychologist* (1986) entitled "Attributional Conceptions in Clinical Psychology," summarized the principles of attribution theories. His work is the primary reference for this section. Additional input comes primarily from Martin E. P. Seligman (Seligman, 1975; Trotter, 1987).

It appears to be insufficient that people simply organize cognitive elements into consonant and dissonant groupings. People have a desire/need/penchant to explain. Explaining requires the relating of concepts to one another and the assignment of causality. The pervasive question, "Why?" of the young child persists throughout life. The need to predict and control elements in life requires knowledge of relationships between and among elements. It may be that the base of all science is a quest for answers to Why? questions. Försterling suggests that people assign or *attribute* causal relationships between and among elements, hence the label, attribution theory.

There are several basic principles in attribution theory.

> First, attributional conceptions are based on the premise that external events or stimuli (S) do not directly trigger reactions (R), such as behaviors or emotions, but that these 'S-R' links are mediated by causal ascriptions (more general, C = cognitions). Therefore, attributional conceptions are cognitive models of action, which is frequently described as follows: S-C-R (p. 276).

People think about events; thinking includes figuring out "what" precedes "what else," and "whatever" usually follows "whatever else." Simple sequence is usually elaborated by the belief that things that come first are the cause of the things that usually follow them; the causal conclusions provide data for deciding what can be done to bring about or to cause a desired outcome.

> A second basic assumption central to most attribution approaches is that individuals are generally (with some exceptions) motivated to gain a *realistic* understanding of causes that have led to different events in their personal domain (p. 276).
> ... attribution theorists are guided by the belief that individuals process information rationally and use 'naive' scientific methods in order to arrive at veridical judgments (p. 276).

Conclusions are evolved through mental processes of observing, postulating or hypothesizing causal relationships, and checking out those postulations through further observations. More or less "true" conclusions, to the extent that they are consistent and consonant, are arrived at through this process.

> Third, although not as salient as the previously mentioned two points, attributional approaches also have a distinctive functionalistic 'flavor'; in such approaches, it is assumed that a causal understanding serves the function of attaining personal goals and survival (p. 276).

The way to achieve goals is to know what causes what else, and then to manage those things that cause the results wanted. All success depends on influence or manipulation of the events or the elements that produce the success.

Försterling says that attributions result from observations of covariance of events. Covariance is a correlational principle that indicates the probability of two or more things happening together or in succession. It avoids, in empirical studies, the issue of causality. If two things are highly correlated, they simply show a great deal of common variance, or have a high probability of recurring in the same fashion under the same conditions. Because "B" accompanies or follows "A," with no evidence to demonstrate otherwise, it cannot be concluded empirically that "A" caused "B." It may well be that "B" caused "A" to occur, or that some other factor or condition caused, and predictably continues to cause, the associated occurrence of "A" and "B."

There are three classes of attributions, or three ways in which events (results) get related (attributed) to other events (causes). They are consensus, distinctiveness, and consistency. If many people experience the same effect to a single or the same cause, then an attributional relationship is established. If the effect is experienced by only one person (low consensus) the likelihood of causal attribution is low. Conversely, if a similar sequence or outcome is experienced by a great number of people and if that experience is communicated, then high consensus and a high probability of causal attribution occurs. As an example, if one person becomes ill shortly after eating at a certain restaurant, there is a slight but low probability that eating at that restaurant will be seen as the cause of the illness. If dozens or hundreds of people who eat at that restaurant get sick very soon after their repast, then the probability of connecting the two events in a causal way is very high.

Distinctiveness refers to the intensity or vividness of the connection between two events. "An event will be attributed to the entity if it only occurs in connection with that entity (high distinctiveness) and to other causes when it covaries with many different entities (low distinctiveness)" (p. 276). For example, if in the process of regurgitating the contents of that meal from the restaurant, the most distinctive and overwhelming stimulus is identified as remnants of a grilled cheese sandwich, a causal relationship may become strongly and instantly established such that future encounters with grilled cheese sandwiches are energetically avoided.

The third class of attribution is consistency, the degree to which the relationship between the antecedent and consequent focus is stable: the same effect to the same cause at different times. If subsequent encounters with that restaurant or with grilled cheese sandwiches failed to cause illness, then the attributional relationship would be weakened. If, however, eating grilled cheeses sandwiches at other times and at other places resulted in illness, an explanation of an allergic reaction to grilled cheese may well be concluded. These three classes of attribution are relatively easy to see in simple examples, which are sufficient to identify them. In complex examples or in cases where there may be an interaction of all three, the precise dynamics may be hard to map. Suffice it to say, people assign cause and effect power to events within their experience. The more consistent, distinctive, and common the experience, the higher the likelihood of a causal relationship. The lower the degree of these characteristics, the less likely that there is such a relationship. A person who, contrary to the report of others, experiences, claims, or insists that something exists is believed to be hallucinating, delusional, or in some other way affected, and his or her behavior is believed to be aberrant. This probably is another demonstration of the power of consensus. Whenever the experience is not common and the rationale is unacceptable, there is another attributional conclusion reached, that an unbalanced mind is causing itself to have unreal experiences.

Other consequences of the causal attributions made by people can occur. For example, failure explained as resulting from a lack of ability may elicit feelings of resignation or discouragement. The same failure blamed on interference from someone else may result in anger and aggression. This is an example of how cognitive perceptions and conclusions can determine the response of the person. Seligman categorized attributions into three dichotomies: stable or unstable, global or specific, and internal or external.

> If your relationship breaks up, for example, you can come up with a variety of reasons. If you explain it as something that is stable over time (I always screw up my personal relationships), you will expect it to happen again and you will show signs of helplessness in future relationships. If you explain it as global, rather than specific (I'm incapable of doing anything right), you will expect bad things to happen in all areas of your life and feel even more helpless. If you explain it as internal rather than external (It was all my fault; my lover did everything possible to keep the relationship going), you are likely to show signs of lowered self-esteem (Trotter, 1987, p. 32).

If you explain it as external, specific, and stable (my lover is incurably self-centered and nobody could be successful in accommodating the demands in such a relationship), you will feel disappointed at your negative experience and fortunate to be free of the negative interaction.

Ascription of failure to stable causes (lack of ability, task difficulty) decreases subsequent expectation of success. Attribution of failure to internal causes (lack of effort) maximizes negative esteem feelings following the outcome. Low achievement strivings seem to be associated with preferring stable and internal explanations for failure; high achievement motivation may be the result of external and variable explanations of failure. Loneliness comes from blaming social failure on internal, global, and stable causes. Depression may result from telling oneself that both interpersonal failures and non-interpersonal failures result from internal, global, and stable causes (I am incapable and unworthy in everything I try, and there is no hope for change). Andersen, Horowitz, and French (1983) conclude that "lonely and depressed people ascribe interpersonal failures to unchangeable characterological defects in themselves. . ." (p. 127). Conversely, most of the attributional choices for failure result in somewhat opposite results if they are used as explanations for success. What Seligman called a "positive explanatory style" is preference for using attributions of the unstable, specific, and external types of cause.

To the extent that misery and self-defeat are the result of the beliefs and explanations at which people arrive, it is possible to change that misery and self-defeat by altering the attributions. Försterling calls this process *attribution retraining*. "A certain maladaptive reaction (R1) can be modified to a more adaptive reaction (R2) when the attribution (a1) that leads to the original reaction (R1) can be replaced with a more desirable attribution (a2) that leads to the more adaptive reaction (R2)" (p. 278).

Rokeach: Values Theory

In addition to making sense out of experiences and sorting them into categories (Festinger), and assigning relationships between and among events (Försterling), people have a general tendency to make value judgments about almost everything. Three questions may be used to structure this triad: "What is it?"; "What caused it?"; and "Is it worthwhile, valuable, moral, good?" Milton Rokeach (1973) presented a treatise on values that showed how perceptions and experiences are processed into categories. These categories are progressively more important to the person and progressively

128 Intervention Theories

more resistant to change. The categories—from distant to central—are: thoughts or concepts, beliefs, attitudes, values (terminal and instrumental), and self-cognitions or self-concept (see Figure 8.2).

Thoughts or concepts are interpretations of experience. They may be seen as hypotheses, hunches, or tentative conclusions. Because of their formative nature, they are easily altered or countered by additional or opposing data.

Beliefs are thoughts or concepts that have been tested or that have been held for some time without challenge. Because of the tendency for people to preserve their cognitive organization, some beliefs require considerable or strong challenge or confrontation in order to produce change.

Attitudes are beliefs combined with personal preference. They serve as a precursor to action; they predispose a person to interpret data in a prescribed way. Prejudice is an example of attitude. Attitudes are especially strong when there is room to give personal interpretation to data: "Given no compelling evidence to the contrary and/or no strong reason to change, I prefer/choose to believe the following." The stronger the attitude, the more compelling or forceful the reason to change must be if any alteration is to be made. The illogical self-statements of Ellis (1969) and the illogical thoughts of Beck (Burns, 1980) fit into this frame.

"A value is an enduring belief that a specific mode of conduct or end-state of existence is personally or socially preferable to an opposite or converse mode of conduct or end-state of existence. A value system is an enduring organization of beliefs concerning preferable modes of conduct or end-states of existence along a continuum of relative importance" (Rokeach, 1973, p. 5). An alternate definition of value is an arrange-

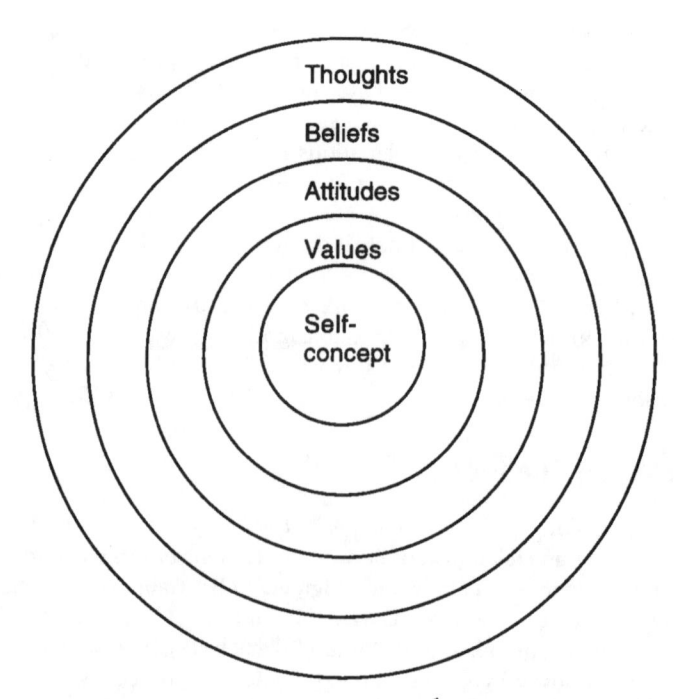

FIGURE 8.2. Comparison of Thoughts, Beliefs, Attitudes, Values, and Self-Concept.

ment of sets of cognitive elements that are strung together in presumed causal relationships, and that can be compared one to another for the purpose of choosing the more preferred. The chosen elements are often evaluated against some external, social standard.

Values are enduring cognitive structures having significance affectively and behaviorally, as well as cognitively. They are a conception of the desirable about which a person can feel emotional and, as a result of which, responses are activated. End-states of existence refer to terminal values—what to become: a good parent, a successful business person, a "righteous soul." Modes of conduct refer to instrumental values—how to act. These are moral and competency guides. They tell a person how to be during the process of accomplishing what to be. *Sensitive, honest, diligent, enthusiastic, unwaivering* are terms that indicate ways of being that are more or less sanctioned by a particular value system.

Such systems, if they are the result of teaching from parents or society, directly or vicariously through modeling, may very well start out as concepts, then move through the belief and attitude stages prior to being internalized as values. Presumably, there is a personal sense to values that comes from experience with and testing of beliefs and attitudes. Those that are most severely challenged with little or no change are the strongest. An untested value may really be little more than an attitude or a belief.

Self-cognitions are the most important of all cognitive elements. The many conceptions or cognitions that a person has about him/herself "are more central than his values" (Rokeach, 1973, p. 215).

> Self-conceptions include all one's cognitions, conscious and unconscious, about one's physical image; intellectual and moral abilities and weaknesses; socioeconomic position in society; national, regional, ethnic, racial and religious identity; the sexual, generational, occupational, marital, and parental roles that one plays in society; and how well or poorly one plays such roles. In short, a person's total conception of himself is an organization of all the distinctive cognitions, negative as well as positive, and the affective connotations of these conditions that would be displayed if a full answer to the question 'Who am I?' were forthcoming" (pp. 215–216).

The contents or structure of the self-cognitions impact everything a person does. They form the basic personality style or script that gives uniqueness to the individual. A change in the self-cognitions will produce changes in all of the less-central belief segments, whereas a change in any one of them will not necessarily impact the self-cognitions. The result is that the more superficial changes will be transitory such that a person may say that he or she believes in your point of view and may promise to act accordingly, yet not do so at a later time. People often "regress" to the values of their childhood home; in truth, they probably never let go of them.

The distinguishing factor of a two-stage model is the existence of mental processing systems and the belief that action is intentional and results from that processing. If thought precedes action, then changes in thought will produce different actions. The task of the cognitive interventionist is either to (a) install a cognitive structure in the case where the client literally does not know what to think, or (b) replace a faulty structure in cases where the action logically follows the existing structure, yet is self-defeating. These options fit, respectively, cognitive deficit and cognitive surplus conditions.

A pattern for intervention similar to that of perceptual intervention exists in the cognitive sphere. Applied theorists will include these steps:

A. Answer the following questions:
   - What is the client doing or not doing that is self-defeating?
   - What is the experiential context in which the undesirable response occurs?
   - What rationale does the client have to explain his or her response? This question is misleading in its simplicity. In many, perhaps most, cases the client will not verbalize clearly or accurately the rationale. It must be deduced by the therapist from an analysis of the context and the response. The interventionist may ask himself or herself, "What rationale logically precedes the response in this context?" A basis for Ellis's Rational-Emotive-Behavioral Therapy (previously, RET) and for Beck's Cognitive Therapy (both of which will be considered in the following section) is that the client must be taught to recognize what "sentences he is telling himself" or the nature of the deeper schemas that underlie his or her cognitive distortions.
   - Is the rationale ill-defined, whimsical, nonsensical? Go to step B.
   - Is the rationale loose and weak, or strong and well-defended? If weak, go to step B. If strong, go to step C.
B. Treat as a cognitive deficit and teach/install a cognitive structure that will direct self-enhancing behavior. Both non-existent and weak structures will give way readily to a strong, contextually appropriate and logical structure.
C. First, work to loosen the structure. It is at this juncture that Festinger's cognitive dissonance principles are invoked. The interventionist recognizes that direct confrontation often results in a client increasing defense of himself or herself and of his or her behavior. Introducing dissonant information (doubt) produces an "I'm not so sure" state that is more receptive to a new structure—particularly if the new structure eliminates the dissonance. Differences across interventions that focus on cognitive restructuring occur most often in their approaches to loosening the existing structures. Rokeach gives additional support for selecting structure-loosening attempts at peripheral levels where resistance is weak. Second, introduce a competing structure, the use of which rules out the initial structure (mutually exclusive where possible), and that is contextually appropriate and logically sound.
D. Because the pattern of cognitive self-defeat tends to be generalized across many client responses, cognitive intervention includes a teaching phase intended to help the client invoke the intervention process in his or her own behalf. Direction and practice in identifying illogical self-statements or cognitive distortions, and direction and practice in confronting one's own illogicality and substituting alternate structures are provided. In essence, the client is given "on the job training" in the development and use of a new cognitive processing skill.

☐ Applied Theories

Four applied theorists will be the focus of this section: David Ausubel, Albert Ellis, Aaron Beck, and Eric Berne. Ausubel emphasizes instructional theory, Ellis and Beck are psychotherapists, and Berne has applied his model to therapy as well as to institutional and corporate consulting. The dynamics of cognitive deficit are more clearly addressed by Ausubel. Ellis and Beck deal with the restructuring of cognitive surpluses. Berne focuses on intrapersonal psychodynamics with a goal of establishing dominance in the "Adult," that part of the person that operates on logical, principle-mediated, problem-solving strategies. His work appears to incorporate Ausubelian principles in counseling and consulting settings.

Ausubel

David Ausubel is identified with Expository Teaching. To some extent his work is seen more clearly in contrast to Bruner's. This is consistent with his precept that learning is enhanced by contrast and discrimination. Recall the Brunerian insistence that learning comes from direct experience. The cognitive closet of the learner, according to Bruner, is organized according to the unique style of its owner. Much like the clothes closet of a young child left to his or her own devices, what is used gets thrown on the floor. Eventually, the frequently used items rise to the top and others find their position elsewhere. The child, and many adults who operate in this manner, seems to find, uncannily, whatever he or she looks for, though to the observer there is no pattern to the organization. In contrast, the Ausubelian cognitive closet is one with racks, drawers, shelves, and rods, all expertly designed and hung with but minor modification to suit the whims of the owner.

Ausubel emphasized the top of families of abstractions and taught for cognitive clarity. An example might be the concept of "mammal." With children who are old enough to do formal operations, to deal with high levels of abstraction, it is possible to teach labels and organizations in the absence of or with reliance on relatively few referents. If a person is taught that there are five elements or criteria for defining mammalness, and if the person understands the elements, called criterial elements by Ausubel, he or she can navigate through life and correctly classify life forms that he or she encounters into two categories: mammals and non-mammals. The criterial elements of mammals are:

- air breathing
- with hair
- warm-blooded
- give birth to live young
- suckle their young

There is a peg labelled "mammal" on which successively lower classifications can be hung—such as land mammals and sea mammals—eventually ending with a place for direct experience with numerous referents of the concept, mammal.

It is Ausubel's contention that conceptual training can prepare people in advance for an incredible variety of life experiences and, if one waits to have first-hand experience, one will be ill-prepared to cope with the complex demands of everyday life. He believed the mission of schools is to install a functional organizing system in the students' cognitive closets and to label the pegs and drawers in a way to facilitate coping successfully with future experiences.

Given an established abstraction such as, "mammal," the learner "subsumes" new information or experience into the appropriate category or label. If the new something is similar to but not identical to an existing abstraction, it gets "correlatively subsumed" close to the original abstraction. Forgetting happens when a new experience is so similar to the previous that the two cannot be distinguished; one or the other becomes "obliteratively subsumed" on the same peg. Learning is enhanced when information or experiences can be presented with clear distinction from previous or companion material—maximum dissociability. Many students find that studying a chart or model of, say, a part of the human anatomy helps them put the physiological name and its relationship clearly in their cognitive awareness so that actual discrimination on a cadaver is aided, even though the borders of anatomical parts are not clearly discernible in the real context.

For the relatively discrete segments of knowledge for which a given professor teaches, it is assumed that his or her students arrive at the outset in a state of cognitive deficit. The professor's task is to install cognitive structures that are valid, complete, and functionally adequate to permit the graduate to use such new structures for advanced study or for practical application. To the extent that clients experience demands from life for which they have no previous experience or teaching, the dynamics of therapy are similar to the classroom. The domain of instruction would not be as vast nor as complicated; the application would be apparent and immediate. Both in and out of the classroom, it is foolish to expect someone to do something that he or she has not been taught to do. In cases of cognitive deficit, formal as in the classroom or informal as in the clinic, the most efficient intervention is to install the absent structure—to teach the student or client what he or she needs to know.

Ellis

Albert Ellis established an approach called "Rational-Emotive Therapy" and an institute for the training therein. In the recent past, recognizing added gains from the *en vivo* practice of therapeutic reorientations, he added a term to his approach, calling it "Rational-Emotive-Behavioral Therapy." Ellis was born in Pittsburgh, Pennsylvania, in 1913. His family moved to New York City while Ellis was quite young. He has lived most of his life in New York City. He almost died from tonsillitis at age five, and subsequently suffered from acute nephritis and diabetes (Dryden, 1989; Morris & Kanitz, 1975). His parents divorced when Ellis was 12 years old, adding some turmoil to his life, though he had operated with a relative minimum of parental structure for several years prior to this time. Graduating in business from the City College of New York in 1934, he worked in the business world for a time, also trying to write and publish some works of fiction. His interest turned to psychology, leading him to a Masters degree in 1943 and the Ph.D. in clinical psychology in 1947 from Columbia University. Subsequently he took training in psychoanalysis and started to practice from that model. Becoming unsatisfied with that approach, he evolved his own strategy, primarily cognitive (Gladding, 1992). Here is Ellis's response to the question, "What is Rational-Emotive Therapy?"

> Briefly, it is a comprehensive approach to psychological treatment that unusually stresses the cognitive aspect of human disturbance, but also importantly deals with its emotive and its behavioral aspects. For human beings are exceptionally complex and there does not seem to be any simple way in which they become what we call "emotionally disturbed" nor does there seem to be a single monolithic way in which they can be helped to be less self-defeating. Their psychological problems arise from their misperceptions and their mistaken cognitions about what they perceive; from their emotional underreactions or overreactions to normal and unusual stimuli; and from their dysfunctional motorial or behavioral patterns, which enable them to keep repeating nonadjustive responses even when they know that they are behaving badly.
>
> On the cognitive side, rational-emotive therapy is strong in both theory and practice. It hypothesizes that most of what we label our "emotional reactions" are caused by our

conscious and unconscious evaluations, interpretations, and philosophies (1969, pp. 83–84).

From another source (Ellis, 1958) comes a list of twelve of the illogical beliefs that commonly lead people into emotional and behavioral self-defeat:

1. The idea that it is a dire necessity for an adult to be loved or approved of by everyone for everything he does—instead of his concentrating on his own self-respect, on winning approval for necessary purposes (such as job advancement) and on loving rather than being loved.
2. The idea that certain acts are wrong, or wicked, or villainous, and that people who perform such acts should be severely punished—instead of the idea that certain acts are inappropriate or antisocial, and that people who perform such acts are invariably stupid, ignorant, or emotionally disturbed.
3. The idea that it is terrible, horrible, and catastrophic when things are not the way one would like them to be—instead of the idea that it is too bad when things are not the way one would like them to be, and one should certainly try to change or control conditions so that they become more satisfactory, but that if changing or controlling uncomfortable situations is impossible, one had better become resigned to their existence and stop telling oneself how awful they are.
4. The idea that much human unhappiness is externally caused and is forced on one by outside people and events—instead of the idea that virtually all human unhappiness is caused or sustained by the view one takes of things rather than the things themselves.
5. The idea that if something is or may be dangerous or fearsome one should be terribly concerned about it—instead of the idea that if something is or may be dangerous or fearsome one should frankly face it and try to render it non-dangerous and, when that is impossible, think of other things and stop telling oneself what a terrible situation one is, or may be, in.
6. The idea that it is easier to avoid than to face life difficulties and self-responsibilities—instead of the idea that the so-called easy way is invariably the much harder way in the long run and that the only way to solve difficult problems is to face them squarely.
7. The idea that one needs something other or stronger or greater than oneself on which to rely—instead of the idea that it is usually far better to stand on one's own feet and gain faith in oneself and one's ability to meet difficult circumstances of living.
8. The idea that one should be thoroughly competent, adequate, intelligent, and achieving in all possible respects—instead of the idea that one should do rather than always try to do well, and that one should accept oneself as a quite imperfect creature, who has general human limitations and specific fallibilities.
9. The idea that because something once strongly affected one's life, it should indefinitely affect it—instead of the idea that one should learn from one's past experiences but not be overly attached to or prejudiced by them.
10. The idea that it is vitally important to our existence what other people do, and that we should make great efforts to change them in the direction we would like them to be—instead of the idea that other people's deficiencies are largely their problems and that putting pressure on them to change is usually least likely to help them do so.

11. The idea that human happiness can be achieved by inertia and inaction—instead of the idea that humans tend to be happiest when they are actively and vitally absorbed in creative pursuits, or when they are devoting themselves to people or projects outside themselves.
12. The idea that one has virtually no control over one's emotions and that one cannot help feeling certain things—instead of the idea that one has enormous control over one's emotions if one chooses to work at controlling them and to practice saying the right kinds of sentences to oneself (p. 39).

That Ellis is a cognitive therapist is firmly established by his firm language relative to the foolish and damaging conclusions that people draw about themselves and their conditions.

> Rational-emotive therapy, then, takes the radical but hardly revolutionary view (since it was first propounded by the Roman philosopher, Epictetus, some two thousand years ago) that there are virtually no legitimate reasons why human beings need to make themselves terribly upset, hysterical, or emotionally disturbed, no matter what kind of negative stimuli are impinging on them. It gives them full leeway to feel strong emotions, including those of sorrow, regret, displeasure, irritation, annoyance, rebellion, and determination to change social conditions; but it believes that when they experience certain self-defeating and inappropriate emotions as inordinate guilt, depression, anxiety, worthlessness, alienation, and rage, they are almost invariably adding a magical, mystical, and unverifiable hypothesis to their empirically-based view that their own acts or those of others stink and that something had better be done about changing them for the better (1969, p. 84).

The Ellis approach to intervention can be organized mnemonically by the letters *A, B, C, D,* and *E*. For all responses, there is an *A*ctivating event or a stimulus event. For all clients, by definition, there is a Consequent action that is self-defeating; often it is this action or feeling that prompts clients to seek therapy. Unlike the single-stage model that says the response is a result of the stimulus, Ellis recognizes and emphasizes a cognitive mediation referred to as the *B*elief system when the response is adjustive, or the B.S. we tell ourselves when the response is maladaptive. Given a clear definition of C (the consequent act) and the context in which it occurs, and having identified A (the activating event), the therapist looks for B (the belief) that is a logical precursor of C. This belief, illogical in nature if it leads to self-defeat, is then *D*isputed. The disputation/confrontation/challenge is the loosening of structure necessary to make the client receptive to change. After the disputation has produced the loosened structure, the therapist *E*ffects change. This is done by installing a superior and more functional structure and by assigning the client homework to practice its application.

Beck

Aaron T. Beck is a psychiatrist, initially of psychoanalytic persuasion. He was born in July of 1921 in Providence, Rhode Island, to his Russian Jewish immigrant parents. An injury and resulting surgery with near fatal consequences at age seven was prominent in a childhood marked by anxieties. He graduated from Brown University in 1942 and entered Yale for his medical training, which he finished in 1946. At first put off by the psychoanalytic approach to psychiatry, he specialized in neurology. A required rotation as part of his residency took him into psychiatry for six months. Once again he was disappointed in the analytic-dominated program he experienced, yet he was intrigued by the seemingly unitary mindset that was apparent in that approach. Subsequently he accepted a two-year fellowship in psychiatry at the Austin Riggs Center in Massachusetts. Later, after completing board-certification in psychiatry, he became an assistant professor at the University of Pennsylvania. His prior experiences as a psychotherapist for the Army during the Korean conflict provided a broad experiential base for his future work and theorizing (Weishaar, 1993). Growing out of attempts to empiricize Freudian approaches to treatment of depression, he observed consistent discrepancies between client aspiration and client accomplishment. Clients tended to see themselves in a negative light (losers). There often were marked discrepancies between the depressed person's self-evaluation and his or her actual achievements. The obvious conclusion for Dr. Beck was that depression resulted from disturbed thinking—idiosyncratic and negative conclusions about self, situation, and future. This mind set caused or was accompanied by mood, motivation, and response to other people typical of the depressive syndrome.

> Dr. Beck's thesis was simple: (1) When you are depressed or anxious, you are *thinking* in an illogical, negative manner, and you inadvertently act in a self-defeating way. (2) With a little effort you can train yourself to straighten your twisted thought patterns. (3) As your painful symptoms are eliminated, you will become productive and happy again, and you will respect yourself. (4) These aims can usually be accomplished in a relatively brief period of time, using straightforward methods (Burns, 1981, p. 4).

Several principles of cognitive therapy ala Beck include:

- Your emotional as well behavioral responses are created by your cognitions: thoughts and/or perceptions.
- When you are feeling depressed or doing wrong, or poorly, your thoughts are dominated by a pervasive and persistent negativity.
- The negative thoughts that cause your emotional turmoil and problem behavior nearly always contain gross distortions.
- It is possible to feel better; this can occur spontaneously without getting better. Getting better comes from systematically applying and reapplying the methods that produce self-enhancing responses.

Beck identified ten categories of cognitive distortion. They are useful in understanding his model as well as in the process of teaching clients about their own particular ways of sabotaging themselves.

1. ALL-OR-NOTHING THINKING: The tendency to dichotomize conclusions. If not completely successful, then a total disappointment.
2. OVERGENERALIZATION: A single unacceptable event defines the future. One rejection leads to a belief that there will be no acceptances—like asking for a date or sending a book to a publisher.
3. MENTAL FILTER: Focus on a single detail that then becomes the value index for the entire experience. This is common for a musician who ignores 100 well-played measures and dwells on one or two mistakes.
4. DISQUALIFYING THE POSITIVE: Failure to accept the results of successful performance by rationalizing it as lucky, "in the right place at the right time," "the judge felt sorry for me," or that others have done it better or more quickly.

5. JUMPING TO CONCLUSIONS: Arriving at a negative interpretation without data to support the conclusion.
   a. Mind Reading. Attribution of negative and intentional action on the part of another and, usually, no attempt to verify the conclusion (e.g., "You are angry at me", "Why doesn't he do what pleases me? He should know").
   b. The Fortune Teller Error. Predicting a negative outcome and then acting as though the prediction is already true.
6. MAGNIFICATION (CATASTROPHIZING) or MINIMIZATION: An exaggeration of the significance of a personal miscue or of someone else's success, or the opposite—underestimation of one's own positive characteristics and a diminution of the importance of someone else's shortcomings.
7. EMOTIONAL REASONING: The assumption that feelings are an infallible barometer of conditions (e.g., "I feel dumb; therefore I must be").
8. SHOULD STATEMENTS: Assumption of external standards as directives for personal performance. Should, should have, shouldn't have, ought to, must, and must not are self-imposed imperatives that play on shortcomings and elicit guilt feelings. (This is common to Ellis: "I will not should on myself." "Musterbation is self-abuse").
9. LABELLING and MISLABELLING: The tendency to overgeneralize a negative and to attribute personal traits by the use of labels—loser, jerk, nerd, fool. The label miscommunicates the negative action or outcome and attributes unacceptable qulities to the person.
10. PERSONALIZATION: Acceptance of blame for some negative external event for which you were not responsible (e.g., "Something goes wrong every time I am in a hurry.", "This always happens to me.").

Dr. Arthur Freedman, an associate of Dr. Beck, in a workshop setting, explained the relationship between cognitive distortions and underlying schema that gives rise to frequent variations in distortions (see Figure 8.3). In regard to depression, one self-defeating condition for which cognitive therapy has demonstrated success, he indicated that depressed people have distorted cognitions based on maladaptive schemas that provide a downward cycle in the cognitive triad. The cognitive triad includes the person's view of (a) himself or herself, (b) his or her future, and of (c) the world (see Figure 8.4).

The focus of therapy is to help the individual to better understand his or her schemas

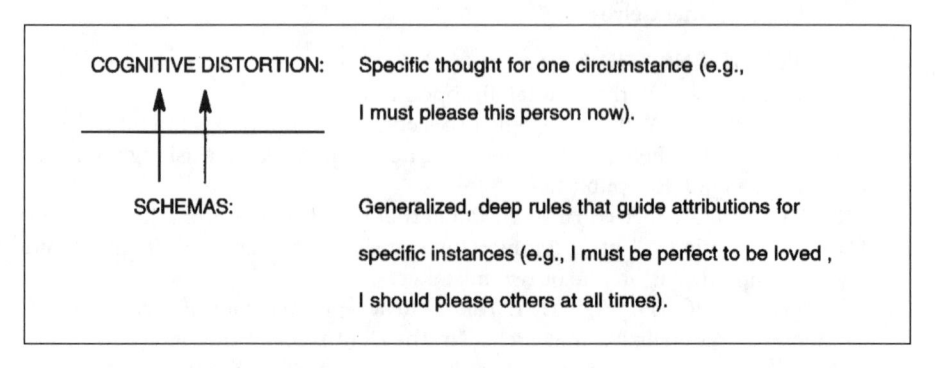

COGNITIVE DISTORTION: Specific thought for one circumstance (e.g.,
                        I must please this person now).

SCHEMAS: Generalized, deep rules that guide attributions for
                        specific instances (e.g., I must be perfect to be loved,
                        I should please others at all times).

FIGURE 8.3. Relationship Between Schemas and Cognitive Distortions.

View of self (Negative)

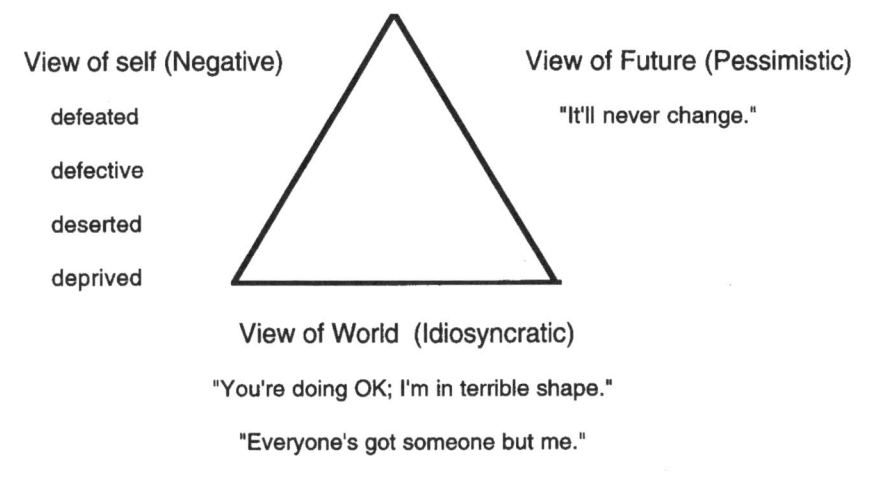

defeated

defective

deserted

deprived

View of Future (Pessimistic)

"It'll never change."

View of World (Idiosyncratic)

"You're doing OK; I'm in terrible shape."

"Everyone's got someone but me."

FIGURE 8.4. Maladaptive Schemas in Depression.

so that he or she can better deal with the distortion. There are four major steps to Beck's approach:

1. Learn to recognize and write down the client's self-critical thoughts.
2. Learn why these thoughts are distorted (label them; give them identity; make them the problem and focus on them).
3. Use a variety of techniques to challenge, weaken, and alter the distortion(s).
4. Teach the client to do the same.

The three-column technique is a good start because thoughts (distortions) often come in bunches. This may explain why a person persists in a negative response set when a friend or other person attacks one's irrationality, as in "Don't be silly! You aren't always incompetent." The triple column helps to sort out and identify the distortions. The client begins with a focus on an undesirable emotional or behavioral response and then identifies the automatic thought that accompanies the response. This thought is categorized into one of the ten types of cognitive distortions and then is restructured into a rational response. Using a chart with three labelled columns is a technique for prompting this sequence (see figure 8.5).

For important conditions, those that occur over time, a daily record of dysfunctional thoughts may provide an indication of patterns that are clues to schemas. An

Automatic Thought	Cognitive Distortion	Rational Response
1.		
2.		
3.		

FIGURE 8.5. Three-Column Technique. Adapted from Burns, 1980, p. 60.

expanded format for recording patterns over an extended period of time includes six column headings: Situation, Emotion(s)/Action(s), Automatic Thought(s), Cognitive Distortion(s), Rational Response(s), and Outcomes.

After recognizing self-centered thoughts, and identifying the distortions, therapy procedures fall into basically two categories: disputing the irrationality (see Figure 8.6) and scaling (see figure 8.7). Additional techniques and examples of their application are in Burns (1981), Chapter 5.

1. But Rebuttal: Write down your "but" statements, then write a rebuttal.

But Column	But Rebuttal
I should... but I'm not in the mood.	I'll feel more like it once I get started.

2. Self-Endorsement: Counter self-downing statements with self-endorsing ones.

Self-downing statement	Self-endorsing statement
It was just luck the way my speech turned out.	It wasn't a matter of luck at all. I prepared well and delivered my speech effectively. I did a damn good job.

3. TIC-TOC Technique: Identify distortions in thinking of task-interfering cognitions and substitute task oriented cognitions.

TICs	TOCs
I'll never be able to get the garage cleaned out. The stuffs been piling up for years.	Overgeneralization; all or nothing thinking. Just do a little bit and get started. There's no reason I have to get it all done today.
My work isn't very important	Disqualifying the positive. It may seem routine to me, but it's quite important to people who depend on its being done. Many people do routine work but that doesn't make them unimportant human beings.

FIGURE 8.6. Methods for Disputing Irrationality (after Burns, 1980, pp. 99–101).

4. Test Your Can'ts: Don't accept self-defeating thoughts of the "I can't..." nature.

   Test them out.

"I Can't" statement.	Putting it to the test.
I'm so upset I can't read anything at all.	Read one sentence from today's newspaper. Summarize it out loud.
But I could never read and understand a whole paragraph.	Read a paragraph and summarize.

5. "Verbal Judo": This is an approach for dealing with criticism from others. It also is a good model for self-disputation.

   a. Identify the negative thoughts you have when you are being criticized, either by someone else or by yourself.

   b. Ask questions to ascertain the critic's motives; try to see the situation through his/her eyes, remembering he/she might be right, wrong, or somewhere in-between.

   "What did I do that...?"   "What is there about me that...?"

   "On what are you basing that conclusion/evaluation...?"

   c. Disarm the critic

   1) Initially find some way to agree with the critic (whether right or wrong).

   2) Avoid sarcasm or defensiveness.

   3) Always speak the truth.

   "You are right. I can be insensitive. Thank you for calling this to my attention."

   d. Feedback and Negotiation: Explain your perceptions and look for a common ground for proceeding.

FIGURE 8.6. Methods for Disputing Irrationality (continued).

Berne

Eric Berne has postulated a personality model, the study of which he called Structural Analysis, and an interpersonal interactions model, the study of which is Transactional Analysis (Berne, 1961). He was born in Montreal, Canada, in 1910. Reportedly, he was close to his father, a doctor, who died at the age of 38 when Eric was nine years old. Berne graduated from McGill University with the M.D. in 1935 and did a psychiatric residency at Yale. He practiced psychoanalysis, having trained with Erik Erikson, until about 1950 when he was rejected for membership in the Psychoanalytic Institute.

The power in scaling is that it demonstrates change without requiring total solution. Complete cure may be inconceivable so improvement is the goal.

1. Pleasure Prediction: To test negative expectations regarding potential future activities, use a pleasure prediction chart and put those perceptions to the test. For example, the prediction might be, "Doing things alone, by myself, is no fun."

Date	Activity for Satisfaction (Sense of achievement or pleasure).	Who did you do this with? If alone, specify self.	Predicted Satisfaction 0-100%	Actual Satisfaction 0-100%

2. Antiprocrastination Sheet: This is a scale for dealing with tasks that tend to get put off because of anticipated difficulty or predicted dissatisfaction. As with other scaling techniques, the task is written down and a prediction of its difficulty and degree of satisfaction is made. The task is then done and evaluated on the same two criteria.

Date	Activity (Break each task down into small steps)	Predicted Difficulty (0-100%)	Predicted Satisfaction (0-100%)	Actual Difficulty (0-100%)	Actual Satisfaction (0-100%)
	1. 2. 3.				

FIGURE 8.7. Scaling Methods. Adapted from Burns, 1980, p. 96.

He then turned to the development of Transactional Analysis (Gladding, 1992). While his structural model is psychodynamic in nature, the objective of his interpersonal interactions model, that which is most appropriate to therapy, is to stabilize control of a person's ego states in the Adult, that part which operates largely on cognitive principles, that is, a logical, principle-mediated, problem-solver. There are three stages in Berne's approach:

1. Teach a cognitive structure that will give the client some awareness and eventual control over his or her psychodynamics and behavior. This involves describing the three ego states—Child, Parent, and Adult—and giving examples of how they inter-

act to define an individual's behavior. This provides clients with definitions and a classification scheme for tracking their own responses and for understanding the responses of others.
2. Help the client to identify referents of each ego state from his or her own behavior. While the actions of the ego states are within consciousness, most clients do not realize that they "come from different places" from time to time. Becoming aware of the psychodynamics of the ego states and labelling their own responses and reactions provides a cognitive model for explaining their own behavior, both of a self-enhancing and of a self-defeating nature.
3. Establish the "executive" power in the Adult ego state and strengthen its functioning therein. While it is psychologically healthy to show a range of responses, including those originating in the Child and in the Parent, it is preferable to have the executive in the Adult for the majority of the time. People who exhibit self-defeating responses often have a weak Adult or a tendency for the executive to reside mostly in either the Child or the Parent. The therapist must teach the client, both cognitively and experientially to "come from the Adult." This is done by the counselor consistently responding from his or her Adult and toward the Adult of the client. The counselor responses are demonstrative of a logical, problem-oriented nature and include instructions to the client as to preferred client behavior.

The interactions between and among most people are marked by a random interrelatedness between ego states of the people involved. If person A comes from his Child with an implicit request to be parented, and if person B comes from her Parent in response, then a consonant transaction occurs. Whenever person B comes from an undesired state, a crossed transaction results along with dissatisfaction and turmoil. In most interrelationships, neither person is in control, hence, the transactions either are fortuitously consonant or unfortunately crossed. Learning to identify one's responses as to ego state of origin and, further, learning to manifest Adult dominance gives the client the power to script successful interactions and to reduce self-defeating actions.

Other Cognitive Interventions

There are several other techniques that operate on cognitive principles and that are used by practitioners of various theoretical persuasions. One of these is an abbreviated approach to restructuring by having a client substitute words prescribed by the counselor for words the client has just used. The following is a list of some words and prescribed substitutions:

Original statement	Substituted statement
"I have to . . ."	"I choose to . . ."
"I must . . ."	"It would be good for me to . . ."
"I should . . ."	"I want to . . ."
"I can't . . ."	"I don't want to . . ."
"Everybody feels . . ."	"I feel . . ."
"You make me (angry)"	"I am feeling (angry)"
"It is terrible . . ."	"It is unfortunate . . ."

Self-help books that are descriptive of problem circumstances and descriptive of procedures for resolution form another somewhat generic cognitive approach. A strength of using such books is in saving therapy time and in providing a manual that can be read and studied according to the client's time schedule and learning style. The major drawbacks are two: (a) many are written to be more entertaining that useful and (b) all must be broad enough to cover a range of readers. If they are used, they must be pre-read by the therapist and prescribed (even structured) for those clients for whom they have a good fit. In other words, they must be used as an adjunct to an ongoing strategy, not as a stand-alone, self-help tool.

☐ Examples

A helpful framework for understanding the following examples is a summary of the intervention strategy given earlier in the chapter:

- Determine the cognitive component and decide if it is a deficit or a surplus concern.
- Identify what the client is doing or not doing that is self-defeating.
- Identify the experiential context in which the undesirable response occurs.
- Determine what rationale the client has to explain his or her response. What rationale is inferred from the behavioral response.
- If the rationale is ill-defined, whimsical, or nonsensical, treat it as a cognitive deficit condition. Teach a cognitive structure that will direct self-enhancing behavior.
- If the rationale is strong and well-defended, treat it as a cognitive surplus condition (i.e., the person believes something that leads to self-defeating responses). The initial step is to loosen the existing cognitive structure, then to introduce a competing structure that is contextually appropriate and logically sound, the use of which rules out the initial structure (mutually exclusive where possible).

Conditions of cognitive deficit seem unusually easy to remedy. They involve a relatively simple process of teaching the client what is missing. It may be that the difficulty comes in recognizing that a deficit occurs. Because the intervention is so simple, in many situations it is employed at the outset. If it works, then the deficit has been filled. If it doesn't work, then the problem is more assuredly a cognitive surplus or an affective or behavioral one.

Clinic: Individual Application, Cognitive Deficit

As an easily identified situation of cognitive deficit, consider the experience of a recent immigrant or of a foreign exchange student from an Eastern European country. The person experiences responses from others of a confusing or mixed acceptance/rejection nature. The person expresses feelings of unsureness, confusion, disappointment, or maybe even anger. When asked about his or her rationale, the person says something like, "I am angry because they are rude, racist, or intolerant. I can't understand why they don't like me." The counselor widens the conceptual focus to consider two sets of dynamics (see Figure 8.8).

Upon further interaction, the counselor discovers that the immigrant bathes infrequently by local standards and has never heard of deodorant. The counselor explains the Western penchant for cleanliness, particularly the tendency to be offended by

Cognitive Learning Approaches 143

Activating event for "others"	➤ The immigrant emits body odor.
Belief of "others"	➤ The immigrant should be like us.
Consequential action of "others"	➤ They act ambivalently toward the immigrant.
Activating event for immigrant	➤ "Others" being ambivalent toward him or her.
Belief of immigrant	➤ No belief or inconsistent conclusion--deficit.
Consequential action of immigrant	➤ Feelings of unsureness, confusion, disappointment

FIGURE 8.8. Immigrant Cognitive Deficit.

odor, and teaches the immigrant about customary hygienic practices and the use of toiletries. The counselor is careful to express no value judgments of either culture's standard of hygiene and schedules several contacts over the following few days to monitor the immigrant's social stimulus effect and to give feedback about hygiene and any other culturally-bound action that may result in mixed responses from others.

Clinic: Individual Application, Cognitive Surplus

Jane completed her training to become a nurse and took the state examination four months ago. Since that time she has experienced personal illness and has had to deal with several family crises that prevented her from seeking a job. Now her circumstances are favorable but she cannot bring herself to complete applications for work. She says things such as, "I don't think I'm competent enough to be a nurse. I can't handle the responsibility. The patients will know that I am insecure. The supervisors will get on my case for mistakes and will have me fired." The following explanation of intervention uses the Consequence, Activating event, Belief system, and Disputation structure of REBT.

C: Resistance to completing application; statements critical of her ability; negative predictions of performance and conditions (catastrophizing).
A: Opportunity to apply for work.
B: As verbalized by Jane, "I am not good enough." As inferred by the counselor, "I have to be perfect."

The counselor used several questioning and challenging techniques to loosen Jane's cognitive structure (D). For example:

C: *"Did you go through a good training program?"*
J: *"Yes, a very good program."*
C: *"How well did you complete the requirements?"*
J: *"I was second in my class."*
C: *"How did you do in the state exam?"*
J: *"They told me 95th percentile. I think that's pretty good isn't it?"*

C: "Do you know any of your classmates who are working as nurses?"

J: "Yes, most of them got jobs right after the exam."

C: "Some who did less well than you are working?"

J: "Yes."

C: "In your training, did you hear of any nurses making mistakes?"

J: "Yes. Nurses are human and fallible at times."

C: "Have you ever been yelled at for making a mistake?"

J: "Yes."

C: "Did you live through it? Did it leave scars?"

J: "No. In fact, I needed the feedback. I'd rather be yelled at than to be allowed to continue to make the mistake."

C: "So you're telling me that you are well-trained; you passed the exam with a high score; you aren't perfect, but then you know of nurses who have made mistakes; you've been corrected in the past with positive results. Your credentials suggest that you are qualified to begin your career, and you predict that you will have strict supervisors who will correct you over the rough spots. The probability is that you won't be perfect, and that you will continue to do as well or better than most. How are you really going to know whether or not you can do it?"

J: "I guess by trying it out. But it will be so hard!"

C: "Have you ever tried to do anything hard before?"

J: "Yes. Nurses training was really hard."

C: "And you succeeded, even though it was hard?"

With Jane's structure effectively loosened, it was relatively simple to install a functional structure and to support her in her effort to get a job. The counselor said something like, "You are as well educated as most new applicants. You are a hard worker and have accomplished difficult tasks. You see advantages to having strict supervisors who will hold you to a high level of performance. You probably will make some mistakes at first; you're human and fallible, like other nurses. The probability is that you won't be the perfect nurse at first, and that you will develop your competence with experience."

Clinic: Group Application, Cognitive Deficit

It is important to remember that group intervention is really individual intervention in a group setting. Not all participants will have the same consequential responses nor the same beliefs. Effectiveness will be a function of the similarities in participants and/or the competence and flexibility of the group leader in managing several different interactions alternatively.

You have been contracted to conduct a pre-retirement seminar for a group of company employees who are three to five years away from retirement. If they are typical, they have big gaps in their knowledge about retirement. You will arrange for a financial planner to educate them on options within the pension plan. They will need to anticipate projections in inflation, and to realize that the health insurance that was provided by the employer will continue only if they pay for it, a several thousand dollar per year expenditure. You will educate them regarding the increased probability of physical decline and illness. You will give them insight regarding changes in social interactions; for example, their vocation—that which gave so much structure to their time and identity will carry virtually no weight in future interactions; after the 30 second response to the question, "What did you used to be/do?", the substance of what one is at this time comes into play. You will install a cognitive structure about the advantages of planning now for the predictable adjustments, and you may provide some resources to help them plan.

Clinic: Group Application, Cognitive Surplus

Stanley agreed to conduct seminars in human communication training to a group of career non-commissioned personnel at the local military base. Because of limited funds, the officer in charge determined that those needing it the most would be selected to participate. The seminars were to be offered during regular duty hours and without any extra help to the units represented by the participants; this meant that the same amount of work had to be accomplished even though the participants, many of them supervisors in charge, would be absent three hours a day for two weeks. At the opening session, even before introduction were completed, it became obvious to Stanley that there was intense resistance on the part of the participants to being required to attend without their compliance and having to maintain work quotas in their absence. Once again the adaptation of Ellis's A, B, C, D system is used to organize the intervention dynamics.

> C: Surly looks, gruff and brief replies, criticism of the system, challenges to Stanley's initiatives in getting the program going.
> A: A seminar to which they had been directed and taught by a person they didn't know. Required absence from their work setting without compensating help or reduction in expectations.
> B: Beliefs of participants: "The officers are stupid. The system is messed up. Other people who are not as important as I should be here. This is another waste of time and resources."
> B: Participants' beliefs, as inferred by Stanley: "They must think I need this stuff, that I am not doing my job well. I am here to be corrected or punished."

Stanley made some paraphrases of the situation to the participants. He said things such as, "You are not too pleased to be here. It's almost like your superiors think you need to be fixed, that something is wrong with you. It's unfair to send you away for treatment and not give you any help in getting the work done. How foolish of them to believe you are not competent and, at the same time, make it harder to be effective by taking you off the job for three hours a day." This line of statements was validated by a change in attention on the part of participants and comments such as, "Right on!" "You got that right."

The next step was to loosen the structure (D). Stanley said, "I wonder if there is another explanation for your being here. Maybe it's because you are weak or incompetent in these areas, in which case I really have my work cut out for me. I've got two weeks to fix you, and you don't want to be fixed. Another possibility is that only those people were selected who showed the most promise of making significant improvement in a relatively short time and, also, those who are capable of managing their work requirements effectively under hardship conditions. Maybe your presence here is a compliment. In that case, I have a delightful task."

Effecting change (E) consisted of creating a structure that resolved some of the dissonance that Stanley had just created and providing a functional structure that would maximize his success and that of the participants. He said, "Maybe you are here to be fixed. Maybe you are here to make a meaningful contribution to the mission. Maybe some of you are here for one reason and some for the other. Maybe there is another reason, totally different from those we've considered. I don't suppose we'll ever know for sure. I suppose that, whatever the reason for our selection, we have the opportunity to make the most of it or to sabotage it. My guess is that each of us stands to benefit more, personally, if we work at getting some benefit from the experience. My choice is to believe that you have the potential to learn and to apply these important and useful skills, so I'm going to give it my best shot in teaching you."

Classroom: Individual Application, Cognitive Deficit

Sandra Smythe is the teacher of a fourth grade class in the Bennion Elementary School. It was the middle of the fourth week since school began. She was feeling pretty comfortable with her perception of most of the students. One in particular, Joan Jantzen, baffled her. Joan was a little taller than the other girls in the class, though not extremely so. Developmentally, she appeared to be showing secondary sexual characteristics and Sandra noted that she was one of the older children in the class. Developmentally, she appeared to be on or ahead of schedule. She was not very responsive in class, electing to let others participate (which not as many did as Sandra was used to). When Sandra called on her to answer questions or contribute her opinion from the reading assignment, she did so without much hesitation and with generally correct or constructive responses. When Sandra stopped her after class and said, "I noticed you do not take part in class unless called upon, and I was wondering why," she just shrugged her shoulders and said, "I don't know," and walked out. Sandra consulted the school psychologist for help with Joan.

C: Absence of spontaneous class participation.
A: Periods of open class discussion or of teacher-initiated, general questions directed to no particular student.
B: "I don't know." [This could be an indication of cognitive deficit or of a typical ten-year old's way of avoiding the issue. The teacher could engage the student in further exploratory interactions, such as talking with her about past classes and how she responded in them.]
D: With no evidence of a competing cognitive structure and a hesitancy to assume one that may be incorrect, the school psychologist recommended that no disputation be made. Instead it was decided to move ahead as though it were a cognitive deficit.
E: The teacher was directed to tell Joan, or even to make it a general class instruction, the following: "Teaching is a very interesting and challenging job. I want to do it well because I care about you and your accomplishments. There is one thing you can do to help me. You see, I can't know what is going on in your mind unless you tell me. I don't always remember to call on each student often enough, and there are times when you have something to contribute to the class or can help me understand what you are learning even when I don't call on you. I would like you to raise your hand at least twice or until I have called on you during general participation periods. Will you do that to help me?"

Within a few weeks, Joan frequently was offering to answer questions and she was giving multiple word responses. Sandra was pleased with Joan's progress and had to remind herself not to favor Joan with more attention at the expense of other students. The teacher invited Joan to journal her responses when she wasn't called on and to include them in written assignments.

Classroom: Individual Application, Cognitive Surplus

The same apparent behavioral manifestation may arise from a different set of dynamics. Shortly after Sandra's success with Joan, Sandra's spouse, Sam, also a teacher, encountered a similar lack of responsiveness in one of his eighth grade students, Jasper. Like Joan, Jasper was physically ahead of his classmates and he tested above average on the scholastic aptitude tests. Though in the eighth grade, Jasper actively affiliated with a group of ninth grade students, none of whom were academically accomplished. There was almost a duality in his responses when Sam called upon him; his answers were complete and accurate, yet his delivery of them was almost sarcastic in nature. Without further analysis, Sam applied his wife's strategy to the class as a whole. The effect was to increase the enthusiasm and involvement of the already active students, and to reduce Jasper's voluntary involvement.

Sam consulted the school counselor, who promptly reviewed Jasper's records, made some classroom observations and interviewed Jasper. Jasper's responses indicated some turmoil relative to academics with a very strong statement that his friends disapproved of any energy invested in academic achievement and especially belittled "showing-off and kissing-up behavior." There also were indications of strong peer-group loyalty norms.

- C: Absence of spontaneous class participation and sullen or sarcastic yet correct answers when pushed to respond.
- A: Periods of open class discussion or of teacher-initiated, general questions directed to no particular student and/or direct quizzing of students in group setting.
- B: Of Jasper: "It's not good to show off in class. It's not okay to get good grades. It's not good to be liked by your teacher."
- B: Jasper's beliefs as inferred by the school counselor: "My friends will reject me if I do well in school. I must maintain my affiliation with this particular group."
- D: Given the presence of strong mediating beliefs with behavior that was consistent with those beliefs, the strategy for cognitive surplus was indicated. (This could be dealt with as a perceptual issue of competing frames—one suggested by the correctness of responses and the other by the sarcastic response style. The counselor could work the split in order to contrast the wish to do well and get adult approval against the wish to do poorly and get peer approval. Developmentally, these dynamics represent a time of strong influence by peers with one option being to tolerate Jasper's performance, assuming that he will grow out of it. It can be seen, also, as an opportune time to structure internal locus of control, though developmentally this is a bit premature. The counselor elected to work through the teacher to build a non-contingent relationship, loosen Jasper's structure, give several alternatives, and to help Jasper through the decision-making and to follow his progress.)

The lines of structural loosening went something like this:
(a) "Your friends will reject you if you do well in school? How do you know? Have you tried? What have you tried? You haven't negotiated with them?"
(b) "It would be terrible if your friends rejected you. You couldn't get along without them. Has there ever been a time that you didn't have a group? And what happened? Apparently you lived through it. It was tough, but you managed relatively well?"
(c) "What would be the *worst* thing that could happen if you honestly put lots of effort into school work? You probably would do very well? I would give you lots of attention and your friends would make fun of you and stop letting you go places with them. And if that happened . . .? What is the *best* thing that could happen if you honestly put lots of effort into school work? You probably would do very well? I would give you lots of attention and your friends would say that they wished they could do as well as you and accept you as you are? And if that happened...? What *probably* would happen if you honestly put lots of effort into school work? You probably would do very well? I would give you lots of attention and some of your friends would make fun of you while others wouldn't care; eventually you would grow away from that group? And if that happened . . .?

E: The teacher then phrased some conclusions that would help reduce the dissonance for Jasper and, hopefully give Jasper some way of moving from his "stuck" position: "You are being dishonest with me, with your friends, and mostly with yourself by not being how you really are. If you be yourself more openly, your friends might reject you, or they might make fun of you but still accept you, or they might not care. If they reject you, it would feel bad for awhile and you would get over it. You could make a deal with me to not call on you in class and to let you do written work so your friends would not know, but that would be dishonest. It's hard to be yourself when others want you to be different. It's hard not to be the person you know you are. It's hard to know what to do, and yet you want to do the right thing, right now. What if we work together on this for the rest of the year? You can think it over; you can try some different ways of being; we can discuss what is going on. I am going to like you and to do what I can to help you be successful, whether or not you choose to participate in class. Maybe I can be sort of a friend to help you work through this."

The counselor could have chosen to work directly with Jasper, moving the strategy outside of the classroom. She chose to involve Sam in the therapy because of his frequent contact with Jasper, because he had a supportive attitude and students generally liked him, and because she believed Jasper would respond better to a man than to her at this time. Sam continued to call on Jasper with about the same frequency as before, but qualified his requests to give Jasper a choice whether or not to respond: "Jasper, would you be willing to share your answer?" "Jasper, can you help us out with this answer?", etc. Jasper declined to respond for a time, yet the sullen and sarcastic tone faded. Gradually he contributed when asked; eventually he volunteered. Concurrent with his gradual change in class, Jasper shifted his involvement from the previous group to another group in which he was more compatible.

Classroom: Group Application, Cognitive Deficit

There is a tendency for people in general to operate as though everyone has the same perception of a universal reality. Teachers with this tendency become concerned or disturbed at students whose behavior doesn't fit their perceptual frame. One approach to the beginning of a new school year that is touted informally by veteran teachers is, "Be really tough, really strict for the first six weeks, then you can ease up and the students will behave." This is a behavioral method that works for many teachers. Six weeks of conditioning, even when poorly managed—inconsistently applied reinforcers—will condition most students. An alternative approach is to recognize that every beginning is a new experience, that each teacher operates differently from every other teacher, and that it is necessary to teach students how to be "your" students. In other words, students will not know the ground rules until they are taught the ground rules. With upper elementary and secondary students, the installation of cognitive guidelines generally enables the students to work the rules in their own behalf and to assimilate them more quickly than through the six week trial-and-error approach.

With any system of rules there comes a system of outcomes—contingencies. Perhaps the difference in filling a cognitive deficit and doing a behavioral intervention comes in enlisting the awareness of the students in installing the system. The contingencies still need to function in order to maintain the system.

Establishing ground rules need be no more complicated than saying to the students something like, "Every successful venture has rules to govern it. My rules for this class probably are a little different from others you may have experienced before. There are a few set rules and there are some areas in which you will have a say. The set rules include:

- We will address each other with respect . . .
- You are responsible for . . .
- I will . . .

"The positive and negative results from response to the basic rules are . . .

"The rules and consequences are posted on the bulletin board near the door. Additional rules we make as a class will be posted with them.

"Here are several areas in which rules can be created by the class. Let's spend some time suggesting ways we can manage them. During the coming few days we will review and refine them. Periodically we will discuss how they are working for us."

Classroom: Group Application, Cognitive Surplus

While cognitive intervention is ultimately a personal focus, there occurs shared conclusions in groups of people for which a group intervention is appropriate. Many times the result of such group indoctrination is inaction: "The environment is in danger but nobody can do anything about it, or we can't do anything about it, or somebody else has the power to fix it and they aren't doing anything about it." "Television fare is regressive and teaches anti-social behavior, but we can't do anything about it." If, in fact, nothing can be done about it, then doing nothing is the logical response whenever concern is focused on the issue. Much of the time this remains an untested belief.

150 Intervention Theories

There are examples of indoctrination that produce action, including the sacrifice of life as a logical extension of the belief. Whether the actions of Kamikaze pilots were an act of honor or of stupidity can be evaluated only from within a belief system that supports it or refutes it. Perhaps most acts of war happen as an extension of a belief system that says, "We are right and they are wrong," and that come under analysis as the perception of history changes in light of successive events or of successive societal biases.

An example of a belief system that is less controversial than war or media evils or environmental abuses is the belief that "Since nothing good has ever come out of Hilliard High School, nothing ever will." For students caught in such an ideological delusion, depressed efforts and low expectations are logical responses: "Why should I aspire? It's hopeless. I am inadequate. If I were worth anything, I would be somewhere else. Since I am here with all these losers, I must be a loser too."

There are two potential cognitive surplus beliefs in this pattern, neither of which is being tested, nor is the combination being tested.

C: Absence of effort to accomplish even low academic goals, let alone to excel. Generalized self-criticism and excuse making for lack of achievement in all areas of life and across all students.
   A: School settings, and generalized to non-school opportunities.
   B: (1) "Nothing good has ever come out of Hilliard High School."
   (2) "Nothing good ever will come out of Hilliard High School."
   These stated beliefs are a collective conclusion for the individual beliefs that include: "I will not/cannot succeed. It is hopeless for me to try. There is no way I can break the pattern."
D: The disputation of the first conclusion is to ask, "How do you know that nothing good has ever come out of Hilliard High School?" Then have the students conduct a thorough follow-up study of former students. This is an empirical reality check, the likely outcome of which is that many exceptions to the assumed rule would be found. The second conclusion can be disputed independently of the first. It is an "if . . . then" proposition: "If I go to Hilliard High School, then I will be a failure in life." Students can be asked to generate other "if . . . then" experiences that have been violated: "Who can give an example of expectations that were violated?" This could result in a wide range of examples such as, "Everybody said the movie was terrible, but I enjoyed it"; "I expected Hawaii to be wonderful, but when I went there with my family I was really disappointed."
E: The dissonance of a presumed inviolable rule with lots of examples of exceptions to rules lays the foundation for a resolution such as, "There is an exception to every rule. Whether or not anything good has ever come out of Hilliard High School, it is possible for me to be an exception; it is possible for all of us to be exceptions; it is possible to change the rule." These are hypotheses to be tested. A group of students challenged to help each other test the rule would increase the probability of improved performance on the part of all of them and some truly outstanding accomplishments on the part of some of them.

☐ Sample Problem Situations

Again there is a prescribed pattern for approaching the following situations. It is recommended that you (a) list the principles involved in resolution of cognitive deficit or cognitive surplus problems, (b) create change procedures for a given sample problem, and (c) review the steps of your procedure with your list of dynamics.

It Won't Happen To Me

You are part of a multi-disciplinary team assigned to work with a group of at-risk teenagers concerning pregnancy, sexually transmitted disease, and drug abuse. Although all of the teens are knowledgeable about prevention and abuse in these areas, all behave as though they believe, "It won't happen to me."

It's a Mistake

You are the therapist in a hospital for the mentally ill. You are running a group with a variety of patients. One, a newcomer, says to you, "I'm here by mistake. This group is for crazy people and I'm not like them."

My Children Won't Like Me

Mary Beth is caught up in a competition with her ex-spouse over who is the better parent. She complains to you about being unable to control her children and resists any suggestions regarding the setting and monitoring of limits because if she does so, "My children won't like me."

Nobody Can Ever Love Me

John is a university senior, approaching graduation. He has distinguished himself for academic excellence in two majors: philosophy and computer science. Throughout his life he has had to cope with extreme and gross physical deformities resulting from a congenital malady. Though he seems to have compensated well in academics, he believes that employers will not hire him and that finding a mate is a hopeless task. He wants desperately to be close to others, but avoids any but the most superficial of social interactions because, "Nobody can ever love me."

I'm Just No Good

Jason has just been released from prison, paroled after seven years of a twenty-years-to-life sentence for killing his two-year-old child while in a drunken stupor. Even though he was a model prisoner, did the twelve-step recovery routine, and completed one year of college work by correspondence while in "the joint," he is depressed and despondent upon being released. He says, "What's the use? I'm just no good."

He's Got No Sense

Buford is a fourth-generation Georgian. His grandfather, an inveterate raccoon hunter, used to relate stories about the great hunts in his day, giving incredible detail to the finer points of the sport. Not inclined himself to be very talkative and not having hunted for several years because of work conflicts, he was now excitedly engaged, with his older brothers, their sons, and his own 12-year old son (a first timer) in the first stages of the hunt. His son has been making numerous mistakes and shows no sensitivity to hunting etiquette nor to the other hunters. Buford says to his brother, "I don't know what's wrong with that kid. He's just got no hunting sense, nohow!"

I'm Really Stuck

It is the fourth week of the term. Suzette is taking a research class. One of the assignments is to come up with a research question and at least one testable hypothesis by the fourth week of the term. She has been trying hard for the entire four weeks and has made no progress at all.

What's the Triad?

Sam Brown's company transferred him from its Juneau office to its plant in Greensboro, North Carolina. He and his family made the relocation just in time for school to start in September. It was his belief that the adjustment was going very well, even though he had put most of his energy and time into professional concerns. Earlier today, as he was getting ready to leave for work, he encountered a major conflict between his wife and their 10-year old son. Andrew, the son, had been slow to get out of bed, had dragged through breakfast and getting ready, and then refused to go to school. Sam didn't have time to work through the problem, but he did get from his son the information that, "I have to do a report on the Piedmont Triad. When I asked 'What is that?' my teacher and friends laughed at me and said 'Go home. It'll come to you'." Not having an immediate answer for his son, Sam told him and his mother to work it out, and he left for work.

Divorce Is Not An Option

Sandra is a thirty-year old student in her junior year. In the process of discussing her career plans, she breaks down and discloses some major marital problems. Her husband has been physically abusive for several years. The most graphic example she gave was of a recent episode where, in the middle of the night with sub-zero temperatures and snow on the ground, he pushed her onto the front porch, locked the doors and went to bed. She was clad only in her nightgown. Somehow she made it to a friend's house, made an excuse for her circumstance and stayed the night with the friend. When asked about her options, she had none, stating especially and emphatically, "We have not had a divorce in our family for thirty generations!"

PART III

CONTEXTUAL CONCERNS

CHAPTER 9

Contextual Issues: Circumstance and Style—Personality and Developmental Dynamics

People learn their way through life. Development of skills, abilities, and behavioral repertoire comes through learning. Self-defeating responses and inappropriate ways of dealing with challenges are learned. Intervention techniques are little more than teaching techniques geared to produce self-enhancing learned responses to replace problematic ones. So far, this text has described four major types of learning families, each with slightly different dynamics and each particularly useful for producing specific types of response. It would be relatively easy to identify cognitive deficits or surpluses, or behavioral deficits or surpluses, and then apply an integrally-sound intervention to rectify the identified condition were it not for a number of confounding variables. People are individual, unique, and different one from another in many ways, all of which impact the intervention process. Four categories of individual differences will be considered as contextual issues, things that need to be taken into account when personalizing an intervention strategy for each particular client. These are personality, developmental, social, and spiritual dynamics. The first two will be treated in this chapter, with social and spiritual dynamics being the focus of Chapter 10.

Contextual issues are client variables that mandate modification of learning-based intervention strategies. They further define the circumstance and style of the client. Personality models are included in this category, even though they may not be a pure representation of current context. In actuality, personality models reflect what a client brings to his or her circumstance as a result of past experience and as a manifestation of personal style dynamics. Personality is an inclusive overlay that permeates individual perception, interpretation, and response across contexts. Because it is a modifier of intervention strategy, it is included here along with the three areas that have previously been identified as "contexts." Because it provides clarity for the counselor in understanding client behavior, an understanding of some personality models is considered to be of importance to the practicing therapist.

☐ Personality

Chapter 2 introduced the idea of individual problem-solving style and suggested that there are four types: cognitive, affective, behavioral, and perceptual. Adler (Ansbacher & Ansbacher, 1956) indicated that each person has a particular life style that is established early in life and usually as a result of family context. Seligman (1991a) spoke of attributional styles, the knowledge of which allows an understanding of why certain individuals behave as they do. Fromm (1941) posited two prime motivational needs in people: (a) the need to join, and (b) the need to individuate. External versus internal locus of control, field dependency versus field independency in perception, and continuing negative influence from childhood trauma versus the individual's ability to adapt and move on are all observations about personality dynamics that may affect therapeutic intervention.

Maddi (1968) categorized many personality theories into three groups, according to the basic motivation or tension perceived to exist within each model: conflict models, fulfillment models, and consistency models. The first group, conflict models, included Freud, Murray, Sullivan, and Rank. The basic motivational power comes from the presence of oppositional forces within the individual. Behavior is an expression of the person's attempt to manage those oppositional forces. Freud postulated an *id* and a *superego*, both unconscious and both driving forces for the individual. Murray subscribed to a psychoanalytic position of the person trying to maximize instinctual gratification while minimizing punishment and guilt. He softened the classical Freudian position by positing a broader number of basic needs and allowing for motivation to spring from conscious awareness of needs. He allowed for rational thought and accurate perception as dynamics in resolution of life problems. Sullivan was not as firmly oppositional as were Freud and Murray. His force comes largely from a need to achieve satisfaction (biological), gain security (psychological), and maneuver in a social context (sociological). Rank wrote of two opposing fears: the fear of life and the fear of death. These are loosely translated with life representing separation from others and individuation, and death meaning union, fusion, dependency (becoming lost in others).

Fulfillment models include those of Rogers, Maslow, Adler, Allport, and Fromm. Rogers talked of "becoming" (1961) in reference to an inborn motivation to fulfill the nature of one's existence, having to combat defensiveness and the restraints of environment on the path of becoming. Similarly, Maslow (1962) put self-actualization at the top of his developmental model (to be considered later in this chapter). There are instinctoid needs and the need to actualize; pursuit of "B-values," or being-values, is the force at the top of his system—we strive to actualize, to be our uniqueness. Adler believed in a striving toward superiority or perfection, as embodied in his concept of fictional finalism. Forces that militate against this accomplishment include family constellation factors, organ inferiority translated to skills and talents, and perceptions of inferiority leading to compensation or overcompensation. Allport put the *proprium* or self at the center of his system and saw the basic motivation as functioning in a manner so as to be expressive of the self. He talked of constructs such as sense of body, self-identity, self-esteem, self-extension, rational coping, self-image, and propriate striving. Fromm (1941) postulated turmoil between the inevitability of being separate from others and the desire to be a comfortable part of something. The escape from freedom could be seen as a universal striving toward fulfillment of a human nature, which is pro-social.

Consistency models include those of Kelly and McClelland, who share the belief that people are motivated to resolve inconsistencies in living, dissonances, by which biological and emotional resolution are achieved. This is a kind of experiential homeostasis model. Kelly describes the adjustment process in terms of cognitive constructs that result from encountering problems, gathering data, making hypotheses, testing these hypotheses, and thus evolving a set of responses that produce or maintain consistency. McClelland focuses on positive affect as an indicator of satisfaction and recognizes that small discrepancies often are sought out and enjoyed, whereas large inconsistensies threaten stability, produce negative affect, and are to be avoided. The consistency aspect for McClelland is between expectation and experience. The highest degree of consistency is experienced by individuals who create expectations (hypotheses?) that are realistic in terms of their abilities and their contexts. The similarity of parts of these models with learning theories such as Festinger's and Försterling's is obvious and stands as one example of the need to consider both personality and learning models in the creation and application of intervention strategies.

In educational psychology there has been an evolution of focus on learning styles. Kagan (1971) was an early theorist who postulated two continua of learning approaches—thematic/analytic and impulsive/reflective—and classified individuals according to their behavior on each. For instance, they might be thematic–impulsive or analytic–reflective. Dunn (1978, 1995), Dunn and Dunn (1977, 1988), and Dunn and Griggs (1995) identified 21 factors of influence on learning style.

Obviously there is an incredible amount of information represented in the foregoing summary. Less obvious, yet important, is the fact that any abstraction that incorporates diverse theories into few categories may do injustice to some or all. The Maddi categories, the learning styles references, and the brief introductions serve to call attention to personality and learning style factors that need to be accounted for in selection or modification of intervention strategies. More, and more thorough, study of some or all of the above models is warranted. For the purpose of this treatise, and as a general referent for personality theory, the following brief description is given for Personal Commitment, an integrative model (Gerber, 1991):

> There are four parts to the Personal Commitment model, each representing a qualitatively different reason for behavior. The first represents what is probably a near absence of commitment or, perhaps, a primitive commitment to emotional self-preservation. It is best described by the concept of learned helplessness (Seligman, 1975). Overt behavior is limited or severely restricted. Emotional response is avoided or suppressed. The pattern is one of clinical depression. "My actions will be futile, so I won't take any action at all." The self-preservation nature of this position is that it's better to expect nothing and be correct in my expectation than to believe that I will be successful in my efforts and be disappointed.
>
> The second type to be considered is reactional or other-directed behavior. This is evidenced by an extreme sensitivity to social situations. Fitting in, doing the "right things", and avoidance of unacceptable or gauche behavior describes the objective for people who operate within this style. The structure or direction exists in the environment. The person is sensitive and reactive to cues for propriety which are communicated by the environment. Situational ethics provide the value base for this type of commitment. The ultimate in other-directedness is to be flexible enough to satisfy the expectations of a frequently changing environment. Such adaptability precludes any kind of internal consistency, hence this type is also addressed by the label, empty people.
>
> Third is a style of response labelled conditioned commitment. Based on influence early

in life, this type of person shows incredible persistence and goal directedness. Many of the world's great achievers behave as though they were scripted or programmed for one purpose in life. The corporate clones which Gail Sheehy addresses in *Passages* (1976), the Mozarts and Joan of Arcs of the world, all represent high intensity, *conditioned* commitment. The model of transactional analysis (Berne, 1961) will serve well to elucidate this style, in particular the references to parental ego states which direct the behavior of some people. To a certain extent, conditioned commitment is an other-directed style. The impetus and direction come from outside the person; however, they are implanted deeply into the value and motivational systems so that there is a very high degree of internal consistency and inflexibility in the behavior of the person. That the response set is free from immediate environmental influence can be seen, for example, in frequent encounters with people who are ensnared in attempts to please a parent, even though that parent is long since deceased.

Personal commitment is marked by behavior that has a unifying theme or style, but which is selectively variable. There is a well-developed internal system, but it is in process and open to selective modification. The personally committed person shows neither the chameleon adaptability of the other-directed nor the inflexibility of the conditioned style. Personal responsibility and decision, a process orientation, marks personal commitment. This person believes in choice, uses opportunities to choose, and accepts responsibility for the choices made (pp. 139–140).

The use of a personality and or learning styles model is helpful in understanding individual differences in clients, and for successful modification of the appropriate learning-based intervention.

In years past, therapy was seen as a process directed at bringing about changes in personality. Whether it was because therapeutic approaches were inefficient or that personality change required a protracted period of therapy, it was not unusual for therapy to be conducted on a weekly or more frequent schedule for four or five years. The current emphasis on brief therapy precludes working toward personality change, although any kind of learning that reduces self-defeat will have some impact on personality. Whether or not personality change is the target, it is important to take personal style factors into consideration when developing intervention strategies.

☐ Development

One of the abstract definitional differences between clinical and counseling psychology is the preference of the latter to ground itself in the normal process of human development and deal with clients as people who have varied from the norm, as opposed to seeing clients as people who possess some malady, illness, or trait which identifies them as deviant. As people develop through the various ages and stages of life, they meet challenges or crises (Gilligan, 1982; Havighurst, 1949; Levinson, 1978; Sheehy, 1976) that sometimes require outside assistance. Preventive mental health is concerned with anticipating and teaching for such transitions.

Developmental status is significant in identifying the problem dynamics encountered by people at various stages of progress, as well as clarifying anomalies of development which may typify a given client. It is also significant in classifying the kinds of abilities available to people of different ages. Piaget (1952) and his disciples have empirically demonstrated that there are qualitative differences in the cognitive abilities of children as they grow from very young to at least adolescence. Such data as that produced by Piaget supports the author's contention that the intervention of choice for children up to 8 years of age (+/- 2 years) and of people with corresponding mental capacity is either some form of operant conditioning or perceptual framing.

Five models of development that are useful as general referents in counseling interventions are Havighurst, Piaget, Erickson, Maslow, and Perry. Brief biographical data will be provided for each theorist and some implication of each relative to modifications across stages or ages in intervention strategies will be given.

Havighurst

Robert Havighurst (1949, 1959, 1973) is known for his emphasis on developmental tasks. Of basic importance is his belief that people learn their way through life. Development is a product of physiological maturation combined with experience and learning. Formally, the developmental task is defined as:

> a task which arises at or about a certain period in the life of the individual, successful achievement of which leads to his happiness and to success with later tasks, while failure leads to unhappiness in the individual, disapproval by society, and difficulty with later tasks (Havighurst, 1949, p. 2).

Havighurst uses observations from embryology as the analog or metaphor for his theorizing. He writes:

> The prototype of the developmental task is the purely biological formation of organs in the embryo. In this development each organ has its time of origin and this time factor is as important as the place of origin. If the eye, for example, does not arise at the appointed time it will never be able to express itself fully, since the time for the rapid outgrowth of some other part will have arrived, and this will tend to dominate the less active region, and suppress the tendency for belated eye expression (Havighurst, 1949, p. 2).

Some tasks arise from physical maturation. Others come from cultural pressures of society. A third source is comprised of the personal values and aspirations of the individual, from the personality. An awareness of typical developmental concerns at various stages of development provides a counselor with a broadened awareness of the developmental context, of issues that impinge on the client. Some of these may be delayed and problematic developmental tasks while others comprise "competition" for the resolution of the problem tasks or of other difficulties of personal adjustment.

Havighurst provides lists of developmental tasks according to six periods. The periods and their tasks are as follows:

Infancy and Early Childhood (birth to 6 years)
1. Learning to take solid foods
2. Learning to walk
3. Learning to talk
4. Learning to control the elimination of body wastes
5. Learning sex differences and sexual modesty
6. Achieving physiological stability
7. Forming simple concepts of social and physical reality
8. Learning to relate oneself emotionally to parents, siblings, and other people
9. Learning to distinguish right and wrong and developing a conscience

Middle Childhood (6 to 12 years)
1. Learning physical skills necessary for ordinary games
2. Building wholesome attitudes toward oneself as a growing organism
3. Learning to get along with age-mates
4. Learning an appropriate masculine or feminine social role
5. Developing fundamental skills in reading, writing, and calculating
6. Developing concepts necessary for everyday living
7. Developing conscience, morality, and a scale of values
8. Achieveing personal independence
9. Developing atitudes toward social groups and institutions

Adolescence (12 years to ?)
1. Achieving new and more mature relations with age-mates of both sexes
2. Achieving a masculine or feminine social role
3. Accepting one's physique and using the body effectively
4. Achieving emotional independence of parents and other adults
5. Achieving assurance of economic independence
6. Selecting and preparing for an occupation
7. Preparing for marriage and family life
8. Developing intellectual skills and concepts necessary for civic competence
9. Desiring and achieving socially responsible behavior
10. Acquiring a set of values and an ethical system as a guide to behavior

Early Adulthood
1. Selecting a mate
2. Learning to live with a marriage partner
3. Starting a family
4. Rearing children
5. Managing a home
6. Getting started in an occupation
7. Taking on civic responsibility
8. Finding a congenial social group

Middle Age
1. Achieving adult civic and social responsibility
2. Establishing and maintaining an economic standard of living
3. Assisting teen-age children to become responsible and happy adults
4. Developing adult leisure-time activities
5. Relating to one's spouse as a person
6. Accepting and adjusting to the physiological changes of middle age
7. Adjusting to aging parents

Later Maturity
1. Adjusting to decreasing physical strength and health
2. Adjusting to retirement and reduced income
3. Adjusting to death of friends and/or spouse
4. Increased leisure time and new friends
5. Meeting social and civic obligations/new social roles
6. Establishing satisfactory physical living arrangements (Havighurst, 1949, 1959).

There is not much empirical support for all of Havighurst's developmental tasks. Changes in societal morés likely would result in restatement or even in changes of some of them. The power for counselors in viewing this approach is to recognize that there are common challenges at various ages or developmental levels and to be broad enough or flexible enough to consider a context beyond the presenting problem.

Piaget

The structure of the intellect is a phrase commonly attached to Piaget's model. He categorized qualitative changes in intellectual development into periods or stages (Phillips, 1969), each identified by behavior that is progressive, new, and absent in earlier periods or stages. The mechanisms that Piaget constructed as explanations for what is happening intellectually are schemata (mental organizations) that are accomplished through assimilation and accommodation, and that occur as a result of disequilibrium. There are four major divisions or developmental periods in Piaget's model.

Sensorimotor Period (0–2 years). This period extends from birth to the acquisition of language. It is marked by mastery of sensory experience and of bringing motor responses under control and coordinated with sensory experiences. This period is marked by behavior that is relatively restricted to direct interactions with the environment.

Stage 1. exercising the ready-made sensorimotor schemes (0–1 month).
Stage 2. primary circular reactions (1–4 months).
Stage 3. secondary circular reactions (4–8 months).
Stage 4. coordination of secondary schemes (8–12 months).
Stage 5. tertiary circular reactions (12–18 months).
Stage 6. invention of new means through mental combinations (18–24 months).

Preoperational Period (2–7 years). With the acquisition of language, the child gains the ability to manipulate symbols that represent the environment. The process of attaching words to environmental referents remains focused on the correlation of present sensory impressions with acceptable labels. It does not yet incorporate reasoning of the transformational type, nor of induction nor deduction.

Concrete Operations Period (7–11 years). While still limited to observational interaction with concrete experience, the child now can grasp relationships and transformations. Conservation of quantity and number, even though an intermediate operation has rearranged the visual representation, is possible. Classification and numbering are accomplished.

Formal Operations Period (11–15 years). Logic, relationships, mental transformations, hypotheses, ability to perform mental operations become functional in this period.

The Concrete Operational child always starts with experience and makes limited interpolations and extrapolations from the data available to his senses. The adolescent, however, begins with the *possible* and then checks various possibilities against memorable representations of past experience, and perhaps against sensory feedback from the concrete manipulations that are suggested by his hypotheses. A final reason that cognition is relatively independent of concrete reality is that the *content* of a problem has at last been subordinated to the *form* of relations within it (Phillips, 1969, p. 134).

From the standpoint of the Piagetian model, interventions need to match the developmental level of the client. "Talk" therapies work best with formal operations clients. Concrete, tangible activities will get through to the concrete operations-level client, and younger clients need interventions that address their level of developmental status. Interventions that do not fit the client create major frustrations for the therapist and, at best, do no damage to the client.

Erikson

Erik Erikson (1950, 1963, 1968, 1980; Coles, 1970; Stevens, 1983) was born on June 15, 1902, near Frankfurt, Germany. His parents were Danish, and had separated before he was born. His mother later married a Jewish pediatrician, Homburger, in Karlsruhe, Germany. In the *gymnasium*, he studied Latin, Greek, and German literature as part of a classical, liberal arts program. Following *gymnasium*, he wandered for a year, returning home to pursue training and a careeer as an artist. After several years of study, artistic production, and much more wandering, Erikson found himself in Vienna, teaching in an alternative school. Anna Freud was a colleague at the school and, among others, influenced Erikson toward an interest in observing the developing children, and became his psychoanalyst. During his stay in Vienna he took schooling in psychoanalysis and in Montessori educational methods, and met and married Joan Serson, a Canadian-American who was highly educated and artistic. Erikson graduated from the Vienna Psychoanalytic Society and became a practicing analyst. In 1933, Erikson moved, first to Denmark and then to the United States, settling in Boston and, later going to New Haven where he became a faculy member of the Yale Medical School. His career in the USA was diverse and varied, befitting the artist-observer and wanderer. Erikson died on May 12, 1994.

> Erikson's work very much follows the pattern of his life and experiences. His first paper—on psychoanalysis and education—was written in Austria, arose from his work as a teacher. His initial publications in the USA were concerned with the observations he had made of children's play and of education in Sioux and Yurok societies. The ideas contained in several of these early papers were drawn together in his first and probably best known book *Childhood and Society* (1950), which was published when Erikson was forty-eight. The book focuses on the complex relationship between individual development and cultural and historical context and the mediating influence played in the process by methods of child rearing and education. It also introduces several other themes including his conceptions of the life cycle and identity . . . (Stevens, 1983, p. 8).

Erikson was a psychoanalyst by training and by inclination. He subscribed to the developmental stages as proposed by Freud and elaborated the influence of the social context of people as a major factor in psychosocial development. He postulated eight stages through which people progress as they express psychological and biological needs toward their environment. The receptiveness or responsiveness of the social environment provides the context in which individuals work out their response patterns. The eight stages are formulated as ranges with polar opposite extremes. The preferred or ideal outcome is stated first with less than perfect accomplishment falling in the direction of the second outcome label.

Basic Trust *versus* Basic Mistrust. This happens in the first year of life and is an attitude toward oneself and the world, an expectation for constancy and beneficence. During this stage the individual is in an incorporative mode dictated by the oral nature of development; that is, the child waits for nutriment, for example, and incorporates it through the mouth. Other experiences are incorporated through other sensory modalities. What the child incorporates is a function of what adults offer or supply. If the relationship between child and adult(s) is marked by reciprocity or what Erikson called *mutual regulation*, basic trust is accomplished. The critical period in this stage seems to be when the child gets teeth and can exercise aggressive response to the adult, namely, biting. If the adult withdraws or punishes or if the child does not learn to incorporate food and other things cooperatively, distrust is generated. Successful accomplishment of trust during the first year of life is the foundation for manifestation in the adult of a combination of faith and realism.

Autonomy *versus* Shame and Doubt. "The over-all significance of this stage lies in the maturation of the muscle system, the consequent ability (and doubly felt inability) to coordinate a number of highly conflicting action patterns such as 'holding on' and 'letting go,' and the enormous value with which the still highly dependent child begins to endow his autonomous will" (Erikson, 1980, p. 68). Obviously this explanation reflects the dynamics of the anal personality of Freudian theory, with the opposing processes of expulsion and retention, and the personality distortions of impulsivity and of compulsivity. "From a sense of self-control without the loss of self-esteem comes a lasting sense of autonomy and pride; from a sense of muscular and anal impotence, of loss of control, and of parental overcontrol comes a lasting sense of doubt and shame" (pp. 70–71). This sense of autonomy grows out of experience centered on toilet training, around age two on the average.

Initiative *versus* Guilt. At age four or five, the individual ventures into refinement of awareness of autonony toward individuality, toward finding out what kind of a person he or she is going to be. This is a function of being able to move around more freely, with a range of movement from acceptable to unacceptable. Language proceeds to the level of understanding more and the risk of not understanding enough. Imagination carries the child beyond the limitations of movement and language to an area of extension into pleasurable fantasy and nightmares. As the child moves through the potentially diverse experiences and emerges with a sense of success at having ventured into potentially hazardous areas, he or she gets a sense of inititative. This time corresponds to Freud's latency period, a time of reduced internal strife and turmoil between desires of the *id* and restrictions of the *superego*. Either punishment for behavioral or language excesses or the self-denigration of oedipal desires creates a sense of guilt. Conscience becomes firmly established at this stage. "The consequences of the guilt aroused at this stage (. . . a deep-seated conviction that the child . . . is essentially bad) . . . may find expression in a self-restriction which keeps an individual from living up to his inner capacities . . ." (p. 85). The focus is on what the person does as opposed to what the person is. Behavior becomes the definition of worth. Many of the ego defense mechanisms grow out of attempts to deal with guilt.

Industry *versus* Inferiority. "One might say that personality at the first stage crystallizes around the conviction 'I am what I am given,' and that of the second, 'I am what I will.' The third can be characterized by 'I am what I can imagine I will be.' . . . the fourth: 'I am what I learn' " (p. 87). This period begins with formal schooling, and especially with the confusing vascillation in most schools of moving from task-oriented, quality-controlled behavior to activities that are an extension of the natural child. Those who are successful in meeting the demands of the situation, as a result of expressing energy willfully, develop a sense of industry. Those who don't, acquire a sense of inferiority. This is obviously reinforced by the shift from parental validation to peer group comparisons. In the realm of the school where success is met with a higher level of expectation, the frame of comparison with peers, as in "I'm as good as, or better than you," becomes a survival skill.

Identity *versus* Identity Diffusion. This stage begins with puberty and adolescence. It is a time of turmoil, fed mostly by rapid physical and hormonal change.

> The growing and developing young people, faced with this physiological revolution within them, are now primarily concerned with attempts at consolidating their social roles. They are ... preoccupied with what they appear to be in the eyes of others as compared with what they feel they are, and with the question of how to connect the earlier cultivated roles and skills with the ideal prototypes of the day.... The sense of ego identity, then, is the accrued confidence that one's ability to maintain inner sameness and continuity (one's ego in the psychological sense) is matched by the sameness and continuity of one's meaning for others (p. 94).

Successful accomplishment of ego identity is contingent upon success at previous levels. Without trust, autonomy, and industry, the person does not have an inner something on which to base sameness and continuity. Absence of success at earlier stages and/or reactions from the social environment that militate against reinforcement of previous accomplishments undergird problems of identity diffusion that are manifest in overidentification with a model or with extreme conformity to peer, sometimes gang, ways of being. They avoid identity confusion by fitting the prescription of a social context, not as a contributor but rather in response to the external frame of reference. A key to the development of ego identity is a validation of the inner self with the resultant confidence to work, increasingly, from an internal frame of reference.

Intimacy and Distantiation *versus* Self-absorption. Once a reasonable sense of identity is established, it becomes possible to move toward intimacy with others who are or may become mates, and distantiate from those who are a threat to continued progress. This drawing closer or creating distance is much deeper than just sexual union or avoidance of the unfamiliar or foreign. Some major problems of development occur when sexual intimaces are experienced prior to the formation of true and mutual psychological intimacy with another person. "... the condition of a true twoness is that one must first become oneself" (p. 101). The psychoanalytic genital stage underlies this period. It is marked by "orgasmic mutuality" that implies at least as much caring for the mate as for the self. Falling short of a sense of intimacy, the individual becomes stuck in the phallic stage and focused on selfish gratification. Pornography addiction, sexual psychopathy, and sexual exploitation are indications of failure at intimacy and of being stuck in self-absorption.

Generativity *versus* Stagnation. The usual outgrowth of a truly intimate relationship is a wish of the couple to "combine their personalities and energies in the production and care of common offspring" (p. 103). This is an extension outward from interest in self to interest in mate to interest in others—the next generation. Generativity isn't limited to having children or only to one's own children. It may be expressed in

> altruistic concern and ... creativity.... The principle thing is to realize that this is a stage of growth of the healthy personality and that where such enrichment fails ... regression from generativity to an obsessive need for psuedo intimacy takes place, often with a pervading sense of stagnation and interpersonal impoverishment (p. 103).

Integrity *versus* Despair and Disgust. This stage is a result of success at the previous seven stages. It is an amalgamation of strengths and satisfactions, marked by confidence, non-defensiveness, of "having it all together" and of a personal validation of one's life and life style. It is not an end, rather, an acceptance and confirmation of direction. The person continues to be productive and to derive joy from his or her activities. Erikson had difficulty with clear definition of this construct and described it in this way:

> It is the acceptance of one's own and only life cycle and of the people who have become significant to it as something that had to be and that, by necessity, permitted of no substitutions. It thus means a new different love of one's parents, free of the wish that they should have been different, and an acceptance of the fact that one's life is one's own responsibility. It is a sense of comradeship with men and women of distant times and of different pursuits, who have created orders and objects and sayings conveying human dignity and love. Although aware of the relativity of all the various life styles which have given meaning to human striving, the possessor of integrity is ready to defend the dignity of his [or her] own life style against all physical and economic threats. For he [or she] knows that an individual life is the accidental coincidence of but one life cycle with but one segment of history; and that for him [or her] all human integrity stands and falls with the one style of integrity of which he [or she] partakes (p. 104).

The midlife crisis described by Sheehy (1976), wherein people deviate strongly and energetically from their previous patterns in a desperate attempt to find or create meaning, is an example of failure to achieve generativity. It involves an awareness that the previous patterns have not and will not result in integrity. It is difficult to validate a self that has been born out of failure and of stagnation. These people react, often in a fashion polar opposite to their previous existence, out of desperation, fueled by disgust with their present state and the perception that time is running out. Erikson's reference to failure at achieving integrity, resulting in despair, seems to be a realistic observation and an appropriate label.

Client behavior that is self-defeating or socially problematic often is a result of the client's unsuccessful attempts to meet his or her developmental challenges. If behavior can be described in terms of basic mistrust, shame and doubt, guilt, inferiority, identity diffusion, self-absorption, stagnation, or despair and disgust, then a developmental crisis is present and attention to development at the age-appropriate or lower levels is warranted. Because Erikson's model is psychosocial, it presumes that some client problems are a manifestation of limitations or distortions in the social context. He says, "We have learned not to stunt a child's growing body with child labor; we must now learn not to break his [or her] growing spirit by making him [or her] the victim of our own anxieties. If we will only learn to let live, the plan for growth is all there" (Erikson, 1980, p. 107). Erickson's model, obviously, is a fulfillment model. Therapeutic intervention is necessary to remedy contextual problems that have resulted in self-defeating behavior.

Maslow

Abraham Maslow was born in 1908 in New York City, the first of seven children. His relationship with his parents is said to be neither intimate nor loving (DeCarvalho, 1991). Maslow described the first part of his life as extremely neurotic. He was shy, nervous, depressed, lonely, and self-reflecting. After beginning college in pre-law, he dropped out, later to enroll in the University of Wisconsin-Madison where he received the BA (1930), MA (1931), and Ph.D. (1934) in psychology. His early work was on dogs and apes, focusing on the emotion of disgust in dogs and on the learning process in apes. After working at Columbia University and Brooklyn College, he became the department chair at Brandeis University. After ten years there, he accepted a fellowship at the Laughlin Foundation in Menlo Park, California. Maslow died in June of 1970.

> In his epoch-making 1943 article, "A Theory of Human Motivation," and more explicitly in *Motivation and Personality* (1954), Maslow argued that there are higher and lower needs in human motivation. Both are "instinctoid" and arranged in a heirarchy. These needs are, in order: physiological wellbeing, safety, love, esteem, and self-actualization. Each group of needs relies on prior satisfaction of previous needs (DeCarvalho, 1991, pp. 26–27).

Maslow's is a combination of personality and developmental theory—a personality model in its postulation of a life force or motivation, developmental in its specification of a hierarchy of levels of need gratification that begin in childhood and are additive with age, experience, and learning. Maslow posits that people are born with a set of instinctoid needs, not instincts in the sense of sucking or grasping, yet powerful in their automatic push toward satisfaction and well-being. The first four—physiological, safety, love and belonging, and self-esteem—are deficiency needs; that is, in a homeostatic sense, without their gratification the individual is unbalanced and incomplete. Self-actualization, with its sometimes added divisions of a desire to know and understand and of aesthetic needs, is a growth need, a striving for what might be, a move toward fulfillment of potential, maybe not necessary for well-being but definitely necessary for fulfillment and maximal satisfaction in life.

A basic need was considered by Maslow to include the following criteria (Maslow, 1962):

1. Its absence breeds illness.
2. Its presence prevents illness.
3. Its restoration cures illness.
4. Under certain, very complex, free-choice situations, it is preferred by the deprived person over other satisfactions.
5. It is found to be inactive, at a low ebb, or functionally absent in the healthy person.

Physiological Needs. The most basic of all needs are survival needs: food, liquid, shelter, sleep, and oxygen. Higher level needs give way to pursuit of satifaction of basic physiologicl needs. Consider the behavior by some poverty-stricken and desperate people who rummage through garbage containers for food, giving little or no thought to whether or not the food is safe to eat. The author had an experience wherein his older brother, while at a swimming party, held him under water for an unusually long time. Where he previously was aware of the colors and forms of people and objects underwater, under conditions of a strong hand holding him down, nothing captured his attention more than the urge to breathe. While people cycle through various levels of needs in each category, an assurance or expectation of satisfying physiological needs usually occurs early in life and frees energy to move to needs higher on the scale.

Safety Needs. Obviously, when physical safety is threatened, the well-known fight or flight pattern becomes primary. Nothing else matters much until the threat is lessened. To a lesser degree, the anticipation of harm or the absence of a sense of security motivates people to seek safety.

> Child psychologists . . . have found that children need a predictable world; a child prefers consistency, fairness and a certain amount of routine. When these elements are absent he [or she] becomes anxious and insecure. Freedom within limits rather than total permissiveness is preferred. . . . The insecure person has a compulsive need for order and stability and goes to great lengths to avoid the strange and the unexpected. The healthy person also seeks order and stability, but it is not the life or death necessity that it is for the neurotic. The mature individual also has an interest in the new and the mysterious (Goble, 1970, pp. 38–39).

Belongingness and Love Needs. Once safety is generally assured, the person becomes compelled toward affectionate relationships, for a place in his or her family or group or social context. Maslow makes a major distinction between love-motivation and sex-motivation, the latter being purely physiological. Sometimes, however, sexual behavior is determined by love-motivation (i.e., sexual intimacy as an expression of love). That love and belongingness is a category of need, he asserts, believing that the absence of love stifles growth and development of potential. Love includes mutual trust, lack of fear, a dropping of defenses, and it involves both giving and receiving.

Absence of the satisfaction of love and belonging needs during early years of development when the family is the primary social context, and continuing in many people well into adulthood, can be seen as a primary definition of affective deficit. An important dynamic in understanding love needs and differentiating them from the next higher level, esteem needs, is that love is given, not earned. There is some correspondence with the achievement by parents of Harris's (1967) "I'm okay—you're okay" dynamics. Such a parent can communicate to his or her child a personal validation, a sense of okay-ness even when the child is at a level of obvious imperfection. If so validated, the child can move on to attempting and succeeding in the gratification of esteem needs. Further explanation of affective deficit, the inability to feel loved and wanted, often compounded by contingency based relationships, follows.

> This state is not marked by absence of emotions; rather, it indicates a vacancy of vital feelings of worth and of personal validation. Expressions such as "I feel so empty," and "My life is going well in every respect; how come I feel so incomplete or so dissatisfied?" indicate a deficit state. A theoretical referent for this condition is Maslow's need hierarchy (1954), specifically what he described as the middle section—need for love and belonging. These needs are usually fulfilled through position in an integrated, accepting, functional family wherein a person has a place simply by virtue of being born into that family unit. Unfortunately, many families are dysfunctional, providing an insufficient structure of valid belongingness, and teaching the propogation of the same dynamics into the second and third generation.
>
> In Western society, this also occurs from an overreliance on achievement as the mark of success, i.e., personal value. It happens subtly and automatically when the parent or parent surrogate communicates "I like/love it/you when you clean your room/get good grades/make winning touchdowns/win beauty awards, etc." In contrast, personal validation, the antidote for affective deficit, occurs through expressions of love and acceptance even at times of disappointing failure, violation of parental hopes and expectations, and

mediocre performance. Contingent validation is a self-esteem strategy which, according to Maslow, will work only if the prerequisite need for love and belonging is satisfied. This may explain why so many admirable, high achieving, successful people engage in serial marriages, struggle through disruptive mid-life transitions, and commit suicide. If world class achievement fails to produce happiness, if the American success dream and promise of happiness through success turns out to be a lie, then desperate options must be exercised. Affective deficit is a widespread condition, especially in highly educated populations. Their plight is further exacerbated by their practiced tendency to try to solve everything by thinking about it (Gerber, Pederson, & Selby, 1996, pp. 7–8).

Esteem Needs. The dynamics of self-esteem appear to be an internalized picture of confidence obtained from performance-derived feedback from important people in one's social context. For children, performance validation comes from parents and/or other significant adults. As the child grows into middle childhood, continuing through much of adolescence, the reference group for validation becomes the peers. Looking "right," sounding "right," doing "right," or in words of recurring cyclical vernacular, "being cool," are the coin of the esteem realm. With a considerable amassing of success experiences, the person internalizes an image of self that is at least acceptable if not commendable from the external reference group. It is important to recognize the contingency dynamics in this pattern.

Problems of inadequate self-esteem are seen as a sense of inferiority and helplessness, discouragement, and possibly neurotic manifestations (Goble, 1970). These tend to be less marked in a person who is secure at the previous need level, love and belonging. Of interest to therapists is a pattern of client discouragement, and statements of inferiority when, from most outside observers, his or her performance would be described as exemplary. The continued striving for validation by the over-achieving client suggests that the client is employing a self-esteem strategy (earn respect and adulation) to fulfill a love and belonging need (personal validation that is given, not earned). When this is the case, creating more success experiences for the client will not assuage the emptiness of the affective deficit.

Self-actualization Needs. The previous needs are deficit needs. When they are unfulfilled there is a homeostatic-like drive toward satisfaction. Beyond self-esteem, the growth need, or the motivation for pursuit of potential becomes active. Each individual has an innate potential, unique to self and somewhat compelling, once the deficiency needs are satisfied (or that the expectation for a reasonable satisfaction level has been reinforced frequently enough to create an assurance of continuation). An apparent curiosity in people and the seeking of beauty are seen as foundations for adding two categories within the self-actualization level—the desire to know and to understand, and the aesthetic motivations. Maslow further attempted to circumscribe self-actualization by proposing a list of "Being-values" the presence of which marked the relatively small proportion of personkind that advanced to the top of his system. These values are not dichotomous nor independent. They form a matrix of development and indicate the seeking for and/or manifestation of each and of all.

1. Wholeness: integration, interconnectedness, meaningful gestalt.
2. Perfection: a just-rightness in relation to a personal standard as well as the gestalt.
3. Completion: reasonable and satisfying end-ness.
4. Justice: fairness, lawfulness.

5. Aliveness: spontaneity, vitality.
6. Richness: complexity, intricacy.
7. Simplicity: essentiality, undue elaboration of simple structure.
8. Beauty: artistic rightness, honest expression of good form.
9. Goodness: rightness, benevolence.
10. Uniqueness: novelty, non-comparability, idiosynchracy.
11. Effortlessness: gracefulness, purposefulness, absence of wasted motion.
12. Playfulness: joy, exhuberance.
13. Truth, honesty: unadulterated, essential, complete.
14. Self-sufficiency: autononous, independent, self-evaluated.

One of the major perceptions of client circumstance and style of importance to a therapist is a differentiation of environmental press and individual motivation. Frequently the needs of the context do not match the strivings of the individual. For example, if the client is having trouble with stress, the symptoms may result from an excessive number or weight of external demands, or from absence of emotional input relative to a sense of well-being. Determining what the client needs from a developmental standpoint and comparing its fit with client behavior in the press of his or her context often results in identification of two or more separate problems requiring separate interventions.

Perry

William Perry (1970) has focused much of his career and his theorizing on higher education. Though still in the process of refinement, his work has received considerable attention by college and university educators. The Perry Scheme is a model for explaining intellectual and ethical development. Its unique contribution to development theory is a focus on "Meaning Making." This section relies heavily on a workshop presentation by William S. Moore (1992).

Overview. There are nine distinct positions from which to view the world. The first five are primarily intellectual; they are systematic, cognitive, and structural. Positions six through nine are ethical concerns. As elaborations on a theme of personal meaning in a relativistic world, they deal with identity and commitment. The following phrases are descriptive of people who are in the stages indicated:

Dualism: Positions one and two
1. Completely unquestioned view of truth as Absolute Truth, understood only by authorities.
2. Different perspectives and beliefs are acknowledged but are simply wrong. Thinking is characterized by dichotomies: We–right–good *versus* They–wrong–evil. The world consists of two boxes—rights and wrongs.

Multiplicity: Positions three and four
3. Acknowledgement of legitimate uncertainty. There are three boxes: right, wrong, and "not-yet-known." The not-yet-known is knowable and will be known sometime. Learning changes focus from data to processes and methodology. One myth at this level is that hard work should pay off in good grades.
4. Small area of rights and wrongs, much larger area of "No one knows." Since we'll never know for sure, what becomes most important is one's own thinking. Quality

versus quantity becomes an issue. Focus shifts from process and method to how to think—independent thinking as a means for making sense of some things.

Contextual Relativism: Positions five through nine

5. Shift from a view of the world as essentially dualistic, with a growing number of exceptions to the rule, to a view of the world as essentially relativistic and context-bound with a few right/wrong exceptions; self is a legitimate source of knowledge along with authority. Self is an active maker of meaning.
6. Awareness of a need for making a major Commitment in one's life.

Commitment Within Relativism: Positions seven through nine

7. Making major commitment
   a. chosen in the face of legitimate alternatives.
   b. chosen after experiencing genuine doubt.
   c. chosen as a clear affirmation of one's self or identity.
8 & 9. Focus on the person coping with and synthesizing solutions to the consequences of his/her commitment(s). Initially assuming that making a commitment will take care of everything, one soon discovers that multiple commitments are necessary (e.g., career, partner, lifestyle)—and that rather than being complimentary, they are sometimes competing or even contradictory.

Overall, the Perry Scheme reflects two central interwoven dynamics:

1. Confronting and coping with diversity and uncertainty, and
2. The attendant evolution of meaning-making about learning and self.

As depicted in the positions of the Perry Scheme, learners cycle through three increasingly complex encounters with diversity in the form of multiples:

- multiple opinions about a given subject or issue (positions 1 through 3);
- multiple contexts/perspectives from which to understand or analyze issues or arguments (positions 4 through 6);
- multiple commitments through which one defines his or her values and identity (positions 7 through 9).

As learners confront these levels of "multiplicity," their meaning-making evolves; most significantly, knowledge is seen as increasingly conjectural and uncertain, open to (and requiring) interpretation. This central epistemology about knowledge and learning triggers parallel shifts in the learner's views about the role of the teacher—moving from seeing an authority as the source of "truth" to seeing an authority as a resource with specific expertise to share—as well as altering his or her views about the role of the student—moving from being a passive receptor of facts to an active agent in defining arguments and creating new "knowledge." This meaning-making has a critical role to play in the learning process (Moore, 1992, p. 6).

As with most developmental models, there is a gradient from less to more developed that parallels, generally, age of client from younger to older. It is important to recognize great differences in developmental status, allowing the possibility for some chronologically older clients to be functioning at a level more typical of a younger age. Also implicit to most developmental models is the valuing of higher levels of development, hence a covert directive for therapists to move their clients up the scale. In the Perry Scheme, clients who are at the lower levels will expect counselors to be much more authoritative with their pronouncements, and will not deal with ambiguity very well. Clients at the upper levels benefit from much more of a collaborative approach that recognizes their ability and responsibility to create their own adjustment.

Often clients of progressively higher chronological age encounter problems in adjusting to complexities of life because they prefer or insist on seeing the world in the dichotomous, two-boxes fashion instead of seeing it as it is—essentially relativistic and context-bound with a few right/wrong exceptions. For clients stuck at a lower level, a case-management mentality that requires the counselor to make decisions and monitor compliance is more effective than a normal development mind set that mandates requiring clients to do everything possible by themselves and in their own behalf. The converse is true at higher levels of development where overmanagement of cases creates either resistance on the part of clients or wasteful dependency.

☐ Conclusion

Identifying client circumstance relative to surplus and deficit dynamics in the perceptual, cognitive, affective, or behavioral families is a relatively straightforward task. Selecting or creating an intervention strategy for each client that is responsive to that surplus or deficit state, likewise, is straightforward. There are factors that complicate those straightforward actions. They are individual difference variables that go beyond learning style to include personality, developmental level, and relative completion of developmental issues, the press of social context, and the effect of spiritual or religious identity and group context. Those aspects of personality and development described in this chapter will be joined by additional, complexity-producing characteristics of the social and spiritual contexts described in Chapter 10.

CHAPTER 10

Contextual Issues: Circumstance and Style— Social and Spiritual Dynamics

Clients are magnificent and frustrating in their myriad manifestations of individual differences. Not only do they exhibit differences in perceptual and cognitive styles, preferred approaches to problem solving, and a range of communication abilities, they are impacted by their surroundings, by their contexts. In addition to the personality and developmental contexts treated in Chapter 9, there are at least two more that are the focus of this chapter: social context and spiritual context.

☐ Social Dynamics

One of the major tenets of the systems theorists is that it is counterproductive to isolate the "identified client" for treatment and then introduce that client back into an unchanged context (Bateson, 1958; Minuchin, 1974; Minuchin & Fishman, 1981; Ruesch & Bateson, 1968). The system is the client. From the emphasis on multiculturalism (Sue & Sue, 1990) comes the awareness that group morés, ethics, customs, and traditions set restrictions on the accessibility of client or system to intervention. They also limit the kinds of therapist-initiated activities that will be tolerated.

Studies of group influence, including peer group dominance for adolescents, family dynamics (Ansbacher & Ansbacher, 1956), groupthink (Janis, 1967), and the Abilene paradox (Harvey, 1974) indicate that consideration of the social context is a critical component to effective therapy. Popular therapeutic classifications such as adult children of alcoholics and co-dependency, with the coining of terms such as "enabling," gives further focus on social context. One definition of social psychology describes it as, "an attempt to understand and explain how the thoughts, feelings, and behavior of individuals are influenced by the actual, imagined, implied presence of others" (Albrecht, Chadwick, & Jacobsen, 1987, p. 6). Leon Festinger (Aron & Aron, 1986; Deutch & Krauss, 1965) posits a theory of social comparison. Since people have no objective and scientific way to evaluate their abilities, opinions, or actions, they judge themselves by comparison with other people. The more uncertain they are, the more they will rely on those comparisons for definition and validation. As this theoretical position is expanded, it can be said that individuals resolve their uncertainties by reference to groups, and that group definition often comes from comparison with other groups. The family is seen by Adler (Ansbacher & Ansbacher, 1956) to be the primary and most influential group for comparison and for establishment of lifestyle. Other groupings can be seen as of major importance to the identity of clients; these would include gender, racial, cultural, regional, and socioeconomic classifications. As with other contextual concerns, some knowledge of major identity characteristics common to such groups may be helpful in working with a particular client. An important caution in this regard is that reliance on stereotypical group characteristics may serve to blur what is uniquely important about the client. Continual reference to the client's disclosure and definition of what his or her affiliations mean is of prime significance.

Family

In the evolution of psychotherapy, a major shift occurred away from biological determinism and toward social factors either as major determinants or at least as important influences on the formation of personality. Adler (Ansbacher and Ansbacher, 1956) posited social interest as a basic motivator in the development of lifestyle. The family is the first social context a child experiences. Similarly, Harris (1967) indicated that the parents are of primary significance in overcoming the universal position of childhood, "I'm not okay—you're okay," so that the child can develop a healthy personality. That the family context is important from the standpoint of primacy, of so many initial and formative experiences occurring in that setting, is generally accepted. While it is true that something once was a major influence, of necessity it does not need to continue its influence. In fact, the ongoing family context either provides or contributes to client experiential and behavioral dynamics.

It is possible to perceive the family in several frameworks. From a causative standpoint, an individual can be explained as a product of his or her upbringing. A sometimes overt and sometimes implied excuse for misbehavior or maladaptation is the dysfunctional nature of the person's family. While it is true that some patterns of family dynamics are correlated with patterns of self-defeat or of psychopathology, it also is true that many individuals sharing such patterns manage to mature normally and to live productively. An alternate view is that each individual creates his or her own response sets from some internal locus of control, and that the family is little more than the arena in which individuality takes form and is expressed. A third frame shows an interaction between individual disposition and environmental control: client behavior results from the interaction of personal tendencies and environmental influences. It is this third view that is consonant with a phenomenological approach to counseling. As with so many of the contextual concerns, the abilities and the perceptions of the individual client must be the primary focus in selection of interventions. There are some noteworthy theories of family dynamics that may explain client behavior and that may predispose the client to specific intervention strategies. An examination of family therapy approaches may give insight into these.

Becvar and Becvar (1988) made a case for a systemic approach to family or relational counseling. They suggested that a focus on what is happening in a relationship (the reciprocal nature of influence—a holistic rather than analytic perceptual set—and looking at patterns of interaction) provides a superior base for therapy to that of a traditional and limited focus on intrapsychic, client-focused intervention. This requires working with systems in order to support changes for individuals within those systems. From an integrational standpoint, some circumstances are more responsive to systemic interventions, while others might be more effectively addressed through direct and client-limited strategies. Taking into account the context provides a bridge between these two ideologies. Understanding contextual dynamics provides the basis for choice of whole system, partial system, or individual client techniques. Six divisions of family therapy are elaborated by the Becvars: Communications, Strategic, Structural, Psychodynamic, Behavioral, and Experiential.

An apparent common root for the various approaches to systemic family intervention was the work of Wiener (1948) dealing with cybernetics. He and his associates focused on the interactive nature of people and events and on the process of feedback and self-correction. Individuals within systems are constantly presented with information as a result of their behavior; such information provides feedback for successive actions or reactions. Each of the specialty approaches emphasizes different strategies for intervention.

The focus of communication therapies (Bateson, 1971, 1974; Satir, 1964, 1972; Watzlawick, Beavin, & Jackson, 1967; Watzlawick, Weakland, & Fisch, 1974) generally deals with the interplay of messages within a communication matrix and with changing behavior as a product of changing communication.

> The rule for therapy is that you change behavior by changing communication. Specifically, hidden messages are brought out into the open and rules governing faulty or paradoxical communication are altered. (Becvar & Becvar, 1988, p. 213)

Strategic therapy (Haley, 1976; Selvini Palazzoli, Boscolo, Cecchin, & Prata, 1978) follows a belief that client behavior is a representation of a logical problem-solving approach within the phenomenal frame of the client. The therapist works to reframe the client's perception in order to enable a change in behavior.

> The strategic therapist believes that things are not the way they are. Rather, they are the way they are because we have perceived and conceptualized them. The therapist therefore behaves in a manner consistent with this belief in order to move people to a different perspective of the same situation . . . The perspective that the map is not the territory and that any phenomenon can be given any number of alternative, equally valid explanations also describes the essence of reframing, an important intervention in strategic therapy.
>
> In strategic theory and therapy, symptoms are seen as interpersonal strategies or efforts to define the nature of relationships . . . They are embedded in the family's network of relationships and serve an important purpose in the family. Thus the maintenance of a symptom is associated with complex, reciprocal feedback mechanisms within and between systems (Becvar & Becvar, 1988, p. 226).

The therapist works to get the family out of the pattern that has it "stuck," by the use of straightforward, cognitive injunction or by more intricate use of paradox, either in verbal or experiential form. The selection of the technique is based on the particular family pattern and its degree of intractability.

Structural family therapy (Minuchin, 1974) focuses on repetitive patterns of interaction (structures), that seem to follow covert rules, and occur between and among subgroups or subsystems within the family. Three subsystems are of primary concern: the spousal subsystem, the parental subsystem, and the sibling subsystem. Ideally the boundaries between and among subsystems are clear and functional. When the boundaries are confusing, varying degrees of enmeshment occur. Rigid boundaries produce disengagement. Clarifying boundaries permits a free and orderly interchange between and among subsystems.

In the psychodynamic approaches (Bowen, 1976; Guerin & Pendagast, 1976) the emphasis is on moving clients to intellectual processing rather than letting emotions dominate or unduly influence the family interactions. A particularly prominent tool for helping parents become aware of dynamics such as triangulation is the genogram, a map of the three-generation family structure and primary characteristics.

The application of behavioral principles and techniques to family therapy (Chamberlain, Patterson, Reid, Kavanaugh, & Forgatch, 1984) resulted in a focus on goal setting and skills acquisition. Behavior occurs and persists because it pays off for some member of the family. Determining what is happening that is undesirable, indentifying a more desirable alternative, and extinguishing the old while reinforcing the new is a well-known strategy.

Experiential approaches (Kempler, 1982; Whitaker, 1976) are employed to provide perceptual insight to family members. Fantasy, sculpting, role-playing, psychodrama, and mediated techniques like sand-tray and doll play are examples of the variety of experiences that may be employed. A distinct Gestalt flavor is present in experiential approaches.

As with individual therapies, systems approaches are varied. It seems likely that an integrational mindset can be applied relatively to them with the conclusion that none works universally well and that a careful understanding of the unique family dynamics would predispose a given approach to be successful and would not support another approach. The major contribution of family therapies is to broaden the focus from an individual, identified client, to consideration of the system as the focus for intervention.

Culture

Wehrly (1995) makes a point of recognizing diversity as a broad frame in which race, culture, ethnicity and other categories of experience fit. She indicates a difference between the construct, culture, and the client manifestations of their cultural context. There may be modal descriptors for cultural groups; yet individuals seldom conform to the cultural norm. Ethnicity is another frame, based on national origin and distinctive cultural patterns, that permits discussion of modal differences between ethnic groups that may not be an accurate representation of a given client. The term, race, incorporates physical or biological differences. It tends to be of more importance to those who are obvious representatives of a racial group, such as people of color. She confirms the necessity of being sensitive to cultural or ethnic influences while at the same time being careful to avoid stereotyping clients in reference to modal characteristics of their identity group.

Sue, Ivey, and Pedersen (1996) took a markedly different approach from Wehrly's concern for honoring the client's individuality. They proposed a theory, a "fourth force" conceptualization, as a better way to work with clients. They made a mistake in equating eclecticism with integrationism and then discounted it with anti-eclecticism arguments. A metatheory is proposed as superior to other extant approaches. Growing out of their position is an awareness of multiple cultural contexts for each client, and of the importance for each client to become aware of his or her cultural press, historically, in the present, and as he or she projects into yet different cultural domains in the future. They recognize that clients may bring different ways of framing their world and of their role within it, and that the emphasis of Western psychology has been toward individual responsibility. They also recognize the client as the major player in his or her life drama, and work to empower the individual toward self-enhancement. Several of their propositions and corollaries will give a flavor of this position. No attempt is made to represent their model in its entirety.

Proposition 2

Both counselor and client identities are formed and embedded in multiple levels of experiences (individual, group, and universal) and contexts (individual, family, and cultural milieu). The totality and interrelationships of experiences and contexts must be the focus of treatment (Sue, et al., 1996, p. 15).

Corollary 2B

A person's identity is formed and continually influenced by his or her context. Working effectively with clients requires an understanding of how the individual is embedded in the family, which in turn requires an understanding of how the family is affected by its place in a pluralistic culture (p. 15).

Corollary 2E

Culture is a complex construct that one can define in multiple ways but is defined here as any group that shares a theme or issue(s). Language, gender, ethnicity/race, spirituality, sexual preference, age, physical issues, socioeconomic class, and survivors of trauma are a few examples of cultural groups with whom counselors and therapists work. Virtually all clients who come for help have cultural issues underlying their concerns (p. 16). [This definition of culture is so broad as to incorporate virtually all contextual concerns.]

Corollary 3A

Developing a cultural identity represents a cognitive, emotional, and behavioral progression through . . . levels of consciousness, or stages. . . . (1) naiveté and embedded awareness of self as a cultural being, (2) encountering the reality of cultural issues, (3) naming of these cultural issues, (4) reflection on the meaning of self as a cultural being, and (5) some form of internalization and multiperspective thought about self-in-system. With each stage comes a different attitude toward oneself (self-identity) and others (reference-group identity of differences) (p. 17).

Corollary 3C

. . . it seems appropriate to change the traditional wording *self-concept* to *conceptions of self-in-relation* (p. 17).

The most basic question for clinical practice is how to move from a traditional focus on the individual to examining the use of cultural concepts in the sessions. Counselors and therapists therefore need to focus part of their interviews on family and cultural issues. If one is to consider self-in-relation, one needs to consider what "in-relation" means to each client.

Counselors and therapists also need to balance their self-oriented helping approach with a self-in-relation orientation (p. 36).

These authors make an impassioned plea for moving from an individual focus to one that strongly emphasizes the context over the individual, at least for a portion of the interview. Integrationism would suggest that undue emphasis on either is fraught with potential problems, and that taking both into consideration is preferable. A responsive approach would entail "reading the client" as opposed to looking for data in prescribed categories. Both recognize the need to be aware of context and to work with it rather than in oppostion to it.

Multicultural issues transcend psychological services. In an article directed at speech-language pathologists and audiologists, Crane (1997) shared some examples of potential difficulties.

> In some cultures it is considered inappropriate for a female to make any physical contact with a male client . . . This presents obvious hurdles to an assessment and intervention (p. 7).
>
> Families from cultures that believe in seniority and authority based on age may defer final decisions regarding assessment and intervention to grandparents. Clinicians also may want to research the view of disabilities held by a particular culture. . . . Some families may not [believe] that "invisible" disabilities, such as language learning disorders or attention deficits, merit treatment. Children with invisible disabilities may be viewed within their culture as lacking motivation and as not working hard enough (p. 7).
>
> Many cultures appear to be fatalistic in their views of disabilities . . . [Dr. Roseberry-McKibbin says], "They believe that an individual lives with a disability and that intervention is not necessary." . . . Still others look at disabilities as being a privilege. For example, some Native American tribes believe that disability is a gift from the Great Spirit (p. 7).
>
> American clinicians should not view their own ways as the only way. Instead they should try to work in accordance with the medical and spiritual beliefs of their client's culture. Clinicians can incorporate the family's point of view into treatment without compromising its efficacy . . . (p. 7).

Several references (Aponte, Rivers, & Wohl, 1995; Axelson, 1993; Ewalt, Freeman, Kirk, & Poole (Eds.), 1996; Sue et al., 1996; Wehrly, 1995) point to the necessity for counselors to be sensitive to potential blind spots resulting from their own cultural contexts and to look for, be aware of, recognize cultural factors that determine or influence client perceptions and responses. Of frequent reference is the precaution against imposition of counselor values through inflicting his or her cultural restraints on clients. Since there are many and different manifestations of cultural context across individuals and across cultural groupings, stereotypical response sets are to be avoided. Broadly based study of cultures is recommended.

As one example of the complexity of multicultural work, consider Dinges and Cherry (in Aponte, Rivers, & Wohl, 1995) as they looked at variations in the expression of symptoms. Borrowing a five point analysis from Good and Good (1986), they stated:

1. *Normative uncertainty* refers to specific cultural assumptions about abnormal behavior and symptoms that are used to inform interpretation of individual symptoms and of their threshold, level, and duration. Good and Good (1986) cite as an example the consistent finding of higher levels of psychological symptoms among Puerto Ricans and the difficulty of determining whether this represents actual differences in psychopathology or culturally patterned variations in the expression of distress.
2. *Centricultural bias* is by now a well-known problem, in which criteria defined and validated in one culture are used to determine the extent of a psychological disor-

der in another culture. In addition to cultural differences in the type, frequency, severity, and duration of symptoms, the additional problem exists of failing to recognize the attributed sources and culturally unique expressions of symptoms.

3. *Indeterminacy of meaning* occurs in the search for semantic equivalents when symptoms are presumed to have universal referents but are in fact expressed differently, thus producing confusion in the interpretation of symptom similarity across ethnic groups. This is most clearly seen in culturally weighted concepts such as guilt and shame, which take on different symptomatic significance for different cultures . . . and which have been amply demonstrated by Kinzie et al. (1982) in the development and validation of the Vietnamese Depression Scale.

4. *Narrative context* refers to the impact of the location and setting in which client symptoms are discussed. The candor and completeness of symptom disclosure can vary significantly depending on who is asking (e.g., clinician, friend, elder, native healer), what the person is asking about (e.g., dreams, contact with spirits, taboo objects, family tensions), and how (e.g., directly, or through trance mediums, relatives, or friends; in English or through bilingual interpreters).

5. *Category validity* is seen most clearly in the differential expression of symptoms that are presumed to reflect a common psychological disorder. Perhaps the best example is that provided by Kleinmen and Good (1985) in which they pose the question of whether depression expressed primarily in psychological terms associated with strong feelings of remorse and guilt can be equated with depression experienced primarily in somatic terms, as clinical lore suggests is common among Asian Americans (pp. 42–43).

Gender

Nobody argues that there are no differences between male and female physiology. From the child's first awareness that his or her external "plumbing" is different from another's to the impressive events surrounding conception, pregnancy, delivery, and the initial nurturance of a baby, the evidence is incontestable. The significance of those differences, and the more complex manifestations of gender—masculinity and feminity—do not experience magnanimity (Notman & Nadelson, 1991). There are numerous popular works that focus on stereotypical differences and offer direction from a psuedo-esoteric stance; for example, Baber's, *Naked At Gendergap: A Man's View of the War Between the Sexes* (1992) and Gray's, *Men Are From Mars, Women Are From Venus* (1993). The following two sections deal with the foundations and expressions of gender and with principal variations to the norm—homosexuality and alternate expression of gender preference.

The author remembers, back many years ago to an undergraduate anatomy class, the instructor saying that if you were to arrange 1,000 university students, nude, facing away from you, and in a line, from most feminine to most masculine, you would not be able to identify the sex of any but the most extreme ends of the continuum. Furthermore, there would be great overlap, with many males located well toward the feminine end and many females being found well over into the masculine portion of the group. This apparently is true with other gender-related differences. ". . . one male differs from another and one female from another as much as the mythical average female differs from the average male" (Hoyenga & Hoyenga, 1993, p. xiii). As will be demonstrated in the following section, stereotypical responses to men and women, and the rapidly changing roles of women in our society make it imperative to recognize and account for gender-related issues while, at the same time, preserving the unique identity of each individual client.

Foundations and Expressions of Gender. The word "gender" refers to many things. It denotes subcultures when modified by female or male, or when followed by preference. It is a biological condition, a genetic predisposition. It can be an expression of developmental outcome, from super-masculine to effeminate for a biological male and from super-feminine to amazon for a biological female. It is used to refer to a lifestyle, perceived as chosen by some, as conditioned by others.

A major genetic argument exists for the establishment of gender. Certainly the physiological manifestations of maleness and femaleness correlate very highly with genetic factors. Yet there exist many variations in genetic pattern, well beyond the simple XX, XY chromosomal patterns (Hoyenga & Hoyenga, 1993). Additionally, the chemical and hormonal environment of the body, especially during the perinatal and postpubertal periods contributes to both structure and function of the brain, such changes being correlated with gender-related differences.

Influence from the physical and social environment is seen as contributing to gender. Learning is a major factor, along with physical maturation in human development. In addition to the formative aspects of learning (i.e., identity formation) are the social constraints to behavior. These may override natural tendencies and result in stereotyped behavior. Furthermore, these social influences may be transitory and easily modified.

> From the moment of birth, your environment responded to you, at least in part, in ways that were based on your gender. Because the sexes are reared in systematically different environments, they learn somewhat different things, especially through observational learning (Hoyenga & Hoyenga, 1993, p. 207).
>
> In the past, both psychologists and other people assumed that individuals' behavior and achievements reflected their stable, internal personality traits. In contrast, current research shows that behavior and achievement, and even our personality traits, are heavily influenced by other's beliefs, perceptions, expectations, and treatment, as well as by our knowledge of expectations for members of our sex. . . . Both men's and women's behavior, achievements, and personality traits are far more quickly responsive to social situational forces than was previously supposed (Beall & Sternberg, 1993, pp. 33-34).

Probably it is more important for therapists to focus on differences in social stereotypes as they impinge on clients than to be concerned with group member differences. The popularity of trade books that play on these differences suggests that many people believe and act on such stereotypes, much to the disrespect and coercion of any who dare to express their variation from the stereotypical norm.

> From the social psychological perspective, gender beliefs and behavior can be understood as an overall self-fulfilling prophecy consisting of a cluster of related and mutually reinforcing specific self-fulfilling prophecies. Gender stereotypes operate as unconscious expectations or prophecies . . . In the broadest outline, gender stereotypes operating as implicit expectations bias perception and treatment of women and men, and the results of the discriminatory perceptions and treatment—sex differences in behavior and achievement—then seemingly confirm that the stereotypes were true all along (Beall & Sternberg, 1993, p. 37).

Relative to dealing with sex and gender group differences, Hoyenga and Hoyenga conclude that the demonstration of differences on the basis of empirical research is of little practical consequence. Rejection of the null hypothesis may justify believing that measurable differences do, in fact, occur. The meaning of those differences and their practical significance is seldom very clear.

> Even though one can conclude that males significantly differ from females along some particular trait dimension, that difference in and of itself is essentially meaningless. There are at least two reasons for this. First, gender differences are often small, especially compared to the variability of that trait within each gender. Often far larger differences exist among men alone, and among women alone, compared to the size of the sex difference in most personality and cognitive traits . . . Because of this, *significant* does not necessarily mean *important*.
>
> Second, one needs to know more about the test before the sex differences can be interpreted. Just knowing the scores on some trait that reveals statistically significant gender differences does not mean that one knows what that difference means. Sometimes getting a given score does not mean the same thing in women as it does in men . . . (1993, p. 35).

Contemporary research supports the contention that there are sex-related differences, that gender is a complicated product of genetics and socialization, and that social expectations and stereotypes influence the expression of behavior along gender lines. That there are differences is noncontestable. The significance of these differences for large groups of men or women is debatable, and for individuals they are nearly inconsequential. Because the individual differences within gender groupings are so great as to overlap group averages, it is necessary to be responsive to the client's unique expression of these variables. The knowledge of differences between and within gender groups makes it imperative to be sensitive to the fact of difference, while avoiding the limitations of acting on our stereotypes. Counselors must allow clients to express themselves freely, and to understand and accept the unique patterns of expression.

Homosexuality/Alternate Expression of Gender Preference. Such a section as this usually requires a qualifying paragraph. The explanations for homosexual or lesbian sexual expression have undergone marked reformulation over the past thirty years (Marmor, 1965; Masters & Johnson, 1979; McNaught, 1988; Minton, 1992; Nungesser, 1983). Homosexuality has variously been seen as a disease to be cured, an anomaly to be corrected, a context to be respected, a condition to be accepted, a manifestation of self to be discovered and celebrated, and a social and psychological characteristic to be protected by law and studied as a formalized academic curriculum. It is explained variously as a matter of choice, a result of fixation at a particular level of development, a manifestation of social suppression, a biologically influenced expression of hormonal levels, and a genetically determined state—a genotye of the first order. Some of the authors, after stating their preferred position, allow that it may be the result of some complex interworking of all of the above.

Weak, mostly correlational, empirical evidence supports the various positions, and there is considerable emotionality expressed in support of the different positions. As yet another position, one might consider truth in each of the diverse arguments. This is another application of an integrational mindset. It allows that different individuals may express homosexuality for different reasons, and as a result of different developmental or experiential backgrounds. Consider a few excerpts that represent the breadth of literature in the homosexual arena.

> Homosexuality as psychopathological:
> The clinical homosexual [is] one who is motivated, in adult life, by a definite preferential erotic attraction to members of the same sex and who usually (but not necessarily) engages in overt sexual relations with them (Marmor, 1965, p. 4).
>
> We are probably dealing with a condition that is not only multiply determined by psychodynamic, sociocultural, biological, and situational factors but also reflects the significance of subtle temporal, qualitative, and quantitative variables. For a homosexual adaptation to occur, in our time and culture, these factors must combine to (1) create an impaired gender identity, (2) create a fear of intimate contact with members of the opposite sex, and (3) provide opportunities for sexual release with members of the same sex (Marmor, 1965, p. 5).

Marmor reported studies that support genetic implications, with one conclusion being that homosexuality is like left-handedness. It is genetically controlled but its manifestation may be limited or suppressed by conditioning in a context that is predominantly right-handed. He also reports correlational results that implicate lateness in birth order, early socialization experiences, crowding, and body morphology.

> The clinicians represented in this volume present convincing evidence that homosexuality is a potentially reversible condition. There is little doubt that much of the recent success in the treatment of homosexuals stems from the growing recognition among psychoanalysts that homosexuality is a disorder of adaptation (p. 21).

In a shift to the opposite polarity is Nungesser. He makes homophobia into a broad-based cause of societal ills in his personal crusade of combatting anti-homosexuality.

> It has been my personal and professional goal to expose the origins and foundations of antihomosexual attitudes. I feel that such knowledge will lead to the resolution of fear and prejudice toward homosexual acts and actors. This resolution of fear will create a condition for human growth and social development. Antihomosexual attitudes are the crux of many of the social ills experienced in the United States, including sexism, gender role conformity, spiritual oppression, and crime (1983, p. ix).

LeVay and Nonas defined sexual orientation as a dimension of personality manifest in the predominant focus of sexual attraction. They indicated it

> is not necessarily a fixed, life-long attribute. Sexual orientation can change: for example, a woman may be predominantly attracted to men for many years, and perhaps have a happy marriage and children during that time, and then become increasingly aware of same-sex attraction in her thirties, forties, or later. This does not mean that she was concealing or repressing her homosexuality during the earlier period. To argue that she was "really" homosexual all the time would be to change the definition of sexual orientation into something murky or inaccessible. The same would be true even if there were some marker (in her genes or her brain, for example) that could be used to predict that she would ultimately become homosexual (1995, pp. 5–6).

In a position that begs the issue of homosexuality as a normal or abnormal state, Masters and Johnson opted instead to focus on their clinical expertise and treat the client without regard to his or her sexual preference.

Millions of men and women have interacted sexually with same-sex partners. A significant percentage of these individuals, like those interacting with opposite-sex partners, have developed varying symptoms of sexual distress, but for them adequate treatment has not been readily available.

A homosexual man or woman who is sexually dysfunctional or dissatisfied is entitled to evaluation and treatment with the same clinical objectivity accorded to the sexually dysfunctional heterosexual individual (1979, p. ix).

Whatever the etiology and dynamics of homosexuality, there has been concern over prejudicial treatment of members of sexual minorities—gay men, lesbians, bisexuals, and transgenderals or transexuals. Concerns such as access and barriers to service, special resources for sexual minorities, and attitudes and perceptions of agency employees toward sexual minorities have been addressed by governmental agencies and executive orders. Administrative policies have been issued by state governments to rectify problems of prejudice (Washington State Department of Social and Health Services, 1993). In order to cope with such issues, societal subgroups have formed to provide members social, economic, and health support (LeVay & Nonas, 1995).

One of the conundrums of the biological and social sciences is the relative significance of heredity and environment in determining or influencing behavior. This nature–nurture battle is renewed in the isolation of genetic factors that correlate with behavioral manifestations such as schizophrenia and homosexuality. One can expect the tide of opinion to shift from time to time. One person's enlightenment is another's folly, and it's not always the same person who enjoys enlightenment or suffers misdirection. In this area, as with other contextual areas, it is important to not lose the client in the confusion or ambivalence of society. It is important to respect the client's position even though it may run counter to the preference of the therapist. In this regard, as well as that of spirituality, social response, honesty, or other value discrepancies between client and counselor, it is important for the therapist to know his or her own level of advocacy or of tolerance and to make referrals of clients who elicit negative emotionality. A cooperative relationship, one that focuses on client–counselor collaboration in the identification of client circumstance and style, usually includes emphasis on open exploration of elements and options. In such a relationship the client owns his or her concerns and has ultimate responsibility for making choices and working to validate those choices.

Geographical/Regional Difference

An extensive examination will not be made of this contextual subset. Casual and empirical observations of groups of people support the existence of different environmental dynamics associated with different locales. Some of these have to do with access to or breadth of experience. This may be mitigated by the pervasive, homogenizing influence of television. Social and political attitudes of liberalism or conservatism may be important. The influence of a major occupational setting, such as a "railroad" town or a mining-based community, or an amalgamation of hospital and health care institutions, can be significant in dominating the phenomenal reality of the client.

Some geographical contexts appear, on the surface, to predispose inhabitants to particular patterns of behavior. Native American reservations, inner-city ghettos, military installations, foreign societies, or distinctive regions within the United States are examples of locations sometimes implicated in geographically mediated or moderated behavior. Whatever the geographical context, a wide range of individual differences emerge. This suggests that even in the most influential of environments, individual client dynamics are of prime importance.

Whether concerned with family, culture, gender, or geography, it is necessary to be sensitive to the client's social context without forcing stereotypes on him or her from popular or educated impressions of the social group or condition to which he or she belongs. While it is important to be sensitive to group identities and differences between groups, the wide range of variability within all group contexts suggests the importance of giving primary consideration to the individual client.

☐ Spirituality

Part of the context of clients is their response to spirituality. This may or may not include religiosity, though a large proportion of clients belong to a church or identify with a group for whom spirituality is of high interest. Even response to the term "religiosity" varies across individuals. At one end of a continuum, some see it in reference to a facilitative organization or "container" for their spiritual experience and expression. At the other end of the continuum it is seen as a series of barriers or impediments to the full experience of spirituality. This varied, individual, and personally unique response to religion is but an expression of a major theme in consideration of a client's spiritual context.

Focus

Consideration of two major emphases seems warranted: (a) The extent to which clients define themselves relative to religious principles, indoctrination, and practices as evidenced in self-descriptions such as, "I am a devout Christian" or "I am not a very good Methodist" or "I am an avid Buddhist" or "My parents/priest would be disappointed in me"; and (b) The reliance on a relationship with a higher power, informally as a support or more formally through prayer or meditation.

There is some confusion across individuals as to the domains of spirituality and of religion. Some see them as one and the same. Others argue that one need not be religious in order to be spiritual; indeed, organized religion is sometimes seen as an obstruction to spirituality. On the other hand, many consider religion to be a vehicle, a structure for the expression of spirituality.

> This may be a moot point. Consider that Religious faith, both in individually packaged and communal forms, while it may not always be deep, is so widespread that it commends itself for study by anyone who wants to understand humans. My source, "The International Bulletin of Missionary Research" (January 1996), projects 6,158,051,000 global citizens in 2000. All but 915,714,000 "nonreligious" and 231,515,000 "atheists" will be in the at-least nominal camps of the religious . . . (Marty, 1996, pp. 15–16).

Membership in a church is not synonymous with a high degree of religiosity or of spirituality; however, the large portion of the world population projected to be church affiliated is sufficient cause to recognize and to legitimize religious or spiritual factors either as determinants or as modifiers of human thought, attitude, emotion, and behavior. Even people who profess anti-religious or anti-spiritual sentiment are defined, at least in part, by the religious context they oppose. The practical significance of this is expressed by Marty:

> In intimate personal relations, such as providing medical care, promoting support groups against addiction, or making sense of the person to whom one is married, some understanding of religious impulses and religion is practical. Even the widespread religious indifference and ignorance in much of the culture demands study: if people abandon religion or are abandoned by it, academics *get* to study what takes place. Something will (1996, p. 17).

If one accepts as given that clients do not exist in a spiritual or religious vacuum and, instead, that their experiences and manifest behavior are extensions of or modifications of spiritual or religious factors, then it is imperative that therapists allow for and account for such factors. Two foundation blocks are necessary to establish a structure that will excuse counselors from studying all religions evidenced in their clientele, while holding them responsible for sensitivity to client characteristics of and concern for spirituality. The first is the tradition of pluralism and of political and legal validation of individual differences. The second is the viewpoint from Existential philosophy that perception is intensely personal and that individual definition comes from personally grappling with dissonance and making decision-based responses.

Relative to the pluralistic tradition in the United States of America and in reference to the responsibility of higher education, Green (1996) wrote:

> Consider one critical respect in which religion differs from nearly all other academic subject areas and aspects of culture. Because of the First Ammendment, religion is a fundamental and unquestioned taxonomic concept that Americans use, routinely and unthinkingly, to sort out, comprehend, and explain the complexity of human experience. Religion is a native category in American life. The self-evidence and cultural meaning that Americans attach to the category "religion" are replicated almost nowhere else, even in societies that have multiple religions. That there is religion, and that religion matters, are axioms of American life. The status of religion as a privileged cultural category has important implications for its place in a higher education enterprise concerned with difference and tolerance.
>
> By mandating both freedom of and freedom from religion, the First Ammendment guarantees that America will have more than one religion. It establishes religion as a legitimate, legally protected form of difference in American society and thereby makes difference itself a defining trait of American life. Because the category of religion includes both individual conscience—the freedom to believe—and collective behavior—the freedom (within some limits) to live out those beliefs, the Constitution extends the freedom to be different to groups as well as to individuals. The First Ammendment shapes a distinctive American attitude toward diversity by implicitly depicting difference—particularly on questions of values—as a cultural good. It is highly likely that America's ability to affirm difference as a social benefit derives in some significant way from the Constitution's commitment to religious freedom. If this is even partially correct, then to educate responsibly about American pluralism we must take religion seriously. But for students to understand what is at stake in religious freedom, they must understand what is at stake in religion itself (p. 27).

And further, he concluded:

> Religion is powerful because, unlike art, politics, or even philosophy, religion tends to expand its reach, to be comprehensive in scope, and to exhibit an enormous range of expres-

sion. It makes demands on the entire human person and claims to provide definitive answers to the urgent questions of life and death. True, religion has a great capacity for oppression. But it has an equal ability to liberate and transform. Whether we like it or not, religion has been and yet remains a tremendously potent force in American social, political, and economic life. The power of religious convictions exposes the irreconcilable differences of belief, behaviors, and values that human beings hold and shows us—again and again—why pluralism is both necessary and difficult. We do our students no educational service by pretending that religion isn't out there and doesn't matter. We cannot promote the tolerance of something we trivialize (p. 28).

Individual differences, freedom of and freedom from religion, ways to sort out, comprehend, and explain the complexity of human experience—all undergird the value of pluralism in our society, a political structure for validating individuality. But what of the individual motivation toward religion or spirituality? Fromm (1941) postulates an inner turmoil between the urge to individuate and the urge to combine. The ultimate state of humanity is isolation. It is freedom from being subsumed into a larger whole. One objective of communication is to reduce that isolation, to verify that others have common experiences with oneself. Much of the social fabric is composed of individual, group, and societal efforts to move toward one another or to move away from one another. This reflects Horney's (1945) postulation of basic personality dynamics that motivate individuals in such a manner.

Paloutzian (1996) made an interesting case for a "religious" drive, a need to reconnect. His line of reasoning goes thusly: the word *religion* comes from the Latin word, *legare,* that means to bind or connect. Re-ligion refers to the rebinding or reconnecting of two entities that have become disconnected.

> The universality of religion suggests that the need to repair some kind of basic brokenness is present in all peoples. An etymological look at religion, therefore, would lead one to the idea that religion involves people's striving for a sense of wholeness or completeness or to that which has a claim on one's commitment (p. 8).
>
> Emilie Durkheim saw religion as a social institution that helped bring people together and stabilize society. This was accomplished by religious functioning as that which contained and perpetuated necessary social and moral codes and that which made it possible for people to overcome "anomie" or isolation. Anything that did these things could be said to serve a religious function (p. 10).

Some sentiment exists for a biological basis to religion. Wesley Wells (Wulff, 1991) suggested that:

> The biological foundations of religious belief are essentially twofold. On the one hand, religious beliefs rest in the primary instincts of curiosity, self-abasement, flight, and parental caretaking, and on the parallel emotions of wonder, negative self-feeling, fear, and tenderness. On the other hand, beliefs possess direct survival value through the subjective effects they have on biological wellbeing. Wells illustrates the enormously powerful influence of deeply held beliefs with the phenomenon of sudden death among nonliterate people who learn that they have violated some fundamental taboo (p. 114).

Whether or not the cause and effect of Wells' observation can be empirically verified, the implication of religious belief and well-being is worthy of consideration. Another aspect of religion that has significance in the context of individual differences and cognitive well-being is the creation or the facilitation of dissonance-reducing attributions and of structures for individual meaning. Frankl (1962) made a big point of supporting an existential drive within people, the resolution of which is an understanding or awareness of their purpose in life. He chronicled variations in the survival and style of life of prisoners, with a marked contrast between those who respond to external exigencies and those whose locus of control is within, who have a "why" to live.

From May and Yalom (1955) came the description of universal striving for order and meaning in four areas: death, freedom, isolation, and meaningless. Particularly they stressed fear of death as an impetus for personal struggle. Often it results in one of two cognitive solutions: (a) a belief that death cannot happen to me—I am invincible (often manifest in youth), and (b) a belief in a "personal omnipotent servant who eternally guards and protects our welfare, who may let us get to the edge of the abyss but who will always bring us back" (p. 277). Religious dogma provides answers for the difficult contemplation of the cessation of conscious interaction with deceased family members or acquaintances. Frost (1962) asserted that "throughout the history of mankind there has persisted a conviction . . . that death cannot be the end. In every age there have been millions firm in the belief that what is truest in humanity persists in some form or state after death" (p. 153).

An explanation of this existential struggle that undergirds a spiritual assumption, from the view of Kierkegaard, is that

> one goes through it all to arrive at faith, the faith that one's very creatureliness has some meaning to a Creator; that despite one's true insignificance, weakness, death, one's existence has meaning in some intimate sense because it exists within an eternal and infinite scheme of things brought about and maintained to some kind of design by some creative force (Becker, 1973, p. 90).

In a partial reprise of Chapter 7, the Gestalt Law of Prägnanz seems to be germane. If the foundation for insight is the perceptual realization of "good form" or of the universal structure that undergirds all understanding, then there is order in the universe—a universality that can be discovered. The origin of universality often is attributed to an act of creation by an omnipotent being, diety, or god. Whether it is an accurate attribution or mythical conclusion is debatable. For the client who believes in a spiritual power, such belief is sufficient to provide motivation to pursue insight and to reframe perceptions until the universal, self-validating "good form" is achieved.

A model of development of recent formulation, the Perry Scheme (Moore, 1992), can be interpreted in such a way as to provide additional support for client religiosity as a functional adjustment mechanism. William Perry proposed that there is an orderly process of development through nine stages. The first two fit under the rubric, dualism. The perception of people at this level is that there is truth and that right and wrong are viable, discrete, value positions. In today's world, the source of truth for this level tends to be seen either as God or science. Levels three and four are classified under "multiplicity." Whatever the source of truth, it is seen as progressively fallible in the face of exceptions to the rules, at first, and then as insufficient or unreliable.

Multiplicity: Positions three and four
3. Acknowledgement of legitimate uncertainty. There are three boxes: right, wrong, and "not-yet-known." The not-yet-known is knowable and will be known sometime.

4. Small area of rights and wrongs, much larger area of "No one knows." Since we'll never know for sure, what becomes most important is one's own thinking. Focus shifts from process and method to how to think—independent thinking as a means for making sense of some things.

The next jump in Perry's scheme is of major importance in consideration of spirituality as a haven for people overtaken by the explosion of information and its apparent counterthemes. Contextual relativism, as a category, suggests that truth is either plural with the appropriate truth needing to be discovered for each separate context, or that there is no universal truth and each person must create his or her own meaning relative to each context.

Contextual Relativism: Positions five through nine
5. Shift from a view of the world as essentially dualistic, with a growing number of exceptions to the rule, to a view of the world as essentially relativistic and context-bound with a few right/wrong exceptions; self is a legitimate source of knowledge along with authority. Self is an active maker of meaning.
6. Awareness of a need for making a major commitment in one's life.

One could posit a full circle in the evolution of thought from pre-Enlightenment times, when information was scarce, illiteracy was high, and stability in thought and in life was a product of a relatively few opinion leaders whose views originated from or were dictated by God or a spiritual source. The message of purpose and unity in the universe was reassuring and, at least in the mind of believers, progressive and good. Today's world presents a hyper-load of data, too much for any person to master, too much in any specialty area of endeavor for even the professionals to manage. Furthermore, knowledge is changing so rapidly that it is only a matter of time before what was reassuringly true one day has been effaced by subsequent discovery or reinterpretation. Earlier, people did not know what to believe because they had limited access to information. They were ignorant. Today, people do not know what to believe because they are confused by the overabundance of contradictory information. If, as Perry suggested, people become aware of the opportunity/need to make commitments, and if they lack a stable anchor from which to evaluate options, then turning to tradition or to a spiritual or a religious source enables them to set a more or less consistent direction for their lives.

Some religious or spiritual conceptions serve well as a base for people who never progress up Perry's scale. They will serve equally well for those who retreat to lower levels as a result of their frustrating venture into confusion. There is a multiplicity of spiritual and religious views, some of which support the need for individuals to make choices and to determine their own existence. For them, spirituality is an influence and a support, more than a coercive force or even an infallible guide. For this latter population, the top three positions in Perry's model still have relevance.

Commitment Within Relativism: Positions seven through nine
7. Making major commitment
    a. chosen in the face of legitimate alternatives.
    b. chosen after experiencing genuine doubt.
    c. chosen as a clear affirmation of one's self or identity.
8. & 9. Focus on the person coping with and synthesizing solutions to the conse-

quences of his/her commitment/s. Initially assuming that making a commitment will take care of everything, one soon discovers that multiple commitments are necessary (e.g., career, partner, lifestyle)—and that rather than being complimentary, they are sometimes competing or even contradictory.

From the scientist's viewpoint, it is important to verify, empirically, the existence of spiritual entities. It is important to establish causal relationships between religious practices and the results claimed by the practitioners. From a clinical standpoint this is less important, especially recognizing the power for direction within the client's phenomenal experience and from the client's cognitive structure. Whether or not they have been empirically isolated and their veracity and power demonstrated, spiritual beliefs have significance for clients. For example, consider this analysis of prayer:

> Praying persists as a habit simply because that was what was practiced under distress and nothing else. The greater the variety of circumstances under which prayer alone was resorted to the more likely it is that it will be elicited and persisted in. And on the basis of the processes called by the Russian experimenters "higher order conditioning" the activity of praying itself comes to speed up the process of emotional equilibrium formerly completely dependent upon regulatory organic processes alone. In this way, prayers come to have important emotional effects upon those who practice them. By virtue of the conditioning process, the saying of prayers can early induce the emotional states or resignations that once waited upon a favorable turn of events or upon the exhaustion of states of grief or frustration (Wulff, 1991, p. 122).

Because something is hard to empiricize does not rule out its existence or its importance. One possibility is that spiritual entities and events exist outside of the domain of the physical scientist. Perhaps some type of construct validation will emerge and form the basis of a spiritual science. Until that time, the term *spiritual science* will remain a non sequitur.

Spirituality and Professional Counseling Literature

The power of religious or spiritual interventions may come from a basic spiritual reality, from a conditioned and helpful reflex, or from some kind of placebo effect. It is potentially beneficial for the therapist to honor, consider, and encourage the application of such interventions by his or her believing clients. The use of such techniques can be discounted as unparsimonious. The therapist could be accused of complicity in furthering the belief and practice of mythical, neurotic, or hallucinatory lapses. The practice might be seen as professionally irresponsible, or as a manifestation of enabling or co-dependant behavior, and therefore unethical. That can be countered by the rationale that there is no empirical evidence denying the veracity of such an approach. To insist that clients operate exclusively on research-based empiricism in preference to their phenomenal data is to inflict the values of the scientist-practitioner on the client. Values imposition is unethical. It would appear that sensitivity to the contextual dynamics of spirituality for a given client is warranted and wise. Involvement of the client's spiritual and/or religious resources also is indicated. Authors such as Bergin (1988, 1991), Shafranske and Malony (1990), and Richards and Potts (1995) lend legitimacy and support to the importance of the spiritual context, both from the standpoint of client and of therapist. "It has become clear that for many people, religious influences were therapeutic. Religious involvement negatively correlated with problems of social conduct and positively correlated with self-esteem, family cohesion, and perceived well-being" (Bergin, 1991, p. 401).

Attention to a client's spiritual context may simply result in content differences in interventions; that is, allowing spiritual concerns and beliefs to be verbalized and to become the focus of therapy. The spiritual context may also have deeper implications for client well-being. There may be certain "generic" interventions that are particularly useful in this domain, especially in perceptual and cognitive approaches. There likely are some techniques that may be unique to this context. Richards and Potts (1995) and Bergin (1988, 1989, 1991) described the use of prayer, scripture study, rituals, spiritual relaxation techniques, spiritual self-disclosure, spiritual homework, and inspirational counseling. One unique application is called the transitional figure. The client is taught that even though he or she is the victim of pathologizing events, it is important to adopt a forgiving attitude in order to break the cycle of transmission of pain. The transitional figure "sacrifices" to absorb the "generational pain" instead of seeking retribution, thus becoming a positive change in the next generation. This technique involves principles and processes of forgiveness, sacrifice, suffering, and redemption.

A combination of or modification of techniques from the perceptual learning family may be especially powerful in addressing more directly the spiritual experience of clients. Susan Zajonc (1996) proposed the following:

> [for] the client who understands God through the vitality of the relationship [and who] would benefit from perceptual interventions. These interventions might include certain homework assignments such as remaining quiet in a meditative fashion in order to be sensitive to insights. Another response to spiritual need is 'dialoguing without words' with one's higher power and reflecting on the feelings which come as a result. Communicating or reconnecting with what is spiritual through art expression such as clay modeling, drawing, painting, or dramatic expression are also approaches to deepening a spiritual relationship. Using vocalizations to spontaneously access the depths of one's existence in the forms of singing and talking can lessen the sense of isolation and give expression to deep spiritual need. Likewise, chanting the mantra may reconnect the transcendental meditator with a sense of calm and peace.
>
> Perhaps a client suffers from a spiritually based perceptual deficit. This person simply has never witnessed faith in others, nor has been driven to grapple with the existential questions of life. When circumstances abruptly change and this formerly well-defended human can no longer "make sense" of life with its changing realities, the therapist has an opportunity to intervene with the goal of filling the deficit. Guided imagery may be used as an experiential teaching tool, as well as recommending particular biographies and autobiographies of people who have lived as spiritual beings . . . Role-playing and psychodrama also can aid in the effort to expand perceptions and possibilities for creating a satisfying spiritual life.
>
> Some clients may enter therapy encumbered unnecessarily by a perceptual surplus of a spiritual nature. An example of this is someone with inhibited expression due to fear of reprisal from the religious sect to which they belong. Reframing the perception of this client's self-image from fearful and dependent to strong and autonomous creates a mutually exclusive experience to what the client brought to therapy. Role reversal, looking at the problem from a different perspective, identifying the positive, and memory substitution would all be methods effectively employed for interventions in this circumstance (pp. 6–7).

From an assessment standpoint, Bergin (1989, 1991) and Masters and Bergin (1991) reported the use of Allport's Religious Orientation Scale. Subjects are scored relative to extrinsic (negative) religiousness and intrinsic (positive) religiousness. The extrinsic orientation is manifest by the desire to gain status, security, and self-gratification, this orientation being defined as spiritual or religious immaturity. Intrinsic religiosity, in contrast, is characterized by internalized beliefs that are adhered to regardless of external consequences. There is some correlational evidence that a positive relationship exists between intrinsic scores and positive adjustment. Similarly, extrinsic scores manifest a significant degree of covariance with indicators of pathology.

There is a third orientation, different from the extrinsic and intrinsic duality of Allport. It is called religion as quest.

> [The] characteristics of complexity, doubt, and tentativeness [in contemplation of complex issues such as ethical responsibility and evil] suggest a way of being religious that is very different from either the extrinsic or the intrinsic orientation . . . ; they suggest an approach that involves honestly facing existential questions in all their complexity, while resisting clear-cut answers. An individual who approaches religion in this way recognizes that he or she does not know, and probably never will know, the final truth about such matters. But still the questions are deemed important, and however tentative and subject to change, answers are sought. There may not be a clear belief in a transcendent reality, but there is a transcendent, religious dimension to the individual's life (Batson & Ventis, 1982, pp. 149–150).

The quest position seems to reflect a reverence for the complexity of existence and a comfortable fixation on the process of drawing nearer to an unperceived and probably unreachable end. This position could be posited to lie between the extrinsic and intrinsic, and at a level four of the Perry Scheme with a very large area of "No one knows," and a favoring of contemplation over observation. This is the beginning of an internal locus of control in the context of a spiritual or transcendent reality that is too big and too important to trust to a premature, hasty, or incorrect resolution. It is a cautious and enjoyable pondering of the suspectedly imponderable.

There appears to be a rising interest on the part of counselor educators to recognize the spiritual realm as a legitimate area for study and for training (Fukuyama & Sevig, 1997; Ingersoll, 1997). The existence of a division of the American Counseling Association with an emphasis on spiritual and religious values (the Association for Spiritual, Ethical, and Religious Values in Counseling) establishes a *de facto* and formal interest on the part of some counseling professionals. Inclusion of a diagnostic category for spiritual and religious problems in the *Diagnostic and Statistical Manual of Mental Disorders,* Fourth Edition (American Psychiatric Association, 1994) legitimizes this area for serious consideration.

"Generic" Religious Principles and Practices

With conscious awareness of the number of cautions in this text relative to avoiding stereotypes and the number of directives to focus on the individual over and above his or her contexts, there are some dynamics of a religious or spiritual nature that can be identified and watched for in therapeutic practice. Once again it must be realized that each individual, from the most thoroughly indoctrinated, to the Christian who expresses religiosity only at Christmas and Easter, has his or her own phenomenal grounding in each of these areas. The conclusions in this section and the next are based on the author's clinical experience and from discussions with colleagues.

Most religions incorporate explanations of the meaning of life and death. From clinical experience, it is apparent that experiences involving the birth, life-threatening illness or accident, and/or the death of a family member, relative, or close friend elicit references to a higher power, purpose, and self-efficacy regarding those events.

A system of values, initially imposed and often internalized, is provided by religious systems. These may be manifest in family traditions, in verbal injunctions, and in canonized scripture. Such sources are often invoked by clients when being pressed to answer, in a cognitive restructuring confrontation, "Where is it written?" The value system or moral code transmitted by religious systems presents a strong foundation of shoulds, oughts, and musts that show up in the parent tapes of transactional analysis or in the alleged irrationalities of the cognitive therapies.

Along with a strongly established and energetically indoctrinated set of moral imperatives, most religious systems incorporate a repentence strategy that permits the believers to recover from forays into mortality. As a repentence ritual, most involve a confession of sinful behavior to an authority figure who exacts evidence in the penitent person of realization of wrongdoing, a feeling of remorse, restitution to the person who was either the object of or a partner in the confessed violation, and a conviction of restraint from repeating the same offense. Whether or not the therapist believes in such a procedure, the use of ritual to resolve problems of affective surplus has been established in previous chapters. Furthermore, the avoidance by a believer or the obstruction by the therapist of such a process often precludes or retards problem resolution.

Another common feature of clients who subscribe to a religious position is the belief in/experience of a relationship with Diety. "Somebody" cares. Somebody hears and answers prayers. There is a perceived connectedness, especially at times of isolation. There is a sense of specialness—either because of the belief in having a corrupt nature with the potential for salvation, or of being an extension of Diety and therefore good.

For those actively involved in a church or a synagogue, there are the products of tradition and of ritual. Some of these products may be good, such as a sense of belonging and support. Similarly, the same dynamics and experiences may be expressed as a sense of being trapped, limited, or oppressed.

Often, religious clients, at least those who admit to or profess being religious, will talk about faith, faith healing, and the place of prayer in coping with trials. Whether or not a counselor feels compelled to comply when asked by a client to pray for him or her, there is in the asking of that question, a statement of prayer's importance to the client. Such phenomenally important dynamics, if respected, may have a beneficial influence on the treatment of that particular client.

Client Issues with Spiritual or Religious Implications

While any topic for a given client may have intense spiritual meaning, there are some topics or areas of client concern that often carry religious or spiritual implications. These would include suicide, extramarital sex, criminality, homosexuality, poor self image, questions of self-worth, coping with death, rebellion against and feelings of disrespect for parents, and family break-up.

These are more or less apparent in clients who claim a degree of spirituality but no religious affiliation. But the conceptualizations tend to be ill-defined and vague (religion puts words on them, with the risk of distorting and being dogmatic). The resident expert on an individual, in all aspects and most certainly as regards his or her spirituality, is that person. Having an exhaustive knowledge of his or her professed religious affiliation or spiritual philosophy provides the individual with a stereotypical and dogmatic structure of his or her abstract spiritual nature, to which somebody else believes he or she should believe and subscribe. Of more importance is the meaning and experience of the client's spiritual context from his or her phenomenal viewpoint.

☐ Conclusion

Personality, development, social and spiritual dynamics—each requires two levels of awareness for the counselor. First, it is necessary to have a well-developed position in each of these areas. It is good to have a personal investment of principle and experience. The second level of awareness is that not all people see these areas the same way as the counselor. This requires a respect for the client's position relative to each and a sensitivity to how he or she interweaves them into the fabric of his or her life. Each client is a separate symphony that can be better appreciated by a counselor who is knowledgeable about themes, structures, timbres, and cadences. This can be accomplished through the counselor paying attention to his or her own symphony.

There is a slant in the profession that says that a counselor must be trained specifically for each special class of client, in areas such as gender, sexuality, marriage and family issues, or alcohol/drug abuse. It is impossible to be a specialist in each unique area presented by clients; yet it is possible to be personally grounded and comfortable enough to let clients be themselves and to understand and appreciate their sense of being. The burgeoning of special interest areas in counseling has been so rapid and so great as to make it impossible for the therapist to be conversant with all areas. Some degree of specialization may be demanded as the profession matures; yet the individual client variations within the diverse contexts makes the "medical specialty" model less appropriate and less functional. For the present, and perhaps as a long-term strategy, therapists need to study enough instances of diversity to permit them to work outside of their own parochial mindset. They are well advised to study much more deeply the contexts of client groups that appear with frequency in their individual practice setting, while maintaining enough objectivity to permit client variation from the group norms.

A focus on contextual elements is necessary for tailoring the chosen, learning-based intervention to the specific client. Contextual elements are modifiers of learning dynamics. The major thrust of intervention must continue to be the change of responses based on learning models.

PART IV

ASSESSMENT, STRATEGY SELECTION, AND IMPLEMENTATION

CHAPTER 11

Assessment and Strategy Selection

There are two axioms that undergird the most powerful and most effective form of human service intervention: technique follows understanding, and the power of an intervention comes from its theoretical context.

Therapists encounter a wide variety of clients who represent many different circumstances. These clients may have been selected informally so that many or most have similar patterns; for example, students making the transition from middle school to high school, graduate students in a highly selective program, first-time mothers in a parenting class. Professionals who work in settings with a generally homogeneous clientele tend to develop a restricted perception and often deal less effectively with those clients who don't fit the pattern. They may also gloss over the unique differences existing within a seemingly homogeneous clientele. Other therapists or teachers, the "general practitioners" of human service, encounter extreme ranges of client types and circumstances.

If technique indeed follows understanding, then each and every client or client system (e.g., family, class, group) needs to be assessed very carefully. Under present pressures of short-term therapy, there is the tendency to perform a quick intake, focus on the "obvious" problem, and apply a quick-fix intervention. So often the cry of, "I don't have time to help clients with real problems" is a transparent admission of incompetence. The amount of time invested in a peripheral issue or symptom often is greater than the time required to resolve the major concern and, by virtue of its application, either delays or prevents treatment of the more important concern. Nowhere is the adage, "haste makes waste," more true than in human services. Unfortunately, much counseling is "reactive" to the demands of the counselor's situation rather than responsive to the needs of the client.

While not every client or student or group requires extensive treatment, each deserves competent and professional care. The challenge offered by every client is, "I'm giving you the opportunity to make a difference in my life." The responsive therapist takes that challenge seriously.

The first step in any intervention strategy is to learn, from the client's framework, his or her circumstances (challenges and resources) and personal style for addressing problems. This is more than a standard intake or pre-service review of files. This requires communication with and observation of the client or system of concern. From such an assessment, it is possible to identify those learning or intervention dynamics that present the highest probability of being effective, thus allowing for the use of theoretically powerful techniques.

The power of an intervention comes from its theoretical context. This chapter continues with the model that has already been elaborated. The major difference is an emphasis on client assessment, perception of unique circumstance and style, and application of intervention strategies that most nearly fit the circumstance and style of the particular client. Because clients are complex, it is possible to frame their situation from several different perspectives. The student of this chapter will be presented with numerous client scenarios, and be encouraged to arrive at alternate strategies, to compare and contrast those of potential applicability to the scenario at hand, and to make defensible decisions regarding which approach to use. It is recognized that human service work is more analogous to an advanced art form than to an empirical science, and that the most logically defensible strategy may not always work. Because of this aspect of reality, it is extremely useful to have considered alternate approaches that may serve as back-up to the selected strategy.

By way of caution and, perhaps, disclaimer, the case vignettes give a limited view of client experience. They are sufficiently complete to permit analysis and to project treatment interventions. It is to be recognized that in working with an actual client, much of what here has to be inferred, there, can be verified through progressive interaction with the client. In the actual situation, there will be less room for speculation and a higher probability of homing in on critical elements that will lead to better interventions.

There are four primary divisions in this chapter. At first, several cases are given with two or three plausible alternative interpretations regarding client circumstance and style. These cases are processed according to the four categories of style and of circumstance, with deficit and surplus qualities (see Figure 11.1).

Based on conclusions from the initial assessments, categorical descriptions of intervention strategies are given, each showing logical consistency in the connection of client circumstance, style, and theory-pure intervention. The intent is for this section to demonstrate thinking within the upper two levels of Blosser's system: Level 3, divergent thinking (given a problem, select strategies from each of two different families of theory and defend their use); and Level 4, evaluative thinking (given a problem, select two appropriate approaches and compare/contrast/evaluate them). These two levels of thinking are critical to the successful application of intervention principles.

The second primary division is concerned with complexities often encountered in

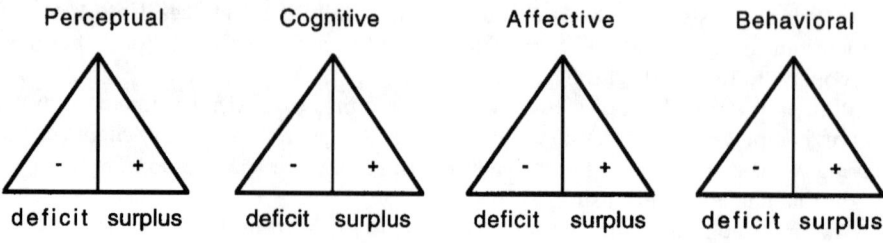

FIGURE 11.1. Four Categories of Style and of Circumstance.

human services intervention. The third section includes several client vignettes for practice and discussion. The chapter will end with a section of brief summary and conclusions.

☐ Demonstration Scenarios
Vignette 1: Special Program Student

Carey is a ten year-old girl who was diagnosed as learning disabled. She attends a combination of special education and regular classes. You attended an individualized educational program meeting, attended also by teachers from both the special education and regular classes, the school social worker, school nurse, and vice-principal. Information that surfaced in the meeting included:

- Carey is often disruptive, non-attentive, and non-compliant in all of her classes.
- She is currently living with her maternal grandparents who recently have obtained permanent custody.
- Born to a single parent, she spent the first eight years with her mother, who has a long history of substance abuse. On numerous occasions her mother was reported to Child Protective Services for alleged neglect of Carey.
- Following her eighth year, she spent twenty months bouncing from one foster home to another before going to her grandparents' home.
- She has a history of malnutrition; at present her health is stable and well within the normal range.

You have been assigned as primary case manager and asked to bring your recommendations back to the IEP Committee in two weeks. Your initial strategy is to make several classroom observations, to talk with Carey's grandparents, and to interview Carey.

From your visits to Carey's classes, you observed that she generally showed age-appropriate behavior. She socialized well with girls in both settings. She joined into activities a little hesitantly at first, but then became fully invested. Her class disruptions bordered on being "cute," never so bad as to cause major problems and yet were too obvious to ignore. Her attention varied without any discernible pattern, and her non-compliance was most evident when challenged with misbehavior or when struggling with a difficult task. The special education teacher used a continuous measurement, frequent reinforcement approach for most tasks. Carey was inconsistent in her responses, on some occasions jumping right into active involvement with moderate success, on other occasions showing either daydreaming or off-task activity. Of seeming curiosity was her insistence to sit close to her regular classroom teacher during story time—sitting at the feet of the teacher and often leaning against the teacher's leg. In another class activity, as the teacher was going down the row asking students to respond sequentially to questions in their math books, Carey was not aware of which problems she was to answer, yet, when oriented to a specific item, she gave a marginally correct answer.

The grandparents indicated that the transition for them in accepting Carey into their home had been difficult. At first, Carey would eat more than necessary, almost as though she didn't trust that there would be more; this was especially true with desserts. Carey lied about nonconsequential things such as what she was watching on television. The grandparents had worked with a counselor to build some ground rules, to chart Carey's responses, and to contract for privileges. This approach had some moderating effect but was not working consistently. Grandmother seemed to be quite concerned about Carey. Grandfather tended to say, "She'll be okay. Just give her time." He particularly enjoyed having Carey follow him around the farm as he did his evening chores.

In the interview with Carey, most of her responses and actions were typical for her age. She answered questions haltingly, watching you intently as she answered. Purposefully you rephrased the same question and elicited inconsistent responses. When you asked her to describe freely an imaginary situation regarding school, she started readily then hesitated, changing her story frequently, again watching you intently as though for guidance or affirmation of her story.

Interpretation and Strategy I: Behavioral Deficit and Behavioral Surplus in the Circumstance, Behavioral Style. Because of the developmental level of the student, age 8 +/- two years, influenced by the diagnosis of a learning disability, she will respond best to an operant system. She has grown up through nine plus years of her life responding to an inconsistent reality. Her mother's history of substance abuse suggests a parental environment alternating from good to bad, with no readily apparent way of anticipating the "rule of the game" from moment-to-moment. Carey had been conditioned to live in the moment, to take what she could get, to buy time through lying. Inconsistencies in her responses at school and home are due to three problems in application of operant procedures: (a) inconsistency on the part of teachers and grandparents, (b) absence of system adjustments to maintain progress in target response, and (c) lack of working programs for important target responses such as staying on task, appropriately responding to adults, increased production between reinforcements, monitoring or "staying with" class assignments and being ready to respond at her turn.

The strategy is to identify one or two unwanted responses in each setting—regular classroom, special education classroom, grandparent's home—and build a behavior management program for each, with emphasis on the positive reinforcement of mutually exclusive and wanted responses. Continued reinforcement will be given for the other behavior that is desired, and other responses—present and unwanted, not present and wanted—will be ignored temporarily until the conditioning of selected target responses has them successfully under control and on a variable reinforcement schedule. At that time, additional wanted and not present responses will be programmed for reinforcement.

Interpretation and Strategy II: Affective Deficit Circumstance, Behavioral Style. Based on the young age of the client, compounded by a lifetime of near-noncontingency relationships between activity and success, it appears that Carey has been striving to earn acceptance in a world of changing rules. From a developmental standpoint, Carey was neither valued nor accepted as a person, no matter what her condition and no matter what her response. She was not even consistently reinforced with negative attention. In the world mediated by substance abuse, her existence was nonconsequential. The inconsistency in attention; the variability in responses, both acceptable and unacceptable to the same situation; the seeking of personal closeness and physical contact in the nonthreatening story context; and the fitting in as a companion in farm chores all indicate a need for personal validation.

The strategy is to create periods of time and activities for which quantity or quality of performance doesn't matter. The story time in the regular classroom is an example. Carey should have some time, every day at home, when she can receive adult attention and acceptance, no matter what her actions have been, such as accompanying her grandfather on his chores, having him focus on her or at least involve her as an active participant with no standards for acceptable performance. As she develops a feeling of security and worth in these settings, the desperation to be okay in other situations will subside and she will naturally pay attention more consistently and perform more often within the limits of acceptability. From a Maslovian perspective, once she has learned that she is okay, fulfilled her love and belonging needs, and accomplished personal validation, she will be able to function at the higher level of contingency-based, self-esteem activities.

Comparison, Evaluation, Decision. Both interpretations and strategies focus on Carey's formative experiences in an environment wherein it was impossible to predict which of her actions might result in success and satisfaction. In a drug- or alcohol-mediated relationship, often the same responses on different occasions result in markedly different results. Carey was taught that no matter what she did (outside of hypervigilance and doing whatever would produce immediate gratification or avoidance of punishment), nothing would result in her being accepted or rejected or ignored. Children develop best in conditions of consistency.

Strategy I, behavioral intervention, is based on the principle of simplifying a few desirable relationships between situation, response, and reinforcement, and managing them over a sufficiently long time-period so as to condition Carey to the predictability of success coming from the desired response. The immediate and manageable reinforcers of charts, checks, prizes, or privileges would gradually give way to social reinforcers of positive attention and praise on a variable reinforcement schedule. The success of this approach lies in teaching the teachers and grandparents to work the system—to observe the target response in the appropriate conditions and consistently apply reinforcers. Such a program, over time, will teach Carey that there is some order in her universe and that she can "control" the outcomes by performing acceptably.

Strategy II, affective deficit, rests on some assumptions regarding human development. First, children need to experience noncontingent and positive socialization as a foundation of their self-concept. Through unconditional positive relationships, usually with a parent, they feel validated; they have value simply because they are. This is consistent with Maslow's third-level hierarchical need for love and belonging. Second, other and higher levels of personal growth are based on accomplishment of requisite, basic ones, in this case personal validation. Esteem dynamics involve performance to some external standard with resultant attention, praise, adulation—"success" experiences. In this case, success is contingent on the response of others, that is, external locus of control. It is the external responses that become internalized to form a positive self-concept. Such esteem dynamics parallel operant conditioning ones. Theoretically, they will be ineffective in fulfilling the requisite personal validation need.

To the extent that one believes in the personality development dynamics underlying Strategy II, they will favor its use over Strategy I. It is possible to use both strategies during the same time frame if applied by separate people in different conditions. For example, the school counselor and the grandfather may work on the affective deficit–personal validation approach while the teacher and grandmother carefully monitor a target response, contingency management program.

Vignette 2: He Makes Me Sick

Virginia is a sophomore at the university. She went to the student health center with complaints of nervousness, difficulty in holding down food, and frequent headaches. She was given some medications to palliate her physical symptoms and referred to you by the physician at the center. The physician's referral note indicated that the medication would provide only temporary relief and that, based on what she said during the examination, she needed psychological help. As she started the interview, she said, "I don't know why the doctor sent me to you. I guess I'm supposed to figure out why I'm getting sick, but the medicine is supposed to make me feel better. I don't know why I have to see a counselor."

You told her that sometimes our bodies react with illness to conditions that aren't going well in our lives. Then you invited her to share what it's like being her. You notice that she was "plain" in appearance, a little overweight, and that she was dressed in clean and unfashionable clothing. She told you that she was a sophomore, majoring in elementary education. Until this term, she was typically taking general university requirements, that her grades were generally around a 2.5 g.p.a., and that she had to work hard to keep up with the pace of instruction. She believed that she would do better in her major classes.

Her parents and high school counselor in a small neighboring community impressed on her the necessity of having a career, though her main life goal was to be a wife and a mother. She related that she is having trouble spending time with her boyfriend due to tension to the point of, "I don't enjoy his company," and, "Sometimes it's easier to be alone." She stated that her boyfriend often gets upset and pouts. He reacts negatively and irrationally. For instance, on being told that his hair was out of place, he pouted and gave her the "silent treatment." She had thought that maybe it would be helpful to talk through this problem because it is very upsetting to her, but her father was very "anti-psychology" and believed that personal problems do not go outside the family.

Interpretation and Strategy I: Behavioral Deficit Circumstance, Cognitive Style.

This looks like a straightforward boundary management circumstance. She has adapted herself to a reactive style of permitting others to take an action to which she then tries to respond—external locus of control. There are hints that her father dominated interactions in her family of origin and that she is casting her boyfriend in a similar role. Group therapy in an assertion skills group would be a good intervention strategy. By participating in such a program, she would learn through reinforced experience that it is possible to assert boundaries, to say "no," to allow others to be different without capitulating to their strength. Ideologically, her cognitive style would not be of concern, assuming that as she experienced success in boundary setting and maintenance, she would rationalize her new position.

There is a strong possibility that her present boyfriend would respond unfavorably to a shift in her response style, resulting in his ending the relationship. This is a potential outcome of any therapeutic intervention that is successful in changing her behavior. Therefore, it is of no particular consequence to the behavioral therapist. It is possible that his behavior is conditioned by her responses and that, as she changes, there will be a corresponding alteration in his behavior. This would be facilitated if he also were to engage in therapy. Similar dynamics exist in her relationship with her parents. As she establishes her own boundaries and asserts them, some stress may result from the reactions of her parents.

Interpretation and Strategy II: Cognitive Surplus Circumstance, Cognitive Style.

Basic to a cognitive restructuring approach, appropriate in a cognitive surplus circumstance, is the assumption that thought precedes action, that all responses are a result of, or are mediated by, cognitive assumptions or self-statements. Using a simple ABC approach, Virginia's cognitive structure might look like this (recognizing that the "real" structure would evolve in interaction with the client on these very points):

Activating event	Belief System	Consequent Response
Boyfriend	Happiness results from getting married and pleasing my husband.	Persisting in face of punishing relationship.
	I can't be happy if he's unpleased or unhappy.	Depressed, discouraged.
	I must make it work.	Somatic symptoms.
	It's my fault he's unhappy or It's my job to make him happy.	Tension.
Counselor	I'm betraying my father.	Resistance.
	I should do what my father says. Father knows best.	Uneasiness.
School	I must please my parents. I should follow the school counselor's advice.	Pursuing degree.
Average grades	I can't do well if I'm not interested.	Disappointment, rationalization.

The intervention would consist of challenging each of the self-statements or defeating beliefs and replacing them with self-enhancing beliefs. For example, to the first one of "happiness results from getting married and pleasing my husband," dialogue and challenges might be made such as: "Have you ever been happy? Even though you didn't have a husband at the time? Where is it written that you should, or even could if you wanted to, cause an unhappy person to be happy? Who gave you the responsibility for your boyfriend's emotional states? One possibility is that you erred in letting him know his hair was messed up. Another possibility is that he responded in an incredibly immature manner." "If you were to manage your own happiness successfully, what kind of impact would that have on others? What kind of friends would you attract if you were a happy person?" "Have you ever been happy or feeling at least neutral? With and without the company of a man?"

The re-structured conclusions would be something like, "My happiness is my responsibility; a happy me will do better in attracting a happy mate. My mate's happiness is his responsibility; if I want my mate to be happy, I should find a happy person to be a mate." Similar sequences would have to be done in regard to her responses to her parents, her school pursuits and her school performance.

Comparison, Evaluation, Decision. Of importance to the decision in this case is a determination of whether or not the current relationship has the potential of becoming workable. At present, it is self-defeating to Virginia and probably to her partner. If she is convinced that he is a potential long-term partner and that she, for reasons of not seeing herself attractive enough to find a more suitable mate or of the belief that he is a worthy "catch," then Strategy I is appealing because it helps her to establish personal strength with the hope that he will adapt positively to her change. Of course, there is no guarantee that he will stay with her when she behaves differently.

If she, or that part of her that genuinely is turned off by him, decides that a clean break holds promise for a more effective and more successful adjustment, then Strategy II has merit. Because her style is cognitive and because there are so many self-defeating self-statements in her belief system, there is relatively more reason to favor Strategy II. Once she has learned the procedure of identifying and challenging the defeating conclusions, and replacing them with enhancing ones, she can be readily directed to repeat the process on successive, defeating cognitive structures.

Complexities and Exceptions to the Rules

Very often, client circumstances are complex, with simultaneous concerns in more than one category. In such instances, it is necessary to isolate the different problems, identify their learning dynamics, project tentative strategies for each separately, and then look at the composite to decide which problem to tackle first and whether or not to work on two or more at the same time. Compound strategies often are enhanced by use of two or more therapists, each working on a separate concern. Consider for example the following case vignettes.

Vignette 1: Athletic Star. John Grandy has been referred to you by his basketball coach because John's grades are marginal and, if they drop any lower, he will be ruled ineligible to play in the state tournament. In your initial, brief conference with John, his attitude is one of impertinence. He says he is interested only in basketball; school is boring—a waste of time; and that the teachers won't flunk the "star" of the basketball team. Your immediate reaction is to enlighten John about the need to get good grades in order to play college basketball and that problems such as these will only increase in the college setting. You stifle your inclination and make an appointment to talk with him the next day, when you can devote more than just a few minutes to him.

Upon entering your office the next day, he says, "I bet you're going to give me that B.S. about college ball and more pressure to get grades. Those schools have tutors and people who cover for the good athletes, so save your breath." After recognizing and honoring John's discomfort and resistance at talking with you, you engage him in some description of his circumstance more broadly. You learn from him that he is 6'6" tall, still growing, and that he holds the league records in scoring and rebounding. He just received his college entrance examination scores and was average or above in all categories. His father, who is a manual laborer, played high school ball but saw limited action as the eighth player in the rotation. He is very excited about John's basketball success. John's mother sometimes nags him about grades, but often is countered by his father's admonitions to "Lay off! He's fine!" John's older brother, Sam, graduated last year with honors, received a National Merit Scholarship, and was accepted to

M.I.T. with a dual-track program in structural engineering and experimental mathematics. Although he enjoys the attention he gets on the court, John is extremely nervous about speaking in front of class groups. He is romantically involved with a girl who is in five of his classes; he knows that his career precludes any serious involvement for a number of years, yet he finds himself to be "extremely in love." For the past six months, he has affiliated with a group of guys who eschew grade games and anything smacking of conformity. While he doesn't indulge with them in smoking and use of drugs and alcohol, John finds them accepting of him and more fun than his athlete associates or other groups.

Some tentative conclusions about John's circumstances might include:

Affective deficit: Performance-based value.
Affective surplus: Impertinence, discomfort in talking, ambivalence in relationship with girl— approach/avoidance—resentment/jealousy of brother's success.
Behavioral surplus: Father and friends reinforce basketball and anti-school responses.
Cognitive surplus: School is a waste of time; teachers will carry athletes; the only value of school is access to basketball.

John's style is obscured by the limited data. It shows evidence for both behavioral and cognitive styles. It is possible that the cognitive indicators are simply conditioned responses to demanding stimuli in his environment. It is expected that further interaction with John will simplify the dynamics; however, he may represent an amalgamation of circumstances and of styles.

Vignette II: Marriage Dissolution. Brandon reluctantly has come to see you upon the advice of a close friend who told him he would not listen any more to Brandon's concerns because they were too severe for him to handle. Brandon's divorce became final last November. Following his separation a year earlier, he had lived with his parents and siblings. After living there for six months, he became withdrawn, depressed, and estranged from his family members, with whom he previously had been very close.

Brandon said that his parents and siblings blame him for the divorce and for deserting his children (two daughters and a step-son). He believes his family has taken his ex-wife's point of view and that nobody knows what it is like for him. He says that he would never do anything to hurt the kids and that he resents his parents and siblings for believing him to be a bad parent.

A somewhat closed person, Brandon believes that he should be able to work out his personal problems on his own, that his divorce concerns only him and his ex-wife, and that only weak or crazy people—of which he is neither—need to go to a counselor.

Recently, Brandon moved back in with his ex-wife and children, but has not told his parents because he is "taking things one day at a time." He wants things to get better, but doesn't really think that they will.

In response to Brandon's disclosures, it is possible to see circumstances leading to differing conclusions or to multiple conclusions; for example:

Affective surplus: Withdrawn, depressed, resentful of family members, pessimistic.
Cognitive surplus: "I must please my parents; you should do it yourself; only weak or crazy people need help"

Cognitive deficit: No obvious knowledge about conflict resolution; no knowledge about the counseling process.
Behavioral surplus: Withdraws when challenged, runs away, blames, external locus of control, wants "things" to get better, came at insistence of friend, looking for positive strokes.

Obviously, Brandon will need a counselor to teach and reinforce talking, looking for alternatives, and working from an internal locus of control. He needs better situational observation and assessment skills, and major help in human relations. Family counseling is indicated; however, he is not likely to experience success in that context without some prior individual work. Too much time devoted to individual work before addressing the family interactions may result in further dissolution of the family. Multiple problems involving several people require careful identification and separation of problems, identification of appropriate interventions for each, and a synthesis of efforts in order to manage the complex circumstance.

It is important to recognize the great diversity in circumstance and style of clients. Each one is unique. Each one requires and deserves utmost care in the exploration of phenomenal reality so as to serve each in a professional and efficient way. It is impossible to catch the richness and diversity of clients on the printed page, and it is problematical to "solve" problems without interaction with the actual client. The following practice vignettes have been selected because they permit more than one analysis and because they are relatively uncomplicated. They are intended to provide the opportunity for the reader to create two or more interventions from different conclusions regarding circumstance and style. The different analyses and interventions give an arena for comparison and contrast, for selection and defense of the preferred approach.

☐ Practice Vignettes

Vignette I: Metropolitan Opera Star

Christina is a moderately talented singer from a family of professional musicians. Beginning with her senior recital and progressively in auditions since that time, she has experienced some laryngitis and other conditions such as headaches and skin rash. Some statements she made in your initial interview include:

- "My father is a world class conductor. I didn't ever spend much time with him because he was gone a lot, and when home he didn't seem to have much time for me."
- "Mother is extremely organized and disciplined. As I was growing up she constantly reminded me to study and practice; she takes extreme pleasure in my successes—a 3.97 g.p.a., numerous singing awards, scholarships, etc."
- "I just can't understand why I have these health problems. It is frustrating and embarrassing to cancel auditions, or worse—to do poorly in them. What's more, I'll probably lose my scholarship and maybe even have to leave the conservatory since I can't seem to perform. I really have to get my act together."

Vignette II: Architect

Jonathan is a first-term college freshman in a pre-architecture program. His father runs a highly successful architectural firm in Dallas, and in recent years had devoted much of his energy to running the business because he has not kept abreast of the technical revolution. It is readily understood that the techniques in drafting, design, and construction will have changed significantly by the time Jon graduates, and that they will undergo major alterations during each four or five years for the foreseeable future.

Jon's dream is to work in his father's firm, eventually taking over when his father retires. Jon was a good B+/A- student in high school, getting his grades with little effort. He played football and basketball, usually second-string, apparently reaching that level with relatively little dedication and effort.

He has just taken his mid-term exams and is worried that his grades will be too low to qualify for fraternity rush and eligibility for spring football. Also, he has been working about 20 hours/week in his father's firm and has been telling everyone how great it is to be at the university and how well he is doing.

Vignette III: I See the Future

Aaron is in his last year at the community college where you work as a counselor. You know of him primarily from his athletic reputation. He plays forward on the basketball team and has a 14-point scoring average and pulls down an average 11 rebounds per game. As you've watched him play, you were curious or concerned about his reckless style. He seemed fearless, rash, even explosive in his intense competitiveness.

One of the psychology teachers asked you to talk with Aaron because, in a class paper, Aaron disclosed that at some time in the future he likely will kill himself by placing a loaded shotgun in his mouth and pulling the trigger. He indicated that both his father and grandfather had killed themselves in that way.

In your first meeting with Aaron, you found him to be quite open and frank about this information as well as being somewhat proud of the strong and forceful lifestyle of his progenitors.

☐ Summary and Conclusions

Consistent throughout this book have been two assumptions: Technique follows understanding, and the strength of an intervention comes from its theoretical context. The keys to translating theory into application are having a thorough knowledge of the theoretical dynamics and an understanding of client circumstance and style. Different intervention strategies are based on varying theoretical dynamics; many appear to have experiential and empirical support for their effectiveness. It is probable that different theories support those interventions that are differentially effective for clients whose circumstance and style fit the dynamics of the intervention strategy. It is asserted that effective therapy, doing what is most efficient and effective for a particular client, is a function of identifying the unique client circumstances and preferred problem-solving styles, and selecting or creating the intervention strategy that is most responsive to the client circumstance and style. Such an intervention strategy will be effective to the extent it is applied correctly, completely, and in a theory-pure way.

It is possible to manipulate intervention principles cognitively, to be able to "talk a good game" without being able to apply them well. This corresponds to the lowest level of Blosser's taxonomy (cognitive learning). A functional mastery of intervention is enhanced by learning to apply specific intervention approaches to appropriate conditions (convergent thinking); to be able to identify from client disclosures one or two from many possible interventions (divergent thinking); and to be able to analyze, compare, evaluate, select, and defend a particular strategy from several that seem applicable (evaluative thinking).

Client reality is often obscure and complex, and often defies a simple, linear diagnosis and prescription approach to amelioration of problems. The maxim, "If what you are doing isn't working, do something else," is strengthened by a knowledge and experiential base that frames client circumstance and style in alternate ways, each based in a theoretical context. When the identified intervention strategy does not produce the desired results, a plausible alternative is readily available. This permits doing a selective "something else," not merely anything else.

An integrationist approach to theory and to intervention is one that allows for many different theory-based interventions to be valid, effective, "true." It recognizes that some therapists are specialists and that they operate exclusively within one theory and apply one intervention strategy to all of their clients. Those who are established and well-known collect a clientele that is primarily self-selected. Most therapists are not so widely known that their clients will accurately seek them out. These are the "general practitioners" of psychotherapy and counseling. In order to treat a wider variety of clients with diverse concerns, they either must tolerate a larger-than-wanted number of failures or partial successes from using a single and narrow strategy; use bits and pieces of several strategies in an amalgamation of theory-weak combinations; or they can learn and apply any of several specialized, theory-pure interventions differentially to clients for whom their repertoire fits. Ideally, counselors will use the strongest approach that provides the best fit with client circumstance and style. The integrationist approach has the highest probability of producing this outcome.

Technique follows understanding. The strength of an intervention comes from its theoretical context.

REFERENCES

Abramson, L., Seligman, M., & Teasdale, J. (1978). Learned helplessness in humans: Critique and reformulation. *Journal of Abnormal Psychology, 87,* 49–74.
Albrecht, S., Chadwick, B., & Jacobsen, C. (1987). *Social psychology* (2nd ed.). Englewood Cliffs, NJ: Prentice-Hall.
American Psychiatric Association. (1994). *Diagnostic and statistical manual of mental disorders* (4th ed.). Washington, DC: Author.
Anderson, C., Horowitz, C., & French, R. (1983). Attributional style of lonely and depressed people. *Journal of Personality and Social Psychology, 45,* 127–136.
Ansbacher, H., & Ansbacher, R. (1956). *The individual psychology of Alfred Adler.* New York: Basic Books.
Aponte, J., Rivers, R., & Wohl, J. (1995). *Psychological interventions and cultural diversity.* Boston: Allyn and Bacon.
Aron, A., & Aron, E. (1986). *The heart of social psychology.* Canada: Aron & Aron.
Ausubel, D. (1963). *The psychology of meaningful verbal learning: An introduction to school learning.* New York: Grune & Stratton.
Axelson, J. (1993). *Counseling and development in a multicultural society, 2nd ed.* Pacific Grove, CA: Brooks/Cole.
Baber, A. (1992). *Naked at gendergap: A man's view of the war between the sexes.* New York: Carol Publishing Group.
Bandler, R., & Grinder, J. (1975). *The structure of magic.* Palo Alto, CA: Science and Behavioral Books.
Bandura, A. (1969). *Principles of behavior modification.* New York: Holt, Rinehart, and Winston.
Bandura, A. (1974, December). Behavior theory and the models of man. *American Psychologist,* 859–869.
Bandura, A., & Walters, R. (1963). *Social learning and personal development.* New York: Holt, Rinehart & Winston.
Barnhardt, C. (Ed.). (1955). *The American college dictionary.* New York: Random House.
Bateson, G. (1958). *Naven, a survey of the problems suggested by a composite picture of a New Guinea tribe drawn from three points of view.* Stanford, CA: Stanford University Press.
Bateson, G. (1971). The cybernetics of "self": A theory of alcoholism. *Psychiatry, 34,* 1–18.
Bateson, G. (1974). Double bind. In S. Brand (Ed.), *II cybernetic frontiers* (pp. 9–33). New York: Random House.
Batson, C. D., & Ventis, W. L. (1982). *The religious experience: A social-psychological perspective.* New York: Oxford University Press.
Beall, A., & Sternberg, R. (1993). *The psychology of gender.* New York: Guilford Press.
Beck, A., Rush, A., Shaw, B., & Emery, G. (1979). *Cognitive therapy of depression.* New York: Guilford Press.
Becker, E. (1973). *The denial of death.* New York: The Free Press.
Becvar, D., & Becvar, R. (1988). *Family therapy: A systemic integration* (3rd ed.). Boston: Allyn and Bacon.
Bergin, A. (1988). Three contributions of a spiritual perspective to counseling, psychotherapy, and behavior change. *Counseling and Values, 33,* 21–31.
Bergin, A. (1989). Religious faith and counseling: A commentary on Worthington. *The Counseling Psychologist, 17.* 621–623
Bergin, A. (1991). Values and religious issues in psychotherapy and mental health. *American Psychologist, 46*(4). 397–403.
Berndt, T. (1997). *Child development* (2nd ed.). Chicago: Brown & Benchmark.
Berne, E. (1961) *Transactional analysis in psychotherapy,* New York: Grove Press.
Bigge, M. (1964). *Learning theory for teachers.* New York: Harper & Rowe.
Blosser, P. (1973). *Handbook of effective questioning techniques.* Worthington, OH: Educational Associates.
Blosser, P. (1975). *Ask the right question.* Washington, DC: National Science Teachers Association.
Bowen, M. (1976). Theory in the practice of psychotherapy. In P. J. Guerin (Ed.), *Family therapy: theory and practice* (pp. 42–90). New York: Gardner Press.

Bower, G., & Hilgard, E. (1981). *Theories of learning* (5th ed.). Englewood Cliffs, NJ: Prentice-Hall.
Bruner, J. (1966). *Toward a theory of instruction*. New York: W. W. Norton.
Burns, D. (1980). *Feeling good: The new mood therapy*. New York: Signet.
Chamberlain, P., Patterson, G., Reid, J., Kavanaugh, K., & Forgatch, M. (1984). Observation of client resistance. *Behavior Therapy, 15*, 144–155.
Chomsky, N. (1975). *The logical structure of linguistic theory*. New York: Plenum Press.
Chomsky, N. (1997). *Essays on form and interpretation*. New York: North Holland.
Coles, R. (1970). *Erik H. Erikson: The growth of his work*. Boston: Little, Brown & Company.
Combs, A. & Soper, D. (1963). The perceptual organization of effective counselors. *Journal of Counseling Psychology. 10*(3), 222–226.
Crane, R. (1997, February 10). Counseling multicultural clients. *Advance: for Speech-Language Pathologists & Audiologists, 7*. King of Prussia, PA: Merion.
Dawson, M., & Furedy, J. (1974). *The role of relational awareness in human autonomic discrimination classical conditioning*. Unpublished manuscript, University of Toronto.
DeCarvalho, R. (1991). *The growth hypothesis in psychology: The humanistic psychology of Abraham Maslow and Carl Rogers*. San Francisco: EM Text.
Deutch, M., & Kraus, R. (1965). *Theories in social psychology*. New York: Basic Books.
Dryden, W. (1989). Albert Ellis: An efficient and passionate life. *Journal of Counseling and Development, 67*, 539–546.
Dunn, R. (1978). *Teaching students through their individual learning styles*. Reston, VA: Reston Pub. Co.
Dunn, R. (1995). *Strategies for educating diverse learners*. Bloomington, IN: Phi Delta Kappa Educational Foundation.
Dunn, R., & Dunn, K. (1977). *Administrator's guide to new programs for faculty management and evaluation*. West Nyack, NY: Parker.
Dunn, R., & Dunn, K. (1988) *Learning styles: Quiet revolution in American secondary schools*. Reston, VA: National Association of Secondary School Principals.
Dunn, R., & Griggs, S. (1995). *Multiculturalism and learning style: Teaching and counseling adolescents*. Westport, CN: Praeger.
Ebbinghaus, H. (1913). *Memory: A contribution to experimental psychology* (H. Ruger & C. Bussenius, Trans.). New York: Teachers College, Columbia University.
Ellis, A. (1958). Rational psychotherapy. *Journal of General Psychology, 59*(1), 35–49.
Ellis, A. (1962). *Reason and emotion in psychotherapy*. New York: Lyle Stuart and Citadel Press.
Ellis, A. (1969). Rational-emotive therapy. *Contemporary Psychotherapy, 1*(2), 82–90.
Ellis, A. (1971). *Growth through reason: Verbatim cases in rational-emotive therapy*. Palo Alto, CA: Science and Behavior Book.
Ellis, A. (1982). Major systems. *The Personnel and Guidance Journal, 61*, 6–7.
Erickson, M. (1967). *Advanced techniques of hypnosis and therapy: Selected papers of Milton H. Erickson* (J. Haley, Ed.). New York: Grune & Stratton.
Erickson, M. (1980). *The collected papers of Milton H. Erickson on hypnosis* (E. Rossi, Ed.). New York: Irvington.
Erikson, E. (1950). *Childhood and society*. New York: W. W. Norton.
Erikson, E. (1963). *Childhood and society, 2nd Ed*. New York: W. W. Norton.
Erikson, E. (1968). *Identity: Youth and crisis*. New York: W. W. Norton.
Erikson, E. (1980). *Identity and the life cycle*. New York: W. W. Norton.
Ewalt, P., Freeman, E., Kirk, S., & Poole, D. (Eds.). (1996). *Multicultural issues in social work*. Washington, DC: NASW Press.
Festinger, L. (1957). *A theory of cognitive dissonance*. Stanford, CA: Stanford University Press.
Försterling, F. (1986). Attributional conceptions in clinical psychology. *American Psychologist, 41*(3), 275–285.
Frankl, (1962). *Man's search for meaning: An introduction to logotherapy* (I. Lasch, Trans.). Boston: Beacon Press.
Fromm, E. (1941). *Escape from freedom*. New York: Rinehart.
Fromm, E. (1956). *The art of loving*. New York: Harper.
Frost, S. Jr. (1962). *Basic teachings of the great philosophers: A survey of their basic ideas*. New York: Doubleday.

References

Fukuyama, M., & Sevig, T. (1997). Spiritual issues in counseling: A new course. *Counselor Education and Supervision, 36,* 224–232.
Gaines, J. (1979). *Fritz Perls: Here and now.* Tiburon, CA: Integrated Press.
Gazda, G., & Corsini, R. (1980). *Theories of learning: A comparative approach.* Itasca, IL: Peacock.
Gagné, R. (1965). *The conditions of learning.* New York: Holt, Rinehart and Winston.
Gengerelli, J. (1976, October). Graduate school reminiscences: Hull and Koffka. *American Psychologist,* 685–688.
Gerber, S. (1986). *Responsive therapy: A systematic approach to counseling skills.* New York: Human Sciences Press.
Gerber, S. (1991). The psychology of personal commitment: A new personality model. *National Social Science Journal,* 138–149.
Gerber, S., Pederson, D., & Selby, P. (1996). Affective deficit in clients: The role of the therapist. In *Resources in Education* (Report No. CG027306). Greensboro, NC: Center for Research on Counseling and Personnel Services. (ERIC Document Reproduction Service No. ED 398 514)
Gilligan, C. (1982). *In a different voice: Psychological theory and women's development.* Cambridge, MA: Harvard University Press.
Gladding, S. (1992). *Counseling: A comprehensive profession.* New York: Merrill.
Goble, F. (1970). *The third force: The psychology of Abraham Maslow.* New York: Grossman.
Good, B., & Good, M. (1986) The cultural context of diagnosis and therapy: A view from medical anthropology. In M. Miranda & H. Kitano (Eds.), *Mental health research and practice in minority communities: Development of culturally sensitive training programs* (DHHS Publication No. ADM 86-1466, pp. 1–28). Rockville, MD: National Institute of Mental Health.
Gray, J. (1993). *Men are from mars, women are from venus: A practical guide for improving communication and getting what you want in your relationships.* Glenview, IL: HarperCollins.
Green, W. (1996). Religion within the limits. *Academe, 82*(6), 24–28.
Grings, W. (1973). The role of consciousness and cognition in autonomous behavior change. In F. J. McGuigan and R. Schoonover (Eds.), *The psychophysiology of thinking.* New York: Academic Press.
Guerin, P., & Pendagast, E. (1976). Evaluation of family system and genogram. In P. J. Guerin (Ed.), *Family therapy: Theory and practice* (pp. 450–464). New York: Gardner Press.
Guthrie, E. (1952). *The psychology of learning.* New York: Harper & Brothers.
Haley, J. (1976). *Problem-solving therapy.* New York: Harper Colophon.
Harvey, J. (1974). The abilene paradox: the management of agreement. *Organizational Dynamics, 3*(1).
Harris, T. (1967). *I'm ok—you're ok: A practical guide to transactional analysis.* New York: Harper & Row.
Havighurst, R. (1949). *Developmental tasks and education.* Chicago: University of Chicago Press.
Havighurst, R. (1959). Social and psychological needs of the aging. In L. Gordow & W. Katkovsky (Eds.), *Readings in the psychology of adjustment* (pp. 443–447). New York: McGraw-Hill.
Havighurst, R. (1972). *Developmental tasks and education.* New York: McKay.
Holt, E. (1915). Response and cognition. *Journal of Philosophy, Psychology, and Scientific Methods, 12,* 365–373.
Horney, K. (1945). *Our inner conflicts.* New York: Norton.
Horney, K. (1950). *Neurosis and human growth.* New York: Norton.
Hoyenga, K., & Hoyenga, K. (1993). *Gender-related differences: Origins and outcomes.* Boston: Allyn and Bacon.
Huxley, A. (1956). *The doors of perception.* New York: Harper & Row.
Ingersoll, E. (1997). Teaching a course on counseling and spirituality. *Counselor Education and Supervision, 36,* 224–232.
James, W. (1960). *The varieties of religious experience.* London: Collins Clear-Type Press.
Janis, I. (1967). *Victims of groupthink: A psychological study of foreign policy decisions and fiascos.* Boston: Houghton-Mifflin.
Jourard, S. (1968). *Disclosing man to himself.* Princeton, NJ: Van Nostrand.
Kagan, J. (1971). *Understanding children: Behavior, motives, and thought.* New York: Harcourt, Brace & Jovanovich.
Kellermann, P. (1992). *Focus on psychodrama: The therapeutic aspects of psychodrama.* Philadelphia: Kingsley.
Kelly, H. (1971). *Attribution in social interaction.* Morristown, NJ: General Learning Press.

Kelley, H., & Michela, J. (1980). Attribution theory and research. *Annual Review of Psychology, 31,* 457–501.
Kempler, W. (1982). Gestalt family therapy. In A. M. Horne & M. M. Ohlsen (Eds.), *Family counseling and therapy* (pp. 141–174). Itasca, IL: F. E. Peacock.
Kinzie, J., Manson, S., Vinh, D., Nguyen, T., Anh, B., & Pho, T. (1982). Development and validation of a Vietnamese-language depression rating scale. *American Journal of Psychiatry, 139,* 1276–1281.
Kleinmen, A., & Good, B. (1985). Introduction: Culture and depression. In A. Kleinman & B. Good (Eds.), *Culture and depression* (pp. 1–33). Berkeley, CA: University of California Press.
Kohler, W. (1925). *The mentality of apes* (E. Winter, Trans.). New York: Harcourt, Brace, & World. (Original work published 1917).
Koffka, K. (1963). *Principles of gestalt psychology.* New York: Harcourt, Brace.
Lashley, K. (1929). *Brain mechanisms and intelligence: A quantitative study of injuries to the brain.* Chicago: Chicago University Press.
LDS Church. (1830). *The book of Mormon.* Salt Lake City, UT: Church of Jesus Christ of Latter-day Saints.
LeVay, S., & Nonas, E. (1995). *City of friends: A portrait of the gay and lesbian community in America.* Cambridge, MA: M.I.T. Press.
Levinson, D. (with Darrow, C., Klein, M., and McKee, B.). (1978). *The seasons of a man's life.* New York: Alfred A. Knopf.
Lovinger, R. (1984). *Working with religious issues in therapy.* New York: Aronson.
MacDonald, F. (1965). *Educational psychology* (2nd ed.). Belmont, CA: Wadsworth.
Macfarlane, D. (1930). The role of kinesthesis in maze learning. *University of California Publications in Psychology, 4,* 277–305.
Maddi, S. (1968). *Personality theories: A comparative analysis.* Homewood, IL: Dorsey.
Mager, R. (1962). *Preparing objectives for programmed instruction.* San Francisco: Fearon.
Mager, R. (1972). *Goal analysis.* Belmont, CA: Fearon.
Marmor, J. (Ed.). (1965). *Sexual inversion: The multiple roots of homosexuality.* New York: Basic Books.
Marty, M. (1996). You get to teach and study religion. *Academe, 82*(6), 14–17.
Maslow, A. (1954). *Motivation and personality.* New York: Harper.
Maslow, A. (1962). *Toward a psychology of being.* Princeton, NJ: Van Nostrand.
Maslow, A. (1966). *The psychology of science: A reconnaissance.* New York: Harper & Row.
Masters, K., & Bergin, A. (1991). Religious life-styles and mental health: A follow-up study. *Counseling and Values, 35,* 211–224.
Masters, W., & Johnson, V. (1979). *Homosexuality in perspective.* Boston: Little, Brown & Company.
May, R., Angel, E., & Ellenberger, H. (Ed.). (1958). *Existence: A new dimension in psychiatry and psychology.* New York: Basic Books.
May, R., & Yalom, I. (1955). Existential psychotherapy. In R. Corsini & D. Wedding (Eds.). *Current psychotherapies* (5th ed., pp. 262–291). Itasca, IL: F. E. Peacock.
McNaught, B. (1988). *On being gay: Thoughts on family, faith, and love.* New York: St. Martin's Press.
Mink, O. (1970). *The behavior change process.* New York: Harper & Row.
Minton, H. (Ed.). (1992). *Gay and lesbian studies.* New York: Haworth.
Minuchin, S. (1974). *Families and family therapy.* Cambridge, MA: Harvard University Press.
Minuchin, S. (1984). *Families kaleidoscope.* Cambridge, MA: Harvard University Press.
Minuchin, S., & Fishman, H. (1981). *Family therapy techniques.* Cambridge, MA: Harvard University Press.
Moore, W. (1992). *Student and faculty epistemology in the college classroom: The Perry scheme of intellectual and ethical development.* Unpublished manuscript.
Morris, K., & Kanitz, M. (1975). *Rational-emotive therapy.* Boston: Houghton Mifflin.
Mueller, R., Dupuy, P., & Hutchins, D. (1995). A review of the tfa counseling system: From theory construction to application. *The Journal of Counseling and Development, 72,* 573–577.
Neill, A. (1964). *Summerhill: A radical approach to child rearing.* New York: Hart.
Notman, M., & Nadelson, C. (1991). *Men and women: New perspectives on gender differences.* Washington, DC: American Psychiatric Press.
Nungesser, L. (1983). *Homosexual acts, actors, and identities.* New York: Praeger.

Paloutzian, R. (1996). *Invitation to the psychology of religion.* Boston: Allyn & Bacon.
Passons, W. (1975). *Gestalt approaches in counseling.* New York: Holt, Rinehart, & Winston.
Pavlov, I. (1955). Lectures on the work of the principle digestive glands. In *Selected Works, I. P. Pavlov,* pp. 81–126. Moscow: Foreign Languages Publishing House. (Original work published 1897).
Perls, F. (1969). *Gestalt therapy verbatim.* Moab, UT: Real People Press.
Perry, W., Jr. (1970). *Forms of intellectual and ethical development in the college years.* New York: Holt, Rinehart & Winston.
Phillips, J. (1969). *The origin of intellect: Piaget's theory.* San Francisco: Freeman.
Piaget, J. (1952). *The origins of intelligence in children.* New York: International Universities Press [original French edition, 1936].
Piaget, J., & Inhelder, B. (1969). *The psychology of the child.* New York: Basic Books.
Richards, P., & Potts, R. (1995). Using spiritual interventions in psychotherapy: Practices, successes, failures, and ethical concerns for Mormon psychotherapists. *Professional Psychology Research and Practice, 26*(1), 163–170.
Rogers, C. (1942). *Counseling and psychotherapy.* Boston: Houghton-Mifflin.
Rogers, C. (1951). *Client-centered therapy.* Boston: Houghton Mifflin.
Rogers, C. (1961). *On becoming a person.* Boston: Houghton-Mifflin.
Rogers, C. (1969). *Freedom to learn.* Columbus, OH: Merrill.
Rokeach, M. (1973). *The nature of human values.* New York: Free Press.
Rudestam, K. (1980). *Methods of self-change: An abc primer.* Belmont, CA: Wadsworth.
Ruesch, J., & Bateson, G. (1968). Communication: The social matrix of psychiatry. New York: W. W. Norton.
Sahakian, W. (1976). *Introduction to the psychology of learning.* Chicago: Rand McNally.
Sahakian, W. (1979). *Psychology of learning: Systems, models, and theories.* Chicago: Markham.
Sahakian, W. (1984). *Introduction to the psychology of learning* (2nd. ed.). Itasca, NY: F. E. Peacock.
Satir, V. (1964). *Conjoint family therapy.* Palo Alto, CA: Science and Behavior Books.
Satir, V. (1972). *Peoplemaking.* Palo Alto, CA: Science and Behavior Books.
Schachtel, E. (1961). *Metamorphosis.* New York: Basic Books.
Schutz, W. (1958). *Firo: A three-dimensional theory of interpersonal behavior.* New York: Rinehart.
Schutz, W. (1966). *The interpersonal underworld.* Palo Alto, CA: Science and Behavior Books.
Schutz, W. (1973). *Elements of encounter.* New York: Bantam.
Sechenov, I. (1965). *Reflexes of the Brain* (S. Belsky, Trans.). Cambridge, MA: M.I.T. Press (original work published 1863)
Seligman, M. (1975). *Helplessness: On depression, development, and death.* San Francisco: Freeman.
Seligman, M. (1991a). *Learned optimism.* New York: Alfred A. Knopf.
Seligman, M. (1991b). *What you can change and what you can't: The complete guide to successful self-improvement.* New York: Alfred A. Knopf.
Selvini Palazzoli, M., Boscolo, L., Cecchin, G., & Prata, G. (1978). *Paradox and counterparadox.* New York: Jason Aronson.
Shafranske, E., & Malony, H. (1990). Clinical psychologists' religions and spiritual orientations and their practice of psychotherapy. *Psychotherapy, 27*(1), 72–78.
Sheehy, G. (1976). *Passages: Predictable crises of adult life.* New York: Bantam Books.
Sherman, A. (1973). *Behavior modification: Theory and practice.* Belmont, CA: Wadsworth.
Skinner, B. F. (1953). *Science and human behavior.* New York: MacMillan.
Snelbecker, G. (1985). *Learning theory, instructional theory, and psychoeducational design.* Lanham, MD: Univ. Press of America.
Spence, K., & Lippitt, R. (1940). "Latent" learning of a simple maze problem with relevant needs satiated. *Psychological Bulletin, 37,* 429.
Stevens, R. (1983). *Erik Erikson: An introduction.* New York: St. Martin's.
Sue, D., Ivey, A., & Pedersen, P. (1996). *A theroy of multicultural counseling and therapy.* Pacific Grove, CA: Brooks/Cole.
Sue, D., & Sue, D. (1990). *Counseling the culturally different: Theory and practice.* New York: Wiley.
Sullivan, H. S. (1953). *The interpersonal theory of personality.* New York: W. W. Norton.
Thorndike, E. (1913a). *The original nature of man.* New York: Teachers College, Columbia University.
Thorndike, E. (1913b). *The psychology of learning.* New York: Teachers College, Columbia University.

Thorndike, E. (1918). *The nature, purposes, and general methods of measurement of educational products.* In G. M. Whipple (Ed.), *The measurement of educational products. The seventeenth yearbook of the national society for the study of education, Part II.* Bloomingdale, IL: Public School Publishing.

Thorndike, E. (1932). *The fundamentals of learning.* New York: Teachers College, Columbia University.

Tolman, E., & Gleitman, H. (1949). Studies in learning and motivation: I. Equal reinforcements in both end-boxes, followed by shock in one end-box. *Journal of Experimental Psychology, 39,* 810–819.

Tolman, E. (1948). Cognitive maps in rats and men. *Psychological Review, 55,* 189–208.

Tolman, E. (1949). *Purposive behavior in animals and men.* Berkeley, CA: University of California Press.

Trotter, R. (1987, February). Stop blaming yourself. *Psychology Today,* 30–42.

Wadsworth, B. (1971). *Piaget's theory of cognitive development.* New York: McKay.

Washington State Department of Social and Health Services. (1993). *Final report 1993 task force on gay and lesbian concerns.* Olympia, WA: Author.

Watzlawick, P. (1978). *The language of change: Elements of therapeutic communication.* Palo Alto, CA: Basic Books.

Watzlawick, P., Beavin, J., & Jackson, D. (1967). *Pragmatics of human communication.* New York: W. W. Norton.

Watzlawick, P., Weakland, J., & Fisch, R. (1974). *Change: Principles of problem formation and problem resolution.* New York: W. W. Norton.

Wehrly, B. (1995). *Pathways to multicultural counseling competence: A developmental journey.* Pacific Grove, CA: Brooks/Cole.

Weishaar, M. (1993). *Aaron T. Beck.* Thousand Oaks, CA: Sage.

Wertheimer, M. (1945). *Productive thinking.* New York: Harper.

Wertheimer, M. (1959). *Productive thinking* (enlarged edition). New York: Harper.

Whitaker, C. (1976). Family is a four-dimensional relationship. In P. J. Guerin (Ed.), *Family therapy: Theory and practice* (pp. 182–192). New York: Gardner Press.

Wiener, N. (1948). Cybernetics. *Scientific American, 179*(5), 14–18.

Wolpe, J. (1969). *The practice of behavior therapy.* New York: Pergammon Press.

Wulff, D. (1991). *Psychology of religion.* New York: Wiley & Sons.

Zajonc, S. (1996). *Spirituality and counseling.* Unpublished manuscript, Eastern Washington University at Cheney.

INDEX

A
Abilene Paradox, 12
Accommodation, 15, 120
Adaptive organism, 38–39
Adler
 on family, 173
 on personality, 156
Advertising, commercial, 56
Affective deficit, 17–18, 198–199
 interventions for, 26
Affective learning, 11
Affective style, 28
Affective surplus, 20–21
 interventions for, 26
Alcohol treatment with Antabuse, 53
Alcoholics Anonymous, 12-Steps of, 13
All-or-nothing thinking, 135
Allport, 156
Allport's Religious Orientation Scale, 190
Allusions, 106
Ambiguities, 106
Analogy, law of, 37
Anchoring, 55–56
Antabuse, alcohol treatment with, 53
Antecedent events, 69–70
Aphorisms, 105
Architect, 204–205
Asceticism, 23
Asian religions, 23–24
Assessment and strategy selection, 195–206
 demonstration scenarios in, 197–205
  complexities in, 202–204
  exceptions to the rules in, 202–204
  vignette 1 in, 202–203
  vignette 2 in, 203–204
 practice vignettes in, 204–205
Assimilation, 15, 120
 law of, 37
Association, unintentional, 64

Association theories, 44–45
Associative learning approaches, 50–67
 focus of, 50
 foundation theories in, 59–66
  of Guthrie, 59–66 (*See also* Guthrie, Edwin R.)
  of Pavlov, 51–58 (*See also* Pavlovian-type association learning)
 sample problem situations in, 66–67
Associative shifting, law of, 37–38
Athletic star, 202–203
Attention, in Guthrian model, 60
Attention deficit, reinforcement learning approach to, 83
Attention deficit hyperactivity disorder (ADHD)
 environmental control in, 53
 reinforcement learning approach to, 82–83
Attitude(s), 128–129
 law of, 37
Attribution retraining, 127
Attribution theory, 120–121, 125–127
Ausubel, David, 11, 131–132
 on subsumption, 16
Autonomy, *vs.* shame and doubt, 163

B
Bad-Active, 33
Bandura, Albert, 4, 12, 96–99, 110
 on perceptual deficits, 17
Basic needs, 166
Basic trust, *vs.* basic mistrust, 162
Beck, Aaron T., 134–138
Becvar, D. and Becvar, R., 173–174
Bedwetting, 54
Behavior
 error in predicting, 60
 target, 19, 45
Behavior modification, 20

213

Index

Behavior qua behavior, 93
Behavioral approaches, 15–16
Behavioral deficit, 20, 197
  interventions for, 25–26
Behavioral learning, 11
Behavioral style, 29–30
  affective deficit in, 198–199
  behavioral deficit and surplus in, 198
  comparison, evaluation, decision in, 199–200
Behavioral surplus, 20, 198
  interventions for, 26
Behavioral therapy, family in, 173
Behaviorism, 34
  purposive, 94–96
  radical, 10
Beliefs, 127–128
  illogical, 133–134
Belongingness, 167–168
Bergin, A., 188–189
Berne, Eric, 110, 133–137
Bigge, Morris, 32–33
Biofeedback, in reinforcement learning approach, 80–81
Bond, 44
Books, self-help, 142
Broad, C.D., 3–4
Bruner, Jerome, 108–109

C

Catastrophizing, 135–136
Categorizing intervention theories, 47–48
Category validity, 178
Causality, in Guthrian model, 60
Centricultural bias, 177
Change, language of, 105
Cherry, 177
Chomsky, N., 11
Christian counselors, 23
Circumstance, four categories of, 196
Circumstance and style, 155–191. *See also* Contextual issues
  development in, 158–171 (*See also* Development)
  personality in, 156–157
  social dynamics in, 172–183 (*See also* Social Dynamics)
  spirituality in, 183–192 (*See also* Spirituality)
Classroom management, 63
Client styles, congruence and, 28–29
Closure, 90, 91
Clueless, 23
Cognition, elements of, 123
Cognitive deficit, 17

cognitive learning approach to
  group, classroom, 149–150
  group, clinic, 144–145
  individual, classroom, 147–148
  individual, clinic, 143–144
interventions for, 27
Cognitive dissonance, 123–124
Cognitive distortions
  categories of, 135–136
  schema and, 136
Cognitive learning, 11–12, 96, 120–152
  applied theories in, 130–142
    of Ausubel, 131–132
    of Beck, 134–139
    of Berne, 139–141
    of Ellis, 132–134
    other cognitive interventions as, 141
  examples of, 142
    group, classroom, 149–150
    group, clinic, 144–146
    individual, classroom, 147–148
    individual, clinic, 146–147
  focus of, 120–123
  foundation theories in, 123–130
    of Festinger, 123–124
    of Försterling, 125–127
    of Rokeach, 127–130
  sample problem situations in, 150–152
Cognitive maps, 94
Cognitive restructuring, of depression, 6–7
Cognitive style, 28
  behavioral deficit in, 198
  cognitive surplus in, 198–199
  comparison, evaluation, decision in, 199
Cognitive surplus, 18, 198–199
  cognitive learning approach to
    group, classroom, 149–150
    group, clinic, 144–145
    individual, classroom, 147–148
    individual, clinic, 142–144
  interventions for, 27–28
Cognitive theories, 47
Cognitive-behavioral therapists, 9
Cognitivists, 9
Combined stimuli, 52
Commitment within relativism, 166, 187–188
Common fate, 91
Communication, of experience, 4
Communication therapies, 174
Complexities, 202–204
Compulsive shopper, 113–114
Concept, 128–129

Concept maker, 102
Conceptual training, 131–132
Conceptualization, 176
Condensations, 105
Conditioned stimulus, 51–52
Conditioning
 in association theory, 44
 Bandura on, 96–97
 in cognition theory, 47
 higher order, 52
 inhibitory, 62
 in perception theory, 46
 place, 64
 in reinforcement theory, 45
Conditioning formula, classical, 51–52
Congruence, 14–29
 client style considerations and, 28–29
 definition of, 14
 intervention strategies and, 24–28
 mental health model of, 14–17
 patterns of incongruence and, 17–24
Connection, 44
Consensus, 125
Consequent events, 70–74
Consistency, 126
Consistency models, 156–157
Consonance, 124
Contextual issues, 155–171
 definition of, 155
 development in, 158–159 (*See also* Development)
 personality in, 156–158
 social dynamics in, 172–183 (*See also* Social Dynamics)
 spirituality in, 183–192 (*See also* Spirituality)
Contextual relativism, 170, 187
Contiguity, 44
 in Guthrian model, 60
 in Pavlovian paradigm, 60
Contingency relationships, 19
Continuity, 91, 92
Co-parenting, 118
Counselor training programs, 8
Covariance, 125
Cues, conflicting, in Guthrian model, 60
Cuing, multiple, 63–64
Cultural diversity, 118
Culture, 21, 175–178

D
Decision making, dynamics of, 120–121
Deficit. *See also* specific types, e.g., Affective deficit
 vs. surplus, 17–18

Deficit conditions, 17
Definitions, of learning, 30–31
Deity, 191
Depression
 cognitive restructuring of, 6–7
 maladaptive schemas in, 136–137
Desensitization, systematic, 57–58
Determinism
 reciprocal, 97
 vs. free will, 6–7
Development, 158–171
 Erikson on, 162–165
 Havighurst on, 159–161
 Maslow on, 165–166
 Perry on, 169–171
 Piaget on, 161
Developmental deficit, 21
Developmental psychology, 21–22
Developmental surplus, 22
Developmental tasks, 159–160
Developmentalists, 21
Dinges, 177
Direction, 89
Discovery learning, 108
Disqualifying the positive, 135
Distinctiveness, 125–126
Diversity, 175
Dualism, 169
Dunn, R., 157

E
Ebbinghaus, H., 122
Effect, law of, 36–37
Eight Humanistic Assumptions of Behavior, 103–104
Ellis, Albert, 9, 132–134
Emotional reasoning, 136
Emotions, learning and, 12
Empiricism, 102
Encopresis, reinforcement learning approach to, 86
Enuresis, 54
Environmental control, in ADHD, 53
Erikson, Erik, 162–165
 on autonomy, *vs.* shame and doubt, 163
 on basic trust, *vs.* basic mistrust, 162
 on generativity, *vs.* stagnation, 164
 on identity, *vs.* identity diffusion, 163
 on industry, *vs.* inferiority, 163
 on initiative, *vs.* guilt, 163
 on integrity, *vs.* despair and disgust, 165
 on intimacy and distantiation, *vs.* self-absorption, 164
Esteem needs, 168
Ethnicity, 175

Evaluative system, 121–122
Exceptionality, 21
Exceptions to the rule, 202–204
Exercise, law of, 36
Existential struggle, 184
Expectancy theory, 94
Experience, in cognition theory, 47
Experiential approaches, to family, 174
Experiential learning, 11, 116
Expository Teaching, 131–132
Extinction, 52

F
Families, of intervention theories, 43–47
Family, 173–175
Festinger, Leon, 123–124
Figurative language, 105
Figure and ground, 91, 109
Forgetting, 15, 60, 131
Försterling, Friedrich, 11, 15, 125–127
Fourth force, 175–176
Frankl, 186
Free will, *vs.* determinism, 6–7
Freedman, Arthur, 136
Freud, Sigmund, 34
  on psychodynamics, 110
Fromm, E., 156
Fulfillment models, 156
Functionalism, 34

G
Gagné, R., 11, 18
Galton, Sir Francis, 34
Gender, 21, 178–179
  foundations and expressions of, 179–180
  homosexuality/alternative expression of, 180–182
  meaning of, 178
Generativity, *vs.* stagnation, 164
Geographical difference, 182–183
Gestalt concepts, 89–93
  insight in, 89
  productive thinking in, 90–01
  relational theory of learning in, 90
  trace theory in, 92–93
Gestalt Law of Prägnanz, 91, 101–102, 186
Gestalt psychology, 34
Gestalt rules of perception, 106–108
Gestalt Therapy, 110–111
Good, 177
Good-Active, 33
"Grandma law," 46
Green, 184–185

"Groupthink ," 12
Guthrie, Edwin R., 44, 59–66
  examples of association learning of, 62–66
    breaking multiple-cued responses, 64
    classroom management, 63
    habit breaking, 65–66
    multiple cuing, 63–64
    place conditioning, 64
    unintentional association, 64–65
  model of, 60–62

H
Habit, in Guthrian model, 60–62
Habit breaking, Guthrie on, 65–66
Harris, 18
  on family, 173
Harvey, J., 12
Havighurst, Robert, 21, 159–161
Helplessness model, 109
Hierarchy of needs, 19–20
Higher order conditioning, 52
Historical roots, 33–35
Homosexuality, 180–182
Hoyenga, K., 178–179
Hull, Clark L., 38–39
Humanistic learning models, 103–104
Humanists, 9
Huxley, Aldous, 3–4, 5

I
Identity, *vs.* identity diffusion, 164
Imitation learning, 46
Inclusiveness, 91
Incongruence, patterns of, 17–24
Indeterminacy of meaning, 178
Industry, *vs.* inferiority, 163
Inhelder, B., 16
Inhibitory conditioning, 62
Initiative, *vs.* guilt, 163
Input, reduction/elimination of, 3–4, 5
Insight, 88, 89
  law of Prägnanz and, 91, 107
Instructional theory, 7–8
Integrationism, 3–13
  basis of, 4–5
  definition of, 3
  parts *vs.* whole in, 9–10
  philosophy and, 6–7
  practice of, 5–6
  Psychoeducational Design and, 7–8
  types of learning and, 11–13
Integrity, *vs.* despair and disgust, 165
Interpretive system, 120–121
Intervening variables, 94–95

Intervention, learning-based areas for, 15–16
Intervention theories, 43–49
  association, 44–45
  categorizing, 47–48
  cognitive, 47
  one-stage and two-stage models, 43–44
  perception, 46–47
  reinforcement, 45–46
Intimacy and distantiation, *vs.* self-absorption, 164
Irrationality, methods for disputing, 138–139
Ivey, A., 175–176

J
Janis, I., 12
Johnson, V., 180
Jourard, S., 102
Jumping to conclusions, 136

K
Kagan, J, 157
Kelly, H., 157
Kierkegaard, S., 186
Knowing. *See also* Learning
  five ways of, 14–15
Koffka, Kurt, 89
Köhler, Wolfgang, 88–89

L
Labelling, 136
Lamaze birthing, 53
Language
  of change, 105
  in cognition theory, 47
  figurative, 105
  Huxley on, 4, 5
  limitations of, 4
Latent learning, 94
Law of assimilation or analogy, 37
Law of associative shifting, 36
Law of disruption, 96
Law of effect, 36–37
Law of emphasis, 96
Law of exercise, 36
Law of motivation, 96
Law of multiple response or varied reaction, 37
Law of partial activity, 37
Law of readiness, 36
Law of set or attitude, 37
Learning, 15. *See also* Knowing
  affective, 12
  in association theory, 44

behavioral, 12
cognitive, 10–11, 97
definitions of, 30–31
discovery, 106
in Guthrian model, 59–61
latent, 94
observational, 96–99
  vicarious, 106
in perception theory, 46
perceptual, 11, 46
place, 95
productive, 88
in reinforcement theory, 45
relational theory of, 90
significant, 101
social and spiritual, 12
types of, 11–13
Learning styles, 158
Learning theory, 7–8, 31–32
  1930s perspectives on, 16–17
Learning-based focus, 21
Learning-based intervention areas, 15–16
Lesbianism, 180–182
LeVay, S., 181–182
Literature, professional counseling, spirituality and, 188–190
Littering, 118
Locke, John, 33
Locus of control, external, 23
Love needs, 167–168
Lovinger, R., 31

M
Maddi, on personality theories, 156
Magnification, 136
Marmor, J., 180
Marriage dissolution, 203–204
Maslow, Abraham, 100–101, 156, 165–167
  on basic needs, 166
  on belongingness and love needs, 167–168
  on esteem needs, 168
  on hierarchy of needs, 19–20
  on physiologic needs, 166
  on safety needs, 167
  on self-actualization needs, 168–169
Masters, W., 180
May, Rollo, 4, 186–187
  on philosophy, 32
McClelland, 157
McDonald model, 120–123
Memory drum, 122
Memory system, 121
Mental filter, 135

Mescalin, Huxley on, 3–4
Metropolitan Opera star, 204
Mind at Large, 4
Minimization, 136
Mislabelling, 136
Monolithic theory, 38
Moral imperatives, 189
Motivation, 99, 99
Motivational system, 122
Movement, in Guthrian model, 60
Multicultural issues, 175–176
Multiple cuing, 63–64
   breaking responses to, 64
Multiple response, law of, 37
Multiplicity, 169, 186

N
Narrative context, 178
Needs
   hierarchy of, 19–20
   Maslow on, 165–168
Negative reinforcement, 72
Neill, A. S., 33
Neutral-Passive, 33
Neuro-linguistic programming (NLP), 55–56
Nonas, E., 181
Normative uncertainty, 177
Nungesser, L., 180

O
Objective set, 91, 92
Object-Relations therapy, 94
Observational, vicarious learning, 106
Observational learning, 96–99
One-stage models, 43–44
Operant techniques, 19
Organizational scheme, 47–48
Overgeneralization, 135

P
Paloutzian, R., 185
Pars pro toto, 105
Partial activity, law of, 37
Parts, *vs.* whole, 9–10
Pavlov, Ivan Petrovich, 44, 50, 51–58
   examples of association learning of, 51–58 (*See also* Pavlovian-type association learning)
   theory of, 51–52
Pavlovian-type association learning, 53–58
   in advertising, 56
   in alcohol treatment with Antabuse, 53
   in enuresis, 54
   in environmental control (ADHD), 53
   in Lamaze birthing, 53
   in neuro-linguistic programming, 55–56
   in systematic desensitization and reciprocal inhibition, 57–58
Pedersen, P., 175–176
Perception, 120
Perception learning, 87–119
   applied theories in, 101–108
      of Bandura, 110
      of Bruner, 108–109
      of Gestalt rules of perception, 106–108
      of perceptual processing system, 104–106
      of phenomenology, 102–104
      of psychodynamics, 110–111
      of Seligmen, 109
   examples of, 111–112
      experiential learning, 116
     group, classroom, 115–116
     group, clinic, 114–115
     individual, classroom, 115
     individual, clinic, 112–113
   focus of, 87
   foundation theories in, 87–101
      of Bandura, 96–99
      Gestalt concepts as, 89–93
      humanistic learning models in, 100–101
      of Koffka, 89
      of Köhler, 88–89
      of Tolman, 93–96
      of Wertheimer, 88
   sample problem situations in, 117–119
Perception theories, 46
Perceptual deficit, 17
   interventions for, 26–27
Perceptual learning, 11, 46
Perceptual processing system, 104–105
Perceptual sorting, 91
Perceptual style, 29
Perceptual surplus, 17
   interventions for, 27
Perceptual trace theory, 92
Perceptual-cognitive approaches, 14–15
Perls, Frederic, 110–111
Perry, WIlliam, 169–171, 186–188
Perry Scheme. *See* Perry, William
Personal Commitment model, 157–158
Personality, 156–158
Personality models, 155
Personalization, 136

Perspective, 30–49
  definitions in, 30–31
  historical roots in, 33–35
  philosophy in, 32–33
  theorists in, 35–39
  theory in, 31–32
Phenomenology, 102–103
Phenomenon, 102
Philosophy, 32–33
Phobia, 44–45
  reciprocal inhibition for, 57–58
  school, 66–67
Physiologic needs, 166
Piaget, J., 15, 161
Pill taking, 86
Place conditioning, 64
Place learning, 96
Pluralism, religious, 183–184
Positive reinforcement, 72
Potts, R., 188
Prägnanz, 89, 107–108, 185
Prepotency of elements, 37
Probabilistic expectancy, 99
Procrastination, 85
Productive learning, 88
Productive thinking, 88, 90–91
Professional, *vs.* technician, 7–8
Proximity, 91, 92
Psychoanalysis, 34
Psychodynamics, 9, 110–111
  family in, 173–175
Psychoeducational Design, 7–8
Punishment, in Guthrian model, 62
Punishment paradigms, of Skinner, 73–74
Puns, 106
Purpose, 90
Purposive behaviorism, 93–96

R
Rational-Emotive Therapy, 9, 132–134
Rational-Emotive-Behavioral Therapy, 132
Readiness, law of, 36
Real learning, 101
Realism, 102
Reality base, 90
Reasoning skills, 48
Reciprocal determinism, 97
Reciprocal inhibition, 57–58
Recycling, 117
Reference, 90
Reframing, 27
Regional difference, 182–183
Reinforcement
  Bandura on, 96, 97
  negative, 72–73
  positive, 72
  in Purposive Behaviorism, 94–96
Reinforcement contingencies, 69
Reinforcement learning approaches, 68–86
  applied theories in, 75–77
  examples of, 77–84
    group, classroom, 83–84
    group, clinic, 81–82
    individual, classroom, 82–83
    individual, clinic, 77–81
  focus of, 68
  foundation theory of, 69
    antecedent events in, 69–70
    consequent events in, 70–74
    responses in, 74–75
  sample problem situations and, 84–86
  six-step method in, 76–77
Reinforcement theories, 45–46
Reinforcers, 45, 70–74
Relational theory of learning, 90
Religion. *See also* Spirituality
  as quest, 189–190
Repentance strategy, 191
Response(s)
  desired, 45
  in Guthrian model, 60–61
  in reinforcement learning, 74–75
Restructuring, abbreviated approach to, 141
Reward, in Guthrian model, 66
Richards, P., 188
Ritual, religious, 191
Rogers, Carl, 9, 33, 99
  cognitive learning and, 11
  on congruence, 14
Rokeach, Milton, 127–130
Rousseau, H., 33
R-R conditioning, 50. *See also* Guthrie, Edwin R.
Rudestam, Kjell E., 9–21
Rules of perception, Gestalt, 106–108
Rumpelstiltskin Effect, 28

S
Safety needs, 167
Scaling Methods, 140, 141
School phobia, 66–67
Schutz, W., 12
Seat belt use, 84
Self-actualization, 156, 165
Self-actualization needs, 166
Self-concept, 128–129

Self-defeat, illogical beliefs in, 133–134
Self-help books, 142
Seligmen, Martin E. P., 109–110
Set, law of, 34
Sexual harassment, 117
Shopper, compulsive, 113–114
Should statements, 136
Sign-gestalts, 94
Significant learning, 101
Similarity, 91, 92
Simulus-response theories, 43–44
Six-step method, 76–77
Skinner, B. F., 45, 63. *See also* Reinforcement learning approaches
Smoking, 86
Social deficit, 23
Social dynamics, 172–183
 of culture, 175–178
 of family, 173–175
 of gender, 178–182
 of geographical/regional difference, 182–183
Social isolation, 85
Social learning, 12
Social personality, 22
Social psychology, 22, 172–173
Social surplus, 22
Sorting, 90
 perceptual, 90–91
Special program student, 197–204
Speeding, 84–85
Spelling challenge, 78–79
Spiral curriculum, 108–109
Spiritual context, 183
Spiritual deficit, 24
Spiritual learning, 12
Spiritual surplus, 24
Spiritual techniques, 23–24
Spirituality, 14, 183–192
 biological basis of, 185
 church membership and, 183–184
 client issues with, 191–192
 existential struggle in, 186
 focus of, 183–188
 "generic" religious principles/practices in, 190–191
 pluralistic tradition of, 184–185
 professional counseling literature and, 188–189
 universal striving for, 183–184
Spontaneous recovery, 52
S-S conditioning, 50. *See also* Pavlovian-type association learning
Stimulus(i)
 in associative learning approaches, 50
 conditioned, 51–52
 environmental, limiting, 53
 in Guthrian model, 60
 in reinforcement theory, 45
 unconditioned, 51
Stimulus discrimination, 52
Stimulus generalization, 52
Stimulus substitution, 50. *See also* Pavlovian-type association learning
Strategic therapy, 173
Structural Analysis, 139–141
Structural family therapy, 173
Structuralism, 34
Style(s). *See also* Circumstance and style
 affective, 28
 behavioral, 28–29, 198–199
 client, congruence and, 28–29
 cognitive, 28, 200–201
 four categories of, 196
 learning, 158
 perceptual, 27
Subsumption, 16
Sue, E., 175–176
Surplus, 18. *See also* specific types, e.g., Affective surplus
vs. deficit, 17–18
Surplus conditions, 18
Systematic desensitization, 57–58
Systems approaches, to family, 174

T
Target behavior, 19, 45
Teaching
 in association theory, 44
 in cognition theory, 47
 in perception theory, 46
 in reinforcement theory, 45
Technician, *vs.* professional, 7–8
Television domination, 78
TFA Counseling System, 10
Theorists, 35–39
Theory, 31–32
Thinking
 all-or-nothing, 135
 productive, 88, 90–92
Third order conditioning, 53
Thorndike, Edward L., 35–36
Thoughts, 128–129
Three-column technique, 137
Tolman, Edward Chance, 93–96
Trace theory, 89, 92–93
Tradition, religious, 189
Training, of counselors, 9
Transactional Analysis, 110–111, 136–141

12-Steps, 13
Two-stage models, 43–44

U
Unconditioned stimulus, 51–52
Unintentional association, 64–65

V
Values, 127–129
Values system, 191
Values theory, 127–130
Varied reaction, law of, 37
Verbal abstractions, 123

W
Walters, R., on perceptual deficits, 18
Wampum, 83–84

Watson, John, 34
Watzlawick, Paul, 16, 104
Wehrly, B., 175
Weight control, 79–80, 85
Wells, Wesley, 185
Wertheimer, Max, 88
Whole, *vs.* parts, 9–10
Wiener, N., 174
Wolpé, Joseph, 57
Wundt, Wilhelm, 33

Y
Yalom, I., 186–187

Z
Zajonc, Susan, 189

ABOUT THE AUTHOR

Dr. Sterling Gerber is a Professor of Applied Psychology at Eastern Washingon University. He received his Ph.D. from the University of Utah and holds the ABPP diploma in Counseling Psychology. Dr. Gerber is the originator and major proponent of Reponsive Therapy, an integrational approach to counseling. A counselor educator for most of his career, his most notable endeavor outside the classroom has been the creation and management of a communication training program for military supervisors. The program was presented at locations in Europe, Asia, and the United States.

DATE DUE

APR '59			
JUN 15 '59			
AUG 19 '59			
APR 26 '60			

HCLC J 398 F48m

Fillmore, Parker
  Hoysted, 1878-
Mighty Mikko; a book of
  Finnish fairy tales and
     [c1922]

MIGHTY MIKKO

BY PARKER FILLMORE
CZECHOSLOVAK FAIRY TALES
THE SHOEMAKER'S APRON
Both Illustrated by Jan Matulka

THE LAUGHING PRINCE
Illustrated by Jay Van Everen

THE HICKORY LIMB
Illustrated by Rose Cecil O'Neill

THE ROSIE WORLD
Illustrated by Maginal Wright Enright

MIGHTY MIKKO

A Book of Finnish Fairy Tales and Folk Tales

BY

PARKER FILLMORE

WITH ILLUSTRATIONS AND DECORATIONS
BY
JAY VAN EVEREN

NEW YORK
HARCOURT, BRACE AND COMPANY

COPYRIGHT, 1922, BY
PARKER FILLMORE

Seventh printing, August, 1940

PRINTED IN THE UNITED STATES OF AMERICA
BY QUINN & BODEN COMPANY, INC., RAHWAY, N. J.

To my niece
PHYLLIS
These stories of her mother's native land

PUBLIC LIBRARY
KANSAS CITY
MO

NOTE

The spirit of nationalism that swept over the small peoples of Europe in the early nineteenth century touched faraway Finland and started the Finns on the quest of the Finnish. There as elsewhere scholars who were also patriots found that the native tongue, lost to the educated and the well-to-do, had been preserved in the songs and stories which were current among the peasants. Elias Lönnrot spent a long and busy life collecting those ancient *runos* from which he succeeded in building up a national epic, the *Kalevala*. This is Lönnrot's great contribution to his own country and to the world. Beside the material for the *Kalevala* Lönnrot made important collections of lyrics, proverbs, and stories.

During his time and since other patriot scholars have

made faithful records of the songs and tales which the old Finnish minstrels, the *runolaulajat,* chanted to the strains of the *kantele.* The mass of such material now gathered together in the archives of the Society of Finnish Literature at Helsingfors is imposing in bulk and of great importance to the student of comparative folklore.

My own excursions into the Finnish have been made possible through the kindness and endless patience of my friend, Lydia Tulonen (Mrs. Kurt J. Rahlson). With her as a native guide I have been wandering some time through the byways of Finnish folklore. The present volume is the traveler's pack I have brought home with me filled with strange treasures which will, I hope, seem as lovely to others as they seemed to me when first I came upon them.

The stories as I offer them are not translations but my own versions. Literal translations from the Finnish would make small appeal to the general reader. To English ears the Finnish is stiff, bald, and monotonous. One has only to read or attempt to read Kirby's excellent translation of the *Kalevala* to realize the truth of this statement. So I make no apology for retelling these tales in a manner more likely to prove entertaining to the English reader, whether child or adult.

NOTE

In some form or other all the tales in this book may be found in the various folklore collections made by Eero Salmelainen, one of the patriotic young scholars who followed in Lönnrot's footsteps. His books were sponsored by the Society of Finnish Literature and used in its campaign to bring back the Finnish language to the Finns at a time when Swedish was the official language of the country.

Full of local color as these stories are, it would be vain to pretend that they are not, for the most part, variants of stories told the world over. All that I can claim for them is that they are dramatic and picturesque, that they are told with a wealth of charming detail which is essentially Finnish, and that they are certainly new to the generality of English readers. *The Three Chests,* so characteristic in feeling of a country famous for its lakes and marshes, is the variant of a German story which Grimm gives as *Fitcher's Bird.* Of *The Forest Bride* I have found variants in the folklore of many lands. There are several very beautiful ones in the Russian; in other books I myself have retold two, one current among the Czechs and one among the Serbians; Grimm has two different versions in *The Three Feathers* and *The Poor Miller's Boy and the Cat;* and Madame d'Aulnoy has used the same story in her elaborate tale, *The White Cat*. There is a well-known Oriental version of *Mighty Mikko* in which the part of the fox is played by a jackal and I am sure that Mikko's faithful retainer, though neither city-bred nor polished, is after all pretty closely related to that most debonnaire of Frenchmen, *Puss in Boots*. Perrault probably and Madame d'Aulnoy certainly are in turn indebted to Straparola. And so it goes.

The little cycle of animal stories included under *Mikko the Fox* will of course instantly invite comparison with the Beast Epic of *Reynard the Fox*. The two have many episodes in common and both have episodes to be found in Æsop and in those books of animal analogues, widely read in mediæval times, *Physiologus* and the *Disciplina Clericalis* of Petrus Alfonsus. The *Reynard* as we have it is a finished satire on church and state and in its present form has been current in Europe since the twelfth century. It was thought at one time that the animal stories found in Finland were debased versions of the *Reynard* stories, but scholars are now of opinion that they antedate *Reynard* and are similar to the earlier simpler stories upon which the *Reynard* cycle was originally built. This makes the little Finnish tales of great interest to the student. Needless to say I do not present them for this reason but because they seem to me charming merely as fables. The animals here are not the clerics and the judges and the nobles that the *Reynard* animals are, but plain downright Finnish peasants, sometimes stupid, often dull, frequently amusing, and always very human.

I have taken one liberty with spelling. I have transliterated Syöjätär, the name of the dread Finnish witch, as Suyettar. I have been unwilling to translate by the insufficient word, *bath-house* or *vapor bath,* that very characteristic institution of Finnish family life, the *sauna,* but have retained the Finnish word, *sauna,* allowing the context in each case to indicate the meaning.

P. F.

New York
June 19, 1922

CONTENTS

	PAGE
THE TRUE BRIDE: The Story of Ilona and the King's Son	1
MIGHTY MIKKO: The Story of a Poor Woodsman and a Grateful Fox	25
THE THREE CHESTS: The Story of the Wicked Old Man of the Sea	47
LOG: The Story of the Hero Who Released the Sun	67
THE LITTLE SISTER: The Story of Suyettar and the Nine Brothers	99
THE FOREST BRIDE: The Story of a Little Mouse Who was a Princess	121
THE ENCHANTED GROUSE: The Story of Helli and the Little Locked Box	141
THE TERRIBLE OLLI: The Story of an Honest Finn and a Wicked Troll	155
THE DEVIL'S HIDE: The Story of the Boy Who Wouldn't Lose His Temper	171

CONTENTS

THE MYSTERIOUS SERVANT: The Story of a Young Man Who Respected the Dead 193

FAMILIAR FACES:
   I   Mary, Mary, So Contrary! 209
   II Jane, Jane, Don't Complain! 215
   III Susan Walker, What a Talker! 221

MIKKO THE FOX: A Nursery Epic in Sixteen Adventures
   I   The Animals Take a Bite 229
   II The Partners 235
   III The Fox and the Crow 243
   IV The Chief Mourner 251
   V   Mirri, the Cat 257
   VI The Fox's Servant 263
   VII The Wolf Sings 267
   VIII The Clever Goat 273
   IX The Harvest 279
   X   The Porridge 283
   XI Nurse Mikko 287
   XII The Bear Says *North* 293
   XIII Osmo's Share 297
   XIV The Reward of Kindness 301
   XV The Bear and the Mouse 307
   XVI The Last of Osmo 309

THE TRUE BRIDE

The Story of Ilona and the King's Son

THE TRUE BRIDE

There were once two orphans, a brother and a sister, who lived alone in the old farmhouse where their fathers before them had lived for many generations. The brother's name was Osmo, the sister's Ilona. Osmo was an industrious youth, but the farm was small and barren and he was hard put to it to make a livelihood.

"Sister," he said one day, "I think it might be well if I went out into the world and found work."

"Do as you think best, brother," Ilona said. "I'm sure I can manage on here alone."

So Osmo started off, promising to come back for his sister as soon as he could give her a new home. He wandered far and wide and at last got employment from the King's Son as a shepherd.

The King's Son was about Osmo's age, and often when he met Osmo tending his flocks he would stop and talk to him.

One day Osmo told the King's Son about his sister, Ilona.

"I have wandered far over the face of the earth," he said, "and never have I seen so beautiful a maiden as Ilona."

"What does she look like?" the King's Son asked.

Osmo drew a picture of her and she seemed to the King's Son so beautiful that at once he fell in love with her.

"Osmo," he said, "if you will go home and get your sister, I will marry her."

So Osmo hurried home not by the long land route by which he had come but straight over the water in a boat.

"Sister," he cried, as soon as he saw Ilona, "you must come with me at once for the King's Son wishes to marry you!"

He thought Ilona would be overjoyed, but she sighed and shook her head.

"What is it, sister? Why do you sigh?"

"Because it grieves me to leave this old house where our fathers have lived for so many generations."

"Nonsense, Ilona! What is this little old house compared to the King's castle where you will live once you marry the King's Son!"

But Ilona only shook her head.

"It's no use, brother! I can't bear to leave this old house until the grindstone with which our fathers for generations ground their meal is worn out."

When Osmo found she was firm, he went secretly and broke the old grindstone into small pieces. He then put the pieces together so that the stone looked the same as before. But of course the next time Ilona touched it, it fell apart.

"Now, sister, you'll come, will you not?" Osmo asked.

But again Ilona shook her head.

"It's no use, brother. I can't bear to go until the old stool where our mothers have sat spinning these many generations is worn through."

So again Osmo took things into his own hands and going secretly to the old spinning stool he broke it and when Ilona sat on it again it fell to pieces.

Then Ilona said she couldn't go until the old mortar which had been in use for generations should fall to bits at a blow from the pestle. Osmo cracked the mortar and the next time Ilona struck it with the pestle it broke.

Then Ilona said she couldn't go until the old worn doorsill over which so many of their forefathers had walked should fall to splinters at the brush of her skirts. So Osmo secretly split the old doorsill into thin slivers and, when next Ilona stepped over it, the brush of her skirts sent the splinters flying.

"I see now I must go," Ilona said, "for the house of our forefathers no longer holds me."

So she packed all her ribbons and her bodices and skirts in a bright wooden box and, calling her little dog Pilka, she stepped into the boat and Osmo rowed her off in the direction of the King's castle.

Soon they passed a long narrow spit of land at the end of which stood a woman waving her arms. That is she looked like a woman. Really she was Suyettar but they, of course, did not know this.

"Take me in your boat!" she cried.

"Shall we?" Osmo asked his sister.

"I don't think we ought to," Ilona said. "We don't know who she is or what she wants and she may be evil."

So Osmo rowed on. But the woman kept shouting:

"Hi, there! Take me in your boat! Take me!"

A second time Osmo paused and asked his sister:

"Don't you think we ought to take her?"

"No," Ilona said.

So Osmo rowed on again. At this the creature raised

such a pitiful outcry demanding what they meant denying assistance to a poor woman that Osmo was unable longer to refuse and in spite of Ilona's warning he rowed to land.

Suyettar instantly jumped into the boat and seated herself in the middle with her face towards Osmo and her back towards Ilona.

"What a fine young man!" Suyettar said in whining flattering tones. "See how strong he is at the oars! And what a beautiful girl, too! I daresay the King's Son would fall in love with her if ever he saw her!"

Thereupon Osmo very foolishly told Suyettar that the King's Son had already promised to marry Ilona. At that an evil look came into Suyettar's face and she sat silent for a time biting her fingers. Then she began mumbling a spell that made Osmo deaf to what Ilona was saying and Ilona deaf to what Osmo was saying.

At last in the distance the towers of the King's castle appeared.

"Stand up, sister!" Osmo said. "Shake out your skirts and arrange your pretty ribbons! We'll soon be landing now!"

Ilona could see her brother's lips moving but of course she could not hear what he was saying.

"What is it, brother?" she asked.

Suyettar answered for him:

"Osmo orders you to jump headlong into the water!"

"No! No!" Ilona cried. "He couldn't order anything so cruel as that!"

Presently Osmo said:

"Sister, what ails you? Don't you hear me? Shake out your skirts and arrange your pretty ribbons for we'll soon be landing now."

"What is it, brother?" Ilona asked.

As before Suyettar answered for him:

"Osmo orders you to jump headlong into the water!"

"Brother, how can you order so cruel a thing!" Ilona cried, bursting into tears. "Is it for this you made me leave the home of my fathers?"

A third time Osmo said:

"Stand up, sister, and shake out your skirts and arrange your ribbons! We'll soon be landing now!"

"I can't hear you, brother! What is it you say?"

Suyettar turned on her fiercely and screamed:

"Osmo orders you to jump headlong into the water!"

"If he says I must, I must!" poor Ilona sobbed, and with that she leapt overboard.

Osmo tried to save her but Suyettar held him back

and with her own arms rowed off and Ilona was left to sink.

"What will become of me now!" Osmo cried. "When the King's Son finds I have not brought him my sister he will surely order my death!"

"Not at all!" Suyettar said. "Do as I say and no harm will come to you. Offer me to the King's Son and tell him I am your sister. He won't know the difference and anyway I'm sure I'm just as beautiful as Ilona ever was!"

With that Suyettar opened the wooden box that held Ilona's clothes and helped herself to skirt and bodice and gay colored ribbons. She decked herself out in these and for a little while she really did succeed in looking like a pretty young girl.

So Osmo presented Suyettar to the King's Son as Ilona, and the King's Son because he had given his word married her. But before one day was past, he called Osmo to him and asked him angrily:

"What did you mean by telling me your sister was beautiful?"

"Isn't she beautiful?" Osmo faltered.

"No! I thought she was at first but she isn't! She is ugly and evil and you shall pay the penalty for having deceived me!"

Thereupon he ordered that Osmo be shut up in a place filled with serpents.

"If you are innocent," the King's Son said, "the serpents will not harm you. If you are guilty they will devour you!"

Meanwhile poor Ilona when she jumped into the water sank down, down, down, until she reached the Sea King's palace. They received her kindly there and comforted her and the Sea King's Son, touched by her grief and beauty, offered to marry her. But Ilona was homesick for the upper world and would not listen to him.

"I want to see my brother again!" she wept.

They told her that the King's Son had thrown her brother to the serpents and had married Suyettar in her stead, but Ilona still begged so pitifully to be allowed to return to earth that at last the Sea King said:

"Very well, then! For three successive nights I will allow you to return to the upper world. But after that never again!"

So they decked Ilona in the lovely jewels of the sea with great strands of pearls about her neck and to each of her ankles they attached long silver chains. As she rose in the water the sound of the chains was like the chiming of silver bells and could be heard for five miles.

Ilona came to the surface of the water just where Osmo had landed. The first thing she saw was his boat at the water's edge and curled up asleep in the bottom of the boat her own little dog, Pilka.

"Pilka!" Ilona cried, and the little dog woke with a bark of joy and licked Ilona's hand and yelped and frisked.

Then Ilona sang this magic song to Pilka:

> "Peely, peely, Pilka, pide,
> Lift the latch and slip inside!
> Past the watchdog in the yard,
> Past the sleeping men on guard!
> Creep in softly as a snake,
> Then creep out before they wake!
> Peely, peely, Pilka, pide,
> Peely, peely, Pilka!"

Pilka barked and frisked and said:

"Yes, mistress, yes! I'll do whatever you bid me!"

Ilona gave the little dog an embroidered square of gold and silver which she herself had worked down in the Sea King's palace.

"Take this," she said to Pilka, "and put it on the pillow where the King's Son lies asleep. Perhaps when he sees it he will know that it comes from Osmo's true sister and that the frightful creature he has married is Suyettar. Then perhaps he will release Osmo before the serpents devour him. Go now, my faithful Pilka, and come back to me before the dawn."

So Pilka raced off to the King's palace carrying the square of embroidery in her teeth. Ilona waited and half an hour before sunrise the little dog came panting back.

"What news, Pilka? How fares my brother and how is my poor love, the King's Son?"

"Osmo is still with the serpents," Pilka answered, "but they haven't eaten him yet. I left the embroidered square on the pillow where the King's Son's head was lying. Suyettar was asleep on the bed beside him where you should be, dear mistress. Suyettar's awful mouth was open and she was snoring horribly. The King's Son moved uneasily for he was troubled even in his sleep."

"And did you go through the castle, Pilka?"

"Yes, dear mistress."

"And did you see the remains of the wedding feast?"

"Yes, dear mistress, the remains of a feast that shamed the King's Son, for Suyettar served bones instead of meat, fish heads, turnip tops, and bread burned to a cinder."

"Good Pilka!" Ilona said. "Good little dog! You have done well! Now the dawn is coming and I must go back to the Sea King's palace. But I shall come again to-night and also to-morrow night and do you be here waiting for me."

Pilka promised and Ilona sank down into the sea to a clanking of chains that sounded like silver bells. The King's Son heard them in his sleep and for a moment woke and said:

"What's that?"

"What's vhat?" snarled Suyettar. "You're dreaming! Go back to sleep!"

A few hours later when he woke again, he found the lovely square of embroidery on his pillow.

"Who made this?" he cried.

Suyettar was busy combing her snaky locks. She turned on him quickly.

"Who made what?"

When she saw the embroidery she tried to snatch it from him, but he held it tight.

"I made it, of course!" she declared. "Who but me would sit up all night and work while you lay snoring!"

But the King's Son, as he folded the embroidery, muttered to himself:

"It doesn't look to me much like your work!"

After he had breakfasted, the King's Son asked for news of Osmo. A slave was sent to the place of the serpents and when he returned he reported that Osmo was sitting amongst them uninjured.

"The old king snake has made friends with him," he added, "and has wound himself around Osmo's arm."

The King's Son was amazed at this news and also relieved, for the whole affair troubled him sorely and he was beginning to suspect a mystery.

He knew an old wise woman who lived alone in a little hut on the seashore and he decided he would go and consult her. So he went to her and told her about Osmo and how Osmo had deceived him in regard to his sister. Then he told her how the serpents instead of devouring Osmo had made friends with him and last he showed her the square of lovely embroidery he had found on his pillow that morning.

"There is a mystery somewhere, granny," he said in conclusion, "and I know not how to solve it."

The old woman looked at him thoughtfully.

"My son," she said at last, "that is never Osmo's sister that you have married. Take an old woman's word—it is Suyettar! Yet Osmo's sister must be alive and the embroidery must be a token from her. It

The old king snake has wound himself around Osmo's arm

probably means that she begs you to release her brother."

"Suyettar!" repeated the King's Son, aghast.

At first he couldn't believe such a horrible thing possible and yet that, if it were so, would explain much.

"I wonder if you're right," he said. "I must be on my guard!"

That night on the stroke of midnight to the sound of silver chimes Ilona came floating up through the waves and little Pilka, as she appeared, greeted her with barks of joy.

As before Ilona sang:

> "Peely, peely, Pilka, pide,
> Lift the latch and slip inside!
> Past the watchdog in the yard,
> Past the sleeping men on guard!
> Creep in softly as a snake,
> Then creep out before they wake!
> Peely, peely, Pilka, pide,
> Peely, peely, Pilka!"

This time Ilona gave Pilka a shirt for the King's Son. Beautifully embroidered it was in gold and silver and Ilona herself had worked it in the Sea King's palace.

Pilka carried it safely to the castle and left it on the

pillow where the King's Son could see it as soon as he woke. Then Pilka visited the place of the serpents and before the first ray of dawn was back at the seashore to reassure Ilona of Osmo's safety.

Then dawn came and Ilona, as she sank in the waves to the chime of silver bells, called out to Pilka:

"Meet me here to-night at the same hour! Fail me not, dear Pilka, for to-night is the last night that the Sea King will allow me to come to the upper world!"

Pilka, howling with grief, made promise:

"I'll be here, dear mistress, that I will!"

The King's Son that morning, as he opened his eyes, saw the embroidered shirt lying on the pillow at his head. He thought at first he must be dreaming for it was more beautiful than any shirt that had ever been worked by human fingers.

"Ah!" he sighed at last, "who made this?"

"Who made what?" Suyettar demanded rudely.

When she saw the shirt she tried to snatch it, but the King's Son held it from her. Then she pretended to laugh and said:

"Oh, that! I made it, of course! Do you think any one else in the world would sit up all night and work for you while you lie there snoring! And small thanks I get for it, too!"

"It doesn't look to me like your work!" said the King's Son significantly.

Again the slave reported to him that Osmo was alive and unhurt by the serpents.

"Strange!" thought the King's Son.

He took the embroidered shirt and made the old wise woman another visit.

"Ah!" she said, when she saw the shirt, "now I understand! Listen, my Prince: last night at midnight I was awakened by the chime of silver bells and I got up and looked out the door. Just there at the water's edge, close to that little boat, I saw a strange sight. A lovely maiden rose from the waves holding in her hands the very shirt that you now have. A little dog that was lying in the boat greeted her with barks of joy. She sang a magic rime to the dog and gave it the shirt and off it ran. That maid, my Prince, must be Ilona. She must be in the Sea King's power and I think she is begging you to rescue her and to release her brother."

The King's Son slowly nodded his head.

"Granny, I'm sure what you say is true! Help me to rescue Ilona and I shall reward you richly."

"Then, my son, you must act at once, for to-night, I heard Ilona say, is the last night that the Sea King will allow her to come to the upper world. Go now to the smith and have him forge you a strong iron chain and a great strong scythe. Then to-night hide you down yonder in the shadow of the boat. At midnight when you hear the silver chimes and the maiden slowly rises from the waves, throw the iron chain about her and quickly draw her to you. Then, with one sweep of your scythe, cut the silver chains that are fastened to her ankles. But remember, my son, that is not all. She is under enchantment and as you try to grasp her the Sea King will change her to many things—a fish, a bird, a fly, and I know not what, and if in any form she escape you, then all is lost."

At once the King's Son hurried away to the smithy and had the smith forge him a strong iron chain and a heavy sharp scythe. Then when night fell he hid in the shadow of the boat and waited. Pilka snuggled up beside him. Midnight came and to the sweet chiming as of silver bells Ilona slowly rose from the waves. As she came she began singing:

"Peely, peely, Pilka, pide——"

Instantly the King's Son threw the strong iron chain about her and drew her to him. Then with one mighty sweep of the scythe he severed the silver chains that were attached to her ankles and the silver chains fell chiming into the depths. Another instant and the maiden in his arms was no maiden but a slimy fish that squirmed and wriggled and almost slipped through his fingers. He killed the fish and, lo! it was not a fish but a frightened bird that struggled to escape. He killed the bird and, lo! it was not a bird but a writhing lizard. And so on through many transformations, growing finally small and weak until at last there was only a mosquito. He crushed this and in his arms he found again the lovely Ilona.

"Ah, dear one," he said, "you are my true bride and not Suyettar who pretended she was you! Come, we will go at once to the castle and confront her!"

But Ilona cried out at this:

"Not there, my Prince, not there! Suyettar if she saw me would kill me and devour me! Keep me from her!"

"Very well, my dear one," the King's Son said. "We'll wait until to-morrow and after to-morrow there will be no Suyettar to fear."

So for that night they took shelter in the old wise woman's hut, Ilona and the King's Son and faithful little Pilka.

The next morning early the King's Son returned to

the castle and had the *sauna* heated. Just inside the door he had a deep hole dug and filled it with burning tar. Then over the top of the hole he stretched a brown mat and on the brown mat a blue mat. When all was ready he went indoors and roused Suyettar.

"Where have you been all night?" she demanded angrily.

"Forgive me this time," he begged in pretended humility, "and I promise never again to be parted from my own true bride. Come now, my dear, and bathe for the *sauna* is ready."

Then Suyettar, who loved to have people see her go to the *sauna* just as if she were a real human being, put on a long bathrobe and clapped her hands. Four slaves appeared. Two took up the train of her bathrobe and the two others supported her on either side. Slowly she marched out of the castle, across the courtyard, and over to the *sauna*.

"They all really think I'm a human princess!" she said to herself, and she was so sure she was beautiful and admired that she tossed her head and smirked from side to side and took little mincing steps.

When she reached the *sauna* she was ready to drop the bathrobe and jump over the doorsill to the steaming shelf, but the King's Son whispered:

"Nay! Nay! Remember your dignity as a beautiful princess and walk over the blue mat!"

So with one more toss of her head, one more smirk of her ugly face, Suyettar stepped on the blue mat and sank into the hole of burning tar. Then the King's Son quickly locked the door of the *sauna* and left her there to burn in the tar, for burning, you know, is the only way to destroy Suyettar. As she burned the last hateful thing Suyettar did was to tear out handfuls of her hair and scatter them broadcast in the air.

"Let these," she cried, yelling and cursing, "turn into mosquitos and worms and moths and trouble mankind forever!"

Then her yells grew fainter and at last ceased altogether and the King's Son knew that it was now safe to bring Ilona home. First, however, he had Osmo released from the place of the serpents and asked his forgiveness for the unjust punishment.

Then he and Osmo together went to the hut of the old wise woman and there with tears of happiness the brother and sister were reunited. The King's Son to show his gratitude to the old wise woman begged her to accompany them to the castle and presently they all set forth with Pilka frisking ahead and barking for joy.

That day there was a new wedding feast spread at the castle and this time it was not bones and fish heads and burnt crusts but such food as the King's Son had not tasted for many a day.

To celebrate his happy marriage the King's Son made Osmo his chamberlain and gave Pilka a beautiful new collar.

"Now at last," Ilona said, "I am glad I left the house of my forefathers."

MIGHTY MIKKO

The Story of a Poor Woodsman and a Grateful Fox

MIGHTY MIKKO

There was once an old woodsman and his wife who had an only son named Mikko. As the mother lay dying the young man wept bitterly.

"When you are gone, my dear mother," he said, "there will be no one left to think of me."

The poor woman comforted him as best she could and said to him:

"You will still have your father."

Shortly after the woman's death, the old man, too, was taken ill.

"Now, indeed, I shall be left desolate and alone," Mikko thought, as he sat beside his father's bedside and saw him grow weaker and weaker.

"My boy," the old man said just before he died, "I have nothing to leave you but the three snares with which these many years I have caught wild animals. Those snares now belong to you. When I am dead, go into the woods and if you find a wild creature caught in any of them, free it gently and bring it home alive."

After his father's death, Mikko remembered the snares and went out to the woods to see them. The first was empty and also the second, but in the third he found a little red Fox. He carefully lifted the spring that had shut down on one of the Fox's feet and then carried the little creature home in his arms. He shared his supper with it and when he lay down to sleep the Fox curled up at his feet. They lived together some time until they became close friends.

"Mikko," said the Fox one day, "why are you so sad?"

"Because I'm lonely."

"Pooh!" said the Fox. "That's no way for a young man to talk! You ought to get married! Then you wouldn't feel lonely!"

"Married!" Mikko repeated. "How can I get married? I can't marry a poor girl because I'm too poor myself and a rich girl wouldn't marry me."

"Nonsense!" said the Fox. "You're a fine well set up young man and you're kind and gentle. What more could a princess ask?"

Mikko laughed to think of a princess wanting him for a husband.

"I mean what I say!" the Fox insisted. "Take our own Princess now. What would you think of marrying her?"

Mikko laughed louder than before.

"I have heard," he said, "that she is the most beautiful princess in the world! Any man would be happy to marry her!"

"Very well," the Fox said, "if you feel that way about her then I'll arrange the wedding for you."

With that the little Fox actually did trot off to the royal castle and gain audience with the King.

"My master sends you greetings," the Fox said, "and he begs you to loan him your bushel measure."

"My bushel measure!" the King repeated in surprise. "Who is your master and why does he want my bushel measure?"

"Ssh!" the Fox whispered as though he didn't want the courtiers to hear what he was saying. Then slipping up quite close to the King he murmured in his ear:

"Surely you have heard of Mikko, haven't you?— Mighty Mikko as he's called."

The King had never heard of any Mikko who was known as Mighty Mikko but, thinking that perhaps he should have heard of him, he shook his head and murmured:

"H'm! Mikko! Mighty Mikko! Oh, to be sure! Yes, yes, of course!"

"My master is about to start off on a journey and he needs a bushel measure for a very particular reason."

"I understand! I understand!" the King said, although he didn't understand at all, and he gave orders that the bushel measure which they used in the storeroom of the castle be brought in and given to the Fox.

The Fox carried off the measure and hid it in the woods. Then he scurried about to all sorts of little out of the way nooks and crannies where people had hidden their savings and he dug up a gold piece here and a silver piece there until he had a handful. Then he went back to the woods and stuck the various coins in the cracks of the measure. The next day he returned to the King.

"My master, Mighty Mikko," he said, "sends you thanks, O King, for the use of your bushel measure."

The King held out his hand and when the Fox gave him the measure he peeped inside to see if by chance it contained any trace of what had recently been measured. His eye of course at once caught the glint of the gold and silver coins lodged in the cracks.

"Ah!" he said, thinking Mikko must be a very mighty lord indeed to be so careless of his wealth; "I should like to meet your master. Won't you and he come and visit me?"

This was what the Fox wanted the King to say but he pretended to hesitate.

"I thank your Majesty for the kind invitation," he said, "but I fear my master can't accept it just now. He wants to get married soon and we are about to start off on a long journey to inspect a number of foreign princesses."

This made the King all the more anxious to have Mikko visit him at once for he thought that if Mikko should see his daughter before he saw those foreign princesses he might fall in love with her and marry her. So he said to the Fox:

"My dear fellow, you must prevail on your master to make me a visit before he starts out on his travels! You will, won't you?"

The Fox looked this way and that as if he were too embarrassed to speak.

"Your Majesty," he said at last, "I pray you pardon my frankness. The truth is you are not rich enough to entertain my master and your castle isn't big enough to house the immense retinue that always attends him."

The King, who by this time was frantic to see Mikko, lost his head completely.

"My dear Fox," he said, "I'll give you anything in the world if you prevail upon your master to visit me at once! Couldn't you suggest to him to travel with a modest retinue this time?"

The Fox shook his head.

"No. His rule is either to travel with a great retinue or to go on foot disguised as a poor woodsman attended only by me."

"Couldn't you prevail on him to come to me disguised as a poor woodsman?" the King begged. "Once he was here, I could place gorgeous clothes at his disposal."

But still the Fox shook his head.

"I fear Your Majesty's wardrobe doesn't contain the kind of clothes my master is accustomed to."

"I assure you I've got some very good clothes," the King said. "Come along this minute and we'll go through them and I'm sure you'll find some that your master would wear."

So they went to a room which was like a big wardrobe with hundreds and hundreds of hooks upon which were hung hundreds of coats and breeches and embroidered shirts. The King ordered his attendants to bring the costumes down one by one and place them before the Fox.

The King thought that if Mikko should see his daughter

MIGHTY MIKKO

They began with the plainer clothes.

"Good enough for most people," the Fox said, "but not for my master."

Then they took down garments of a finer grade.

"I'm afraid you're going to all this trouble for nothing," the Fox said. "Frankly now, don't you realize that my master couldn't possibly put on any of these things!"

The King, who had hoped to keep for his own use his most gorgeous clothes of all, now ordered these to be shown.

The Fox looked at them sideways, sniffed them critically, and at last said:

"Well, perhaps my master would consent to wear these for a few days. They are not what he is accustomed to wear but I will say this for him: he is not proud."

The King was overjoyed.

"Very well, my dear Fox, I'll have the guest chambers put in readiness for your master's visit and I'll have all these, my finest clothes, laid out for him. You won't disappoint me, will you?"

"I'll do my best," the Fox promised.

With that he bade the King a civil good day and ran home to Mikko.

The next day as the Princess was peeping out of an upper window of the castle, she saw a young woodsman approaching accompanied by a Fox. He was a fine stalwart youth and the Princess, who knew from the presence of the Fox that he must be Mikko, gave a long sigh and confided to her serving maid:

"I think I could fall in love with that young man if he really were only a woodsman!"

Later when she saw him arrayed in her father's finest clothes—which looked so well on Mikko that no one even recognized them as the King's—she lost her heart completely and when Mikko was presented to her she blushed and trembled just as any ordinary girl might before a handsome young man.

All the Court was equally delighted with Mikko. The ladies went into ecstasies over his modest manners, his fine figure, and the gorgeousness of his clothes, and the old graybeard Councilors, nodding their heads in approval, said to each other:

"Nothing of the coxcomb about this young fellow! In spite of his great wealth see how politely he listens to us when we talk!"

The next day the Fox went privately to the King, and said:

"My master is a man of few words and quick judg-

MIGHTY MIKKO

ment. He bids me tell you that your daughter, the Princess, pleases him mightily and that, with your approval, he will make his addresses to her at once."

The King was greatly agitated and began:

"My dear Fox—"

But the Fox interrupted him to say:

"Think the matter over carefully and give me your decision to-morrow."

So the King consulted with the Princess and with his Councilors and in a short time the marriage was arranged and the wedding ceremony actually performed!

"Didn't I tell you?" the Fox said, when he and Mikko were alone after the wedding.

"Yes," Mikko acknowledged, "you did promise that I should marry the Princess. But, tell me, now that I am married what am I to do? I can't live on here forever with my wife."

"Put your mind at rest," the Fox said. "I've thought of everything. Just do as I tell you and you'll have nothing to regret. To-night say to the King: 'It is now only fitting that you should visit me and see for yourself the sort of castle over which your daughter is hereafter to be mistress!'"

When Mikko said this to the King, the King was

overjoyed for now that the marriage had actually taken place he was wondering whether he hadn't perhaps been a little hasty. Mikko's words reassured him and he eagerly accepted the invitation.

On the morrow the Fox said to Mikko:

"Now I'll run on ahead and get things ready for you."

"But where are you going?" Mikko said, frightened at the thought of being deserted by his little friend.

The Fox drew Mikko aside and whispered softly:

"A few days' march from here there is a very gorgeous castle belonging to a wicked old dragon who is known as the Worm. I think the Worm's castle would just about suit you."

"I'm sure it would," Mikko agreed. "But how are we to get it away from the Worm?"

"Trust me," the Fox said. "All you need do is this: lead the King and his courtiers along the main highway until by noon to-morrow you reach a crossroads. Turn there to the left and go straight on until you see the tower of the Worm's castle. If you meet any men by the wayside, shepherds or the like, ask them whose men they are and show no surprise at their answer. So now, dear master, farewell until we meet again at your beautiful castle."

The little Fox trotted off at a smart pace and Mikko and the Princess and the King attended by the whole Court followed in more leisurely fashion.

The little Fox, when he had left the main highway at the crossroads, soon met ten woodsmen with axes over their shoulders. They were all dressed in blue smocks of the same cut.

"Good day," the Fox said politely. "Whose men are you?"

"Our master is known as the Worm," the woodsmen told him.

"My poor, poor lads!" the Fox said, shaking his head sadly.

"What's the matter?" the woodsmen asked.

For a few moments the Fox pretended to be too overcome with emotion to speak. Then he said:

"My poor lads, don't you know that the King is coming with a great force to destroy the Worm and all his people?"

The woodsmen were simple fellows and this news threw them into great consternation.

"Is there no way for us to escape?" they asked.

The Fox put his paw to his head and thought.

"Well," he said at last, "there is one way you might escape and that is by telling every one who asks you that you are the Mighty Mikko's men. But if you value your lives never again say that your master is the Worm."

"We are Mighty Mikko's men!" the woodsmen at once began repeating over and over. "We are Mighty Mikko's men!"

A little farther on the road the Fox met twenty grooms, dressed in the same blue smocks, who were tending a hundred beautiful horses. The Fox talked to the twenty grooms as he had talked to the woodsmen and before he left them they, too, were shouting:

"We are Mighty Mikko's men!"

Next the Fox came to a huge flock of a thousand sheep tended by thirty shepherds all dressed in the Worm's blue smocks. He stopped and talked to them until he had them roaring out:

"We are Mighty Mikko's men!"

Then the Fox trotted on until he reached the castle of the Worm. He found the Worm himself inside lolling lazily about. He was a huge dragon and had been a great warrior in his day. In fact his castle and his lands and his servants and his possessions had all been won in battle. But now for many years no one had cared to fight him and he had grown fat and lazy.

"Good day," the Fox said, pretending to be very

breathless and frightened. "You're the Worm, aren't you?"

"Yes," the dragon said, boastfully, "I am the great Worm!"

The Fox pretended to grow more agitated.

"My poor fellow, I am sorry for you! But of course none of us can expect to live forever. Well, I must hurry along. I thought I would just stop and say good-by."

Made uneasy by the Fox's words, the Worm cried out:

"Wait just a minute! What's the matter?"

The Fox was already at the door but at the Worm's entreaty he paused and said over his shoulder:

"Why, my poor fellow, you surely know, don't you? that the King with a great force is coming to destroy you and all your people!"

"What!" the Worm gasped, turning a sickly green with fright. He knew he was fat and helpless and could never again fight as in the years gone by.

"Don't go just yet!" he begged the Fox. "When is the King coming?"

"He's on the highway now! That's why I must be going! Good-by!"

"My dear Fox, stay just a moment and I'll reward

you richly! Help me to hide so that the King won't find me! What about the shed where the linen is stored? I could crawl under the linen and then if you locked the door from the outside the King could never find me."

"Very well," the Fox agreed, "but we must hurry!"

So they ran outside to the shed where the linen was kept and the Worm hid himself under the linen. The Fox locked the door, then set fire to the shed, and soon there was nothing left of that wicked old dragon, the Worm, but a handful of ashes.

The Fox now called together the dragon's household and talked them over to Mikko as he had the woodsmen and the grooms and the shepherds.

Meanwhile the King and his party were slowly covering the ground over which the Fox had sped so quickly. When they came to the ten woodsmen in blue smocks, the King said:

"I wonder whose woodsmen those are."

One of his attendants asked the woodsmen and the ten of them shouted out at the top of their voices:

"We are Mighty Mikko's men!"

Mikko said nothing and the King and all the Court were impressed anew with his modesty.

A little farther on they met the twenty grooms with

their hundred prancing horses. When the grooms were questioned, they answered with a shout:

"We are Mighty Mikko's men!"

"The Fox certainly spoke the truth," the King thought to himself, "when he told me of Mikko's riches!"

A little later the thirty shepherds when they were questioned made answer in a chorus that was deafening to hear:

"We are Mighty Mikko's men!"

The sight of the thousand sheep that belonged to his son-in-law made the King feel poor and humble in comparison and the courtiers whispered among themselves:

"For all his simple manner, Mighty Mikko must be a richer, more powerful lord than the King himself! In fact it is only a very great lord indeed who could be so simple!"

At last they reached the castle which from the blue smocked soldiers that guarded the gateway they knew to be Mikko's. The Fox came out to welcome the King's party and behind him in two rows all the household servants. These, at a signal from the Fox, cried out in one voice:

"We are Mighty Mikko's men!"

Then Mikko in the same simple manner that he would have used in his father's mean little hut in the woods bade the King and his followers welcome and they all entered the castle where they found a great feast already prepared and waiting.

The King stayed on for several days and the more he saw of Mikko the better pleased he was that he had him for a son-in-law.

When he was leaving he said to Mikko:

"Your castle is so much grander than mine that I hesitate ever asking you back for a visit."

But Mikko reassured the King by saying earnestly:

"My dear father-in-law, when first I entered your castle I thought it was the most beautiful castle in the world!"

The King was flattered and the courtiers whispered among themselves:

'How affable of him to say that when he knows very well how much grander his own castle is!"

When the King and his followers were safely gone, the little red Fox came to Mikko and said:

"Now, my master, you have no reason to feel sad and lonely. You are lord of the most beautiful castle in the world and you have for wife a sweet and lovely Princess. You have no longer any need of me, so I am going to bid you farewell."

Mikko thanked the little Fox for all he had done and the little Fox trotted off to the woods.

So you see that Mikko's poor old father, although he had no wealth to leave his son, was really the cause of all Mikko's good fortune, for it was he who told Mikko in the first place to carry home alive anything he might find caught in the snares.

THE THREE CHESTS

The Story of the Wicked Old Man of the Sea

THE THREE CHESTS

There was once an honest old farmer who had three daughters. His farm ran down to the shores of a deep lake. One day as he leaned over the water to take a drink, wicked old Wetehinen reached up from the bottom of the lake and clutched him by the beard.

"Ouch! Ouch!" the farmer cried. "Let me go!"

Wetehinen only held on more tightly.

"Yes, I'll let you go," he said, "but only on this condition: that you give me one of your daughters for wife!"

"Give you one of my daughters? Never!"

"Very well, then I'll never let go!" wicked old Wetehinen declared and with that he began jerking at the beard as if it were a bellrope.

"Wait! Wait!" the farmer spluttered.

Now he didn't want to give one of his daughters to wicked old Wetehinen—of course not! But at the same time he was in Wetehinen's power and he realized that if he didn't do what the old reprobate demanded he might lose his life and so leave all three of his daughters orphans. Perhaps for the good of all he had better sacrifice one of them.

"All right," he said, "let me go and I'll send you my oldest daughter. I promise."

So Wetehinen let go his beard and the farmer scrambled to his feet and hurried home.

"My dear," he said to his oldest daughter, "I left a bit of the harness down at the lake. Like a good girl will you run down and get it for me."

The eldest daughter went at once and when she reached the water's edge, old Wetehinen reached up and caught her about the waist and carried her down to the bottom of the lake where he lived in a big house.

At first he was kind to her. He made her mistress of the house and gave her the keys to all the rooms and closets. He went very carefully over the keys and pointing to one he said:

"That key you must never use for it opens the door to a room which I forbid you to enter."

The eldest daughter began keeping house for old Wetehinen and spent her time cooking and cleaning and spinning much as she used to at home with her father. The days went by and she grew familiar with the house and began to know what was in every room and every closet.

At first she felt no temptation to open the forbidden door. If old Wetehinen wanted to have a secret room, well and good. But why in the world had he given her the key if he really didn't want her to open the door? The more she thought about it the more she wondered. Every time she passed the room she stopped a moment and stared at the door. It looked just exactly like the doors that led into all the other rooms.

"I wonder why he doesn't want me to open just that door?" she kept asking herself.

Finally one day when old Wetehinen was away she thought:

"I don't believe it would matter if I opened that door just a little crack and peeped in once! No one would know the difference!"

For a few moments she hesitated, then mustered up courage enough to turn the key in the forbidden lock and throw open the door.

The room was a storeroom with boxes and chests and old jars piled up around the wall. That was unexciting enough, but in the middle of the floor was something that made her start when she saw what it was.

It was blood—that's what it was, a pool of dark red blood! She was about to slam the door shut when she saw something else that made her pause. This was a lovely shining ring that lay in the midst of the pool.

"Oh!" she thought to herself, "what a beautiful ring! If I had it I'd wear it on my finger!"

The longer she looked at it, the more she wanted it.

"If I'm very careful," she said, "I know I could reach over and pick it up without touching the blood."

She tiptoed cautiously into the room, wrapped her skirts tightly about her legs, knelt down on the floor, and stretched her arm over the pool. She picked up the ring very carefully but even so she got a few drops of blood on her fingers.

"No matter!" she thought, "I can wash that off! And see the lovely ring!"

But later, after she had the door again locked, when she tried to wash the blood off, she found she couldn't. She tried soap, she tried sand, she tried everything she could think of, but without success.

"I don't care!" she thought to herself. "If Wetehinen sees the blood, I'll just tell him I cut my finger by accident."

So when Wetehinen came home, she hid the ring and pretended nothing was the matter.

THE THREE CHESTS 53

After supper Wetehinen put his head in her lap and said:

"Now, my dear, scratch my head and make me drowsy for bed."

She began scratching his head as she had many nights before but, at the first touch of her fingers, he cried out:

"Stop! You're burning my ear! There must be some blood on your fingers! Let me see!"

He reached up and caught her hand and, when he saw the blood stains, he flew into a towering rage.

"I thought so! You've been in the forbidden room!"

He jumped up and without allowing her time to say a word he just cut off her head then and there with no more concern than if she had been a mosquito! After that he took the body and the severed head and threw them into the forbidden room and locked the door.

"Now then," he growled, "*she* won't disobey me again!"

This was all very well but now he had no one to keep house for him and cook and scratch his head in the evening and soon he decided he'd have to get another wife. He remembered that the farmer had two more daughters, so he thought to himself that now he'd marry the second sister.

He waited his chance and one day when the farmer was out in his boat fishing, old Wetehinen came up from the bottom of the lake and clutched the boat. When the poor old farmer tried to row back to shore he couldn't make the boat move an inch. He worked and worked at the oars and wicked old Wetehinen let him struggle until he was exhausted. Then he put his head up out of the water and over the side of the boat and as though nothing were the matter he said:

"Hullo!"

"Oh!" the farmer cried, wishing he were safe on shore, "it's you, is it? I wondered what was holding my boat."

"Yes," wicked old Wetehinen said, "it's me and I'm going to hold your boat right here on this spot until you promise to give me another of your daughters."

What could the farmer do? He pleaded with Wetehinen but Wetehinen was firm and the upshot was that before the farmer again walked dry land he had promised Wetehinen his second daughter.

Well, when he got home, he pretended he had forgotten his ax in the boat and sent his second daughter

THE THREE CHESTS 55

down to the lake to get it. Wicked old Wetehinen caught her as he had caught her sister and carried her home with him to his house at the bottom of the lake.

Wetehinen treated the second sister just exactly as he had the first, making her mistress of the house and telling her she might use every key but one. Like her sister she, too, after a time gave way to the temptation of looking into the forbidden room and when she saw the shining ring lying in the pool of blood of course she wanted it and of course when she reached to get it she dabbled her fingers in the blood. So that was the end of her, too, for wicked old Wetehinen when he saw the blood stains just cut her head right off and threw her body and the severed head into the forbidden room beside the body and head of her sister and locked the door.

Time went by and the farmer was living happily with his youngest daughter when one day while he was out chopping wood he found a pair of fine birch bark brogues. He put them on and instantly found himself walking away from the woods and down to the lake. He tried to stop but he couldn't. He tried to walk in another direction but the brogues carried him straight down to the water's edge and out into the lake until he was in waist deep.

Then he heard a gruff voice saying:

"Hullo, there! What are you doing with my brogues?"

Of course it was wicked old Wetehinen who had played that trick to get the farmer into his power again.

"What do you want this time?" the poor farmer cried.

"I want your youngest daughter," Wetehinen said.

"What! My youngest daughter!"

"Yes."

"I won't give her up!" the farmer declared. "I don't care what you do to me. I won't give her up!"

"Oh, very well!" Wetehinen said, and immediately the brogues which had been standing still while they talked started walking again. They carried the farmer out into the lake farther and farther until the water was up to his chin.

"Wait—wait a minute!" he cried.

The brogues stopped walking and Wetehinen said:

"Well, do you promise to give her to me?"

"No!" the farmer began. "She's my last daughter and—"

Before he could say more, the brogues walked on and the water rose to his nose. In desperation he threw up his hands and shouted:

"I promise! I promise!"

She fitted the key in the lock

THE THREE CHESTS

So when he got home that day he said to his youngest daughter whose name was Lisa:

"Lisa, my dear, I forgot my brogues at the lake. Like a good girl won't you run and get them for me?"

So Lisa went to the lake and Wetehinen of course caught her and carried her down to his house as he had her two sisters.

Then the same old story was repeated. Wetehinen made Lisa mistress of the house and gave her keys to all the doors and closets with the same prohibition against opening the door of the forbidden room.

"If I am mistress of the house," Lisa said to herself, "why should I not unlock every door?"

She waited until one day when Wetehinen was away from home, then went boldly to the forbidden room, fitted the key in the lock, and flung open the door.

There lay her two poor sisters with their heads cut off. There in the pool of blood sparkled the lovely ring, but Lisa paid no heed to it.

"Wicked old Wetehinen!" Lisa cried. "I suppose he thinks that ring will tempt me but nothing will tempt me to touch that awful blood!"

Then she rummaged about, opening boxes and chests, and turning things over. In a dark corner she found two pitchers, one marked *Water of Life,* the other *Water of Death.*

"Ha! This is what I want!" she cried, taking the pitcher of the *Water of Life.*

She set the severed heads of her sisters in place and then with the magic water brought them back to life. She used up all the *Water of Life,* so she filled the pitcher marked *Water of Life* with the water from the other pitcher, the *Water of Death.* She hid her sisters each in a big wooden chest, she shut and locked the door of the forbidden room, and Wetehinen when he came home found her working at her spinning wheel as though nothing unusual had happened.

After supper Wetehinen said:

"Now scratch my head and make me drowsy for bed."

So Lisa scratched his wicked old head and she did it so well that he grunted with satisfaction.

"Uh! Uh!" he said. "That's good! Now just behind my right ear! That's it! That's it! You're a good girl, you are! You're not like some of them who do what they're told not to do! Now behind the other ear! Oh, that's fine! Yes, you're a good girl and if there's anything you want me to do just tell me what it is."

THE THREE CHESTS

"I want to send a chest of things to my poor old father," Lisa said. "Just a lot of little nothings—odds and ends that I've picked up about the house. I'd be ashamed to have you open the chest and see them. I do wish you'd carry the chest ashore to-morrow and leave it where my father will find it."

"All right, I will," Wetehinen promised.

He was true to his word. The next morning he hoisted one of the chests on his shoulder, the one that had in it the eldest sister, he trudged off with it, and tossed it up on shore at a place where he was sure the farmer would find it.

Lisa then wheedled him into carrying up the second chest that had in it the second sister. This time Wetehinen wasn't so good-natured.

"I don't know what she can always be sending her father!" he grumbled. "If she sends another chest I'll have to look inside and see."

Now Lisa, when the second sister was safely delivered, began to plan her own escape. She pulled out another empty chest and then one evening after she had succeeded in making old Wetehinen comfortable and drowsy she begged him to carry this also to her father. He grumbled and protested but finally promised.

"And you won't look inside, will you? Promise me you won't!" Lisa begged.

Wetehinen said he wouldn't, but he intended to just the same.

Well, the next morning as soon as Wetehinen went out, Lisa took the churn and dressed it up in some of her own clothes. She carried it to the top of the house and perched it on the ridge of the roof before a spinning wheel. Then she herself crept inside the third chest and waited.

When Wetehinen came home he looked up and saw what he thought was Lisa spinning on the roof.

"Hullo!" he shouted. "What are you doing up there?"

Lisa, in the chest, answered in a voice that sounded as if it came from the roof:

"I'm spinning. And you, Wetehinen, my dear, don't forget the chest that you promised to carry to my poor old father. It's standing in the kitchen."

Wetehinen grumbled but because of his promise he hoisted the chest on his shoulder and started off. When he had gone a little way he thought to put it down and take a peep inside. Instantly Lisa's voice, sounding as if it came from the roof, cried out:

"No! No! You promised not to look inside!"

"I'm not looking inside!" Wetehinen called back. "I'm only resting a minute!"

Then he thought to himself:

"I suppose she's sitting up there so she can watch me!"

When he had gone some distance farther, he thought again to set down the chest and open the lid but instantly Lisa's voice, as from a long way off, called out:

"No! No! You promised not to look inside!"

"Who's looking inside?" he called back, pretending again he was only resting.

Every time he thought it would be safe to put down the chest and open the lid, Lisa's voice cried out:

"No! No! You promised not to!"

"Mercy on us!" old Wetehinen fumed to himself, "who would have thought she could see so far!"

On the shore of the lake when he threw down the chest in disgust he tried one last time to raise the lid. Instantly Lisa's voice cried out:

"No! No! You promised not to!"

"I'm not looking inside!" Wetehinen roared, and in a fury he left the chest and started back into the water.

All the way home he grumbled and growled:

"A nice way to treat a man, always making him

carry chests! I won't carry another one no matter how much she begs me!"

When he came near home he saw the spinning wheel still on the roof and the figure still seated before it.

"Why haven't you got my dinner ready?" he called out angrily.

The figure at the spinning wheel made no answer.

"What's the matter with you?" Wetehinen cried. "Why are you sitting there like a wooden image instead of cooking my dinner?"

Still the figure made no answer and in a rage Wetehinen began climbing up the roof. He reached out blindly and clutched at Lisa's skirt and jerked it so hard that the churn came clattering down on his head. It knocked him off the roof and he fell all the way to the ground and cracked his wicked old head wide open.

"Ouch! Ouch!" he roared in pain. "Just wait till I get hold of that Lisa!"

He crawled to the forbidden room and poured over himself the water that was in the pitcher marked *Water of Life*. But it wasn't the *Water of Life* at all, it was the *Water of Death,* and so it didn't help his wicked old cracked head at all. In fact it just made it worse and worse *and* worse.

Lisa and her sisters were never again troubled by him nor was any one else that lived on the shores of that lake.

"Wonder what's become of wicked old Wetehinen?" people began saying.

Lisa thought she knew but she didn't tell.

LOG

The Story of the Hero Who Released the Sun

LOG

There was once a poor couple who had no children. Their neighbors all had boys and girls in plenty but for some reason God didn't send them even one.

"If I can't have a flesh and blood baby," the woman said one day, "I'm going to have a wooden baby."

She went to the woods and cut a log of alder just the size of a nice fat baby. She dressed the log in baby clothes and put it in a cradle. Then for three whole years she and her husband rocked the cradle and sang lullabies to the log baby.

At the end of three years one afternoon, when the man was out chopping wood and the woman was driving the cows home from pasture, the log baby turned into a real baby! It was so strong and hearty that by the time its parents got home it had crawled out of the cradle and was sitting on the floor yelling lustily for food. It ate and ate and ate and the more it ate the faster it grew. It wasn't any time at all in passing from babyhood to childhood, from childhood to youth, and from youth to manhood. From its beginnings it was known in the village as Log and never received any other name.

Log's parents knew from the first that Log was destined to be a great hero. That was why he was so strong and so good. There was no one in the village as strong as he nor any one as kind and gentle.

Now just at this time a great calamity overtook the world. The Sun and the Moon and the Dawn disappeared from the sky and as a result the earth was left in darkness.

"Who have taken from us the Sun and the Moon and the Dawn?" the people cried in terror.

"Whoever they are," the King said, "they shall have to restore them! Where, O where are the heroes who will undertake to find the Sun and the Moon and the Dawn and return them to their places in the sky?"

There were many men willing to offer themselves for the great adventure but the King realized that something more was needed than willingness.

"It is only heroes of exceptional strength and endurance," he said, "who should risk the dangers of so perilous an undertaking."

So he called together all the valiant youths of the kingdom and tested them one by one. He had some waters of great strength and it was his hope to find three heroes the first of whom could drink three bottles of the strong waters, the second six bottles, and the third nine bottles.

Hundreds of youths presented themselves and out of them all the King found at last two, one of whom was able to take three bottles of the strong waters, the other six bottles.

"But we need three heroes!" the King cried. "Is there no one in all this kingdom strong enough to drink nine bottles?"

"Try Log!" some one shouted.

All the youths present instantly took up the cry: "Log! Log! Send for Log!"

So the King sent for Log and sure enough when Log came he was able to drink down nine bottles of the strong waters without any trouble at all.

"Here now," the King proclaimed, "are the three heroes who are to release the Sun and the Moon and the Dawn from whoever are holding them in captivity and restore them to their places in the sky!"

He equipped the three heroes for a long journey furnishing them money and food and drink of the strong waters, each according to his strength. He mounted them each on a mighty horse with sword and arrow and dog.

So the three heroes rode off in the dark and the women of the kingdom wept to see them go and the men cheered and wished that they, too, were going.

They rode on and on for many days that seemed like nights until they had crossed the confines of their own country and entered the boundaries of an unknown kingdom beyond. Here the darkness was less dense. There was no actual daylight but a faint grayness as of approaching dawn.

They rode on until they saw looming up before them the towers of a mighty castle. They dismounted near the castle at the door of a little hut where they found an old woman.

"Good day to you, granny!" Log called out.

"Good day, indeed!" the old woman said. "It's little enough we see of the day since the Evil One cursed the Sun and handed it over to Suyettar's wicked offspring, the Nine-Headed Serpent!"

"The Evil One!" Log exclaimed. "Tell me, granny, why did the Evil One curse the Sun?"

"Because he's evil, my son, that's why! He said the Sun's rays blistered him, so he cursed the Sun and gave him over to the Nine-Headed Serpent. And he cursed the Moon, too, because at night when the Moon shone he could not steal. Yes, my son, he cursed the Moon and handed her over to Suyettar's second offspring, the Six-Headed Serpent. Then he cursed the Dawn because he said he couldn't sleep in the morning because of the Dawn. So he cursed the Dawn and gave her over to Suyettar's third offspring, the Three-Headed Serpent."

"Tell me, granny," Log said, "where do the three Serpents keep prisoner the Sun and the Moon and the Dawn?"

"Listen, my son, and I will tell you: When they go far out in the Ocean they carry with them the Sun and the Moon and the Dawn. The Three-Headed Serpent stays out there one day and then returns at night. The Six-Headed Serpent stays two days and then returns, and the mighty Nine-Headed Monster does not return until the third night. As each returns a faint glow spreads over the land. That is why we are not in utter darkness."

Log thanked the old woman and then he and his companions pushed on towards the castle. As they neared it they saw a strange sight which they could not understand. One half of the great castle was laughing and rocking as if in merriment and the other half was weeping as if in grief.

"What can this mean?" Log cried out. "We had better ask the old woman before we go on."

So they went back to the hut and the old woman told them all she knew.

"It is on account of the dreadful fate that is hanging over the King's three daughters," she said. "Those three evil Monsters are demanding them one by one. To-night when the Three-Headed Serpent comes back from the Ocean he expects to devour the eldest. If the King refuses to give her up, then Suyettar's evil son will devour half the kingdom, half of the castle itself, and half the shining stones. O that some hero would kill the monster and save the princess and at the same time release the Dawn that it might again steal over the world!"

Log and his fellows conferred together and the one they called Three Bottles, because his strength was equal to three bottles of the strong waters, declared that it was his task to fight and conquer the Three-Headed Serpent.

In the castle meanwhile preparations for the sacrifice of the oldest princess were going forward. As the King sewed the poor girl into a great leather sack, his tears fell so fast that he could scarcely see what he was doing.

"My dear child," he said, "it should comfort you greatly to think that the Monster is going to eat you instead of half the kingdom! Not many princesses are considered as important as half the kingdom!"

The princess knew that what her father said must be true and she did her best to look cheerful as they slipped the sack over her head. Once inside, however, she allowed herself to cry for she knew that no one could see her.

The sack with the princess inside was carried down to the beach and put on a high rock near the place where Suyettar's sons were wont to come up out of the water.

"Don't be frightened, my daughter!" the King called out as he and all the Court started back to the castle. "You won't have long to wait, for it will soon be evening."

Log and his companions watched the King's party disappear and then Three Bottles solemnly drank down the three bottles of strong waters with which his own King had equipped him. As he was ready to mount his horse, he handed Log the leash to which his dog was attached.

"If I need help," he said, "I'll throw back my shoe and do you then release my dog."

With that he rode boldly down to the beach, dismounted, and climbed up the rock where the unfortunate princess lay in a sack. With one slash of the sword he ripped open the sack and dragged the princess out. She supposed of course that he was the Three-Headed Serpent and at first was so frightened that she kept her eyes tightly shut not daring to look at him. She expected every minute to have him take a first bite and, when minutes and more minutes and more minutes still went by and he didn't, she opened her eyes a little crack to see what was the matter.

"Oh!" the princess said.

She was so surprised that for a long time she didn't dare to take another peep.

"You thought I was the Three-Headed Serpent, didn't you?" a pleasant voice asked. "But I'm not. I'm only a young man who has come to rescue you."

The princess murmured, "Oh!" again, but this time the "Oh!" expressed happy relief.

"Yes," repeated the young man, "I am the hero who has come to rescue you. My comrades call me Three Bottles and you, too, may call me that. And while we are waiting for the Serpent to come in from the Ocean I wish you would scratch my head."

The princess wasn't in the least surprised at this request. Heroes and monsters and fathers alike seemed always to want their heads scratched.

So Three Bottles stretched himself at the princess' feet and put his head in her lap. He settled himself comfortably and she scratched his head while he gazed out over the dark Ocean waiting for the Serpent to appear.

At first there was nothing to break the glassy surface of the water. They waited and at last far out they saw three swirling masses rolling landward.

"Quick, my princess!" Three Bottles cried. "There comes the Monster now! Get you down behind the rock and hide there while I go meet the creature and chop off his ugly heads!"

The princess, quivering with fright, crouched down behind the rock and Three Bottles, mounting his horse, rode boldly down to the water's edge awaiting the Serpent's coming.

It came nearer and nearer in long easy swirls, slowly lifting its three scaly heads one after another.

As it approached shore it sniffed the air hungrily.

"Fee, fi, fo, fum!" it muttered in a deep voice,

repeating the magic rime it had learned from its evil mother, Suyettar:

> "Fee, fi, fo, fum!
> I smell a Finn!   Yum! Yum!
> I'll fall upon him with a thud!
> I'll pick his bones and drink his blood!
> Fee, fi, fo, fum!
> Yum! Yum!"

"Stop boasting, son of Suyettar!" Three Bottles cried. "You'll have time enough to boast after you fight!"

"Fight?" repeated the Serpent as if in surprise. "Shall we fight, pretty boy, you and I? Very well! Blow then with your sweet breath, blow out a long level platform of red copper whereon we can meet and try our strength each with the other!"

"Nay," answered Three Bottles. "Do you blow with your evil breath and instead of red copper we shall have a platform of black iron."

So the Serpent blew and on the iron platform that came of his breath Three Bottles met him in combat. Back and forth they raged, Three Bottles striking right and left with his mighty sword, the Serpent hitting at Three Bottles with all his scaly heads and belching forth fire and smoke from all his mouths. Three Bottles whacked off one scaly head and at last a second one, but he was unable to touch the third.

"I shall have to have help," he acknowledged to himself finally, and reaching down he took one of his shoes and threw it over his shoulder back to his comrades who were awaiting the outcome of the struggle. Instantly they loosed the dog which bounded forward to its master's assistance and soon with the dog's help Three Bottles was able to dispatch the last head.

He was faint now with weariness and his comrades had to help him back to the old woman's hut where he soon fell asleep.

Night passed and Dawn appeared. A great cry of relief and thanksgiving went up from all the earth.

"The Dawn! The Dawn!" people cried. "God bless the man who has released the Dawn!"

Only at the castle was there sorrow still.

"My poor oldest daughter!" the King cried with tears in his eyes. "It was my sacrifice of her that has released the Dawn!"

Then he called his slaves and gave them orders to gather up his daughter's bones and to bring back the leather sack.

"We shall need it again to-night," he said. He wiped

his eyes and for a moment could say no more. "Yes, to-night we shall have to sew up my second daughter and offer her to the Six-Headed Serpent, him that holds captive the Moon. Otherwise the monster will devour half my kingdom, half the castle, and half the shining stones. Ai! Ai! Ai!"

But the slaves when they went to the high rock on the seashore found, not the princess' bones, but the princess herself, sitting there with her chin in her hand, gazing down on the beach which was strewn with the fragments of the Three-Headed Serpent.

They led her back to her father and reported the marvel they had seen.

"There, O King, lies the monster on the sand with all his heads severed! So huge are the heads that it would need three men with derricks to move one of them!"

"Some unknown hero has rescued my oldest daughter!" the King cried. "Would that another might come to-night to rescue my second child likewise! But, alas! what hero is strong enough to destroy the Six-Headed Monster!"

So when evening came they sewed the second princess in the sack and carried her out to the rock.

Log and his companions saw the procession move down from the castle and they saw that the castle was again disturbed, one half of it laughing and one half weeping.

"It's the second princess to-night," the old woman told them. "Unless her father, the King, gives her to the Six-Headed Serpent, the Monster will come and devour half the kingdom, half the castle, and half the shining stones. He it is that holds the Moon captive and the hero that slays him will release the Moon."

Then he whom his comrades called Six Bottles cried out:

"Here is work for me!"

He drank bottle after bottle of the strong waters until he had emptied six.

"Now I am ready!" he shouted.

He mounted his mighty horse and as he rode off he called to his comrades:

"If I need help I'll throw back a shoe and do you then unleash my dog!"

He rode to the rock on the shore and dismounted. Then he climbed the rock and released the second princess. He told her who he was and as they awaited the arrival of the Six-Headed Serpent he lay at the princess' feet and she scratched his head.

This time the Serpent came in six mighty swirls with six awful heads that reared up one after another.

In terror the second princess hid behind the rock while Six Bottles, mounting his horse, rode boldly down to the water's edge.

Like his brother Serpent this one, too, came sniffing the air hungrily, muttering the magic rime he had learned from his mother, wicked Suyettar:

> "Fee, fi, fo, fum!
> I smell a Finn! Yum! Yum!
> I'll fall upon him with a thud!
> I'll pick his bones and drink his blood!
> Fee, fi, fo, fum!
> Yum! Yum!"

"Stop boasting, son of an evil mother!" Six Bottles cried. "You will have time enough to boast after you fight!"

"Fight?" repeated the Serpent scornfully. "Shall we fight, little one, you and I? Very well! Blow then with your sweet breath, blow out a long level platform of white silver whereon we can meet and try our strength one with the other."

"Nay!" answered Six Bottles. "Do you blow, blow with your evil breath, and instead of white silver we shall have a platform of red copper."

So the Serpent blew and on the copper platform that

came of his breath Six Bottles met him in combat. Back and forth they raged, Six Bottles striking left and right with his mighty sword, the Serpent hitting at Six Bottles with every one of his six scaly heads and belching forth fire and smoke from all his mouths. Six Bottles whacked off one head, then another, then another. At last he had disposed of five heads. He tried hard to strike the last, but by this time the Serpent had grown wary and Six Bottles' own strength was waning. So he reached down and took one of his shoes and threw it over his shoulder back to his comrades who were awaiting the outcome of the struggle. Instantly they loosed the dog which bounded forward to its master's assistance and soon with the dog's help Six Bottles was able to dispatch the last head.

Then his comrades led him, weary from the fight, to the old woman's hut and soon he fell asleep.

While he slept the Moon appeared in the sky and a great cry of relief and thanksgiving went up from all the world:

"The Moon! The Moon! God bless the man who has released the Moon!"

The King who was awakened by the sound looked out the castle window and when he saw the Moon, returned to its place in the sky, his eyes overflowed with grief.

"My poor second daughter!" he cried. "It was my sacrifice of her that has released the Moon! To-morrow morning I will send the slaves to gather up her bones and to bring back the leather sack into which, alas! I must then sew my youngest daughter for evil Suyettar's third son, the Nine-Headed Serpent. Ai! Ai! Ai! How sad it is to be a father!"

But on the morrow when the slaves went to the rock they found the second princess sitting there alone gazing down upon the scattered fragments of the Six-Headed Serpent.

"Here she is, safe and sound!" they reported to the King as they led the second princess into his presence, "and, marvel of marvels! on the beach below the rock lies the body of the Six-Headed Serpent torn to pieces! Its heads, O King, are so monstrous that six men with derricks could scarcely move one of them!"

"God be praised!" the King cried. "Another unknown hero has come and saved the life of my second child! Would that a third might come to-night and rescue the life of my youngest child! Alas, she is dearer to me than both the others, but I fear me that even if there be heroes who could dispatch the first two Serpents, there is never one who can touch him of the Nine Heads that holds the mighty Sun a captive!"

"This last and mightiest battle is for me!"

And the poor King wept, so sure was he that nothing could save the life of his youngest child.

When Log and his companions heard of the King's grief, Log at once stood forth and said:

"This last and mightiest battle is for me!"

He opened the strong waters and drank bottle after bottle until he had emptied nine.

"Now let night come as soon as it will!" he cried. "I am ready for the Monster!"

He started forth telling his comrades he would throw back a shoe if he needed help from his dog.

So it was Log himself who slashed open the sack for the third time and released the Youngest Princess who was much more beautiful than her sisters. She fell in love with the mighty hero on sight and was so thrilled with his godlike beauty that when he put his head in her lap she hardly knew what to do although her father always declared that she scratched his head much better than either of her sisters.

They had not long to wait for soon all the Ocean was a glitter with the swirls of the ninefold Monster who was coming to shore with the captive Sun in his keeping.

"Await me behind the rock!" Log cried to the Princess as he leapt upon his horse and started forward.

"Oh, Log, my hero, be careful!" the Princess cried after him.

Nearer and nearer came the swirls of the nine-coiled Monster. One after another of his nine heads rose and fell as he approached, and every head sniffed more hungrily as it came nearer, and each head rumbled as it sniffed:

> "Fee, fi, fo, fum!
> I smell a Finn! Yum! Yum!
> I'll fall upon him with a thud!
> I'll pick his bones and drink his blood!
> Fee, fi, fo, fum!
> Yum! Yum!"

"Stop boasting, evil son of an evil mother!" Log cried. "You will have time enough to boast after you fight!"

"Fight?" roared the awful Monster. "Shall we fight, poor infant, you and I? Very well! Blow then with your sweet breath, blow out a long level platform of shining gold whereon we can meet and try our strength each with the other!"

"Nay!" Log answered boldly. "Do you blow, blow with your evil breath and instead of shining gold we shall have a platform of white silver."

So the Monster blew and on the silver platform that came of his breath Log met him in combat. Back and forth they raged, Log striking right and left with his mighty sword, the Serpent hitting at Log with all his nine scaly heads and belching forth fire and smoke from all his nine mouths. Log whacked off head after head until six lay gaping on the sand. But the last three he could not get.

Suddenly he pointed behind the Serpent and cried: "Quick! Quick! The Sun! It is escaping!"

The Serpent looked around and Log whacked off a head. Now only two remained, but try as he would Log could get neither of them.

Again he tried a subterfuge.

"Your wife, O Son of Suyettar! See, yonder, they're abusing her!"

The Monster looked and Log whacked off another head. But one now remained and as usual it was the hardest of them all to get. Log felt his strength waning while the Monster seemed more nimble than ever.

"I shall have to have help," Log thought.

He threw back his shoe to his comrades and they at once loosed his dog. With the dog's help Log was soon able to dispatch the last head. Then Three Bottles and Six Bottles helped him off his horse and supported him to the old woman's hut where he soon fell into a deep sleep.

The next morning the blessed Sun rose at his proper time and people all over the world, falling on their knees with thanksgiving and weeping with joy, cried out:

"The Sun! The Sun! God bless the man who has released the Sun!"

At the castle they waked the King with the good news but the King only shook his head and murmured in grief:

"Yes, the Sun is released but what care I since my favorite child, my youngest daughter, has been sacrificed!"

He dispatched the slaves to gather up her bones and presently these returned bringing the Princess herself and telling a marvelous tale of the beach littered with nine severed heads so huge that it would need nine men with derricks to move one of them.

"What manner of heroes are these who have rescued my daughters!" cried the King. "Let them come forth and I will give them my daughters for wives and half my riches for dowry! But they will have to prove themselves the actual heroes by bringing to the castle the heavy heads of the Monsters they have slain."

When Log and his fellows heard this they laughed

with happiness and, strengthening themselves with deep draughts of the strong waters, they gathered together the many heads of the mighty Serpents, bore them to the castle, and piled them up at the King's feet.

Then Log stepped forward and said:

"Here we are, O King, come to claim our reward!"

The King, true to his promise, gave them his daughters in marriage, the oldest to Three Bottles, the second to Six Bottles, and the lovely Youngest to Log. Then he apportioned them the half of his riches and, after much feasting and merrymaking, the heroes took their brides and their riches and bidding the King farewell started homewards.

As they rode through a great forest they sighted a tiny hut and Log, motioning his comrades to wait for him quietly, crept forward to see who was in the hut. It was well he was cautious for inside the hut was Suyettar herself talking to two other old hags.

"Ay," she was saying, "they have slain my three beautiful sons, my mighty offspring that held captive the Sun and the Moon and the Dawn! But I tell you, sisters, they will pay the penalty. . . ."

To hear better Log changed himself into a piece of firewood and slipping inside the hut hid himself in the woodpile near the stove.

"Ay, they will pay the penalty!" Suyettar repeated. "I shall have my revenge on them! A fine supper Suyettar shall soon have, yum, yum!

> I'll fall upon them with a thud!
> I'll pick their bones and drink their blood!

Fools, fools, to think they can escape Suyettar's anger!"

"But sister, sister," the two old hags asked, "how will you get them?"

Suyettar looked this way and that to make sure that no one was listening. Then she whispered:

"This is how I shall get them: As they come through this forest, the three men with their brides, I shall send upon them a terrible hunger. Then they shall come suddenly upon a table spread with tempting food. One bite of that food and they are in my power, he-he! Ay, sisters, to-night Suyettar will have a fine supper! Nothing can save them unless, before they touch the food, some one make the sign of the cross three times over the table. Then table and food would disappear and also the ravening hunger. But even if that happens Suyettar shall still get them!"

"How, sister, how?" the other two asked.

"Presently I should send upon them consuming thirst, and then put in their pathway a spring of cold sparkling water. One drop of that water and they are in my power, he-he! Nothing can save them from me unless, before their lips touch the water, some one make the sign of the cross three times over the spring. At that the spring would disappear and also their thirst. But even if they escape the spring, I shall still get them. I shall send great heaviness on them and a longing for sleep, then let them come upon a row of soft inviting feather beds. If they cast themselves upon the beds, they are mine, he-he! to feast upon as I will! Nothing can save but that some one make the sign of the cross three times over the beds before they touch them. Oh, sisters, I shall get them one way or another for there is no one to warn them. If there was any one to warn them, he wouldn't dare tell them what he knows for he would also know that if he told them he would himself be turned into a blue cross and have to stand forever in the cemetery."

As Log knew now all the dangers that threatened, he slipped away from the woodpile and, when he was outside, took his own shape and hurried back to his comrades.

"Away!" he cried. "We are in great danger!"

They all spurred their horses and rode swiftly on until Three Bottles suddenly cried:

"Hold, comrades, hold! I am faint with hunger!"

"Me, too!" cried Six Bottles.

At that instant a great table, laden with delicious food, appeared before them.

"Look!" cried the one of them.

"Food!" cried the other.

They flung themselves from their horses and ran towards the table. But quick as they were, Log was quicker. He reached the table first and, raising his hand, made the sign of the cross three times. The table disappeared as suddenly as it had come and with it the strange hunger that had but now consumed them.

"Strange!" Three Bottles exclaimed. "I thought I was hungry, but I'm not!"

"I thought I saw food just now," Six Bottles said. "I must have been dreaming."

So they mounted again and pushed on.

"Danger threatens us," said Log. "We must hurry and not dismount no matter what the temptation."

They agreed but presently one of them cried out and then the other:

"Water! Water! We shall soon perish unless we have water!"

Instantly by the wayside appeared a spring of cool sparkling water and it was all Log could do to reach it before his fellows. He did get there first and make the sign of the cross three times whereat the spring disappeared and with it the thirst which had but now consumed them all.

"I thought I was thirsty," Three Bottles said, "but I'm not!"

"Why did we dismount?" Six Bottles asked. "There's no water here."

So again they mounted and went forward and Log, warning them again that danger threatened, begged them not to dismount a third time no matter what the temptation.

They promised they would not but presently, complaining of fatigue, they wanted to. Their brides, too, swayed in the saddle, overcome with weariness and sleep.

"Dear Log," they said, "let us rest for an hour. See, our brides are drooping with fatigue! One hour's sleep and we shall all be refreshed!"

Instantly beside them on the forest floor they saw three soft white feather beds. Log leaped to the ground but before he was able to make the sign of the cross over more than one of the beds, his comrades and their brides had fallen headlong on the other two.

And that was the end of poor Three Bottles and Six Bottles and their two lovely brides. There was no way now of saving them from Suyettar. She had them in her power and nothing would induce her to give them up.

As Log and his bride sadly mounted their horse and rode on they heard an evil voice chanting out in triumph:

> "I'll fall upon them with a thud, he-he!
> I'll pick their bones and drink their blood, he-he!"

"Poor fellows! Poor fellows!" Log said, and the Princess wept to think of the awful fate that had overtaken her two sisters.

Well, Log and his bride reached home without further adventure and were received by the King with great honors.

"I knew my heroes were succeeding," the King said, "when first the Dawn appeared again, and then the Moon, and last the mighty Sun. All hail to you, Log, and to your two comrades! But, by the way, where are Three Bottles and Six Bottles?"

"Your Majesty," Log said, "Three Bottles and Six Bottles were brave men both. By their prowess they released the one the Dawn, the other the Moon. Then in an evil adventure on the way home they perished. I can tell you no more."

"You can tell me no more?" the King said. "Why

can you tell me no more? What was the evil adventure in which they perished?"

"If I told you, O King, then I, too, should perish, for I should be turned into a blue cross and stood forever in the cemetery!"

"What nonsense!" the King exclaimed. "Who would turn you into a blue cross and stand you forever in the cemetery?"

"That is what I cannot tell you," Log said.

The King laughed and pressed Log no further, but the people of the kingdom, scenting a mystery, insisted on knowing in detail what had happened the other two heroes. Presently the rumor began to spread that Log himself had done away with them in order that he might gather to himself all the glory of the undertaking.

The King was forced at last to send for him again and to demand a full account of everything.

Log realized that his end was near. He met it bravely. Commending to the King's protection his lovely bride, the Youngest Princess, Log related how the three mighty Serpents whom they had killed were sons of Suyettar, and how in revenge Suyettar had succeeded in destroying Three Bottles and Six Bottles together with their brides. Then he told the fate about to overtake himself.

He finished speaking and as the King and the Court looked at him, to their amazement he disappeared.

"To the cemetery!" some one cried.

They all went to the cemetery where at once they found a fresh blue cross that had come there nobody knew how. There it stands to this day, a reminder of the life and deeds of the mighty hero, Log.

The King was overcome with sorrow at losing such a hero. He took Log's bride under his protection and he found her so beautiful and so gentle that soon he fell in love with her and married her.

THE LITTLE SISTER

The Story of Suyettar and the Nine Brothers

THE LITTLE SISTER

There was once a woman who had nine sons. They were good boys and loved her dearly but there was one thing about which they were always complaining.

"Why haven't we a little sister?" they kept asking. "Do give us a little sister!"

When the time came that another child was to be born, they said to their mother:

"If the baby is a boy we are going away and you will never see us again, but if it is a little girl then we shall stay home and take care of it."

The mother agreed that if the child were a girl she would have her husband put a spindle outside on the gatepost and, if it were a boy, an ax.

"Just wait," she said, "and see what your father puts on the gatepost and then you will know whether it is another brother God has sent you or a little sister."

The baby turned out to be a girl and the mother was overjoyed.

"Hurry, husband!" she cried, "and put a spindle on the gatepost so that our nine sons may know the good news!"

The man did so and then quickly returned to the mother and baby. The moment he was gone Suyettar slipped up and changed the tokens. She took away the spindle and put in its place an ax. Then with an evil grin she hurried off mumbling to herself:

"Now we'll see what we'll see!"

She hoped to bring trouble and grief and she succeeded. As soon as the nine sons saw the ax on the gatepost they thought their mother had given birth to another son and at once they left home vowing never to return.

The poor mother waited for them and waited.

"What is keeping my sons?" she cried at last. "Go out to the gate, husband, and see if they are coming."

The man went out and soon returned bringing back word that some one had changed the tokens.

"The spindle that I put on the gatepost is gone," he said, "and in its place is an ax."

"Alas!" cried the poor mother, "some evil creature has done this to spite us! Oh, if we could only get word to our sons of the little sister they were so eager to have!"

But there was no way to reach them for no one knew the way they had gone.

In a short time the husband died and the poor woman, abandoned by her nine sons, had only her little daughter left. She named the child Kerttu. Kerttu was a dear little girl and her face was as beautiful as her heart was good. Whenever she found her mother weeping alone she tried to comfort her and, as she grew older, she wanted to know the cause of her mother's grief. At last the mother told her about her nine brothers and how they had gone away never to return owing to the trick of some evil creature.

"My poor mother!" she cried, "how sorry I am that I am the innocent cause of your loss! Let me go out into the world and find my brothers! When once they hear the truth they will gladly come home to you to care for you in your old age!"

At first the mother would not consent to this.

"You are all I have," she said, "and I should indeed be miserable and lonely if anything happened you!"

But Kerttu continued to weep every time she thought of her poor brothers driven unnecessarily from home and at last the mother, realizing that she would nevermore be happy unless she were allowed to go in search of them, gave up opposing her.

"Very well, my daughter, you may go and may God go with you and bring you safely back to me. But before you go I must prepare you a bag of food for the journey and bake you a magic cake that will show you the way."

So she baked a batch of bread and at the same time mixed a little round cake with Kerttu's own tears and baked it, too. Then she said:

"Here now, my child, are provisions for the journey and here is a magic cake that will lead you to your brothers. All you have to do is throw it down in front of you and say:

'Roll, roll, my little cake!
Show me the way that I must take
To find at last the brothers nine
Whose own true mother is also mine!'

Then the little cake will start rolling and do you follow wherever it rolls. But, Kerttu, my child, you must not start out alone. You must have some friend or companion to go with you."

Now it happened that Kerttu had a little dog, Musti, that she loved dearly.

"I'll take Musti with me!" she said. "Musti will protect me!"

THE LITTLE SISTER

So she called Musti and Musti wagged his tail and barked with joy at the prospect of going out into the world with his mistress.

Then Kerttu threw down the magic cake in front of her and sang:

> "Roll, roll, my little cake!
> Show me the way that I must take
> To find at last the brothers nine
> Whose own true mother is also mine!"

At once the cake rolled off like a little wheel and Kerttu and Musti followed it. They walked until they were tired. Then Kerttu picked up the little cake and they rested by the wayside. When they were ready again to start the cake a-rolling, all Kerttu had to do was throw it down in front of her and say the magic rime.

Their first day was without adventure. When night came they ate their supper and went to sleep in a field under a tree.

The second day they overtook an ugly old woman whom Kerttu disliked on sight. But she said to herself:

"Shame on you, Kerttu, not liking this woman just because she's old and ugly!" and she made herself answer the old woman's greetings politely and she made Musti stop snarling and growling.

The old hag asked Kerttu who she was and where she was going and Kerttu told her.

"Ah!" said the old woman, "how fortunate that we have met each other for our ways lie together!"

She smiled and petted Kerttu's arm and Kerttu felt like shuddering. But she restrained herself and told herself severely:

"You're a wicked girl not to feel more friendly to the poor old thing!"

Musti felt much as Kerttu did. He no longer growled for Kerttu had told him not to, but he drooped his tail between his legs and, pressing up close to Kerttu, he trembled with fright. And well he might, too, for the old hag was none other than Suyettar who had been waiting all these years just for this very chance to do further injury to Kerttu and her brothers.

Kerttu, poor child, was, alas! too good and innocent to suspect evil in others. She said to Suyettar:

"Very well, if our ways lie together then we can be companions."

So Suyettar joined Kerttu and Musti and the three of them walked on following the little cake. As the day advanced the sun grew hotter and hotter and at last when they reached a lake Suyettar said:

"My dear, let us sit down here for a few moments and rest."

They all sat down and presently Suyettar said:

"Let us go bathing in the lake. That will refresh us."

Kerttu would have agreed if Musti had not tugged at her skirts and warned her not to.

"Don't do it, dear mistress!" Musti growled softly. "Don't go in bathing with her! She'll bewitch you!"

So Kerttu said:

"No, I don't want to go in bathing."

Suyettar waited until they were again journeying on and then when Kerttu wasn't looking she turned around and kicked Musti and broke one of the poor little dog's legs. Thereafter Musti had to hop along on three legs.

The next afternoon when they passed another lake, Suyettar tried again to tempt Kerttu into the water.

"The sun is very hot," she said, "and it would refresh us both to bathe. Come, Kerttu, my dear, don't refuse me this time!"

But again Musti tugged at Kerttu's skirts and, licking her hand, whispered the warning:

"Don't do it, dear mistress! Don't go in bathing with her or she will bewitch you!"

So again Kerttu said politely:

"No, I don't feel like going in bathing. You go in alone and I'll wait for you here."

But this was not what Suyettar wanted and she said, no, she didn't care to go in alone. She was furious, too, with Musti and later when Kerttu wasn't looking she gave the poor little dog a kick that broke another leg. Thereafter Musti had to hop along on two legs.

They slept the third night by the wayside and the next day they went on again always following the magic cake. In midafternoon they passed a lake and Suyettar said:

"Surely, my dear, you must be tired and hot. Let us both bathe in this cool lake."

But Musti, hopping painfully along on two legs, yelped weakly and said to Kerttu:

"Don't do it, dear mistress! Don't go in bathing with her or she'll bewitch you!"

So for a third time Kerttu refused and later, when she wasn't looking, Suyettar kicked Musti and broke the third of the poor little dog's legs. Thereafter Musti hopped on as best he could on only one leg.

Well, they went on and on. When night came they

slept by the roadside and then next morning they started on again. The sun grew hot and by midafternoon Kerttu was tired and ready to rest. When they reached a lake Suyettar again begged that they both go in bathing. Kerttu was tempted to agree when poor Musti threw himself panting at her feet and whimpered:

"Don't do it, dear mistress! Don't go in bathing with her or she will bewitch you!"

So Kerttu again refused.

"That's right, dear mistress!" Musti panted, "don't do it! I shall soon be dead, I know, for she hates me, but before I die I want to warn you one last time never to go in bathing with her or she will bewitch you!"

"What's that dog saying?" Suyettar demanded angrily, and without waiting for an answer she picked up a heavy piece of wood and struck poor Musti such a blow on the head that it killed him.

"What have you done to my poor little dog?" Kerttu cried.

"Don't mind him, my dear," Suyettar said. "He was sick and lame and it was better to put him out of his misery."

Suyettar tried to soothe Kerttu and make her forget Musti but all afternoon Kerttu wept to think that she would never again see her faithful little friend.

The next afternoon when Suyettar begged her to go in bathing there was no Musti to warn her against it and at last Kerttu allowed herself to be persuaded. She was tired from her many days' wandering and it was true that the first touch of the cool water refreshed her.

"Now splash water in my face!" Suyettar cried.

But Kerttu didn't want to splash water into Suyettar's face for she supposed Suyettar was an old woman and she thought it would be disrespectful to splash water into the face of an old woman.

"Do you hear me!" screamed Suyettar.

When Kerttu still hesitated, Suyettar looked at her with such a terrible, threatening expression that Kerttu did as she was bidden. She splashed water into Suyettar's face and, as the water touched Suyettar's eyes, Suyettar cried out:

> "Your bonny looks give up to me
> And you take mine for all to see!"

Instantly they two changed appearance: Suyettar looked young and beautiful like Kerttu, and Kerttu was changed to a hideous old hag. Then too late she realized that the awful old woman to whom she had been so polite was Suyettar.

Suyettar bewitching Kerttu

THE LITTLE SISTER

"Oh, why," Kerttu cried, "why didn't I heed poor Musti's warning!"

Suyettar dragged her roughly out of the water.

"Come along!" she said. "Dress yourself in those rags of mine and start that cake a-rolling! We ought to reach your brothers' house by to-night."

So poor Kerttu had to dress herself in Suyettar's filthy old garments while Suyettar, looking like a fresh young girl, decked herself out in Kerttu's pretty bodice and skirt.

Unwillingly now and with a heavy heart Kerttu threw down the cake and said:

> "Roll, roll, my little cake!
>   Show me the way that I must take
>   To find at last the brothers nine
>   Whose own true mother is also mine!"

Off rolled the little cake and they two followed it, Kerttu weeping bitterly and Suyettar taunting her with ugly laughs. Then suddenly Kerttu forgot to weep for Suyettar took from her her memory and her tongue.

The little cake led them at last to a farmhouse before which it stopped. This was where the nine brothers were living. Eight of them were out working in the fields but the youngest was at home. He opened the door and when Suyettar told him that she was Kerttu, his sister, he kissed her tenderly and made her welcome. Then he invited her inside and they sat side by side on the bench and talked and Suyettar told him all she had heard from Kerttu about his mother and about the tokens which had been changed at Kerttu's birth. The youngest brother listened eagerly and Suyettar told her story so glibly that of course he supposed that she was his own true sister.

"And who is the awful looking old hag that has come with you?" he asked pointing at Kerttu.

"That? Oh, that's an old serving woman whom our mother sent with me to bear me company. She's dumb and foolish but she's a good herd and we can let her drive the cow out to pasture every day."

The older brothers when they came home were greatly pleased to find what they thought was their sister. They began to love her at once and to pet her and they said that now she must stay with them and keep house for them. She told them that was what she wanted to do and she said that now she was here the youngest brother need no longer stay at home but could go out every morning with the rest of them to work in the fields.

So now began a new life for poor Kerttu. In the

morning after the brothers were gone Suyettar would scold and abuse her. She would bake a cake for her dinner to be eaten in the fields and she would fill the cake with stones and sticks and filth. Then she would take Kerttu as far as the gate where she would give her back her tongue and her memory and order her roughly to drive the cow to pasture and look after it all day long. In the late afternoon when Kerttu drove home the cow, Suyettar would meet her at the gate and take from her her tongue and her memory and then in the evening the brothers would see her as a foolish old woman who couldn't talk. Every morning and every evening Kerttu begged Suyettar to show her a little mercy, but far from showing her any mercy Suyettar grew more cruel from day to day.

Suyettar was very proud to think that nine handsome young men took her for a beautiful girl and she felt sure they would never find out their mistake for only Kerttu knew who she really was and Kerttu was entirely in her power.

At night seated in the shadow in a far corner of the kitchen with her nine brothers laughing and talking Kerttu felt no sorrow for at such times of course she had no memory. But during the day it was different. Then when she was alone in the meadow she had her memory and her tongue and she thought about her poor mother at home anxiously awaiting her return and she thought of her nine sturdy brothers all of whom might now through her mistake fall victims to Suyettar. These thoughts made her weep with grief and as the days went by she put this grief into a song which she sang constantly:

> "I've found at last the brothers nine
> Whose own true mother is also mine,
> But they know me not from stick or stone!
> They leave me here to weep alone,
> While Suyettar sits in my place
> With stolen looks and stolen face!
> She snared me first with evil guile
> And now she mocks me all the while:
> By night she takes my tongue away,
> She feeds me sticks and stones by day! . . .
> Oh, little they guess, the brothers nine,
> That their own true mother is also mine!"

The brothers as they worked in nearby fields used to hear the song and they wondered about it.

"Strange!" they said to one another. "Can that be the old woman singing? In the evening at home she never opens her mouth and our dear sister always says that she's dumb and foolish."

One afternoon when Kerttu's song sounded particularly sad, the youngest brother crept close to the meadow where Kerttu was sitting in order to hear the words. He listened carefully and then hurried back to the others and with frightened face told them what he had heard.

"Nonsense!" the older brothers said. "It can't be so!"

However, they, too, wanted to hear for themselves the words of the strange song, so they all crept near to listen.

It looked like an old hag who was singing but the voice that came out of the withered mouth was the voice of a young girl. As they listened they, too, grew pale:

> "I've found at last the brothers nine
> Whose own true mother is also mine,
> But they know me not from stick or stone!
> They leave me here to weep alone,
> While Suyettar sits in my place
> With stolen looks and stolen face!
> She snared me first with evil guile
> And now she mocks me all the while:
> By night she takes my tongue away,
> She feeds me sticks and stones by day! . . .
> Oh, little they guess, the brothers nine,
> That their own true mother is also mine!"

"Can it be true?" they said, whispering together. They sent the youngest brother to question Kerttu and he, when he had heard her story, believed it true. Then the other brothers went to her one by one and questioned her and finally they were all convinced of the truth of her story.

"It is well for us," they said, "if we do not all fall into the power of that awful creature! How, O how can we rescue our poor little sister!"

"I can never get back my own looks," Kerttu said, "unless Suyettar splashes water into my eyes and unless I cry out a magic rime as she does it."

The brothers discussed one plan after another and at last agreed on one that they thought might deceive Suyettar.

They had Kerttu inflame her eyes with dust and come groping home one midday. The brothers, too, were at home and as Kerttu came stumbling into the kitchen they said to Suyettar:

"Oh, sister, sister, see the poor old woman! Something ails her! Her eyes—they're all red and swollen! Get some water and bathe them!"

"Nonsense!" Suyetter said. "The old hag's well enough! Let her be! She doesn't need any attention!"

"Oh, sister!" the youngest brother said, reproachfully, "is that any way for a human, kindhearted girl like you to talk? If you won't bathe the old creature's eyes, I will myself!"

Then Suyettar who of course wanted them to think that she was a human, kindhearted girl said, no, she would bathe them. So she took a basin of water over to Kerttu and told her to lean down her head. As she splashed the first drop of water into Kerttu's eyes, Kerttu cried out:

> "My own true looks give back to me
> And take your own for all to see!"

Instantly Suyettar was again a hideous old hag though still dressed in Kerttu's pretty bodice and skirt, and Kerttu was herself again, young and fresh and sweet, though still incased in Suyettar's rags. But the brothers pretended that they saw no difference and kept on talking to Suyettar as though they still thought her Kerttu. And Suyettar because her eyes were blinded with the dust supposed that they were still deceived.

Then one of the brothers said to Suyettar:

"Sister dear, the *sauna* is all heated and ready. Don't you want to bathe?"

Suyettar thought that this would be a fine chance to wash the dust from her eyes, so she let them lead her to the *sauna*. Once they got her inside they locked the door and set the *sauna* a-fire. Oh, the noise she made then when she found she had been trapped! She kicked and screamed and cursed and threatened! But Kerttu and the brothers paid no heed to her. They left her burning in the *sauna* while they hurried homewards.

They found their poor old mother seated at the window weeping, for she thought that now Kerttu as well as her sons was lost forever. As Kerttu and the nine handsome young men came in the gate she didn't recognize them until Kerttu sang out:

> "I bring at last the brothers nine
> Whose own true mother is also mine!"

Then she knew who they were and with thanks to God she welcomed them home.

THE FOREST BRIDE

The Story of a Little Mouse Who Was a Princess

THE FOREST BRIDE

There was once a farmer who had three sons. One day when the boys were grown to manhood he said to them:

"My sons, it is high time that you were all married. To-morrow I wish you to go out in search of brides."

"But where shall we go?" the oldest son asked.

"I have thought of that, too," the father said. "Do each of you chop down a tree and then take the direction in which the fallen tree points. I'm sure that each of you if you go far enough in that direction will find a suitable bride."

So the next day the three sons chopped down trees. The oldest son's tree fell pointing north.

"That suits me!" he said, for he knew that to the north lay a farm where a very pretty girl lived.

The tree of the second son when it fell pointed south.

"That suits me!" the second son declared thinking of

a girl that he had often danced with who lived on a farm to the south.

The youngest son's tree—the youngest son's name was Veikko—when it fell pointed straight to the forest.

"Ha! Ha!" the older brothers laughed. "Veikko will have to go courting one of the Wolf girls or one of the Foxes!"

They meant by this that only animals lived in the forest and they thought they were making a good joke at Veikko's expense. But Veikko said he was perfectly willing to take his chances and go where his tree pointed.

The older brothers went gaily off and presented their suits to the two farmers whose daughters they admired. Veikko, too, started off with brave front but after he had gone some distance in the forest his courage began to ebb.

"How can I find a bride," he asked himself, "in a place where there are no human creatures at all!"

Just then he came to a little hut. He pushed open the door and went in. It was empty. To be sure there was a little mouse sitting on the table, daintily combing her whiskers, but a mouse of course doesn't count.

"There's nobody here!" Veikko said aloud.

The little mouse paused in her toilet and turning towards him said reproachfully:

"Why, Veikko, I'm here!"

"But you don't count. You're only a mouse!"

"Of course I count!" the little mouse declared. "But tell me, what were you hoping to find?"

"I was hoping to find a sweetheart."

The little mouse questioned him further and Veikko told her the whole story of his brothers and the trees.

"The two older ones are finding sweethearts easily enough," Veikko said, "but I don't see how I can off here in the forest. And it will shame me to have to go home and confess that I alone have failed."

"See here, Veikko," the little mouse said, "why don't you take me for your sweetheart?"

Veikko laughed heartily.

"But you're only a mouse! Whoever heard of a man having a mouse for a sweetheart!"

The mouse shook her little head solemnly.

"Take my word for it, Veikko, you could do much worse than have me for a sweetheart! Even if I am only a mouse I can love you and be true to you."

She was a dear dainty little mouse and as she sat looking up at Veikko with her little paws under her chin and her bright little eyes sparkling Veikko liked her more and more.

Then she sang Veikko a pretty little song and the song

cheered him so much that he forgot his disappointment at not finding a human sweetheart and as he left her to go home he said:

"Very well, little mouse, I'll take you for my sweetheart!"

At that the mouse made little squeaks of delight and she told him that she'd be true to him and wait for him no matter how long he was in returning.

Well, the older brothers when they got home boasted loudly about their sweethearts.

"Mine," said the oldest, "has the rosiest reddest cheeks you ever saw!"

"And mine," the second announced, "has long yellow hair!"

Veikko said nothing.

"What's the matter, Veikko?" the older brothers asked him, laughing. "Has your sweetheart pretty pointed ears or sharp white teeth?"

You see they were still having their little joke about foxes and wolves.

"You needn't laugh," Veikko said. "I've found a sweetheart. She's a gentle dainty little thing gowned in velvet."

"Gowned in velvet!" echoed the oldest brother with a frown.

"Just like a princess!" the second brother sneered.

"Yes," Veikko repeated, "gowned in velvet like a princess. And when she sits up and sings to me I'm perfectly happy."

"Huh!" grunted the older brothers not at all pleased that Veikko should have so grand a sweetheart.

"Well," said the old farmer after a few days, "now I should like to know what those sweethearts of yours are able to do. Have them each bake me a loaf of bread so that I can see whether they're good housewives."

"Mine will be able to bake bread—I'm sure of that!" the oldest brother declared boastfully.

"So will mine!" chorused the second brother.

Veikko was silent.

"What about the Princess?" they said with a laugh. "Do you think the Princess can bake bread?"

"I don't know," Veikko answered truthfully. "I'll have to ask her."

Of course he had no reason for supposing that the little mouse could bake bread and by the time he reached the hut in the forest he was feeling sad and discouraged.

When he pushed open the door he found the little mouse as before seated on the table daintily combing her whiskers. At sight of Veikko she danced about with delight.

"I'm so glad to see you!" she squeaked. "I knew you would come back!"

Then when she noticed that he was silent she asked him what was the matter. Veikko told her:

"My father wants each of our sweethearts to bake him a loaf of bread. If I come home without a loaf my brothers will laugh at me."

"You won't have to go home without a loaf!" the little mouse said. "I can bake bread."

Veikko was much surprised at this.

"I never heard of a mouse that could bake bread!"

"Well, I can!" the little mouse insisted.

With that she began ringing a small silver bell, *tinkle, tinkle, tinkle*. Instantly there was the sound of hurrying footsteps, tiny scratchy footsteps, and hundreds of mice came running into the hut.

The little Princess mouse sitting up very straight and dignified said to them:

"Each of you go fetch me a grain of the finest wheat."

All the mice scampered quickly away and soon returned one by one, each carrying a grain of the finest wheat. After that it was no trick at all for the Princess mouse to bake a beautiful loaf of wheaten bread.

The next day the three brothers presented their father the loaves of their sweethearts' baking. The oldest one had a loaf of rye bread.

"Very good," the farmer said. "For hardworking people like us rye bread is good."

The loaf the second son had was made of barley.

"Barley bread is also good," the farmer said.

But when Veikko presented his loaf of beautiful wheaten bread, his father cried out:

"What! White bread! Ah, Veikko now must have a sweetheart of wealth!"

"Of course!" the older brothers sneered. "Didn't he tell us she was a Princess? Say, Veikko, when a Princess wants fine white flour, how does she get it?"

Veikko answered simply:

"She rings a little silver bell and when her servants come in she tells them to bring her grains of the finest wheat."

At this the older brothers nearly exploded with envy until their father had to reprove them.

"There! There!" he said. "Don't grudge the boy his good luck! Each girl has baked the loaf she knows how to make and each in her own way will probably make a good wife. But before you bring them home to me I want one further test of their skill in housewifery. Let them each send me a sample of their weaving."

The older brothers were delighted at this for they knew that their sweethearts were skilful weavers.

"We'll see how her ladyship fares this time!" they said, sure in their hearts that Veikko's sweetheart, whoever she was, would not put them to shame with her weaving.

Veikko, too, had serious doubts of the little mouse's ability at the loom.

"Whoever heard of a mouse that could weave?" he said to himself as he pushed open the door of the forest hut.

"Oh, there you are at last!" the little mouse squeaked joyfully.

She reached out her little paws in welcome and then in her excitement she began dancing about on the table.

"Are you really glad to see me, little mouse?" Veikko asked.

"Indeed I am!" the mouse declared. "Am I not your sweetheart? I've been waiting for you and waiting, just wishing that you would return! Does your father want something more this time, Veikko?"

"Yes, and it's something I'm afraid you can't give me, little mouse."

"Perhaps I can. Tell me what it is."

"It's a sample of your weaving. I don't believe you can weave. I never heard of a mouse that could weave."

"Tut! Tut!" said the mouse. "Of course I can weave! It would be a strange thing if Veikko's sweetheart couldn't weave!"

She rang the little silver bell, *tinkle, tinkle, tinkle,* and instantly there was the faint *scratch-scratch* of a hundred little feet as mice came running in from all directions and sat up on their haunches awaiting their Princess' orders.

"Go each of you," she said, "and get me a fiber of flax, the finest there is."

The mice went scurrying off and soon they began returning one by one each bringing a fiber of flax. When they had spun the flax and carded it, the little mouse wove a beautiful piece of fine linen. It was so sheer that she was able when she folded it to put it into an empty nutshell.

"Here, Veikko," she said, "here in this little box is a sample of my weaving. I hope your father will like it."

Veikko when he got home felt almost embarrassed for he was sure that his sweetheart's weaving would shame his brothers. So at first he kept the nutshell hidden in his pocket.

The sweetheart of the oldest brother had sent as a sample of her weaving a square of coarse cotton.

"Not very fine," the farmer said, "but good enough."

The second brother's sample was a square of cotton and linen mixed.

"A little better," the farmer said, nodding his head. Then he turned to Veikko.

"And you, Veikko, has your sweetheart not given you a sample of her weaving?"

Veikko handed his father a nutshell at sight of which his brothers burst out laughing.

"Ha! Ha! Ha!" they laughed. "Veikko's sweetheart gives him a nut when he asks for a sample of her weaving."

But their laughter died as the farmer opened the nutshell and began shaking out a great web of the finest linen.

"Why, Veikko, my boy!" he cried, "however did your sweetheart get threads for so fine a web?"

Veikko answered modestly:

"She rang a little silver bell and ordered her servants

to bring her in fibers of finest flax. They did so and after they had spun the flax and carded it, my sweetheart wove the web you see."

"Wonderful!" gasped the farmer. "I have never known such a weaver! The other girls will be all right for farmers' wives but Veikko's sweetheart might be a Princess! Well," concluded the farmer, "it's time that you all brought your sweethearts home. I want to see them with my own eyes. Suppose you bring them to-morrow."

"She's a good little mouse and I'm very fond of her," Veikko thought to himself as he went out to the forest, "but my brothers will certainly laugh when they find she is only a mouse! Well, I don't care if they do laugh! She's been a good little sweetheart to me and I'm not going to be ashamed of her!"

So when he got to the hut he told the little mouse at once that his father wanted to see her.

The little mouse was greatly excited.

"I must go in proper style!" she said.

She rang the little silver bell and ordered her coach and five. The coach when it came turned out to be an empty nutshell and the five prancing steeds that were drawing it were five black mice. The little mouse seated herself in the coach with a coachman mouse on the box in front of her and a footman mouse on the box behind her.

"Oh, how my brothers will laugh!" thought Veikko.

But he didn't laugh. He walked beside the coach and told the little mouse not to be frightened, that he would take good care of her. His father, he told her, was a gentle old man and would be kind to her.

When they left the forest they came to a river which was spanned by a foot bridge. Just as Veikko and the nutshell coach had reached the middle of the bridge, a man met them coming from the opposite direction.

"Mercy me!" the man exclaimed as he caught sight of the strange little coach that was rolling along beside Veikko. "What's that?"

He stooped down and looked and then with a loud laugh he put out his foot and pushed the coach, the little mouse, her servants, and her five prancing steeds —all off the bridge and into the water below.

"What have you done! What have you done!" Veikko cried. "You've drowned my poor little sweetheart!"

The man thinking Veikko was crazy hurried away.

Veikko with tears in his eyes looked down into the water.

"You poor little mouse!" he said. "How sorry I am

She beckoned to Veikko

that you are drowned! You were a faithful loving sweetheart and now that you are gone I know how much I loved you!"

As he spoke he saw a beautiful coach of gold drawn by five glossy horses go up the far bank of the river. A coachman in gold lace held the reins and a footman in pointed cap sat up stiffly behind. The most beautiful girl in the world was seated in the coach. Her skin was as red as a berry and as white as snow, her long golden hair gleamed with jewels, and she was dressed in pearly velvet. She beckoned to Veikko and when he came close she said:

"Won't you come sit beside me?"

"Me? Me?" Veikko stammered, too dazed to think. The beautiful creature smiled.

"You were not ashamed to have me for a sweetheart when I was a mouse," she said, "and surely now that I am a Princess again you won't desert me!"

"A mouse!" Veikko gasped. "Were you the little mouse?"

The Princess nodded.

"Yes, I was the little mouse under an evil enchantment which could never have been broken if you had not taken me for a sweetheart and if another human being had not drowned me. Now the enchantment is broken forever. So come, we will go to your father and after he has given us his blessing we will get married and go home to my kingdom."

And that's exactly what they did. They drove at once to the farmer's house and when Veikko's father and his brothers and his brothers' sweethearts saw the Princess' coach stopping at their gate they all came out bowing and scraping to see what such grand folk could want of them.

"Father!" Veikko cried, "don't you know me?"

The farmer stopped bowing long enough to look up.

"Why, bless my soul!" he cried, "it's our Veikko!"

"Yes, father, I'm Veikko and this is the Princess that I'm going to marry!"

"A Princess, did you say, Veikko? Mercy me, where did my boy find a Princess?"

"Out in the forest where my tree pointed."

"Well, well, well," the farmer said, "where your tree pointed! I've always heard that was a good way to find a bride."

The older brothers shook their heads gloomily and muttered:

"Just our luck! If only our trees had pointed to the forest we, too, should have found princesses instead of plain country wenches!"

But they were wrong: it wasn't because his tree pointed to the forest that Veikko got the Princess, it was because he was so simple and good that he was kind even to a little mouse.

Well, after they had got the farmer's blessing they rode home to the Princess' kingdom and were married. And they were happy as they should have been for they were good and true to each other and they loved each other dearly.

THE ENCHANTED GROUSE

The Story of Helli and the Little Locked Box

THE ENCHANTED GROUSE

There was once an old couple who lived with their married son and his wife. The son's name was Helli. He was a dutiful son but his wife was a scold. She was always finding fault with the old people and with her husband and for that matter with everybody else as well.

One morning when she saw her husband taking out his bow and arrows she said:

"Where are you going now?"

"I'm going hunting," he told her.

"Isn't that just like you!" she cried. "You're going off to have a good time hunting and you don't give a thought to me who have to stay home alone with two stupid old people!"

"If I didn't go hunting," Helli said, "and shoot something, we'd have nothing to put in the pot for dinner and then you would have reason to scold."

At that the woman burst into tears.

"Of course, as usual blame me! Whatever happens it's my fault!"

Poor Helli hurried off, hoping that by the time he returned his wife would be in a calmer state of mind. He had small success with his hunting. He shot arrow after arrow but always missed his mark. Then when he had only one arrow left he saw a Grouse standing in some brushwood so near that there was little likelihood of his missing it.

He took good aim but before he could fire the Grouse said:

"Don't shoot me, brother! Take me home alive."

Helli paused, then he shook his head.

"I've got to shoot you for we've nothing to put in the pot for dinner."

Again he aimed his arrow and again the Grouse said:

"Don't shoot me, brother! Take me home alive."

For the second time Helli paused.

"I'd like to spare you," he said, "but what would my wife say if I came home empty-handed?"

He took aim again and a third time the Grouse said:

"Don't shoot me, brother! Take me home alive."

At that Helli dropped his arrow.

"I don't care what she says! I can't shoot a creature that begs so pitifully for its life! Very well, Mr.

THE ENCHANTED GROUSE

Grouse, I'll do as you say: I'll take you home alive. But don't blame me if my wife wrings your neck."

He took the Grouse up in his arms and started homewards.

"Feed me for a year," the Grouse said, "and I'll reward you."

When they reached home and Helli's wife saw the Grouse, she cried out petulantly:

"Is that all you've got and out hunting all morning! That won't be dinner enough for four!"

"This Grouse isn't to be killed," Helli announced. "I'm going to keep it for a year and feed it."

"It won't take much to feed a Grouse," the old man remarked.

But the wife flew into a passion.

"What! Feed a useless bird when there isn't enough to feed your own flesh and blood!"

But Helli was firm and despite her threats his wife did not dare to maltreat the Grouse.

At the end of a year the Grouse grew a copper feather in its tail which it dropped in the dooryard. Then it disappeared.

"Ha!" laughed Helli's wife. "A copper feather! That's your reward for feeding that thankless bird a whole year! And now it's escaped!"

But the next day the Grouse returned.

"Feed me for another year," it said to Helli, "and I'll reward you."

His wife raised an awful to-do over this, but Helli was firm and for another year he fed and petted the Grouse.

At the end of the second year the Grouse grew a silver feather in its tail which it dropped in the dooryard. Then it disappeared.

"One silver feather!" Helli's wife cried. "So that's all you get for feeding that thankless bird a whole year! And now it's escaped!"

But it hadn't. It returned the very next day.

"Feed me for another year," it said to Helli, "and I'll reward you."

At the end of the third year the Grouse grew a golden feather in its tail and when it dropped that in the dooryard the scolding wife hadn't so much to say, for a golden feather was after all pretty good pay for a few handfuls of grain.

For a day the Grouse disappeared and then when it returned it said to Helli:

"Get on my back and I'll reward you."

Helli did so and the Grouse, rising high in the air, flew far away. On, on it flew until it reached the broad

On it flew until it reached the broad Ocean

Ocean. Over the Ocean it flew until Helli could see nothing but water in whatever direction he looked.

"Ha!" he said to himself with a shudder, "I hope I can hold on!"

As he spoke, the Grouse slipped from beneath him and he fell down, down, down. However, before he touched water the Grouse swooped under him and caught him up again high into the air. He had this same terrible experience a second time and a third time and each time he thought his last moment had arrived.

"Now," the Grouse told him, "you know what my feelings were when you threatened three times to shoot me with your arrow."

"You have taught me a lesson," Helli said.

After that the Grouse flew on and on. At last it said:

"Look straight ahead, master, and tell me what you see."

Helli shaded his eyes and looked.

"Far, far ahead I see what looks like a copper column."

"Good!" the Grouse said. "That is the home of my oldest sister. She will be overjoyed to see us and when she hears how you have spared my life she will want to make you a present and will offer you various things. Take my advice and tell her that the only thing you want is her little locked box the key to which is lost. If she won't give you that, accept nothing."

The Grouse's oldest sister received them most hospitably and when she had heard their story at once offered Helli anything he might like from among her treasures.

"Then give me your little locked box the key to which is lost," Helli said.

The oldest sister shook her head.

"My little locked box! Who told you about that? I'm sorry, but I cannot give you that! Take anything else!"

"No," Helli said, "that or nothing!"

When the oldest sister could not be prevailed upon to give away her little locked box, the Grouse had Helli mount his back once more and off they flew.

"We'll visit my second sister now," he said. "If she offers you a present, ask her for her little locked box without a key and accept nothing else."

On, on they flew until the oldest sister's castle was far behind.

"Look, master," the Grouse said, "look straight ahead and tell me what you see."

Helli shaded his eyes and looked.

THE ENCHANTED GROUSE

"Far ahead I see something that is like a silver cloud."

"That," said the Grouse, "is the silver castle of my second sister."

At the silver castle the second sister received them with joy and when she heard who Helli was at once declared that she wanted to show him her gratitude by making him a gift.

"Ask from me what you will," she said, "and you shall have it."

But when he asked for her little locked box without a key, she cried out:

"No! No! Not that! Anything else!"

"But I don't want anything else!" Helli said.

When the Grouse saw that his second sister was not to be parted from her little locked box, he bade Helli mount his back and off they flew again.

"We'll go to my youngest sister this time," he said. "If she offers you a present, ask for the same thing."

On, on they flew until the silver castle was lost to view.

"Now, master, look ahead and tell me what you see."

Helli shaded his eyes and looked.

"I seem to see a golden haze like the sun behind a cloud."

"That is the golden castle of my youngest sister."

They arrived and the youngest sister threw her arms about the Grouse for she loved him dearly and had not seen him for a long time.

"Welcome, brother!" she said. "And welcome also to you, Helli!"

Then she offered Helli a present and when he asked for her little locked box without a key she gave it to him at once.

"It is my most precious possession," she said, "but you may have it for you spared my dear brother's life when you might have taken it."

After they had rested and feasted they bade the youngest sister farewell and Helli with his precious box held tightly in one hand mounted the Grouse's back and off they flew towards home.

"Be careful of the box," the Grouse said, "and don't let it out of your hands until we reach some beautiful spot where you'd like always to live."

They passed high mountains and wooded lakes and fertile valleys.

"Shall we stop here?" the Grouse asked. "Or here? Or here?"

But always Helli said:

"No, not here."

At last they reached home and the Grouse told Helli that now they must part forever.

"By sparing my life three times," the Grouse said, "and then feeding me for three years you have broken the enchantment that bound me and now I shall not have to go about any longer as a grouse but shall be able to resume my natural shape. Farewell, Helli, and when you find the spot where you think you would like always to live, drop the box and you will find you have a treasure that will more than reward you for your kindness to me."

The Grouse disappeared and Helli said to himself:

"Where do I want to live always but right here at home with my dear old father and mother and my wife who is my wife even if she does scold me sometimes!"

So there at home after they all had supper together, he dropped the box on the floor. It broke and out of it arose a beautiful castle with servants and riches and everything that Helli had always wanted and never had. And Helli and his old father and mother and his wife lived in it and were happy. And gradually his wife got over her habit of scolding for when you're happy you haven't anything to scold about.

THE TERRIBLE OLLI

The Story of an Honest Finn and a Wicked Troll

THE TERRIBLE OLLI

There was once a wicked rich old Troll who lived on a Mountain that sloped down to a Bay. A decent Finn, a farmer, lived on the opposite side of the Bay. The farmer had three sons. When the boys had reached manhood he said to them one day:

"I should think it would shame you three strong youths that that wicked old Troll over there should live on year after year and no one trouble him. We work hard like honest Finns and are as poor at the end of the year as at the beginning. That old Troll with all his wickedness grows richer and richer. I tell you, if you boys had any real spirit you'd take his riches from him and drive him away!"

His youngest son, whose name was Olli, at once cried out:

"Very well, father, I will!"

But the two older sons, offended at Olli's promptness, declared:

"You'll do no such thing! Don't forget your place in the family! You're the youngest and we're not going to let you push us aside. Now, father, we two will go across the Bay and rout out that old Troll. Olli may come with us if he likes and watch us while we do it."

Olli laughed and said: "All right!" for he was used to his brothers treating him like a baby.

So in a few days the three brothers walked around the Bay and up the Mountain and presented themselves at the Troll's house. The Troll and his old wife were both at home. They received the brothers with great civility.

"You're the sons of the Finn who lives across the Bay, aren't you?" the Troll said. "I've watched you boys grow up. I am certainly glad to see you for I have three daughters who need husbands. Marry my daughters and you'll inherit my riches."

The old Troll made this offer in order to get the young men into his power.

"Be careful!" Olli whispered.

But the brothers were too delighted at the prospect of inheriting the Troll's riches so easily to pay any heed to Olli's warning. Instead they accepted the Troll's offer at once.

Well, the old Troll's wife made them a fine supper and after supper the Troll sent them to bed with his three daughters. But first he put red caps on the three youths and white caps on the three Troll girls. He made a joke about the caps.

"A red cap and a white cap in each bed!" he said.

The older brothers suspected nothing and soon fell asleep. Olli, too, pretended to fall asleep and when he was sure that none of the Troll girls were still awake he got up and quietly changed the caps. He put the white caps on himself and his brothers and the red caps on the Troll girls. Then he crept back to bed and waited.

Presently the old Troll came over to the beds with a long knife in his hand. There was so little light in the room that he couldn't see the faces of the sleepers, but it was easy enough to distinguish the white caps from the red caps. With three swift blows he cut off the heads under the red caps, thinking of course they were the heads of the three Finnish youths. Then he went back to bed with the old Troll wife and Olli could hear them both chuckling and laughing. After a time they went soundly to sleep as Olli could tell from their deep regular breathing and their loud snores.

Olli now roused his brothers and told them what had

happened and the three of them slipped quietly out of the Troll house and hurried home to their father on the other side of the Bay.

After that the older brothers no longer talked of despoiling the Troll. They didn't care to try another encounter with him.

"He might have cut our heads off!" they said, shuddering to think of the awful risk they had run.

Olli laughed at them.

"Come on!" he kept saying to them day after day. "Let's go across the Bay to the Troll's!"

"We'll do no such thing!" they told him. "And you wouldn't suggest it either if you weren't so young and foolish!"

"Well," Olli announced at last, "if you won't come with me I'm going alone. I've heard that the Troll has a horse with hairs of gold and silver. I've decided I want that horse."

"Olli," his father said, "I don't believe you ought to go. You know what your brothers say. That old Troll is an awfully sly one!"

But Olli only laughed.

"Good-by!" he called back as he waved his hand. "When you see me again I'll be riding the Troll's horse!"

Olli and the Troll's horse

The Troll wasn't at home but the old Troll wife was there. When she saw Olli she thought to herself:

"Mercy me, here's that Finnish boy again, the one that changed the caps! What shall I do? I must keep him here on some pretext or other until the Troll comes home!"

So she pretended to be very glad to see him.

"Why, Olli," she said, "is that you? Come right in!"

She talked to him as long as she could and when she could think of nothing more to say she asked him would he take the horse and water it at the Lake.

"That will keep him busy," she thought to herself, "and long before he gets back from the Lake the Troll will be here."

But Olli, instead of leading the horse down to the Lake, jumped on its back and galloped away. By the time the Troll reached home, he was safely on the other side of the Bay.

When the Troll heard from the old Troll wife what had happened, he went down to the shore and hallooed across the Bay:

"Olli! Oh, Olli, are you there?"

Olli made a trumpet of his hands and called back:

"Yes, I'm here! What do you want?"

"Olli, have you got my horse?"

"Yes, I've got your horse but it's my horse now!"

"Olli! Olli!" his father cried. "You mustn't talk that way to the Troll! You'll make him angry!"

And his brothers looking with envy at the horse with gold and silver hairs warned him sourly:

"You better be careful, young man, or the Troll will get you yet!"

A few days later Olli announced:

"I think I'll go over and get the Troll's money-bag."

His father tried to dissuade him.

"Don't be foolhardy, Olli! Your brothers say you had better not go to the Troll's house again."

But Olli only laughed and started gaily off as though he hadn't a fear in the world.

Again he found the old Troll wife alone.

"Mercy me!" she thought to herself as she saw him coming, "here is that terrible Olli again! Whatever shall I do? I mustn't let him off this time before the Troll gets back! I must keep him right here with me in the house."

So when he came in she pretended that she was tired and that her back ached and she asked him would he watch the bread in the oven while she rested a few moments on the bed.

"Certainly I will," Olli said.

So the old Troll wife lay down on the bed and Olli sat quietly in front of the oven. The Troll wife really was tired and before she knew it she fell asleep.

"Ha!" thought Olli, "here's my chance!"

Without disturbing the Troll wife he reached under the bed, pulled out the big money-bag full of silver pieces, threw it over his shoulder, and hurried home.

He was measuring the money when he heard the Troll hallooing across to him:

"Olli! Oh, Olli, are you there?"

"Yes," Olli shouted back, "I'm here! What do you want?"

"Olli, have you got my money-bag?"

"Yes, I've got your money-bag but it's my money-bag now!"

A few days later Olli said:

"Do you know, the Troll has a beautiful coverlet woven of silk and gold. I think I'll go over and get it."

His father as usual protested but Olli laughed at him merrily and went. He took with him an auger and a can of water. He hid until it was dark, then climbed the roof of the Troll's house and bored a hole right over the bed. When the Troll and his wife went to sleep he sprinkled some water on the coverlet and on their faces.

The Troll woke with a start.

"I'm wet!" he said, "and the bed's wet, too!"

The old Troll wife got up to change the covers.

"The roof must be leaking," she said. "It never leaked before. I suppose it was that last wind."

She threw the wet coverlet up over the rafters to dry and put other covers on the bed.

When she and the Troll were again asleep, Olli made the hole a little bigger, reached in his hand, and got the coverlet from the rafters.

The next morning the Troll hallooed across the Bay:

"Olli! Oh, Olli, are you there?"

"Yes," Ollie shouted back, "I'm here! What do you want?"

"Have you got my coverlet woven of silk and gold?"

"Yes," Olli told him, "I've got your coverlet but it's my coverlet now!"

A few days later Olli said:

"There's still one thing in the Troll's house that I think I ought to get. It's a golden bell. If I get that golden bell then there will be nothing left that had better belong to an honest Finn."

So he went again to the Troll's house taking with him a saw and an auger. He hid until night and, when the Troll and his wife were asleep, he cut a hole through

THE TERRIBLE OLLI

the side of the house through which he reached in his hand to get the bell. At the touch of his hand the bell tinkled and woke the Troll. The Troll jumped out of bed and grabbed Olli's hand.

"Ha! Ha!" he cried. "I've got you now and this time you won't get away!"

Olli didn't try to get away. He made no resistance while the Troll dragged him into the house.

"We'll eat him—that's what we'll do!" the Troll said to his wife. "Heat the oven at once and we'll roast him!"

So the Troll wife built a roaring fire in the oven.

"He'll make a fine roast!" the Troll said, pinching Olli's arms and legs. "I think we ought to invite the other Troll folk to come and help us eat him up. Suppose I just go over the Mountain and gather them in. You can manage here without me. As soon as the oven is well heated just take Olli and slip him in and close the door and by the time we come he'll be done."

"Very well," the Troll wife said, "but don't be too long! He's young and tender and will roast quickly!"

So the Troll went out to invite to the feast the Troll folk who lived on the other side of the Mountain and Olli was left alone with the Troll wife.

When the oven was well heated she raked out the coals and said to Olli:

"Now then, my boy, sit down in front of the oven with your back to the opening and I'll push you in nicely."

Olli pretended he didn't quite understand. He sat down first one way and then another, spreading himself out so large that he was too big for the oven door.

"Not that way!" the Troll wife kept saying. "Hunch up little, straight in front of the door!"

"You show me how," Olli begged.

So the old Troll wife sat down before the oven directly in front of the opening, and she hunched herself up very compactly with her chin on her knees and her arms around her legs.

"Oh, that way!" Olli said, "so that you can just take hold of me and push me in and shut the door!"

And as he spoke he took hold of her and pushed her in and slammed the door! And that was the end of the old Troll wife!

Olli let her roast in the oven until she was done to a turn. Then he took her out and put her on the table all ready for the feast.

Then he filled a sack with straw and dressed the sack up in some of the old Troll wife's clothes. He threw the dressed up sack on the bed and, just to glance at it, you'd suppose it was the Troll wife asleep.

Then Olli took the golden bell and went home.

Well, presently the Troll and all the Troll folk from over the Mountain came trooping in.

"Yum! Yum! It certainly smells good!" they said as they got the first whiff from the big roast on the table.

"See!" the Troll said, pointing to the bed. "The old woman's asleep! Well, let her sleep! She's tired! We'll just sit down without her!"

So they set to and feasted and feasted.

"Ha! Ha!" said the Troll. "This is the way to serve a troublesome young Finn!"

Just then his knife struck something hard and he looked down to see what it was.

"Mercy me!" he cried, "if here isn't one of the old woman's beads! What can that mean? You don't suppose the roast is not Olli after all but the old woman! No! No! It can't be!"

He got up and went over to the bed. Then he came back shaking his head sadly.

"My friends," he said, "we've been eating the old woman! However, we've eaten so much of her that I suppose we might as well finish her!"

So the Troll folk sat all night feasting and drinking.

At dawn the Troll went down to the water and hallooed across:

"Olli! Oh, Olli, are you there?"

Olli who was safely home shouted back:

"Yes, I'm here! What do you want?"

"Have you got my golden bell?"

"Yes, I've got your golden bell but it's my golden bell now!"

"One thing more, Olli: did you roast my old woman?"

"Your old woman?" Olli echoed. "Look! Is that she?"

Olli pointed at the rising sun which was coming up behind the Troll.

The Troll turned and looked. He looked straight at the sun and then, of course, he burst!

So that was the end of him!

Well, after that no other Troll ever dared settle on that side of the Mountain. They were all too afraid of the Terrible Olli!

THE DEVIL'S HIDE

The Story of the Boy Who Wouldn't Lose His Temper

THE DEVIL'S HIDE

There was once a Finnish boy who got the best of the Devil. His name was Erkki. Erkki had two brothers who were, of course, older than he. They both tried their luck with the Devil and got the worst of it. Then Erkki tried his luck. They were sure Erkki, too, would be worsted, but he wasn't. Here is the whole story:

One day the oldest brother said:

"It's time for me to go out into the world and earn my living. Do you two younger ones wait here at home until you hear how I get on."

The younger boys agreed to this and the oldest brother started out. He was unable to get employment until by chance he met the Devil. The Devil at once offered him a place but on very strange terms.

"Come work for me," the Devil said, "and I promise that you'll be comfortably housed and well fed. We'll make this bargain: the first of us who loses his temper will forfeit to the other enough of his own hide to sole a pair of boots. If I lose my temper first, you may exact from me a big patch of my hide. If you lose your temper first, I'll exact the same from you."

The oldest brother agreed to this and the Devil at once took him home and set him to work.

"Take this ax," he said, "and go out behind the house and chop me some firewood."

The oldest brother took the ax and went out to the woodpile.

"Chopping wood is easy enough," he thought to himself.

But at the first blow he found that the ax had no edge. Try as he would he couldn't cut a single log.

"I'd be a fool to stay here and waste my time with such an ax!" he cried.

So he threw down the ax and ran away thinking to escape the Devil and get work somewhere else. But the Devil had no intention of letting him escape. He ran after him, overtook him, and asked him what he meant leaving thus without notice.

"I don't want to work for you!" the oldest brother cried, petulantly.

"Very well," the Devil said, "but don't lose your temper about it."

"I will so lose my temper!" the oldest brother declared. "The idea—expecting me to cut wood with such an ax!"

"Well," the Devil remarked, "since you insist on losing your temper, you'll have to forfeit me enough of your hide to sole a pair of boots! That was our bargain."

The oldest brother howled and protested but to no purpose. The Devil was firm. He took out a long knife and slit off enough of the oldest brother's hide to sole a pair of big boots.

"Now then, my boy," he said, "now you may go."

The oldest brother went limping home complaining bitterly at the hard fate that had befallen him.

"I'm tired and sick," he told his brothers, "and I'm going to stay home and rest. One of you will have to go out and get work."

The second brother at once said that he'd be delighted to try his luck in the world. So he started out and he had exactly the same experience. At first he could get no work, then he met the Devil and the Devil made exactly the same bargain with him that he had made with the oldest brother. He took the second brother home with him, gave him the same dull ax, and sent him out to the woodpile. After the first stroke the second brother threw down the ax in disgust and tried to run off and the Devil, of course, wouldn't let him go until he, too, had submitted to the loss of a great patch of hide. So it was no time at all before the second brother came limping home complaining bitterly at fate.

"What ails you two?" Erkki said.

"You go out into the cruel world and hunt work," they told him, "and you'll find out soon enough what ails us! And when you do find out you needn't come limping home expecting sympathy from us for you won't get it!"

So the very next day Erkki started out, leaving his brothers at home nursing their sore backs and their injured feelings.

Well, Erkki had exactly the same experience. At first he could get work nowhere, then later he met the Devil and went into his employ on exactly the same terms as his brothers.

The Devil handed him the same dull ax and sent him out to the woodpile. At the first blow Erkki knew that the ax had lost its edge and would never cut a single log. But instead of being discouraged and losing his temper, he only laughed.

"I suppose the Devil thinks I'll lose my hide over a trifle like this!" he said. "Well, I just won't!"

THE DEVIL'S HIDE 177

He dropped the ax and, going over to the woodpile, began pulling it down. Under all the logs he found the Devil's cat. It was an evil looking creature with a gray head.

"Ha!" thought Erkki, "I bet anything you've got something to do with this!"

He raised the dull ax and with one blow cut off the evil creature's head. Sure enough the ax instantly recovered its edge and after that Erkki had no trouble at all in chopping as much firewood as the Devil wanted.

That night at supper the Devil said:

"Well, Erkki, did you finish the work I gave you?"

"Yes, master, I've chopped all that wood."

The Devil was surprised.

"Really?"

"Yes, master. You can go out and see for yourself."

"Then you found something in the woodpile, didn't you?"

"Nothing but an awful looking old cat."

The Devil started.

"Did you do anything to that cat?"

"I only chopped its head off and threw it away."

"What!" the Devil cried angrily. "Didn't you know that was my cat!"

"There now, master," Erkki said soothingly, "you're

not going to lose your temper over a little thing like a dead cat, are you? Don't forget our bargain!"

The Devil swallowed his anger and murmured:

"No, I'm not going to lose my temper but I must say that was no way to treat my cat."

The next day the Devil ordered Erkki to go out to the forest and bring home some logs on the ox sledge.

"My black dog will go with you," he said, "and as you come home you're to take exactly the same course the dog takes."

Well, Erkki went out to the forest and loaded the ox sledge with logs and then drove the oxen home following the Devil's black dog. As they reached the Devil's house the black dog jumped through a hole in the gate.

"I must follow master's orders," Erkki said to himself.

So he cut up the oxen into small pieces and put them through the same hole in the gate; he chopped up the logs and pitched them through the hole; and he broke up the sledge into pieces small enough to follow the oxen and the logs. Then he crept through the hole himself.

That night at supper the Devil said:

"Well, Erkki, did you come home the way I told you?"

"Yes, master, I followed the black dog."

"What!" the Devil cried. "Do you mean to say you brought the oxen and the sledge and the logs through the hole in the gate?"

"Yes, master, that's what I did."

"But you couldn't!" the Devil declared.

"Well, master," Erkki said, "just go out and see."

The Devil went outside and when he saw the method by which Erkki had carried out his orders he was furious. But Erkki quieted him by saying:

"There now, master, you're not going to lose your temper over a trifling matter like this, are you? Remember our bargain!"

"N-n-no," the Devil said, again swallowing his anger, "I'm not going to lose my temper, but I want you to understand, Erkki, that I think you've acted very badly in this!"

All that evening the Devil fumed and fussed about Erkki.

"We've got to get rid of that boy! That's all there is about it!" he said to his wife.

Of course whenever Erkki was in sight the Devil

tried to smile and look pleasant, but as soon as Erkki was gone he went back at once to his grievance. He declared emphatically:

"There's no living in peace and comfort with such a boy around!"

"Well," his wife said, "if you feel that way about it, why don't you kill him to-night when he's asleep? We could throw his body into the lake and no one be the wiser."

"That's a fine idea!" the Devil said. "Wake me up some time after midnight and I'll do it!"

Now Erkki overheard this little plan, so that night he kept awake. When he knew from their snoring that the Devil and his wife were sound asleep, he slipped over to their bed, quietly lifted the Devil's wife in his arms, and without awakening her placed her gently in his own bed. Then he put on some of her clothes and laid himself down beside the Devil in the wife's place.

Presently he nudged the Devil awake.

"What do you want?" the Devil mumbled.

"Sst!" Erkki whispered. "Isn't it time we got up and killed Erkki?"

"Yes," the Devil answered, "it is. Come along."

They got up quietly and the Devil reached down a great sword from the wall. Then they crept over to

Erkki's bed and the Devil with one blow cut off the head of the person who was lying there asleep.

"Now," he said, "we'll just carry out the bed and all and dump it in the lake."

So Erkki took one end of the bed and the Devil the other and, stumbling and slipping in the darkness, they carried it down to the lake and pitched it in.

"That's a good job done!" the Devil said with a laugh.

Then they went back to bed together and the Devil fell instantly asleep.

The next morning when he got up for breakfast, there was Erkki stirring the porridge.

"How—did you get here?" the Devil asked. "I mean —I mean where is my wife?"

"Your wife? Don't you remember," Erkki said, "you cut off her head last night and then we threw her into the lake, bed and all! But no one will be the wiser!"

"W-wh-what!" the Devil cried, and he was about to fly into an awful rage when Erkki restrained him by saying:

"There now, master, you're not going to lose your temper over a little thing like a wife, are you? Remember our bargain!"

So the Devil was forced again to swallow his anger.

"No, I'm not going to lose my temper," he said, "but I tell you frankly, Erkki, I don't think that was a nice trick for you to play on me!"

Well, the Devil felt lonely not having a wife about the house, so in a few days he decided to go off wooing for a new one.

"And, Erkki," he said, "I expect you to keep busy while I'm gone. Here's a keg of red paint. Now get to work and have the house all blazing red by the time I get back."

"All blazing red," Erkki repeated. "Very well, master, trust me to have it all blazing red by the time you get back!"

As soon as the Devil was gone, Erkki set the house a-fire and in a short time the whole sky was lighted up with the red glow of the flames. In great fright the Devil hurried back and got there in time to see the house one mass of fire.

"You see, master," Erkki said, "I've done as you told me. It looks very pretty, doesn't it? all blazing red!"

The Devil almost choked with rage.

"You—you—" he began, but Erkki restrained him by saying:

"There now, master, you're not going to lose your

From the bones of the cattle he laid three bridges

THE DEVIL'S HIDE

temper over a little thing like a house a-fire, are you? Remember our bargain!"

The Devil swallowed hard and said:

"N—no, I'm not going to lose my temper, but I must say, Erkki, that I'm very much annoyed with you!"

The next day the Devil wanted to go a-wooing again and before he started he said to Erkki:

"Now, no nonsense this time! While I'm gone you're to build three bridges over the lake, but they're not to be built of wood or stone or iron or earth. Do you understand?"

Erkki pretended to be frightened.

"That's a pretty hard task you've given me, master!"

"Hard or easy, see that you get it done!" the Devil said.

Erkki waited until the Devil was gone, then he went out to the field and slaughtered all the Devil's cattle. From the bones of the cattle he laid three bridges across the lake, using the skulls for one bridge, the ribs for another, and the legs and the hoofs for the third. Then when the Devil got back, Erkki met him and pointing to the bridges said:

"See, master, there they are, three bridges put together without stick, stone, iron, or bit of earth!"

When the Devil found out that all his cattle had been slaughtered to give bones for the bridges, he was ready to kill Erkki, but Erkki quieted him by saying:

"There now, master, you're not going to lose your temper over a little thing like the slaughter of a few cattle, are you? Remember our bargain!"

So again the Devil had to swallow his anger.

"No," he said, "I'm not going to lose my temper exactly but I just want to tell you, Erkki, that I don't think you're behaving well!"

The Devil's wooing was successful and pretty soon he brought home a new wife. The new wife didn't like having Erkki about, so the Devil promised her he'd kill the boy.

"I'll do it to-night," he said, "when he's asleep."

Erkki overheard this and that night he put the churn in his bed under the covers, and where his head ordinarily would be he put a big round stone. Then he himself curled up on the stove and went comfortably to sleep.

During the night the Devil took his great sword from the wall and went over to Erkki's bed. His first blow hit the round stone and nicked the sword. His second blow struck sparks.

"Mercy me!" the Devil thought, "he's got a mighty hard head! I better strike lower!"

With the third stroke he hit the churn a mighty blow. The hoops flew apart and the churn collapsed.

The Devil went chuckling back to bed.

"Ha!" he said boastfully to his wife, "I got him that time!"

But the next morning when he woke up he didn't feel like laughing for there was Erkki as lively as ever and pretending that nothing had happened.

"What!" cried the Devil in amazement, "didn't you feel anything strike you last night while you were asleep?"

"Oh, I did feel a few mosquitoes brushing my cheek," Erkki said. "Nothing else."

"Steel doesn't touch him!" the Devil said to his wife. "I think I'll try fire on him."

So that night the Devil told Erkki to sleep in the threshing barn. Erkki carried his cot down to the threshing floor and then when it was dark he shifted it into the hay barn where he slept comfortably all night.

During the night the Devil set fire to the threshing barn. In the early dawn Erkki carried his cot back to the place of the threshing barn and in the morning when the Devil came out the first thing he saw was Erkki unharmed and peacefully sleeping among the smoking ruins.

"Mercy me, Erkki!" he shouted, shaking him awake, "have you been asleep all night?"

Erkki sat up and yawned.

"Yes, I've had a fine night's sleep. But I did feel a little chilly."

"Chilly!" the Devil gasped.

After that the Devil's one thought was to get rid of Erkki.

"That boy's getting on my nerves!" he told his wife. "I just can't stand him much longer! What are we going to do about him?"

They discussed one plan after another and at last decided that the only way they'd ever get rid of him would be to move away and leave him behind.

"I'll send him out to the forest to chop wood all day," the Devil said, "and while he's gone we'll row ourselves and all our belongings out to an island and when he comes back he won't know where we've gone."

Erkki overheard this plan and the next day when they were sure he was safely at work in the forest he slipped back and hid himself in the bedclothes.

THE DEVIL'S HIDE

Well, when they got to the island and began unpacking their things there was Erkki in the bedclothes!

The Devil's new wife complained bitterly.

"If you really loved me," she said, "you'd cut off that boy's head!"

"But I've tried to cut it off!" the Devil declared, "and I never can do it! Plague take such a boy! I've always known the Finns were an obstinate lot but I must say I've never met one as bad as Erkki! He's too much for me!"

But the Devil's wife kept on complaining until at last the Devil promised that he would try once again to cut off Erkki's head.

"Very well," his wife said, "to-night when he's asleep I'll wake you."

Well, what with the moving and everything the wife herself was tired and as soon as she went to bed she fell asleep. That gave Erkki just the very chance he needed to try on the new wife the trick he had played on the old one. Without waking her he carried her to his bed and then laid himself down in her place beside the Devil. Then he waked up the Devil and reminded him that he had promised to cut off Erkki's head.

The poor old Devil got up and went over to Erkki's bed and of course cut off the head of his new wife.

The next morning when he had found out what he had done, he was perfectly furious.

"You get right out of here, Erkki!" he roared. "I never want to see you again!"

"There now, master," Erkki said, "you're not going to lose your temper over a little thing like a dead wife, are you?"

"I am so going to lose my temper!" the Devil shouted. "And what's more it isn't a little thing! I liked this wife, I did, and I don't know where I'll get another one I like as well! So you just clear out of here and be quick about it, too!"

"Very well, master," Erkki said, "I'll go but not until you pay me what you owe me."

"What I owe you!" bellowed the Devil. "What about all you owe me for my house and my cattle and my old wife and my dear new wife and everything!"

"You've lost your temper," Erkki said, "and now you've got to pay me a patch of your hide big enough to sole a pair of boots. That was our bargain!"

The Devil roared and blustered but Erkki was firm. He wouldn't budge a step until the Devil had allowed him to slit a great patch of hide off his back.

That piece of the Devil's hide made the finest soles that a pair of boots ever had. It wore for years and years and years. In fact Erkki is still tramping around on those same soles. The fame of them has spread over all the land and it has got so that now people stop Erkki on the highway to look at his wonderful boots soled with the Devil's hide. Travelers from foreign countries are deeply interested when they hear about the boots and when they meet Erkki they question him closely.

"Tell us," they beg him, "how did you get the Devil's hide in the first place?"

Erkki always laughs and makes the same answer:

"I got it by not losing my temper!"

As for the Devil, he's never again made a bargain like that with a Finn!

THE MYSTERIOUS SERVANT

The Story of a Young Man Who Respected the Dead

THE MYSTERIOUS SERVANT

There was once a rich merchant who had an only son. As he lay dying, he said:

"Matti, my boy, my end is approaching and there are two things I want to say to you: The first is that I am leaving you all my wealth. If you are careful you will have enough to suffice you for life. The second thing I have to say is to beg you never to leave this, your native village. At your birth there was a prophecy which declared that if ever you left this village you would have to marry a woman with horns. Now that I have warned you in time it will be your own fault if ever you have to meet this fate."

The merchant died and Matti was left alone. He had never before wanted to travel but now that he knew of the fate which would overtake him if he did, he couldn't bear the thought of remaining forever a prisoner in his native village.

"What is the use of riches," he asked himself, "if one can't travel over the broad world and see wonderful sights? Besides, if it's my fate to marry a horned woman, I don't see why sitting quietly at home is going to save me. No! I'm going to take my chances like a man and come and go as I like!"

So he gathered his riches together, closed the old house where he had been born, and started out into the bright world. He traveled many days, meeting strange peoples and seeing strange sights. At last he settled down in a large city and became a merchant like his father.

One afternoon as he was out walking, he saw a crowd of men dragging the body of a dead man in the gutter. They were kicking and abusing the dead body and calling it evil names.

Matti stopped them.

"What is this you are doing?" he demanded. "Don't you know that disrespect to the dead is disrespect to God? Give over abusing this poor dead body and bury it decently or God will punish you!"

"Let us alone!" the men cried. "He deserves the abuse we are giving him! When he was alive he borrowed money from us all and then he died without repaying us. Are we to have no satisfaction at all?"

With that they resumed their abuse of the dead body.

"Wait!" Matti cried. "Tell me what the dead man owed you and I will pay it!"

"He owed me ten ducats!" said one.

"And me a hundred!" shouted another.

"And me five hundred!"

"And me a thousand!"

"Come all of you to my house," Matti said, "and I will pay you, but only on condition that first you hand over the body to me and help me give it a decent burial."

The men agreed. They helped Matti bury the dead man and then went home with him.

Each told Matti the amount the dead man owed him and, true to his promise, Matti paid them all.

When he had paid the last man he found that he had nothing left for himself but nine silver kopeks. The dead man's debts had exhausted all the wealth his father had left him.

"No matter!" Matti thought to himself. "My riches would have done me no good if I had stood by and allowed a poor dead man to be abused. What if I have nothing left? I'm young and strong and I can go out into the world and make my livelihood somehow. I'll go home and have one last look at my native village and then begin life anew."

So, dressed in shabby old clothes with nothing in his pockets but the nine silver kopeks, Matti left the city where people were beginning to know him as a merchant and started back to his native village. He was soon met by a man who addressed him respectfully and asked to be engaged as his servant.

"My servant!" Matti repeated with a laugh. "My dear fellow, I'm too poor to have a servant! All I have in the world are nine silver kopeks!"

"No matter, master," the man said. "Take me anyhow. I will serve you well and I promise you will not regret our bargain."

So Matti agreed and they walked on together. The sun was hot and by midafternoon Matti was feeling faint with hunger and fatigue.

"Master," the Servant said, "I will run ahead to the next village and order the landlord at the inn to prepare you a fine dinner. Do you come along slowly and by the time you arrive the dinner will be ready."

"But remember," Mattie warned him, "I have no money to pay for a fine dinner!"

"Trust me!" the Servant said and off he hurried.

At the next village he hunted out the best inn and ordered the landlord to prepare his finest dinner without delay. He was so particular that everything should be the best that the landlord supposed his master must be some great lord.

When Matti arrived on foot, tired and travel-stained and shabby, the landlord was amazed.

"It's fine lords we have nowadays!" he muttered scornfully, and he wished he had not been in such haste to cook the best food in the house. But it was cooked and ready to serve and so, with an ill grace, he served it.

Matti and his man ate their fill of good cabbage soup and fish and fowl tender and juicy.

It quite enraged the landlord to see poor men with such good appetites.

"They eat as if their pockets were lined with gold!" he muttered angrily. "Well, let them eat while they can for they'll lose their appetites once they see the reckoning!"

When they finished eating, they rested and then called for the reckoning. It was much more than it should have been but neither Matti nor the Servant objected.

"Like a good fellow," the Servant said, "will you please to lend me your half peck measure."

"Like a good fellow, indeed!" the landlord muttered to himself. "Who are you to call me a good fellow I'd like to know!"

Nevertheless he went out and got the measure.

"Now, master," the Servant said, "give me three of your nine silver kopeks."

The Servant threw the three silver kopeks into the measure, shook the measure three times and lo! it was filled to the brim with silver kopeks! The Servant counted out the amount of the reckoning and handed the rest of the money to his master. Then he and Matti went on their way leaving the landlord gaping after them with open mouth.

Day after day the Servant paid the reckoning in the same way at the various inns where they stopped until they reached at last Matti's native village and the old house that still belonged to him.

They settled themselves there and one day the Servant said to Matti:

"Now, master, you know your fate: for having left your native village you know you are destined to marry a horned woman. You might as well do it at once for you'll have to do it sooner or later."

"That is true," Mattie said, "and if I knew the whereabouts of the horned woman who is my fate I should marry her at once."

"In that case we'll lose no more time," the Servant said. "The King has three daughters all of whom are horned. This isn't generally known but it is true. Let us go to the palace and present your suit. The King will give friendly ear for there are not many suitors for daughters with horns. He will try to make you take the oldest who has big horns and a hoarse voice. When she sees you, she'll whisper: 'Take me! Take me!' But do you shake your head and answer: 'No! Not this one!' Then the King will send for his second daughter. Her horns are not so big nor is her voice so hoarse. She, too, will whisper you: 'Take me! Take me!' But do you again shake your head and answer: 'No! Not this one!' Be firm and the King will finally have to send for his youngest daughter. Her horns are just soft little baby horns and her voice is just a little husky. Take her and soon all will be well."

So Matti and the Servant went to the palace and got audience with the King.

"My master, Matti," the Servant said, addressing the King, "is desirous of marrying a wife with horns."

The King was interested at once.

"As it happens I have a daughter with horns," he said. "I'll have her come in."

He sent for his oldest daughter and presently she appeared. Her horns were long and thick.

"Take me! Take me!" she whispered hoarsely as she passed Matti.

"See what a fine girl she is!" the King said, "and what well grown horns she has!"

But Matti shook his head.

"No, Your Majesty, I don't think I want to marry this one."

"Of course you must follow the dictates of your heart," the King said drily. "However, come to think of it, my second daughter also has horns. Maybe you'd like to consider her."

So the second daughter was called in. Her horns were not so large as her sister's nor was her voice so hoarse. But Matti, remembering the Servant's warning, refused her, too. The King seemed surprised and even annoyed that Matti should refuse his daughters so glibly, but when he found that Matti was firm he said:

"I have got another daughter, my youngest, but, if it's horns you're looking for, I don't believe you'll be interested in her at all since her horns are so small and soft that they are hardly noticeable at all. However, as you're here, you might as well see her."

So the youngest princess was sent for and at once Matti knew that she was the one he wanted to marry.

"*She is under an evil enchantment and I am delivering her!*"

THE MYSTERIOUS SERVANT

She wasn't as beautiful as a princess should be but she was gentle and modest and when she passed Matti her cheeks flushed and she wasn't able to whisper anything. But Matti felt very sure that if she had whispered her voice would have been scarcely husky.

"This, O King," he said, "is my choice! Let me marry your youngest daughter and I promise to be a faithful husband to her."

The King would have preferred to marry off the older princesses first for their horns were getting to be very troublesome, but as they all had horns he was afraid to refuse Matti's offer.

So after a little talk he gave Matti the youngest and in a short time they were married.

After the wedding feast the King led the young couple to the bridal chamber and closed the door.

Matti's Servant meantime had gone out to the woods and cut some stout switches of birch. When the palace was quiet and all were asleep, he crept softly into the bridal chamber and, dragging the bride out of bed, he beat her unmercifully.

"Oh! Oh!" she cried in pain.

Her screams woke Matti and in fright he jumped out of bed and tried to stop the Servant.

"Wait!" the Servant said. "She is under an evil enchantment and I am delivering her!"

So he kept on beating her until he had drawn blood. Then instantly the horns fell from her head and there she stood a beautiful young girl released from the evil enchantment that had disfigured her.

The Servant handed her over to her husband who fell in love with her on sight and has loved her ever since.

"Now farewell, Matti," the Servant said. "My work is done and you will need me no longer. You have married a beautiful princess and the King will soon make you his heir."

With these words the Servant disappeared and Matti was left alone with his lovely bride.

And that was Matti's reward for having respected the dead. God Himself in the form of the Servant had come down and taken care of him.

FAMILIAR FACES

    I   *Mary, Mary, So Contrary!*
   II   *Jane, Jane, Don't Complain!*
 III   *Susan Walker, What a Talker!*

When she got to the middle of the stream

I

MARY, MARY, SO CONTRARY!

There was once a farmer who was married to the most contrary wife in the world. Her name was Maya. If he expected Maya to say, "Yes," she would always say, "No," and if he expected her to say, "No," she would always say, "Yes." If he said the soup was too hot, Maya would instantly insist that it was too cold. She would do nothing that he wanted her to do, and she always insisted on doing everything that he did not want her to do.

Like most contrary people Maya was really very stupid and the farmer after he had been married to her for a few years knew exactly how to manage her.

For instance at Christmas one year he wanted to make a big feast for his friends and neighbors. Did he tell his wife so? Not he! Instead, a few weeks beforehand he remarked casually:

"Christmas is coming and I suppose every one will

expect us to have fine white bread. But I don't think we ought to. It's too expensive. Black bread is good enough for us."

"Black bread, indeed!" cried Maya. "Not at all! We're going to have white bread and you needn't say any more about it! Black bread at Christmas! To hear you talk people would suppose we are beggars!"

The farmer pretended to be grieved and he said:

"Well, my dear, have white bread if your heart is set on it, but I hope you don't expect to make any pies."

"Not make any pies! Just let me tell you I expect to make all the pies I want!"

"Well, now, Maya, if we have pies I don't think we ought to have any wine."

"No wine! I like that! Of course we'll have wine on Christmas!"

The farmer was much pleased but, still pretending to protest, he said:

"Well, if we spend money on wine, we better not expect to buy any coffee."

"What! No coffee on Christmas! Who ever heard of such a thing! Of course we'll have coffee!"

"Well, I'm not going to quarrel with you! Get a little coffee if you like, but just enough for you and me for I don't think we ought to have any guests."

"What! No guests on Christmas! Indeed and you're wrong if you think we're not going to have a houseful of guests!"

The farmer was overjoyed but, still pretending to grumble, he said:

"If you have the house full of people, you needn't think I'm going to sit at the head of the table, for I'm not!"

"You are, too!" screamed his wife. "That's exactly where you are going to sit!"

"Maya, Maya, don't get so excited! I will sit there if you insist. But if I do you mustn't expect me to pour the wine."

"And why not? It would be a strange thing if you didn't pour the wine at your own table!"

"All right, all right, I'll pour it! But you mustn't expect me to taste it beforehand."

"Of course you're going to taste it beforehand!"

This was exactly what the farmer wanted his wife to say. So you see by pretending to oppose her at every turn he was able to have the big Christmas party that he wanted and he was able to feast to his heart's content with all his friends and relatives and neighbors.

Time went by and Maya grew more and more contrary if such a thing were possible. Summer came and the haymaking season. They were going to a distant meadow to toss hay and had to cross an angry little river on a footbridge made of one slender plank.

The farmer crossed in safety, then he called back to his wife:

"Walk very carefully, Maya, for the plank is not strong!"

"I will not walk carefully!" the wife declared.

She flung herself on the plank with all her weight and when she got to the middle of the stream she jumped up and down just to show her husband how contrary she could be. Well, the plank broke with a snap, Maya fell into the water, the current carried her off, and she was drowned!

Her husband, seeing what had happened, ran madly upstream shouting:

"Help! Help!"

The haymakers heard him and came running to see what was the matter.

"My wife has fallen into the river!" he cried, "and the current has carried her body away!"

"What ails you?" the haymakers said. "Are you mad? If the current has carried your wife away, she's floating downstream, not upstream!"

"Any other woman would float downstream," the

farmer said. "Yes! But you know Maya! She's so contrary she'd float upstream every time!"

"That's true," the haymakers said, "she would!"

So all afternoon the farmer searched upstream for his wife's body but he never found it.

When night came he went home and had a good supper of all the things he liked to eat which Maya would never let him have.

They were so busy eating and drinking

II

JANE, JANE, DON'T COMPLAIN!

There was once a man who was poor and lazy and he had a wife who was even worse. Her name was Jenny. Jenny was so lazy that it was an effort for her to lift one foot after the other. And in addition to her laziness she was an everlasting complainer. "Oh!" she used to grunt in the morning, "I wish we didn't have to get up!" and "Oh!" she used to groan at night, "I wish we didn't have to take our shoes off before going to bed!"

One day when they were both out in the forest collecting faggots, Jenny said:

"I don't see why we're not rich! I don't see why the King should live at his ease while we have to grub for everything we get! I just hate work!"

Of course the trouble both with Jenny and her husband was not that they worked but that they didn't work. It was because they didn't that they had so much time to think about it.

"Drat it all!" Jenny went on, whining, "Adam and Eve are to blame for all our misfortunes! If they hadn't disobeyed God's commandment and eaten that apple, we'd all be living in the Garden of Eden to this day! It's all their fault that we have to moil and toil and hurry and scurry!"

"Yes," the man agreed, "it is, especially Eve's. Of course Adam was to blame, too, for he should have controlled his wife better. But Eve was the more to blame. If I had been Adam I shouldn't have allowed her to touch the apple in the first place."

Now it happened that the King who was out hunting that day overheard this conversation.

"Ha!" he thought to himself, "I've a great mind to teach these two people a lesson!"

He pushed aside the bushes that had hidden him from them and said:

"Good day to you both! I have just heard your complaints and I, too, think it very hard that you should be poor while others are rich. I tell you what I'll do: I'll take you both home with me to the castle and maintain you in ease and luxury provided you obey me in just one thing."

Jenny and her husband agreed to this eagerly and just as they were the King took them home with him to the castle. He lodged them in a room with golden furniture, he gave them fine clothes to wear, and for food he had them served the choicest delicacies in the world.

As they sat eating their first royal meal, he came in to them carrying in his hands a covered dish of silver. He put the dish down in the center of the table.

"Now, my friends," he said, "I promised to maintain you in this ease and luxury provided you obeyed me in one thing. You see this silver dish. I forbid you ever to lift the cover. If you disobey me, that moment I shall take from you your fine clothes and send you back to your poverty and misery."

With that the King left them and they stuffed themselves to their hearts' content with the delicate foods set before them.

They were so busy, eating and drinking and admiring themselves in their fine clothes, that for the first day they didn't give the covered dish a thought. The second day the wife noticed it and said:

"That's the thing we're not to touch. Well, for my part I don't want to touch it. I don't want to do anything but eat and sleep and try on my pretty new clothes."

By the third day they had eaten so much and so

steadily that they were no longer hungry and when they lay down on the big soft bed they no longer fell instantly asleep.

"Dear me," Jenny began whining, "I don't know what's the matter with this food! It doesn't taste as good as it used to! Maybe the cook has grown careless! I think we ought to complain to the King. I'm beginning to feel very uncomfortable and I haven't any appetite at all! I wonder what's in that covered dish. Perhaps it's something to eat, something perfectly delicious! I've half a mind to lift the cover and see."

"Now just you leave that silver dish alone!" the man growled. He, too, had been eating too much and was feeling peevish. "Don't you remember what the King said?"

"Pooh!" cried Jenny. "What do I care what the King said! I think he was just poking fun at us telling us we mustn't lift the cover of that silver dish. After all a dish is a dish and it's no crime to lift a cover even if it is made of silver!"

With that Jenny jumped up and before her husband could stop her she lifted the forbidden cover. Instantly a little white mouse hopped out of the silver dish and scurried away.

"Oh!" Jenny screamed, dropping the cover with a great clatter.

The King who was in an adjoining chamber heard the noise and came in.

"So!" he said, "you have done the one thing that I told you not to do! You haven't been here three days and although you've had everything that heart could wish for yet you couldn't obey me in this one little matter!"

"Your Majesty," the man said, "it was my wife who did it, not I."

"No matter," the King said, "you, too, are to blame. If you had restrained her it wouldn't have happened."

Then he called his servants and had them strip off the fine clothes and dress the couple again in their old rags.

"Now," he said as he drove them from the castle gates, "never again blame Adam and Eve for the misfortunes which you bring upon yourselves!"

They carried home the treasure on their backs

III

SUSAN WALKER, WHAT A TALKER!

There was once a man whose wife was an awful talker. Her name was Susanna. No matter how important it was to keep a matter quiet, if Susanna knew about it, she just had to talk.

She was always running to the neighbors and exclaiming:

"Oh, my dear, have you heard so and so?"

Her husband was an industrious fellow. He set nets in the river, he snared birds in the forest, and he worked at any odd jobs that came along.

It happened one day while he was out in the forest that he found a buried treasure.

"Ah!" he thought to himself, "now I can buy a little farm that will keep me and Susanna comfortable the rest of our days!"

He started home at once to tell his wife the good fortune that had befallen them. He had almost reached home when he stopped, suddenly realizing that the first thing Susanna would do would be to spread the news broadcast throughout the village. Then of course the government would get wind of his find and presently officers of the law would come and confiscate the entire treasure.

"That would never do," he told himself. "I must think out some plan whereby I can let Susanna know about the treasure without risking the loss of it."

He puzzled over the matter for a long time and at last hit upon something that he thought might prove successful.

In his nets that day he had caught a pike and in one of his snares he had found a grouse. He went back now to the river and put the bird in the fishnet, and then he went to the woods and put the fish in the snare. This done he went home and at once told Susanna about the buried treasure which was going to be the means of making their old age comfortable.

She flew at once into great excitement.

"La! La! A buried treasure! Whoever heard of such luck! Oh, how all the neighbors will envy us when they hear about it! I can hardly wait to tell them!"

"But they mustn't hear!" her husband told her. "You don't want the officers of the law coming and taking it all from us, do you?"

"That would be a nice how-do-you-do!" Susanna cried. "What! Come and take our treasure that you found yourself in the forest?"

"Yes, my dear, that's exactly what they'd do if once they heard about it."

"Well, you can depend upon it, my dear husband, not a soul will hear about it from me!"

She shook her head vigorously and repeated this many times and then tried to slip out of the house on some such excuse as needing to borrow a cup of meal from a neighbor.

But the man insisted on her staying beside him all evening. She kept remembering little errands that would take her to the houses of various neighbors but each time she attempted to leave her husband called her back. At last he got her safely to bed.

Early next morning, before she had been able to talk to any one, he said:

"Now, my dear, come with me to the forest and help me to carry home the treasure. On the way we'd better see if we've got anything in the nets and the snares."

They went first to the river and when the man had lifted his nets they found a grouse which he made Susanna reach over and get. Then in the woods he let her make the discovery of a pike in one of the snares.

She was all the while so excited about the treasure that she hadn't mind enough left to be surprised that a bird should be caught in a fishnet and a fish in a birdsnare.

Well, they found the precious treasure and they stowed it away in two sacks which they carried home on their backs. On the way home Susanna could scarcely refrain from calling out to every passerby some hint of their good fortune. As they passed the house of Helmi, her dearest crony, she said to her husband:

"My dear, won't you just wait here a moment while I run in and get a drink of water?"

"You mustn't go in just now," her husband said. "Don't you hear what's going on?"

There was the sound of two dogs fighting and yelping in the kitchen.

"Helmi is getting a beating from her husband," the man said. "Can't you hear her crying? This is no time for an outsider to appear."

All that day and all that night he kept so close to Susanna that the poor woman wasn't able to exchange a word with another human being.

Early next morning she escaped him and ran as fast as her legs could carry her to Helmi's house.

"My dear," she began all out of breath, "such a

wonderful treasure as we've found but I've sworn never to whisper a word about it for fear the government should hear of it! I should have stopped and told you yesterday but your husband was beating you—"

"What's that?" cried Helmi's husband who came in just then and caught the last words.

"It's the treasure we've found!"

"The treasure? What are you talking about? Begin at the beginning."

"Well, my old man and me we started out yesterday morning and first we went to the river to see if there was anything in the nets. We found a grouse—"

"A grouse?"

"Yes, we found a grouse in the nets. Then we went to the forest and looked in the snares and in one we found a pike."

"A pike!"

"Yes. Then we went and dug up the treasure and put it in two sacks and you could have seen us yourself carrying it home on our backs but you were too busy beating poor Helmi."

"I beating poor Helmi! Ho! Ho! Ho! That is a good one! I was busy beating my wife while you were getting birds out of fishnets and fish out of snares! Ho! Ho! Ho!"

"It's so!" Susanna cried. "It is so! You were so beating Helmi! And you sounded just like two dogs fighting! And we did so carry home the treasure!"

But Helmi's husband only laughed the harder. That afternoon when he went to the Inn he was still laughing and when the men there asked him what was so funny he told them Susanna's story and soon the whole village was laughing at the foolish woman who found birds in fishnets and fish in snares and who thought that two yelping dogs were Helmi and her husband fighting.

As for the treasure that wasn't taken any more seriously than the grouse and the pike.

"It must have been two sacks of turnips they carried home on their backs!" the village people decided.

The husband of course said nothing and Susanna, too, was soon forced to keep quiet for now whenever she tried to explain people only laughed.

MIKKO, THE FOX

A Nursery Epic in Sixteen Adventures

Osmo, the Bear, grunted out:
"Huh! That's easy! We'll eat the smallest of us next!"

ADVENTURE I

THE ANIMALS TAKE A BITE

A Farmer once dug a pit to trap the Animals that had been stealing his grain. By a strange chance he fell into his own pit and was killed.

The Ermine found him there.

"H'm," thought the Ermine, "that's the Farmer himself, isn't it? I better take him before any one else gets him."

So the Ermine dragged the Farmer's body out of the pit, put it on a sledge, and then, after taking a bite, began hauling it away.

Presently he met the Squirrel who clapped his hands in surprise.

"God bless you, brother!" the Squirrel exclaimed, "what's that you're hauling behind you?"

"It's the Farmer himself," the Ermine explained. "He fell into the pit that he had digged for us poor forest folk and serve him right, too! Take a bite of him and then come along and help me pull."

"Very well," the Squirrel said.

He took a bite of the Farmer and then marched along beside the Ermine, helping him to pull the sledge.

Presently they met Jussi, the Hare. Jussi looked at then in amazement, his eyes popping out of his head.

"Mercy me!" he cried, "what's that you two are hauling?"

"It's the Farmer," the Ermine explained. "He fell into the pit that he digged for us poor forest folk and serve him right, too! Take a bite of him, Jussi, and then come along and help us pull."

So Jussi, the Hare, took a bite of the Farmer and then marched along beside the Ermine and the Squirrel helping them to pull the sledge.

Next they met Mikko, the Fox.

"Goodness me!" Mikko said, "what's that you three are hauling?"

The Ermine again explained:

"It's the Farmer. He fell into the pit that he had digged for us poor forest folk and serve him right, too! Take a bite of him, Mikko, and then come along and help us pull."

So Mikko, the Fox, took a bite and then marched along beside the Ermine and the Squirrel and the Hare helping them to pull the sledge.

Next they met Pekka, the Wolf.

"Good gracious!" Pekka cried, "what's that you four are hauling?"

The Ermine explained:

"It's the Farmer. He fell into the pit that he had digged for us poor forest folk and serve him right, too! Take a bite of him, Pekka, and then help us pull."

So Pekka, the Wolf, took a bite and then marched along beside the Ermine, the Squirrel, the Hare, and the Fox, helping them to pull the sledge.

Next they met Osmo, the Bear.

"Good heavens!" Osmo rumbled, "what's that you five are hauling?"

"It's the Farmer," the Ermine explained. "He fell into the pit that he had digged for us poor forest folk and serve him right, too! Take a bite of him, Osmo, and then help us pull."

So Osmo, the Bear, took a bite and then marched along beside the Ermine, the Squirrel, the Hare, the Fox, and the Wolf, helping them to pull the sledge.

Well, they pulled and they pulled and whenever they felt tired or hungry they stopped and took a bite until the Farmer was about finished.

Then Pekka, the Wolf, said:

"See here, brothers, we've eaten up every bit of the Farmer except his beard. What are we going to eat now?"

Osmo, the Bear, grunted out:

"Huh! That's easy! We'll eat the smallest of us next!"

He had no sooner spoken than the Squirrel ran up a tree and the Ermine slipped under a stone.

Pekka, the Wolf said:

"But the smallest have escaped!"

Osmo, the Bear, grunted again:

"Huh! The smallest now is that pop-eyed Jussi! Let's—"

At mention of his name the Hare went loping across the field and was soon at a safe distance.

Osmo, the Bear, put his heavy paw on the Fox's shoulder.

"Mikko," he said, "it's your turn now for you're the smallest of us three."

Mikko, the Fox, pretended not to be at all afraid.

"That's true," he said, "I'm the smallest. All right, brothers, I'm ready. But before you eat me I wish you'd take me to the top of the hill. Down here in the valley it's so gloomy."

"Very well," the others agreed, "we'll go where you say. It is more cheerful there."

As they climbed the hill the Fox whispered to the Wolf:

"Sst! Pekka! When you eat me whose turn will it be then? Who will be the smallest then?"

"Mercy me!" the Wolf cried, "it will be my turn then, won't it?"

The terror of the thought quite took his appetite away.

"See here, Osmo," he said to the Bear, "I don't think it would be right for us to eat Mikko. You and I and Mikko ought to be friends and live together in peace. Now let's take a vote on the matter and we'll do whatever the majority says. I vote that we three be friends. What do you say, Mikko?"

The Fox said that he agreed with the Wolf. It

would be much better all around if they three were friends.

"Well," grunted Osmo, the Bear, "it's no use my voting for you two make a majority. But I must say I'm sorry to have you vote this way for I'm hungry."

So the three animals, the Bear, the Wolf, and the Fox, agreed henceforward to be friends and planned to live near each other in the woods behind the Farm.

ADVENTURE II

THE PARTNERS

The Bear and the Wolf and the Fox made houses quite close together and the Wolf and the Fox decided to go into partnership.

"The first thing we ought to do," said Pekka, the Wolf, "is make a clearing in the forest and plant some crops."

The Fox agreed and the very next day they started out to work. Each had a crock with three pats of butter for his dinner. They left their crocks in the cool water of a little spring in the forest not far from the place where they had decided to make a clearing.

It was hard work felling trees and the Fox, soon tiring of it, made some sort of excuse to run off. When he came back he said to the Wolf:

"Pekka, the folks at the Farm are having a christening and have sent me an invitation to attend."

"It's too bad we're so busy to-day," the Wolf said. "Another day you might have gone."

"But I must go," the Fox insisted. "They've been good neighbors to us and they'd be insulted if I refused."

"Very well," the Wolf said, "if you feel that way about it you better go. But hurry back for we have a lot to do."

So the Fox trotted off but he got no farther than the spring where the butter crocks were cooling. He took the Wolf's crock and licked off the top layer of butter. Then after a while he went back to the clearing.

"Well, Mikko," the Wolf said, "is the christening over?"

"Yes, it's over."

"What did they name the child?"

"They named it Top."

"Top? That's a strange name!"

In a few moments the Fox again ran off and returned

with the announcement that there was to be another christening at the Farm and again they wanted him to attend.

"Another christening!" the Wolf exclaimed. "How can that be?"

"This time the daughter has a baby."

"You're not going, are you, Mikko? You can't always be going to christenings."

"That's true, Pekka, that's true," said the Fox, "but I think I must go this time."

The Wolf sighed.

"You will hurry back, won't you? This work is too much for me alone."

"Yes, Pekka dear," the Fox promised, "I'll hurry back as quickly as I can."

So he trotted off again to the spring and the Wolf's butter crock. This time he ate the middle pat of the Wolf's butter, then slowly sauntered back to the clearing.

"Well," said the Wolf, pausing a moment in his work, "what did they name the baby this time?"

"This one they named Middle."

"Middle? That's a strange name to give a baby!"

For a few moments the Fox pretended to work hard. Then he ran off again. When he came back, he said:

"Pekka, do you know they're having another christening at the Farm and they say that I just must come."

"Another christening! Now, Mikko, that's too much! How can they be having another christening?"

"Well, this time it's the daughter-in-law that has a baby."

"I don't care who it is," the Wolf said, "you just can't go. You've got some work to do, you have!"

The Fox agreed:

"You're right, Pekka, you're right! I'm entirely too busy to be running off all the time to christenings! I'd say, 'No!' in a minute if it wasn't that we are new settlers and they are our nearest neighbors. As it is I'm afraid they'd think it wasn't neighborly if I didn't come. But I'll hurry back, I promise you!"

So for the third time the Fox trotted off to the little spring and this time he licked the Wolf's butter crock clean to the bottom. Then he went slowly back to the clearing and told the Wolf about the christening and the baby.

"They've named this one Bottom," he said.

"Bottom!" the Wolf echoed. "What funny names they give children nowadays!"

The Fox pretended to work hard for a few minutes, then threw himself down exhausted.

*"Wake up, Pekka!
Wake up! There's
butter running out of your nose!"*

"Heigh ho!" he said, with a yawn, "I'm so tired and hungry it must be dinner time!"

The Wolf looked at the sun and said:

"Yes, I think we had better rest now and eat."

So they went to the spring and got their butter crocks. The Wolf found that his had already been licked clean.

"Mikko!" he cried, "have you been at my butter?"

"Me?" the Fox said in a tone of great innocence. "How could I have been at your butter when you know perfectly well that I've been working right beside you all morning except when I was away at the christenings? You must have eaten up your butter yourself!"

"Of course I haven't eaten it up myself!" the Wolf declared. "I just bet anything you took it!"

The Fox pretended to be much aggrieved.

"Pekka, I won't have you saying such a thing! We must get at the bottom of this! I tell you what we'll do: we'll both lie down in the sun and the heat of the sun will melt the butter and make it run. Now then, if butter runs out of my nose then I'm the one that has eaten your butter; if it runs out of your nose, then you've eaten it yourself. Do you agree to this test?"

The Wolf said, yes, he agreed, and at once lay down in the sun. He had been working so hard that he was very tired and in a few moments he was sound asleep. Thereupon the Fox slipped over and daubed a little lump of butter on the end of his nose. The sun melted the butter and then, of course, it looked as if it were running out of the Wolf's nose.

"Wake up, Pekka! Wake up!" the Fox cried. "There's butter running out of your nose!"

The Wolf awoke and felt his nose with his tongue.

"Why, Mikko," he said in surprise, "so there is! Well, I suppose I must have eaten that butter myself but I give you my word for it I don't remember doing it!"

"Well," said the Fox, pretending still to feel hurt, "you shouldn't always suspect me."

When they went back to the clearing, the Wolf began pulling the brush together to burn it up and the Fox slipped away and lay down behind some brushes.

"Mikko! Mikko!" the Wolf called. "Aren't you going to help me burn the brush?"

"You set it a-fire," the Fox called back, "and I'll stay here to guard against any flying sparks. We don't want to burn down the whole forest!"

So the Wolf burned up all the brush while the Fox took a pleasant nap.

Then when he was ready to plant the seed in the rich wood ashes, the Wolf again called out to the Fox to come help him.

"You do the planting, Pekka," the Fox called back, "and I'll stay here and frighten off the birds. If I don't they'll come and pick up every seed you plant."

So Mikko, the rascal, took another nap while the poor Wolf planted the field he had already cleared and burned.

ADVENTURE III

THE FOX AND THE CROW

In a short time the field that Pekka, the Wolf, had planted began to sprout. Pekka was delighted.

"See, Mikko," he said to the Fox, "our grain is growing and we shall soon be harvesting it!"

The Fox turned up his nose indifferently.

"If we don't get something to eat before that grain ripens," he said, "we'll starve, both of us! While we wait for the harvest I think we better go out hunting. I'm going this minute for I tell you I'm hungry!"

The Fox went sniffing into the forest and finally came

to the tree where Harakka, the Magpie, had her nest. The Fox, cocking his head, paced slowly round and round the tree, looking at it from every angle. Harakka, the Magpie, sitting on her nest among her fledglings began to feel nervous.

"Say, Mikko," she called down, "what are you looking at?"

At first the Fox made no answer. Deep in thought, apparently, he nodded his head and murmured:

"Yes, the very tree!"

Harakka, the Magpie, again called down:

"What are you looking at, Mikko?"

The Fox started as though he had heard the question for the first time.

"Ah, Harakka, is that you? Good day to you! I hope you are well! I hope the children are all well! I was so busy looking for the right tree that I didn't recognize you at first. You see I have to cut down a tree to get wood for a new pair of *skis*. This tree is just the one I want."

"Oh, mercy me!" the Magpie cried. "You can't cut down this tree! Do you want to kill all my children? This is our home!"

Mikko, the rascal, pretended to be very sympathetic.

"I'm awfully sorry to have to disturb you, truly I am, but I'm afraid I do have to cut down this tree. I can't find another that suits me as well."

The Magpie flapped her wings in despair.

"You hard-hearted wretch! What will you take not to cut down this tree?"

The Fox put his paw to his head and pretended to think hard. After a moment he said:

"Well, Harakka, I'll make you this offer: I'll leave this tree standing provided you throw me down one of your fledglings."

"What!" the poor Magpie shrieked. "Give you one of my babies! I'll never do that! Never! Never! *Never!*"

"Oh, very well! Just as you like! If I cut the tree down I can get them all. But I thought for the sake of old times I'd ask for only one. However, do as you think best."

What could the poor Magpie say? If the tree were felled and her fledglings thrown out of the nest they would certainly all perish. Perhaps it would be wise to sacrifice one to save the rest.

"You promise to let the tree stand," she said, "if I give you one of my children?"

"Yes," the rascal promised, "just drop me one of your

fledglings, a nice plump one, and I won't cut down the tree."

With shaking claw Harakka pushed one of her children over the edge of the nest. It fluttered to the ground and Mikko carried it off.

Well, the next day what did that Fox do but come back and begin pacing around the tree again.

"Yes," he said, pretending to talk to himself, "this is the best tree I can find. I might as well cut it down at once."

"But, Mikko!" cried the Magpie, "you forget! You said you wouldn't cut down this tree if I gave you one of my children and I did give you one!"

The Fox flipped his tail indifferently.

"I know," he said, "I did promise but I thought then I could find another tree that would suit me as well as this one, but I can't. I've looked everywhere and I can't. I'm sorry but I'm afraid that I'll just have to take this tree."

"O dear, O dear, O dear!" the poor distracted Magpie wept. "Will nothing make you leave this tree stand?"

The Fox smacked his lips.

"Well, Harakka, drop me down another of your fledglings and I won't disturb the tree. I promise."

"What! Another of my babies! Oh, you wretch!"

"Well, suit yourself," Mikko said. "One of your fledglings and you can keep the others safe in the nest, or I'll cut the tree down."

What could the poor Magpie do? Wouldn't it be better to sacrifice another fledgling on the chance of saving the rest? Yes, it would! So she pushed another out of the nest. It fluttered to the ground and Mikko, the rascal, carried it off.

That afternoon Varis, the Crow, came to call on the Magpie.

"Why, my dear," she said, looking over the fledglings, "two of your children are missing! Whatever has become of them?"

"It's that rascally Mikko!" the Magpie cried, and thereupon she told her friend the whole story.

Varis, the Crow, listened carefully and then said:

"My dear, that miserable Fox has been fooling you! Why, he can't cut down this tree or any other tree for that matter! He hasn't even got an ax! Don't let him impose on you a third time!"

So the very next day when the Fox came and again tried the same little trick, Harakka, the Magpie, tossed her head scornfully and said:

"Go along, you rascal! You can't fool me again!

How can you cut down this tree or any other for that matter when you haven't even got an ax!"

The Fox was furious at being cheated of his dinner.

"You didn't think that out yourself, Harakka!" he said. "Some one's been talking to you! Who was it?"

"It was my dear friend, Varis," the Magpie said. "She's on to your tricks!"

"I'll teach that Crow to interfere with my affairs!" the Fox muttered to himself as he trotted off.

He went to an open field and lay down with his mouth open, pretending to be dead.

"I'm sure Varis will soon spy me!" he said to himself.

He was right. Presently the Crow began circling above him. She flew nearer and nearer and at last alighted on his head. His tongue was lolling out and Varis decided to have her first bite there. She gave it a sharp peck at which the Fox jumped up and caught her in his paws.

"Ha! Ha!" he cried. "So you're the one who spoiled my little game with Harakka, are you? Well, I'll teach you not to interfere with me! As I haven't got one of Harakka's fledglings for my dinner, I'm going to take you!"

"You don't mean you're going to eat me!" cried the Crow in terror.

"I'll teach that Crow
to interfere with my
affairs!" the Fox muttered
to himself as he trotted off

"That's exactly what I mean!"

"No, no, Mikko! Don't do that!"

"Yes, that's exactly what I'm going to do! I'm going to teach you birds that I'm not an animal to be played jokes on!"

"I suppose," the Crow said, sighing, "if it must be, it must be! But, Mikko, if you really want to use me as a warning to the other birds, you oughtn't to eat me right down. It would be much better if you dragged me along the ground first. Then they'd see a wing here, a leg there, and a long trail of feathers. That really would terrify them."

"I believe you're right," the Fox said.

He put the Crow down on the ground and lifted his paw for a moment to change his hold. The Crow instantly jerked away and escaped.

"Ha! Ha!" she cawed as she flew off. "You were clever enough to catch me, Mikko, but you weren't clever enough to eat me when you had me!"

So this was one time when Mikko, the Fox, was worsted.

ADVENTURE IV

THE CHIEF MOURNER

"Mercy me!" thought Mikko to himself as he watched Varis, the Crow, fly away, "this is certainly my unlucky day! There I had my dinner right in my hand and then lost it!"

Sighing and shaking his head he sauntered slowly back to the forest.

Now it happened that Osmo, the Bear, had just lost his wife and was out looking for some one to bewail her death. The first person he met was Pekka, the Wolf.

"Pekka," he said, "my wife's dead and I'm out looking for a good strong mourner. Can you mourn?"

"Me? Indeed I can! Just listen!"

Pekka, the Wolf, pointed his nose to the sky and let out a long shivery howl.

"There!" he said. "I don't believe you'll find any one that can do any better than that!"

But Osmo, the Bear, shook his head.

"No, Pekka, you won't do. I don't like your mourning at all!"

The Bear ambled on and presently he met the Hare.

"Good day, Jussi," he said. "Are you any good at mourning? Show me what you can do."

The Hare gave some frightened squeaks as his idea of mourning the dead.

"No, no," Osmo said, "I don't like your mourning either."

So he walked on farther until by chance he met the Fox.

"Mikko," he said, "my wife's dead and I'm out looking for a good strong mourner. Can you mourn?"

"Can I? Indeed I can!" the Fox declared. "I'm a marvel at mourning! I can wail high and low and soft and loud and just any way you want! Listen!" And Mikko, beginning with a little whimpering sound,

*And Mikko, beginning with
a little whimpering sound,
slowly rose to a high heartrending cry*

slowly rose to a high heartrending cry. This is what he wailed:

> "*Med! Med! Med!*
> The Bear's Wife is dead!
> *Lax! Lax! Lax!*
> No more she'll spin the flax!
> *Eyes! Eyes! Eyes!*
> No more she'll bake the pies!
> *Air! Air! Air!*
> No more she'll drive the mare!
> *Shakes! Shakes! Shakes!*
> There'll be no more little cakes!
> *Darth! Darth! Darth!*
> Throw the pots on the hearth
> For the Bear's Wife is dead!
> *Med! Med! Med!*"

Osmo, the Bear, was deeply moved.

"Beautiful! Beautiful!" he grunted hoarsely. "How well you knew her! Come along home with me, Mikko, and start right in! Oh, how beautifully you wail!"

So Mikko went home with the Bear. The old Bear Wife was laid out on a bench in the kitchen.

"Now then," the Bear said, "you begin the wailing while I cook the porridge."

"No, no, Osmo," the Fox said, "I couldn't possibly wail in here! The place is full of smoke and my voice would get husky in two minutes! Can't you lay her out in the storehouse?"

The Bear demurred but the Fox insisted and at last had his way. So together they dragged the body of the old Bear Wife out to the storehouse. The Fox stood beside the body ready to begin his wailing and the Bear went back to the kitchen.

The moment the Bear was out of sight Mikko, the rascal, instead of bewailing the old Bear Wife began gobbling her up! He just gobbled and gobbled and gobbled as fast as he could.

"What's the matter?" the Bear called out after a few minutes. "Why don't you begin?"

The Fox made no reply but kept on gobbling as hard as he could.

"Mikko! Mikko!" the Bear called out again. "What's the matter? Why aren't you howling?"

By this time the Fox had made a good dinner, so he called back:

"Don't bother me! I'm busy eating! Yum! Yum! Yum! Bear meat is awful good! Just give me a few more minutes and I'll be finished!"

At that the Bear rushed out of the kitchen in a terrible rage but the Fox was already running off and the Bear was unable to catch him. He did hit the end of his tail with the long spoon with which he had been measuring the meal, but that was all.

Mikko, the rascal, got safely away. However, to this day his tail shows the white mark of the meal.

ADVENTURE V

MIRRI, THE CAT

One day while the Fox was out walking in the forest he met a stranger.

"Good day," he said. "Who are you?"

"I am Mirri," the stranger said, "a poor unfortunate Cat out of employment. I had service in a decent family but I've had to leave them."

"Did they treat you badly?" the Fox asked.

"No, it wasn't that. They were considerate enough but they kept getting poorer and poorer until finally they hadn't food enough to feed us animals. Then I overheard the master say that soon they'd be forced to eat us and that they'd begin with me. At that I decided it was time for me to run away and here I am."

"My poor Cat," Mikko said, "you've had a cruel experience! Why don't you take service with me?"

"Will I be safe with you?" the Cat asked. "Will you protect me?"

"Will I?" the Fox repeated boastfully. "My dear Mirri, once it becomes known that you are Mikko's servant all the animals will show you a wholesome respect."

"Well then, I'll enter your service," the Cat said.

So the bargain was struck and the Fox at once began to train his new servant.

"Now, Mirri, tell me: what would you do if you suddenly met a Bear?"

"There's just one thing I couid do, master: I'd run up a tree."

The Fox laughed.

"You must have more ways than one to meet such a situation! Take me now: there are any of a hundred things that I could do if I met a Bear!"

Just then Osmo, the Bear, ambled softly up behind the Fox. The Cat saw him and instantly flew up a

He jerked quickly away and fled and the Bear was left standing with his mouth wide open

tree. Before the Fox could move Osmo clutched him firmly on the shoulder with his teeth.

"Oh, master, master!" the Cat called down from the tree. "What's this? I with my one way have escaped and you with your hundred are caught!"

But the Fox paid no heed to the Cat. He twisted his head around and looked reproachfully at the Bear.

"Why, Osmo, my dear old friend!" he said, "what in the world do you mean taking hold of me so roughly! Ouch! You're nipping my shoulder, really you are! I don't understand why you're acting this way! Here I've always been such a good friend to you, so faithful, so true, so—"

"What!" rumbled the Bear. "Faithful! True! Oh, you—"

Osmo's feelings overcame him to such an extent that he opened his jaws to roar out freely his denial of the Fox's hypocrisy.

That gave the Fox just the chance he wanted. He jerked quickly away and fled and the Bear was left standing with his mouth wide open.

Later when the Bear had ambled off the Fox returned and called the Cat down from the tree.

"You see, Mirri," he remarked casually, "it wasn't anything at all for me to get the best of the Bear!"

He could see that he had vastly impressed the Cat, so he let the subject drop.

"Come along, Mirri," he said, "it's time for us to go home."

*A terrible creature landed
on his nose and drove it
full of pins and needles*

ADVENTURE VI

THE FOX'S SERVANT

A day or so later the Fox met Pekka, the Wolf. The Fox hadn't seen much of Pekka recently for Pekka had been having a hard time and had been on the verge of starvation. Now he was sleek again and well fed for he had recently killed an Ox.

"Good day, Pekka," the Fox said in a friendly way.

"Good day, Mikko. How are you?"

"Very fine indeed!" the Fox said. "You see I have a new servant. Oh, he's a wonderful servant! He's not big to look at, you know, but he's so strong and quick that he'd jump on you in a minute and eat you up before you knew what was happening!"

"Really, Mikko?"

"Yes, really! You just ought to see him!"

"I'd like to see him," the Wolf said.

"Well, you might slip down now and take a peep in the kitchen. He's at home. But, my dear Pekka, I warn you not to let him see you! If he catches sight of you, I won't be responsible for the consequences!"

The Wolf was deeply impressed with all this. He crept carefully down to the Fox's kitchen and sniffed cautiously at the crack under the door. The Cat inside, seeing the tip of the Wolf's nose and thinking it was a Mouse, pounced on it with all his claws. This gave the Wolf a mighty fright and he bolted madly off into the forest.

He was still panting when he met the Bear.

"Osmo," he said, "have you heard about that awful creature that Mikko has for a servant?"

The Bear had heard nothing, so the Wolf related to him his own terrifying experience.

The Bear's curiosity was aroused.

"I must have a glimpse of this wonderful servant," he said, ambling off in the direction of the Fox's kitchen.

THE FOX'S SERVANT

"I'll wait for you here," the Wolf called after him, "and I warn you, Osmo, be careful!"

The Bear when he got to the Fox's kitchen quietly stuck his nose under the crack of the door and squinted inside. He hardly had time for one squint when a terrible creature with a straight tail that looked like a spear came flying through the air, landed on his nose, and drove it full of pins and needles.

"Ouch! Ouch! Ouch!" the Bear whimpered as he hurried back to the Wolf.

"Did you see him?" the Wolf asked.

"I got just one glimpse of him," the Bear said. "He had a long spear sticking up over his shoulder and he came swooping down through the air just as if he had wings!"

"My! I wish we could really see him!" the Wolf said. "Suppose we ask Mikko to arrange some way we can have a good look at him."

So they went to the Fox and Mikko, the rascal, said:

"Well, now, if you make a feast and invite my servant I think he will come."

"All right," the Wolf said, "that's what we'll do. I've still got some of that ox. It will make a fine feast."

So they roasted the remains of the ox and set it out.

"Now I'll go get my servant," the Fox said. "When

you hear us coming, you two hide some place where you can see us but we can't see you. If my servant once sees you I won't be responsible for the consequences!"

So the Wolf hid in some bushes nearby and the Bear drew himself up into the branches of a tree.

Well, the Fox and the Cat arrived and sat them down to the feast. Now it happened that the Wolf was not able to see, so he tried to twist himself around into a better position. The Cat caught a glimpse of his tail moving in the bushes and instantly pounced on it. With one terrified yelp, the Wolf jumped out of the bushes and fled into the forest as fast as he could.

In fright the Cat scampered up the tree and the Bear, of course, supposed that the awful creature now was after him. In his frantic efforts to escape he tumbled down out of the tree and broke two ribs. But for all that he made off, too terrified to look back.

So the Fox and the Cat were left to finish the ox in peace.

ADVENTURE VII

THE WOLF SINGS

Having sacrificed his ox in order to feast the Fox's servant, the Wolf had nothing left for himself and was soon very hungry. He could find nothing to eat in the forest, so he went prowling around a farm in hopes of getting a pig or a chicken. The only living creature he came upon was a thin old Dog asleep in the sun.

"This is better than nothing," he thought to himself and, taking hold of the Dog, he began dragging it off.

"Cousin! Cousin!" cried the Dog. "Is this any way to treat a relation? Let me go!"

"I'm sorry," the Wolf said, "but I can't let you go. I'm too hungry."

"Let me go," the Dog begged, "and I tell you what I'll do: I'll give you a bottle of vodka."

"Promises come easy," the Wolf said. "Where will you get the vodka?"

"Under the bench in the kitchen. That's where the master keeps his bottle. I've seen him hide it there. Come to-night after the family's asleep and I'll let you in and give you the vodka."

Now Pekka, the Wolf, was very fond of vodka, so he said to the Dog:

"Very well, I'll let you go. But see that you keep your promise!"

Late that night when the family were asleep, the Wolf came scratching at the farmhouse door and the Dog let him in.

"Well, old fellow, you know why I've come," the Wolf said.

At once the Dog crawled under the bench and got the master's bottle of vodka.

"Here, Pekka, here it is!" he said, offering the Wolf the bottle.

The Wolf went staggering around the room howling at the top of his voice

"You drink first," Pekka insisted. "You're the host."

The Dog raised the bottle and took a little sip. Then the Wolf took a deep swallow.

"Ah!" he said, smacking his lips, "that's something like!"

His stomach was empty and the vodka went through his veins like fire. He felt happy and laughed and went capering around the room.

"I feel like singing!" he cried.

"My dear Pekka," the Dog said, "I beg you don't sing! You will wake the folks! Sit down quietly and we'll talk."

So they sat awhile and talked and then the Wolf took another deep swallow of the vodka. Again he wanted to sing and the Dog had trouble in restraining him.

"Do you want to wake the family, Pekka? Be quiet now or you can't have any more vodka!"

The Wolf took another deep drink and after that there was no holding him back. He went staggering around the room howling at the top of his voice.

The Farmer and all his family came hurrying into the kitchen with clubs and pokers and whatever they could pick up.

"It's a Wolf!" the Farmer cried. "The impudent scoundrel, coming right into the house! Give him a good beating!"

If the door hadn't been open they would have clubbed poor Pekka to death. As it was he barely escaped with his life.

In the confusion that followed the Wolves stampeded, running helter-skelter in all directions

ADVENTURE VIII

THE CLEVER GOAT

The truth is Pekka, the Wolf, was a pretty stupid fellow always getting into some scrape or other. With sore ribs and a back aching from the beating which the farm folk had given him he slunk quietly along the forest ways hoping to come upon some easy prey. Suddenly he saw ahead of him a Goat and a Ram.

"What are they doing hereabouts?" he thought to himself. "This is no place for them and if anything happens to them it will be their own fault."

Vuhi, the Goat, and Dinas, the Ram, both knew that the forest was no place for them. But where else could they go? They had recently been turned loose to fend for themselves by their poor old master who was no longer able to feed them.

"This forest rather frightens me," the Ram had said to the Goat. "Do you suppose we'll be able to keep off the Wolves?"

Vuhi, the Goat, flirted his whiskers and said:

"I've got a plan."

Thereupon he took a sack and half filled it with dry chips. Then when he shook the sack the chips made a hollow rattle. He threw the sack over his shoulder and said to the Ram:

"Don't you be frightened, Dinas. We'll be able to hold our own with the forest creatures."

It was just at this moment that Pekka, the Wolf, appeared.

"Ha! Ha!" said Pekka suspiciously. "What's that you've got in that sack? No nonsense now! Answer me at once or I'll have to kill you both!"

Vuhi, the Goat, gave the sack a little rattle.

"In this sack?" he said. "Oh, only the skulls and bones of the Wolves we have eaten. We haven't had any Wolf meat now for some time, have we, Dinas? It's good you've come along for we're hungry. . . . Attention, Dinas! Kill the Wolf!"

The Ram lowered his horns ready for attack and Pekka, the Wolf, too surprised to resist and too stiff to run away, cried out wildly:

"Brothers! Brothers! Don't kill me! I'm your friend! Spare me and I'll do something for you!"

"Attention, Dinas!" the Goat commanded. "Don't kill the Wolf just yet!"

Then he asked Pekka:

"What will you do for us if we spare you?"

"I'll send you twelve Wolves," Pekka promised. "That will give you more meat than you'd have if you killed just me!"

"Twelve," the Goat replied. "You are right: twelve Wolves will give us more meat than one. Very well, we'll let you go on condition that you send us twelve. But see you keep your word!"

So the Wolf went off as fast as his stiff legs could carry him and assembled twelve of his brothers.

"I've called you together," he said, "to warn you of two terrible creatures, a Goat and a Ram, who are here in the forest eating up Wolves! Already they have a sack full of our unfortunate relations' skulls and bones! I saw the sack myself! Don't you think we ought all of us to flee?"

"What!" said the other Wolves, "thirteen Wolves turn tail on one Goat and one Ram? Never! We'll go together and give them battle!"

"Don't count me in!" Pekka said. "I don't want to see those two again!"

So the twelve Wolves marched off without Pekka.

The Goat as he saw them coming ran up a tree. The Ram followed him but couldn't get very high.

The twelve Wolves came under the tree and standing in close formation called out:

"Now then, you two, come on! We're ready for you!"

"Attention, Dinas!" the Goat commanded. "They're all here, so lose no more time! Jump down among them and kill them!"

The Goat himself began climbing down the tree, at the same time making an awful noise with his sack. He gave the Ram a push and the Ram slipped and fell right on the backs of the Wolves.

"That's right, Dinas! Kill them all!" the Goat shouted, rattling his sack more furiously than ever. "Don't let one of them escape!"

THE CLEVER GOAT

In the confusion that followed the Wolves stampeded, running helter-skelter in all directions. Every Wolf there felt that his own escape was a piece of rare good fortune.

"Those terrible two!" he thought.

Thereafter Vuhi, the Goat, and Dinas, the Ram, lived on in the forest untroubled by the Wolves.

"Here are three of us and see, here on the floor is our harvest already divided into three heaps"

ADVENTURE IX

THE HARVEST

Well, the time came when the field of barley which the Fox and the Wolf had planted together was ready to harvest. So the two friends cut the grain and carried the sheaves to the threshing barn where they spread them out to dry.

When it was time to thresh the grain, they asked Osmo, the Bear, to come and help them.

"Certainly," Osmo said.

At the time agreed the three animals met at the threshing barn.

"Now the first thing to decide," Pekka said, "is how to divide the work."

The Fox climbed nimbly up to the rafters.

"I'll stay up here," he called down, "and support the beams and the rafters. In that way there won't be any danger of their falling and injuring either of you. You two work down there without any concern. Trust me! I'll take care of you!"

So Osmo, the Bear, used the flail, and Pekka, the Wolf, winnowed the chaff from the grain. Mikko, the rascal, occasionally dropped down upon them a hunk of wood.

"Take care!" they'd call out. "Do you want to kill us?"

"Indeed, brothers, you have no idea how hard it is for me to hold up all these rafters!" Mikko would say. "You're very lucky it's only a little piece that drops on you now and then! If it weren't for me you'd certainly be killed, both of you!"

Well, the Bear and the Wolf worked steadily. When they were finished Mikko, the rascal, leaped down from the rafters and stretched himself as though he had been working the hardest of them all.

"I'm glad that job of mine is finished!" he said. "I couldn't have held things up much longer!"

"Well now," Pekka asked, "how shall we divide this our harvest?"

"I'll tell you how," Mikko said. "Here are three of us and, see, here on the floor is our harvest already divided into three heaps. The biggest heap will naturally go to the biggest of us. That's Osmo, the Bear. The middle sized heap will go to you, Pekka. I'm the smallest, so the smallest heap comes to me."

The Bear and the Wolf, stupid old things, agreed to this. So Osmo took the great heap of straw, Pekka the pile of chaff, and Mikko, the rascal, got for his share the little mound of clean grain.

Together they all went to the mill to grind their meal.

As the millstone turned on Mikko's grain, it made a rough rasping sound.

"Strange," Osmo said to Pekka, "Mikko's grain sounds different from ours."

"Mix some sand with yours," Mikko said, "then yours will make the same sound."

So the Bear and the Wolf poured some sand in their straw and their chaff and sure enough, when they turned their millstones again, they, too, got a rough rasping sound.

This satisfied them and they went home feeling they had just as good a winter's supply of food as Mikko.

*He dropped it in the water
and of course it spread out
far and wide and the current
carried it off*

ADVENTURE X

THE PORRIDGE

Well, it was only natural that they should all want to see at once what kind of porridge their meal would make.

Osmo's came out black and disgusting. Greatly disturbed he ambled over to Mikko's house for advice. The Fox was stirring his own porridge which was white and smooth.

"What's the matter with my porridge?" the Bear asked. "Yours is white and smooth but mine is black and horrid."

"Did you wash your meal before you put it into the pot?" the Fox asked.

"Wash it? No! How do you wash meal?"

"You take it to the river and drop it in the water. Then when it's clean you take it out."

The Bear at once went home and got his ground up straw and took it to the river. He dropped it in the water and of course it spread out far and wide and the current carried it off.

So that was the end of Osmo's share of the harvest.

Pekka, the Wolf, had as little luck with his porridge. Soon he, too, came to Mikko for advice.

"I don't know what's the matter with me," he said. "I don't seem to be able to make good porridge. Look at yours all white and smooth! I must watch you how you make it. Won't you let me hang my pot on your crane? Then I'll do just as you do."

"Certainly," the Fox said. "Hang your pot on this chain and the two pots can then cook side by side."

"Yours is so white to begin with," Pekka said, "and mine looks no better than dirt."

"Before you came I climbed up the chain and hung over the pot," the Fox said. "The heat of the fire melted the fat in my tail and it dripped down into the

ADVENTURE XI

NURSE MIKKO

The Wolf's wife gave birth to three little cubs and then died.

"You poor children!" Pekka said, "your mother is dead and there is no one to take her place. I must get you a nurse."

So he went through the forest hunting some one to take care of his motherless cubs. The white Grouse offered her services but, when she sang a lullaby to show what a good nurse she could be, Pekka shook his head.

"I don't like your voice," he said. "I can't take you."

Then Jussi, the Hare, applied for the position.

"You know I'm lame," he said, "so quiet work like nursing would suit me."

"Can you sing lullabies?" Pekka asked.

"Oh, yes! Listen!" and Jussi began squealing.

"Stop!" Pekka cried. "I don't like your voice either."

Just then Mikko, the Fox, came running up.

"Good day, Pekka," he said. "I hear you're out looking for a nurse for your sweet babies."

"Yes, Mikko, I am. Can you recommend one?"

"I'd like the job myself," the Fox said.

"You, Mikko?"

"Yes."

"But you can't sing lullabies, can you?"

"Oh, yes! I sing them very beautifully. Listen:

'Hushabye, sweet little cubs,
  Hushabye to sleep!
  Who best loves you, do you think?
  Who will give you food and drink?
  Who on faithful guard will keep?
  Mikko! Mikko!

'Hushabye, sweet little cubs,
  Mikko loves you well,
  Loves each little pointed nose,
  Loves your little scratchy toes,
  Loves you more than he can tell—
  Mikko! Mikko!'"

*He ran after Mikko and was about
to overtake him when Mikko
slipped into a crevice in the rocks.
Only one paw stuck out*

Pekka, the Wolf, was charmed with Mikko's lullaby.

"Beautiful! Beautiful!" he said. "I never heard a sweeter lullaby! You're the very nurse I want! Come home with me at once."

So Mikko went home with Pekka and took over the care of the three little Wolf cubs.

"I'll go off now and get them something to eat," Pekka said.

He came back after a while with the hind leg of a horse.

"This will be enough for them to start on," he said.

The Fox shook his head.

"I'm afraid it won't last them very long. They're beautiful healthy children with fine appetites."

"Poor little dears!" Pekka said. "Let me see them."

"Not just now!" Mikko insisted. "They're asleep and mustn't be disturbed. Go out hunting again and the next time you come home you shall see them."

Pekka felt that the Fox must be a very good nurse indeed to be so strict. So he went off hunting again without seeing his children.

As soon as he was gone Mikko, the rascal, ate up all the horse meat without giving the cubs one bite and then, as he was still hungry, he ate one of the cubs. The next day he ate another cub, and the day following he ate the last of them. He was just finishing that last cub when the Wolf came home and called in at the door:

"Now, nurse, here I am come home to see my dear children! They're well, aren't they?"

"Very well!" the Fox declared. "But they've grown so big under my good care that the house isn't large enough now to hold them and you and me at the same time. If you're coming in, I must get out first."

So the Wolf stood aside as the Fox came out and scampered away.

Then the Wolf went in and of course all he could find of his dear children were their bones.

"You faithless, faithless nurse!" he cried.

In awful rage he ran after Mikko and was about to overtake him when Mikko slipped into a crevice in the rocks. Only one paw stuck out. The Wolf pounced on this paw and began gnawing it.

"Say, Pekka, have you gone crazy?" the Fox asked. "What do you think you're doing biting that old root? I hope you don't think it's one of my paws. I'm sitting on all four paws."

The Wolf looked up to see whether this was true and, quick as a flash, Mikko, the rascal, drew in his paw.

So the poor old Wolf, fooled again, went sadly home.

Of course the instant he opened his mouth the Grouse flew away

ADVENTURE XII

THE BEAR SAYS *NORTH*

One day while Osmo, the Bear, was prowling about the woods he caught a Grouse.

"Pretty good!" he thought to himself. "Wouldn't the other animals be surprised if they knew old Osmo had caught a Grouse!"

He was so proud of his feat that he wanted all the world to know of it. So, holding the Grouse carefully in his teeth without injuring it, he began parading up and down the forest ways.

"They'll all certainly envy me this nice plump Grouse," he thought. "And they won't be so ready to call me awkward and lumbering after this, either!"

Presently Mikko, the Fox, sauntered by. He saw at once that Osmo was showing off and he determined that the Bear would not get the satisfacion of any admiration from him. So he pretended not to see the Grouse at all. Instead he pointed his nose upwards and sniffed.

"Um! Um!" grunted Osmo, trying to attract attention to himself.

"Ah," Mikko remarked, casually, "is that you, Osmo? What way is the wind blowing to-day? Can you tell me?"

Osmo, of course, could not answer without opening his mouth, so he grunted again hoping that Mikko would have to notice why he couldn't answer. But the Fox didn't glance at him at all. With his nose still pointed upwards he kept sniffing the air.

"It seems to me it's from the South," he said. "Isn't it from the South, Osmo?"

"Um! Um! Um!" the Bear grunted.

"You say it is from the South, Osmo? Are you sure?"

"Um! Um!" Osmo repeated, growing every moment more impatient.

"Oh, not from the South, you say. Then from what direction is it blowing?"

By this time the Bear was so exasperated by Mikko's interest in the wind when he should have been admiring the Grouse that he forgot himself, opened his mouth, and roared out:

"North!"

Of course the instant he opened his mouth, the Grouse flew away.

"Now see what you've done!" he stormed angrily. "You've made me lose my fine plump Grouse!"

"I?" Mikko asked. "What had I to do with it?"

"You kept asking me about the wind until I opened my mouth—that's what you did!"

The Fox shrugged his shoulders.

"Why did you open your mouth?"

"Well, you can't say, 'North!' without opening your mouth, can you?" the Bear demanded.

The Fox laughed heartily.

"See here, Osmo, don't blame me. Blame yourself. If I had had that Grouse in my mouth and you had asked me about the wind, I should never have said, 'North!'"

"What would you have said?" the Bear asked.

Mikko, the rascal, laughed harder than ever. Then he clenched his teeth and said:

"East!"

"Why, do you know," he said, "my turnips and my bread don't taste a bit like this!"

ADVENTURE XIII

OSMO'S SHARE

One day Osmo, the Bear, came to a clearing where a Man was plowing.

"Good day," the Bear said. "What are you doing?"

"I'm plowing," the Man answered. "After I finish plowing I'm going to harrow and then plant the field, half in wheat and half in turnips."

"Yum! Yum!" Osmo thought to himself. "Good food that—wheat and turnips!"

Aloud he said:

"I know how to plow and harrow. What do you say to my helping you?"

"If you help me," the Man said, "I'll share the harvest with you."

So Osmo set to work and between them they soon had the field plowed, harrowed, and planted.

When Autumn came they went to get their crops.

At the turnip field the Man said:

"Now what do you want as your share—the part that grows above the ground or the part that grows below?"

Osmo, the Bear, seeing how green and luxuriant the turnip tops were, said:

"Give me the part that grows above ground."

After they had harvested the turnips, they went on to the wheat field where the Man put the same question. The wheat stocks were all dry and shriveled. Osmo looked at them wisely and said:

"This time you better give me the part that grows under the ground."

The Man laughed in his sleeve and agreed.

One day the following winter the two met and the Man invited the Bear to dinner. Osmo who was very hungry accepted the invitation gladly.

First they had baked turnips.

"Oh, but these are good!" Osmo said. "I've never tasted anything better! What are they!"

"Why," the Man said, "they're the turnips from that field that you and I planted together."

The Bear was greatly surprised.

Then they had some freshly baked bread.

"How good! How good!" Osmo exclaimed. "What is it?"

"Just plain bread," the Man said, "baked from the wheat you and I planted together."

Osmo was more surprised than ever.

"Why, do you know," he said, "my turnips and my bread don't taste a bit like this!"

The Man burst out laughing and Osmo wondered why.

The first person they met was an old Horse. They put their case to him

ADVENTURE XIV

THE REWARD OF KINDNESS

Osmo, the Bear, used to go day after day to a field of growing rye and eat as much as he wanted. The Farmer noticed from the Bear's tracks that he always came by the same route.

"I'll teach that Bear a lesson!" the Farmer thought to himself.

So he set a snare made of a strong net and carefully covered it over with leaves and branches.

That day Osmo, when he came as usual to the field, got entangled in the net and was unable to escape.

The Farmer when he came and found him securely caught was overjoyed.

"Now, you brute!" he said, 'I've got you and I'm going to kill you!"

"Oh, master, don't do that!" the Bear implored. "Don't kill me!"

"Why shouldn't I kill you?" the Farmer asked. "Aren't you destroying my rye?"

"Let me off this time!" Osmo begged, "and I'll reward you! I swear I will!"

He begged and begged until at last he prevailed upon the Farmer to open the net and let him out.

"Now then," the Farmer said as soon as the Bear was freed, "how are you going to reward me?"

Osmo put a heavy paw on the Farmer's shoulder.

"This is how I'm going to reward you," he said: "I'm going to eat you up!"

"What!" the Farmer exclaimed, "is that your idea of a reward for kindness?"

"Exactly!" Osmo declared. "In this world that is the reward kindness always gets! Ask any one!"

"I don't believe it! I don't believe it!" the Farmer cried.

"Very well. I'll prove to you that I'm right. We'll ask the first person we meet."

The first person they met was an old Horse. They put their case to him.

THE REWARD OF KINDNESS

"The Bear is right," the old Horse said. "Look at me: For thirty years I gave my master faithful service and just this morning I heard him say: 'It's time we killed that old plug! He's no good for work any more and he's only eating his head off!'"

The Bear squinted his little eyes.

"You see!"

"No, I don't see!" the Farmer insisted. "We must ask some one else."

They walked on a little farther until they met an old Dog. They put their case to him and at once the Dog said:

"The Bear is right! Look at me: I gave my master a life time of faithful service and just this morning I overheard him say: 'It's time we killed that old Dog!' Alas, alas, in this wicked world goodness is always so rewarded!"

But still the Farmer was unsatisfied and to humor him Osmo said that he was willing that they should put their case once more to the judgment of an outsider.

The next person they met was Mikko, the Fox. Mikko listened carefully and then drawing the Farmer aside he whispered:

"If I give judgment in your favor will you let me carry off all the chickens in your hen-house?"

"Indeed I will!" the Farmer promised.

Then Mikko cleared his throat importantly and said:

"H'm! H'm! To give fair judgment in this case I must go over all the ground. First show me the field of rye and the damage Osmo did."

So they went to the field and the Fox, after he had appraised the damage, shook his head seriously.

"It was certainly wicked of Osmo eating all that rye! . . . Now show me the net."

So they went to the snare and the Fox examined it carefully.

"You say the Bear got entangled in this snare. I want to see just how he did it."

Osmo showed just how he had been caught.

"Get all the way in," the Fox said. "I want to make sure that you couldn't possibly get out unaided."

So the Bear entangled himself again in the net and proved that he couldn't possibly get out unaided.

"Well," said Mikko, the rascal, "you deserved to get caught the first time and now that you're in there again you can just stay there! Come on, Mr. Farmer."

So Mikko and the Farmer went off leaving Osmo to his fate.

That night the Fox went to the Farmer's hen-house to claim his reward. When he came in the chickens, of course, set up an awful squawking that aroused the family. The Farmer stayed in bed but he sent his wife out with a stout club.

"It sounds to me," he said, "as if some rascally Fox is trying to steal our hens. If you catch him, don't be gentle with him!"

"Gentle!" repeated the wife significantly.

She hurried out to the hen-house and when she found Mikko inside she gave him an awful beating. In fact he barely escaped with his life.

"Ah!" he said to himself as he limped painfully home, "to think that this is the reward my kindness has received! Oh, what a wicked, wicked world this is!"

With that the Bear lifted his paw and the little mouse scampered off

ADVENTURE XV

THE BEAR AND THE MOUSE

When Osmo, the Bear, was left alone in the net, he thrashed about this way and that until he was exhausted. Then he fell asleep.

While he slept a host of little Mice began playing all over his great body. Their tiny feet tickled him and he woke with a start. The Mice scampered off, all but one that Osmo caught under his paw.

"Tweek! Tweek!" the frightened little Mouse cried. "Let me go! Let me go! Please let me go! If you do I'll reward you some day! I promise I will!"

Osmo let out a great roar of laughter.

"What, little one? You'll reward me! Ha! Ha! That is good! The Mouse will reward the Bear! Well now, that is a joke! However, little one, I will let you go! You're too weak and insignificant for me to kill and too small to eat. So run along!"

With that the Bear lifted his paw and the little Mouse scampered off.

"It will reward me for my kindness!" Osmo repeated, and in spite of the fact that he was fast caught in a net he shook again with laughter.

He was still laughing when the little Mouse returned with a great army of his fellows. All the host at once began gnawing at the ropes of the net and in no time at all they had freed the big Bear.

"You see," the little Mouse said, "although we are weak and insignificant we can reward a kindness!"

Osmo was so ashamed for having laughed at the Mice on account of their size that all he could say as he shambled off into the forest was:

"Thanks!"

ADVENTURE XVI

THE LAST OF OSMO

There was a Farmer that used to drive his sledge into the forest to cut wood. Always as he drove he shouted abusively at his Horse.

"Go along, you old plug!" he'd say.

"What do you think you're good for, anyway? If you don't move along more lively I'll give you to the Bear for his supper—that's what I'll do with you!"

Now Osmo, the Bear, heard about this, how the Farmer was always talking about giving him his Horse, so one afternoon while the Farmer was going through his usual tirade Osmo suddenly stepped out of the bushes and said:

"Well, Mr. Farmer, here I am! Suppose you give me my supper."

The Farmer was greatly taken back.

"I didn't really mean what I was saying," he stammered. "He's a good Horse but he's a little lazy—that's all."

Osmo stood there swaying his shoulders and twisting his head.

"Even if he is lazy he'll taste all right to me. Come along, Mr. Farmer, hand him over as you've promised to do this long time!"

"But I can't afford to give you my Horse!" the Farmer cried. "He's the only Horse I've got!"

But the Bear was firm.

"No matter! You have to keep your word!"

"See here," the Farmer begged, "let me off on giving you my Horse and I tell you what I'll do: I'll give you my Cow. I can spare the Cow better."

"When will you give me the Cow?" the Bear asked.

"To-morrow," the Farmer promised.

"Very well," Osmo said, "if you deliver me the Cow to-morrow I'll let you off on the Horse. But see you keep your word!"

On his way home that afternoon the Farmer visited his traps. In one he found Mikko, the Fox. Mikko, the little rascal, begged for his life so piteously that the Farmer with a laugh freed him.

"You've done me a good turn," Mikko said, "and some day I'll do something for you. Just wait and see if I don't."

Well, early next morning the Farmer put his Cow on the sledge and started off for the forest. On the way he met Mikko.

"Good morning," Mikko said. "Where are you going with your Cow?"

The Farmer stopped and told Mikko about his bargain with the Bear.

"See here," the Fox said, "I promised you yesterday that some day I'd do you a good turn. That day has come! I'm going to save you your Cow and show you how you can kill that old Bear once and for all. But if I do this, you'll have to give me the Bear's carcass after he's dead and gone."

"I'll be glad enough to do that," the Farmer declared. "Save me my Cow and you may have all of that old Bear that you want!"

"Well then," Mikko said, "go home with the Cow as quickly as you can and come back here with ten distaffs.

My plan is to have you put five of the distaffs around my neck and five around my tail. I can make an awful noise rattling them. When the Bear hears me and wonders who I am, do you say to him: 'Oh! That must be my son, the Hunter! Don't you hear the rattle of his musket?' Then between us we'll finish that old Bear."

The Farmer did as the Fox directed. He drove the Cow home and returned to the forest with ten distaffs, five of which he fastened about the Fox's neck and five about his tail. Then he drove the sledge on to the place where he was to meet the Bear and Mikko, the Fox, crept along quietly behind him.

"Where's my Cow?" the Bear demanded as soon as the sledge appeared.

"I've come to talk to you about that," the Farmer began.

Just then there was an awful rattle of something in the bushes behind the Farmer.

"What's that?" the Bear cried.

"Oh," the Farmer said, "that must be my son, the Hunter! Don't you hear the rattle of his musket?"

The Bear shook in terror.

"The Hunter, you say! Mercy me, what shall I do! Oh, Mr. Farmer, save me from the Hunter and I'll forgive you the Cow!"

"Very well," the Farmer promised, "I'll do my best! Lie down and I'll try to make the Hunter believe you're only a log."

So the Bear lay down on the ground and stayed perfectly quiet.

"Father," called the Fox in a voice that sounded like the Hunter's, "what's that big brown thing lying on the ground near you? Is it a Bear?"

"No, son," the Farmer called back, "that isn't a Bear. It's only a log of wood."

"If it's a log of wood, father, chop it up!"

The Farmer raised his ax.

"Don't really chop me!" the Bear begged in a whisper. "Just pretend to."

"This is too good a log to chop up," the Farmer said.

"Well, father," said the voice from the bushes, "if it's such a good log you better put it on your sledge and take it home."

"Lie still," the Farmer whispered, "while I put you on the sledge."

So the Bear lay stiff and quiet and the Farmer dragged him on to the sledge.

"Father," the voice said, "you better tie that log down to keep it from rolling off."

"Don't move," the Farmer whispered, "and I'll tie you down just as if you were a log."

So the Bear lay perfectly still while the Farmer lashed him securely to the sledge.

"Father, are you sure that log can't roll off?"

"Yes, son," the Farmer said, "I'm sure it can't roll off now."

"Then, father, drive your ax into the end of the log and off we'll go!"

At that the Farmer raised his ax and with one mighty blow buried it in the neck of the Bear.

So that was the end of poor old lumbering Osmo!

The Farmer was saved both his Horse and his Cow and Mikko, the rascal, feasted on Bear meat for a week.

So that was THE END